UNIONS
BEFORE THE BAR

UNIONS
BEFORE THE BAR

Historic Trials Showing the Evolution
of Labor Rights in the United States

BY
ELIAS LIEBERMAN
MEMBER OF THE NEW YORK BAR,
AUTHOR OF
"THE COLLECTIVE LABOR AGREEMENT"

HARPER & BROTHERS
PUBLISHERS · NEW YORK

TO THE MEMORIES OF

MORRIS HILLQUIT

WHO ENCOURAGED ME TO STUDY LAW,

AND

JULIAN W. MACK
Judge, United States
Circuit Court of Appeals

WHO SPONSORED MY ADMISSION TO THE BAR

Contents

PREFACE   ix

(1805–1806)
1. THE CONSPIRACY OF THE PHILADELPHIA BOOTMAKERS   1
   Commonwealth (Pa.) v. Cordwainers

(1840–1842)
2. "VIRTUOUS ENDS PURSUED BY VIRTUOUS MEANS"   16
   Commonwealth (Mass.) v. Hunt

(1894–1895)
3. GOVERNMENT BY INJUNCTION—THE PULLMAN STRIKE   29
   United States v. Debs

(1906–1908)
4. THAT "FREEDOM" TO HIRE AND FIRE   44
   United States v. Adair

(1902–1913)
5. THE DANBURY HATTERS FACE THE SHERMAN ACT   56
   Loewe v. Lawlor

(1906–1913)
6. HOW SAMUEL GOMPERS WAS SAVED FROM JAIL   71
   Bucks Stove and Range Co. v. Gompers

(1907–1917)
7. THE "YELLOW-DOG" CONTRACT   84
   Hitchman Coal & Coke Company v. Mitchell

(1913–1921)
8. THE VANISHING "MAGNA CARTA"   96
   Duplex Printing Press Company v. Deering

(1914–1921)
9. "Pink-Tea Picketing"   108
     American Steel Foundries v. Tri-City Central Trades Council

(1916–1921)
10. When Picketing Meets "Due Process"   118
     Truax v. Corrigan

(1920–1925)
11. The Compulsory Arbitration Cure   127
     Charles Wolff Packing Company v. Court of Industrial Relations of the State of Kansas

(1914–1925)
12. The Confusing Coronados (two cases)   141
     Coronado Coal Co. v. United Mine Workers of America, 1922
     Coronado Coal Co. v. United Mine Workers of America, 1925

(1925–1927)
13. The Stone Cutters' Union Strikes a Rock   164
     Bedford Cut Stone Company v. Journeymen Stone Cutters' Association, et al.

(1935–1937)
14. Advertising for Customers: Merchants by Window Display, Union by Picketing   173
     Senn v. Tile Layers Protective Union

(1936–1937)
15. The Supreme Court Sees the Industrial Facts of Life   181
     National Labor Relations Board v. Jones & Laughlin Steel Corporation

(1937–1939)
16. The Sit-Down Strike Boomerangs   204
     National Labor Relations Board v. Fansteel Metallurgical Corporation

(1939–1940)
17. THE "FREE SPEECH" UMBRELLA FOR PEACEFUL PICKETING   217
    State of Alabama v. *Byron Thornhill*

(1937–1940)
18. THE SHERMAN ACT IN MODERN DRESS   225
    Apex Hosiery Company v. *Leader*

(1940–1941)
19. THE PROTECTIVE WINGS OF THE NORRIS-LA GUARDIA ACT   241
    United States v. *Hutcheson*

(1941–1944)
20. "ALL WITHIN THE UNION ARE BRETHREN"   252
    Steele v. *Louisville & Nashville Railroad*

(1942–1944)
21. THERE ARE NO RIGHTS WITHOUT DUTIES   263
    Wallace Corporation v. *National Labor Relations Board*

(1935–1945)
22. LET UNIONS BEWARE OF THE COMPANY THEY KEEP   272
    Allan-Bradley Co., et al. v. *Local Union No. 3, et al.*

(1946–1947)
23. THE HIGH COST OF CONTEMPT   287
    United States v. *John L. Lewis*

(1947–1948)
24. WITH MALICE TOWARD LABOR   303
    The Taft-Hartley Act

(1947–1949)
25. THE OPEN GATES OF THE CLOSED SHOP   330
    (a) *Lincoln Federal Labor Union No. 19129, et al.* v.
        Northwestern Iron and Metal Company, et al.
    (b) *George Whitaker, et al.* v. *State of North Carolina*
    (c) *American Federation of Labor, et al.* v. *American
        Sash & Door Company, et al.*

*(Past and
Future)*
26. LOOKING BOTH WAYS   344
        Comments on the 5 stages in the evolution of labor rights

CASES AND AUTHORITIES CITED   353

BIBLIOGRAPHY   355

INDEX   363

Preface

THIS BOOK is primarily for the layman, for the many men and women who have a genuine interest in the exciting topic of labor rights, but who are not trained to deal with legal technicalities. My aim was to make the book informative without being technical. The court cases were "humanized" without, however, sacrificing legal accuracy. Each chapter is a story of a labor case which helped shape the rights of unions in the United States. As the cases unfold themselves, the reader is likely to become aware of the interplay of the social and economic forces in our economy and of the changing position of labor in our society.

The tremendously important position labor unions occupy in our industrial scene makes them a heated issue in the halls of Congress, the state legislatures, the press, and the courts. This book portrays historic stages in the development of labor rights in our country from the early days of the Republic. It seeks to throw light on the changing attitudes of society and the judiciary toward labor unions.

Out of the welter of legal material during the past one hundred and forty-five years, only twenty-five cases were selected. These are the outstanding cases germane to the main theme—the evolution of union rights—that have been passed upon by the highest court of the land. I deemed it advisable to restrict the book to cases which have been passed upon by the Supreme Court of the United States and, therefore, I omitted state court cases regardless of their importance. I made an exception with respect to the two earliest cases (Chapters 1 and 2) and the controversial Taft-Hartley Act (Chapter 24) because of their significance and direct influence on the main theme—the evolution of labor rights in the United States.

Several people directly and indirectly contributed to my thinking and the shaping of this book but I am especially indebted to:

Dorothy Lieberman, my wife, for inspiring me to write this book and for her enthusiastic encouragement during the preparation of the manuscript.

Helene S. Zahler, for her very intelligent and industrious research, which enabled me to set the cases in their respective backgrounds. In addition thereto, she lightened my burden in connection with proof reading and preparation of the index, for all of which I am very grateful.

Dr. George Simpson, of The City College of New York, for his encouraging endorsement of my plans for this book and for his valuable service and cooperation during its preparation.

Vinson C. Aronson, Esq., with whom I have discussed the manuscript in its various stages, for his criticism and suggestions, which were reflected in the final draft.

Charles O. Gregory, Professor of Law, Chicago University, for his constructive criticism on eleven chapters of the first draft and for his wise suggestion to add two cases which are the basis of Chapters 14 and 22.

Joseph Kovner, Esq., of Washington, for his comments on several chapters dealing with the Sherman Act; Morris P. Glushien, Esq., for his observations on the chapter dealing with the Taft-Hartley Act; and Max D. Danish, for his suggestions in connection with the last chapter, *Looking Both Ways*.

ELIAS LIEBERMAN

New York, October, 1949.

UNIONS
BEFORE THE BAR

THERE is in each of us a stream of tendency, whether you choose to call it philosophy or not, which gives coherence and direction to thought and action. Judges cannot escape that current any more than other mortals. All their lives, forces which they do not recognize and cannot name, have been tugging at them—inherited instincts, traditional beliefs, acquired convictions; and the resultant is an outlook on life, a conception of social needs, a sense in James' phrase of "the total push and pressure of the cosmos," which, when reasons are nicely balanced, must determine where choice shall fall. In this mental background every problem finds its setting.

—BENJAMIN N. CARDOZO,
The Nature of the Judicial Process

- I -

The Conspiracy of the Philadelphia Bootmakers

(1805–1806)

COMMONWEALTH (PA.) V. CORDWAINERS

I

The first recorded labor case in the United States is as dramatic as it is significant. The eight defendants on trial were simple, honest, hard-working bootmakers. They were charged by the commonwealth of Pennsylvania with the crime of *conspiring* to raise their wages. The scene in the courtroom reflected the clash between the two dominant political and social powers of the day—the Federalists and the Jeffersonians. The defendants in the case were mere pawns in the battle between these two contending forces. This is the case of the *Philadelphia Cordwainers*.

When this trial took place—at the beginning of the nineteenth century—there was hardly any labor movement in existence in the United States. There were no mass production industries, there were no large employers, and there was no collective bargaining with labor to speak of. The only type of so-called workers' organizations in existence then were "friendly societies," organized mainly for fraternal purposes to which employers or masters, as well as workers, belonged. Class cleavages occurred much later, with the development of industry. When that occurred, the employers began forming their own trade associations, and the workers turned to their own trade unions.

In no slight sense this *Philadelphia Cordwainers* case was symbolic of things to come in industrial relations. Let us look at the background of the first recorded labor case in the history of the United States.

1

II

The shoemakers were among the first groups of workers in the United States who sought to organize themselves. In this respect they followed in the footsteps of their employers, who were among the first employer groups to form a trade association. As far back as October 16, 1648, the shoemaker employers of Boston formed a trade association, or guild, and secured from the Colony of Massachusetts Bay the first American guild charter.

The ostensible purpose of this guild charter was to enable this association to establish and preserve the standards of quality of shoes produced and to prevent the production of inferior merchandise. The guild had the power to set rigid rules for the trade and to penalize infractions by levying fines up to 40 shillings. In fact, this charter granted the guild members a monopoly over the production of footwear throughout Massachusetts Bay Colony. Without approval by the guild, no one could engage in the trade of shoemaking. The members of the guild, however, were not permitted to refuse to make boots or shoes for a person and his family from leather supplied by such person, and were also prohibited from increasing prices or wages. But their benefits far outweighed these restrictions. The monopoly over production given by this charter enabled the guild members to reap rich rewards from their trade.

In those days, shoemaking was a highly skilled craft, each artisan being required to make the complete boot and shoe. It was customary for the workers to call for the work at the employer's place of business but perform the work in their own homes. The workers' pay was based on piecework, and their earnings consequently depended upon the quantity of work produced by them. Some specialized on "bespoke-work," what is now known as custom work, ordered by individuals for their own use. This type of work was generally of better quality, requiring more care and attention to detail and naturally resulting in small quantity of production. Other workers were engaged on "order work," or what is now known as stock work, and were able to produce relatively greater quantities per week.

In the latter part of the eighteenth century, the employers of the boot and shoe trade in Philadelphia formed an association known as the "Society of Master Cordwainers." The original main purpose of the Masters' Society was to protect themselves from unfair competition, especially from those employers who were likely to offer inferior merchandise at lower prices. But by the end of the eighteenth century this Masters' Society widened its activity. The members of the society acted collectively in their dealings with the journeymen and agreed among themselves on the prices or rates to be paid by them to the cordwainers.

The Philadelphia journeymen, or workers, in this trade also organized themselves. These shoemakers were from the beginning a militant group. They were determined to resist any attempts of their employers to cut their wages or make them bear the burden of price competition. When wage cuts were attempted by the employers, they would spontaneously walk out and by these means resist lowering of piece rates paid to them for their work.

At the time, when journeymen wished to secure a higher price for their labor, it was customary for them to meet among themselves and decide upon the price. The leaders of their society would then notify the masters of the new price list. If the masters refused to pay these prices, a "turnout," a strike, would follow. During such a turnout, no member of the workers' society was expected to work for a master until a settlement was reached. A journeyman who worked for such a master without the society's approval was subject to discipline by the society and if he failed to comply he was subject to what was tantamount to social ostracism by the members of the society. Likewise a master or employer who broke his promise to pay for labor in accordance with the price list was disciplined by the imposition of a fine. If he failed to pay the fine, the Journeymen's Society would advise its members to refuse to work for him.

The shoemakers were well organized and maintained what would be known today as a "union shop." Every journeyman was expected to join the society. When a new journeyman appeared in the locality, the society invited him to join. If he did not, his employer was asked to "turn him off"—that is, not give him any work. If an employer failed to comply with such a request, the members of the society were likely to discontinue working for him.

The level of prices paid for labor was standard and uniform, but fluctuations occurred as the relative strength of the respective organizations of the masters and workers or the demand for the supply of labor waxed or waned. In 1796, the price paid by the masters to the workers in Philadelphia for custom-made, or bespoke, boots was

$2.75 a pair; for stock work, or order work, it was $2.50 a pair. When, two years later, in 1798, an outbreak of cholera weakened the Journeymen's Society, the masters reduced the price for labor to $2.25. When, subsequently, the workers "turned out," demanding restoration of the previous piece rates, the masters acceded, only to reduce the price again the following year. When the workers again turned out, the masters got together, combined, and locked them out.

The events immediately leading to the first labor case were briefly as follows: As a result of a short strike in 1804, the shoemakers of Philadelphia established the price for labor at $2.75 per pair of boots. But after Christmas of that same year the masters reduced the price to $2.50. The workers resented the reduction, waited for a while and then, in 1805, requested that the prices for their work be the same as those prevailing in New York and Baltimore. Their masters refused. The society took a vote and the majority voted for a turnout. During this turnout George Pullis and seven other journeymen were arrested on a preliminary complaint, but were not prosecuted at the time. However, these arrests served their purpose of undermining and defeating the turnout. The workers lost their strike.

This strike caused the master-employers and the dominant political powers in Philadelphia to look with apprehension on the growing strength of workers' organizations. With the aid of the Pennsylvania Federalists and their allies, the Constitutional Republicans, they decided once and for all to suppress and prevent organizations of workers in the commonwealth of Pennsylvania. Accordingly, after the strike was over and the shoemakers were back at work, the eight cordwainers who had been arrested during the strike, but were not prosecuted at the time, were later, in January, 1806, indicted and charged with the crime of "a combination and conspiracy to raise their wages."

III

A few words on the political and social scene at the time are in order.

Thomas Jefferson, who was elected president of the United States in 1800, won his re-election in 1804. The defeated Federalists proclaimed that Jefferson's election sealed America's doom. Their animosity and bitterness toward Jeffersonian democracy went so far as to prompt one of their leaders to say that Jeffersonians aimed "to destroy every trace of civilization in the world and force mankind back into his savage state . . . We have a country governed by blockheads and knaves; the ties of marriage with all its felicities are severed and destroyed; our wives and daughters are thrown into the stews . . . Can the imagination paint anything more dreadful this side of hell?"

Alexander Hamilton was the doctrinaire of the Federalists. He believed in a strong central government and advocated a vigorous policy of industrialization of the American economy. The Federalists had little confidence in the judgment of the common man and they believed that only the strong and the rich were qualified to govern. They were stanchly antilabor and their policy was *the state over the man.*

Jefferson, on the other hand, feared the decline of free men. His followers looked with concern on the growth of industrialism. They distrusted a strong central government in which the common man could not directly participate. They feared that such a government would soon become an oligarchy. Jefferson stood for the principle that the will of the majority should prevail. He believed in the declaration that "all men are created equal." He trusted the common man and the Jeffersonians threw their support on the side of labor.

The clash between these two political philosophies was demonstrated in the Pennsylvania legislature. While the indictment against the eight bootmakers was pending, the Jeffersonians introduced a bill in the legislature to the effect that the English common-law doctrine of conspiracy was not the law of Pennsylvania. Such a law would have disposed of the indictment against the bootmakers. But the Federalists, allied with the Constitutional Republicans, by a vote of 44 to 32, defeated the bill. They wanted the bootmakers to be tried. The Federalists concentrated on retaining their stronghold on the legislature and the judiciary. Having in their control the legislative power to make law, and the judicial power to interpret the law, the Federalists sought to fasten their political and economic views on American society.

This was the background against which the eight Philadelphia boot- and shoemakers were tried. The fight in the courtroom reflected the national struggle between aristocracy and Jeffersonian democracy.

IV

The trial of the eight indicted boot- and shoemakers took place in the Mayor's Court in Philadelphia in March, 1806. The court consisted of five: John Innskeep, the mayor; Pettit, Douglas, and Carswell, three aldermen of the city; and Moses Levy, the recorder, who presided.

The jury consisted of 12 small businessmen; 3 grocers, 3 innkeepers, 1 merchant, 1 watchmaker, 1 tobacconist, 1 hatter, 1 tailor, and 1 bottler.

The defendants were: George Pullis, Peter Pollen, John Harket, John Hepburn, Underl Barnes, John Dubois, George Keimer, and George Snyder.

As the trial opened, Joseph Hopkinson, for the prosecution, read the indictment, which contained three counts.

The first count charged: The defendants, on the 1st day of November, 1805, with force and arms did combine, conspire, and agree "to increase and augment the prices and rates usually paid and allowed to them . . . and unjustly to exact and procure great sums of money for their work and labour . . . to the damage, injury and prejudice of the masters employing them . . ."

The second count charged: The defendants agreed that they "should and would endeavour to prevent by threats, menaces, and other unlawful means . . . other workmen and journeymen in their occupation from working except at certain large prices, and rates set by them for their future work, to the great damage and prejudice of others, artificers and journeymen . . . to the evil example of others, and against the peace and dignity of the Commonwealth of Pennsylvania."

The third count charged: The defendants "unlawfully, perniciously and deceitfully" formed themselves into a club and combination, adopted "unlawful and arbitrary bye-laws, rules and orders" and corruptly agreed that none of them would work for any master who should employ any workman or journeyman who should infringe or break any of their unlawful rules, orders or bylaws.

While the prosecution called thirteen witnesses in support of the indictment, the main testimony was supplied by Job Harrison, a worker, and John Bedford, an employer. The prosecution relied mainly on the law and on the testimony of these witnesses. Under questioning by Hopkinson for the prosecution and occasionally by the recorder, Harrison was led to recite his experiences with the society of the cordwainers from the time he first joined it.

The story went back to 1794, when he came to this country from England. He then lived in Germantown near Philadelphia and for about six or seven weeks he worked for Mr. Bedford. He usually called for work once a week, on Saturday, took the material home, and then brought back the finished product. During one of his Saturday visits, he was informed by Mr. Bedford that the price for the work had been raised and he was paid accordingly. Later, on another occasion, he was told the same thing and was paid the higher price. Some time thereafter, some of the workmen called on Harrison and told him that it was his duty to join the "body" (society). He told them that he knew nothing about the body. He was then told by them that if he would not join, he was likely to be "scabb'd." When he inquired what that meant, he was told that the meaning was that "they would not work in the same shop nor board or lodge in the same house, nor would they work at all for the same employer." He told them that he "was willing to be as good a member of their body as any other man," and he joined.

A few years later, in 1799, there was a turnout on *boots*. Harrison at the time worked for Mr. Bedford on *shoes*. He felt that he should not be included in that strike because he was not able financially to stand it, having a sick wife and a large young family, and besides, since he worked on shoes and not on boots, he had nothing to gain by the strike. His plea did not prevail. He was directed to refuse to make shoes for his employer unless his employer would settle with the bootmakers. Continuing his testimony, he said, "I concluded at that time I would turn a scab, unknown to them, and would continue my work, and not let them know of it." This subsequently was discovered by the society. When the journeymen won that turnout, they informed Mr. Bedford that he must discharge the "scabs," which meant Harrison and another worker by the name of Logan. Mr. Bedford refused to do this because at the beginning of the strike he had promised that he would protect them in their jobs.

At that time Mr. Bedford employed twenty journeymen. His shop was scabbed and they all left. At the suggestion of Mr. Bedford, Harrison and Logan agreed between themselves to go to the society and see if they could adjust the matter by payment of a fine of not more than $8 each. The society, however, took a different view. It fined Logan $18 and fined Harrison $20 "for being a hypocrite." This decision irritated Harrison. "It was like throwing coals of fire in my face." They refused to pay the fine and the shop remained scabbed.

This lasted for about two years. Bedford was greatly handicapped because he could not get any workers and in 1802 he temporarily moved to Trenton, New Jersey. Harrison went there to work for him. While there he met with some local shoemakers and, after a short time, made peace with the Cordwainers' Society by paying a $4 fine in 4 monthly installments.

When the turnout of 1805 occurred, Mr. Bedford first agreed to pay the new price but, after a meeting of the Master Cordwainers, at which it was decided to refuse the society's demand, Mr. Bedford changed his mind. Harrison testified that at this time he was determined not to scab. The strike continued for about six weeks. Strikers in need received strike benefits, which were usually based upon the rate of half a dollar a week for each person in the family. On that basis Harrison was entitled to receive $4 a week. He did not receive it, however, because he did not want to certify that he was in absolute need.

In spite of the testimony given by Harrison, he appeared to be friendly toward the society. He testified that during the strike he received $20 from Mr. Bedford on settlement for his work and out of that sum he lent $10 to the body (society) to give to Cummings, another striker, to enable him financially to continue to stand the turnout. He also manifested his friendly feeling toward the society by stating in court that if the Society "broke down today, I would endeavour to raise it up again tomorrow."

During Harrison's testimony an incident occurred in court, which showed how high feeling ran at this trial between the masters and the workmen. Some noise in the courtroom arose at the time Harrison made his statement that he was determined not to be a scab at this time. The recorder interrupted the hearing and asked who had made that noise. Mr. Ryan (apparently an employer) pointed to the person just behind him as the noisemaker. The recorder then directed Mr. Ryan to be sworn in and to state under oath what he heard that man say. Mr. Ryan then said that he had heard George Alcorn say in a distinct tone of voice, "A scab is a shelter for lice."

After a short consultation on the bench, the recorder said, "George Alcorn, for this contempt of court in interrupting a witness, the court fines you $10 and orders you to pay the money immediately or be committed." (The money was paid immediately.)

John Bedford, the employer for whom Harrison worked, corroborated in many respects the testimony of Harrison. He dwelt upon the losses he had sustained in that first turnout in 1799. He claimed that at the time in an endeavor to secure business he went to Charleston, South Carolina. He got two customers there. Then he got some additional business in Virginia, in Norfolk, Petersburg, Richmond, and Alexandria, but as a result of the increase in the price of labor, which he was obliged to add to the price of the goods, he lost two customers and subsequently lost another one, a shoemaker at Alexandria "who had agreed to take $1,500 worth per annum of me." On the whole he believed he lost $4,000 worth of business per year. He further testified that in 1799, when his shop was scabbed, some violence occurred, but during the turnout of 1805 there were no such difficulties. In reply to a question, he testified that he considered loss of business as a most serious injury, particularly to the commerce of Philadelphia.

Other witnesses for the prosecution corroborated some aspects of Harrison and Bedford's testimony about the society and its attitude toward workers who refused to join, or who disobeyed its rules, or toward employers who refused to abide by their agreement concerning prices, or who employed nonsociety workers.

The defense attorneys, through witnesses of their own and through cross-examination of witnesses for the prosecution, established the following facts:

The direct cause of the turnout of 1805 was the request of the journeymen for an increase in the prices to be paid to them, which request was as follows:

Fancy tops	were	$4.25	proposed to be raised to	$5
Back straps	"	3.75	to " "	4
Long boots	"	2.75	to " "	3
Cossack	"	2.75	to " "	3
Bootees	"	2.50	to " "	3

The defense also proved that the prices asked by the society were those prevailing at that time in New York and Baltimore and that the strikers were willing to accept a compromise but the employers refused to give any increase whatever.

It was further established that the Society of Cordwainers had been in existence for about fifteen years and that the procedure concerning the setting of piece rates and employment of its members had been recognized by their employers; that the sole purpose of the society was to improve the condition of its members and that it had been organized by them for their mutual protection; and that their request for price increases was not unreasonable and was not higher than in the neighboring markets.

The defense further showed that the Master Cordwainers who were behind the prosecution of these eight boot- and shoemakers themselves had combined in a society for the purpose of maintaining prices and other mutual protections for themselves, as shown by the journal of the proceeding of the Masters' Society, which contained the record of their first meeting held in April, 1789. Their rules included the following: (1) The subscribers were to hold four stated general meetings in every year. Absentees to pay a fine of 1s. 6d. (2) Members were to consult for the general good of the trade, and determine upon the most eligible means to prevent irregularities in the same. (5) No person should be elected a member of the society, who offered for sale any boots, shoes, etc., in the public market of that city, or advertised the price of his work in any of the public papers or handbills, so long as he continued in these practices. (6) All fines and penalties to be paid, or for neglect, after notice, to be considered as an unworthy member, and accordingly excluded from the society.

As stated, there was no testimony of any violence in connection with the 1805 turnout for which the eight defendants were indicted. Neither was there any testimony that the eight defendants had done any wrong, except that they had participated in the turnout and agreed to conform to the society's rule not to associate with any scabs. Neither was there any testimony that the defendants, with the exception of one, had been members of the society at the time Harrison was fined or the Bedford shop scabbed in 1799.

Not the facts but rather the law applicable to such labor organization was the main issue at the trial. The respective contentions for the prosecution and the defense in substance seem to have been as follows:

Joseph Hopkinson and Jared Ingersoll for the prosecutor contended:

1. The object of the Society of Cordwainers was to procure large prices for their work and to compel the employers to accede to the cordwainers' terms. The society sought to accomplish this objective by a combination among themselves, by rewarding their followers and by punishing those who opposed them, workers or employers. This was a crime against those whom they injured and against the welfare of the state.

2. Such a combination interfered with the regulation of wages and prices by the "natural law" of supply and demand.

3. A combination of workmen to raise their wages or to compel a worker to join a society by threatening otherwise to refuse to associate with him, or to work for any employer who employed such a worker, was a crime under English common law.

4. English common law as to crimes against governmental authority was also the common law of the state of Pennsylvania.

5. The expansion of manufacturing is beneficial to the community. Conspiracies like those of these boot- and shoemakers would disturb manufacture. Higher prices for labor meant higher prices to the consumers. The courts must protect the community, the consumer, industry, and the individual worker; and therefore must punish the conspirators.

Caesar A. Rodney and Walter Franklin, for the defense, vigorously opposing the prosecution's position as an attack on the basic human rights of employees to combine for mutual protection, contended:

(a) Workers in the state of Pennsylvania were free to associate themselves for the betterment of their conditions. This was an exercise of the freedom guaranteed to Americans.

(b) English common law was neither binding on, nor applicable to, the free and independent commonwealth of Pennsylvania. The English doctrine of common-law conspiracy could not survive as law in the United States after the colonial period, for such doctrine was in derogation of the natural and inalienable rights of men and inconsistent with democracy, as intended by the Declaration of Independence.

(c) Even if our common law were the same as the English, this case is distinguished from the English cases of labor conspiracy. In England, there was a *statute which prohibited* workers from working at a wage above that fixed by that law and made such an act a crime. Therefore, in England a combination of workers to violate that statute might have been regarded as a criminal conspiracy. But no such law existed in Pennsylvania and therefore a combination of workers to raise their wages could not be held to be a criminal conspiracy to violate the law of Pennsylvania.

(d) No master was compelled to give to his employed cordwainers more than he thought their work was worth. It was a matter of bargaining between them. The price of labor would thus be regulated between the masters and the employees.

(e) It was not a crime for a man to refuse to work with another man. The refusal might be considered by some as being not liberal or improper, but it furnished no legal foundation for prosecution. There could be no indictment for that. Every man might choose the company with whom he wished to associate and refuse to associate with anyone whose company might be disagreeable to him, without being obliged to give a reason for it and without violating the laws of the land.

In support of their respective contentions, the attorneys for the prosecution and for the defense cited various cases from English law. They elaborated their arguments with learned and technical dissertations on the meaning of English law, its pertinence and applicability to American law, and its appropriateness to the cordwainers' case. These fine points of law were far above the heads of the grocers, the innkeepers, the merchants, and the others who comprised the jury in this case.

The recorder, Moses Levy, a stanch Federalist, had no difficulty in charging the jury. He frankly favored the rights of those who were "equipped to guide society" and denounced organizations of wage earners which interfered with the exercise of such rights. In harmony with the Federalist doctrine that social control should be in the hands of "the rich, the wise and the good" (as the Federalists liked to describe themselves), the recorder, in his charge to the jury, appealed to prejudice, patriotism, and the economic self-interest of the jurors.

In his long and ardent charge to the jury, he also said: "The measure [turnout] is pregnant with public mischief and private injury—tends to demoralize the workers—destroy the trade of the city and leaves the pockets of the whole community to the discretion of the concerned [strikers]. . . . If they could stand out three or four weeks in winter, they might raise the prices of boots to thirty or forty dollars a pair. . . . It [the turnout] interferes with the 'natural' regulation of wages and prices by *supply and demand* . . . If journeymen may combine to exact 'artificial wages' it follows that masters may combine to exact artificial prices for boots. . ."

To counteract the effect of the defense plea to the jury, that a verdict of guilty would deprive individuals of their inalienable rights to unite for their own protection, the recorder beclouded that plea by charging that an *individual worker* might strike as much as he pleased, as long as he did not do it together with others. The recorder well knew that a strike by an individual worker was economically meaningless and of no effect, but it sounded good. In instructing the jury as to the law, he said: "A combination of workmen to raise their wages may be considered in a two-fold point of view: One is to benefit themselves . . . the other is to injure those who do not join their society. The Rule of law condemns both."

In conformity with procedural formalities and legal amenities, the recorder instructed the jury to disregard any appeal to passion made by the attorneys, but he was not above making such an appeal himself, and said: "Are we to have besides our state legislature a new legislature consisting of journeymen-shoe-makers? The laws of the journeymen leave no individual at liberty to join the society or reject it. They are not the laws of Pennsylvania."

The recorder concluded his charge at the end of a day, and the jury was directed to bring in a sealed verdict. The next morning Mr. Franklin, for the defense, requested that the jury be polled. It was granted by the court. Mr. William Henderson, the fifth juror on the roster, spoke up and said that the signed verdict of the jury would be found on a paper enclosed in the indictment. The clerk read the paper: "We find the defendants guilty of a combination to raise their wages." The court thereupon fined the eight defendants $8 each, with costs of the suit, and directed that the defendants were to stand committed to jail until the fines were paid.

V

The behavior of the recorder and the verdict of the jury met with a blast of criticism from the Jeffersonians. Their newspaper *Aurora*, in its issue of March 31, 1806, commenting on the court proceedings, minced no words. Its comment was: "A man who did not know the purposes for which the law contemplated the appointment of re- corder to preside in the Mayor's court, would unquestionably have concluded that Mr. Recorder Levy had been paid by the master shoemakers for his discourse in the Mayor's court on Friday last. *Never* did we hear a charge to a jury delivered in a more prejudiced and partial manner. From such court recorders and juries, good Lord deliver us."

While the uninformed might not have appreciated the significance of this case, others did, as can be seen from the following:

The case was reported in shorthand and, on May 21, 1806, after transcribing the minutes, the court reporter, Thomas Lloyd, called at the office of the clerk of the court and asked to examine the written paper containing the verdict rendered by the jury. To his surprise he was told that the paper was missing or had been destroyed. The clerk told him that once a verdict was rendered, the paper containing it was of no importance. Obviously, the clerk was not aware of the historic value of this document. The reporter himself, however, was. He forwarded a copy of the transcript with the following note:

To THOMAS M'KEAN, Governor, and
THE GENERAL ASSEMBLY OF PENNSYLVANIA,

Is dedicated the report of the most interesting law case, which has occurred in this state since our revolution . . . with the hope of attracting their particular attention, at the next meeting of the Legislature.

"It is better that the law be known and certain, than that it be right." With respect, I am, fellow citizens, your most obedient,

Thomas Lloyd.

One may seriously question the legal conclusions drawn by the recorder in this case. He took it upon himself to declare what the public policy of the commonwealth of Pennsylvania was toward labor organizations. At that time there was no American public policy toward such combination of workers, and the recorder had no authority, express or implied, to pronounce a public policy for the state of Pennsylvania when its legislation had never adopted such a policy.

Aside from the fact that the common law of England could scarcely be binding on the state of Pennsylvania after the American colonies declared their independence in 1776, the English cases concerning combination of workmen under common law could not be applied to the American situation. As properly pointed out by the defense attorneys, there existed in England a law limiting the workers' wages, therefore, a combination of workmen to raise wages in violation of that law might there have been considered a criminal conspiracy. But since there was no law in Pennsylvania limiting wages, a combination of workmen to raise their wages was not a combination to defeat any existing Pennsylvania law and could not be held to be a criminal conspiracy.

Behind the *Cordwainers* case there was a larger issue, the struggle for power between the Jeffersonian democrats and the Hamiltonian Federalists. The latter, believing in a strong propertied class, with a wealthy merchantry and an expansion of manufacture, also believed that the richer the rich the more employment they would provide and "accumulated private wealth is national power." Hence, they sought to suppress workers' organizations which might obstruct the accumulation of private wealth and interfere with the expansion of national power. The Jeffersonians, on the other hand, believed in a strong middle class, consisting of independent artisans and small farmers. They therefore supported combinations of workmen as a protective shield against concentrated economic wealth. In this *Cordwainers* case, the Federalists succeeded in giving their philosophy the sanctity of law, wrapped in the dignity, tradition, and precedent of the English common law.

The significance of this case in its effect on the development of labor rights in the United States can be seen from the following. During the early decades of the nineteenth century, several states followed the doctrine enunciated in the *Cordwainers* case, namely, that a combination of workmen to raise their wages was a criminal conspiracy to be suppressed by the states. There were nineteen cases (in the states of Connecticut, Maryland, Massachusetts, New York, and Pennsylvania) in which workers' organizations were prosecuted on such conspiracy charges.

2

"*Virtuous Ends Pursued by Virtuous Means*"

(1840–1842)

Commonwealth (Mass.) v. Hunt

I

For almost thirty-six years, the decision of the *Philadelphia Cordwainers* case continued to plague workers' organizations. During these years, about twenty indictments in various states were secured against labor organizations, charging them with "criminal conspiracy" in combining unlawfully to raise their wages. In spite of these indictments, organizations of workers for improvement of their economic conditions sprang up from time to time.

In the year 1842 a radical change occurred in the attitude of the courts toward labor organizations. The ambitions of a district attorney in Boston, and the obstinacy of a Bostonian bootmaker, contrary to the intentions of both, helped to dissolve the taint of crime that was attached to labor organizations by the *Philadelphia Cordwainers* decision. This new attitude of the courts was demonstrated in the case of *Commonwealth v. Hunt* in the state of Massachusetts, which was destined to have a far-reaching effect on the development of labor rights in the United States. Let us look at the background of this case.

II

The economic position of workers about 1830 was not a happy one. There was currency inflation, with its accompaniment of continuous mounting in the cost of living. The country was getting a foretaste of hard times to come and the workers were feeling the effect of incipient economic depression. Some of them were seeking protection against the effects of inflation by joining labor organizations.

About this time, in 1835, Bostonian workers engaged in the making of high-grade boots formed a society under the name of the Boston Journeymen Bootmakers' Society. This society adopted a constitution which recited that its main purpose was to maintain a rate of wages essential to ensure the necessaries of life for its members. The dues of the members were 12½ cents a month. The funds of the society could be used to assist a member who had been on strike for at least ten days. The constitution provided for a Board of Judges which should decide disputes between employers and journeymen. Those who violated the rules of the society were subject to fines. One of the essential clauses in the constitution was that a member in a "society shop" should not work with a journeyman who was not a member of the society, unless the shop did not have a majority of society men at work. In other words, it provided for what subsequently became known as the "closed shop."

Shortly after these workers organized themselves, they went out on strike, demanding an increase in their piece rates. They succeeded. The piece rate for bootmaking, which at the time had been $1.50, was increased to $1.75 per pair. But in the face of the currency inflation of the time, this additional 25 cents proved insufficient to meet the increase in the cost of living, so the following year, again by means of a strike, the society succeeded in raising the price of their work to $2 per pair.

The success of the society did not last long. In 1837 the country was in the throes of an economic panic, which usually weakens workers' organizations. However, the society did succeed in retaining the piece rates of $2 a pair, but not without making various concessions to the employers. If a master furnished the workplace (usually the bootmakers worked in their own homes), he made a deduction of 25 cents for each pair. Furthermore, while nominally the established piece rates prevailed, the masters exacted a higher standard of quality of workmanship without paying additional compensation. Since the bootmakers were employed on piecework, the additional time consumed by them in performing higher quality work was not compensated. The worker who previously would normally produce five pairs of boots in a week could not produce more than four pairs of boots of the higher standard quality. Thus, without nominally reducing the piece rates, the wages or earnings of the workers in reality dropped about 20 per cent.

The society was powerless. It simply did not know how to meet the problem of protecting the earnings of its members against the imposition of higher standards of work without corresponding compensation. The time was not propitious to risk a strike for higher piece rates. The members were advised to be patient and wait for a better opportunity, but they were instructed to be on guard and report any employers who might attempt to exact additional work without additional compensation.

III

In the year 1840 an incident occurred, on its face insignificant, but which turned out to have a tremendous effect on the development of labor rights in this country.

Jeremiah Horne, one of the members of the Boston Journeymen Bootmakers' Society, used to work for a master by the name of Isaac Waite. Horne was a good mechanic. On one occasion his master, Waite, requested him to make a pair of boots which required extra work, but he did not allow extra compensation for the extra work. Horne performed the work without informing the society about it. Upon learning these facts, the society imposed a fine on him. However, after Waite paid Horne for the extra work involved, the society "took off" the fine.

Shortly thereafter, Horne again breached the society's rules. He was fined $1, but refused to pay it. In vain did his master, Waite, urge him to comply with the rules of the society. He even offered him the dollar. Horne, a rugged individualist at heart, not only refused to pay the fine but openly defied the society and passed various derogatory remarks about it. The society then expelled him from membership. As a condition of readmission, the society demanded that Horne "sign the rules" and pay the following fines: for going off the books—$1; for initiation fee—50 cents; for breach of rule—50 cents; and for slandering the society—$5; in all, $7.

Horne remained adamant and would not take the advice of his own master to become a member in good standing. The society demanded his discharge and in accordance with the prevailing practice, Waite discharged him. Horne then lodged a complaint with the district attorney of Boston.

At that time, the district attorney of Boston was Samuel D. Parker, who belonged to the so-called "upper class." The Horne charge presented him with an opportunity to prosecute a labor organization in Massachusetts. The political benefit and professional prestige that might flow to him from successful prosecution of such a case spurred him on. The incident appeared to him especially propitious because the complainant was not an employer but a member of the very society that he, Parker, would have liked to suppress. His ambition was aroused. Accordingly, on October 8, 1840, Parker secured an indictment against Hunt and six other leaders of the Boston Journeymen Bootmakers' Society, charging them with criminal conspiracy. A few days later the case came up for trial in the Municipal Court in Boston before Judge Peter Oxenbridge Thatcher.

IV

The courtroom at this trial reflected the struggle for power between the two contending political parties of the time, the Whigs and the Democrats. The Whigs were represented by the district attorney, Samuel D. Parker. The Jacksonian Democrats were represented by the attorney for the defendants, Robert Rantoul, Jr., formerly Democratic leader in the Massachusetts legislature. The philosophy of these two political parties clashed at this trial.

The heart of the indictment against the defendants consisted of two essential counts, which in substance were:

(*a*) The society, of which the defendants were the leaders, was a criminal conspiracy to oppress and impoverish employers and nonconformist workmen.

(*b*) The defendants conspired together and agreed not to work for any master who, after notice from the society to discharge any workman who was not a member, continued to employ him.

While the district attorney called various witnesses in support of the indictment, surprisingly most of the witnesses called by him were not antagonistic to the society. They did not claim that the society was oppressive or that its members exacted unreasonably high prices for their work. Their testimony did not show that the society called strikes which impoverished the employers. There was no substantial proof that even Jeremiah Horne was impoverished or that as a result of his discharge he was obliged to take lower wages or found it harder to get employment elsewhere. However, the district attorney expected to prove his case in large measure, by so-called documentary evidence. He offered in evidence the constitution of the society, and attacked all its provisions, but most vigorously Article 14, which read: "Any member working for a Society shop, and knowing a journeyman to be at work for the same but who is not a member of this Society, shall immediately give notice to the other journeymen, who, receiving such information, shall quit work for that shop; *provided* such shop shall have a majority of Society men on work, but if their number be less, they may continue until work can be obtained elsewhere."

The district attorney characterized this so-called "closed shop" article as "akin to slavery," the article that provided for fines for violation of the rules as "extortion," and the article that provided for the payment of dues of 12½ cents a month "oppressive and as an illegal tax."

Noting that the preamble of the constitution of the society recited that it is adopted "provided always, in so doing, we do not act in opposition to the laws of this Commonwealth," the district attorney argued that the intention of the defendants was unimportant, that their ignorance of the law did not shield them from punishment. Stressing the law as he interpreted it and propounding his social philosophy, the district attorney, in brief, contended:

(*a*) The common law of England concerning conspiracy was applicable to this case. (*b*) Under the English laws a combination of workmen to raise their wages was an unlawful conspiracy. It was so decided in 1721 in the case of *Rex* v. *Journeymen Taylors of Cambridge*. (*c*) The law concerning combination of workmen in this country was similar, and it was correctly so held in the *Philadelphia Cordwainers* case and in the case of *People* v. *Fisher* in New York State. (*d*) Workers' organizations which adopted rules compelling members to pay dues and compelling employers to employ or not to employ particular workers, were tyrannical, illegal, and were conspiracies and should be suppressed. (*e*) The Boston society was a criminal conspiracy to oppress and impoverish both employers and nonconformist workmen. The objects of such workers' combinations were a threat to the economic welfare of the community and therefore such combinations were unlawful conspiracies and must be suppressed.

As attorney for the defendants, Robert Rantoul, Jr., deemed it advisable not to press the social issues involved in the case, but rather to rely on a strict interpretation of the legal questions. He did not hesitate to make use of highly technical objections. By the use of such objections he succeeded in excluding the testimony of the main complainant, Jeremiah Horne. It is an incident worth recording.

When Horne was called as a witness by the district attorney, Rantoul objected, claiming that Horne was disqualified to give testimony because he was an atheist. In support of his objection he called witnesses who testified that Horne denied the existence of a Supreme Being; that he expected when he died to be thrown into a hole and that would be the end of him; that a man was not any more than dirt or clay; that he did not believe in any "damned Relig;" and that he did not believe in heaven or hell. The evidence concerning Horne's atheism satisfied the judge to disqualify Horne as a witness. Thus, the main complainant, whose charge set in motion the state apparatus of justice against the society, was not permitted to testify at all.

Rantoul endeavored to show that a combination of men for improvement of economic conditions was not a crime and that as a matter of fact such combinations were made in the best of society. To prove this point, he drew an analogy between the society of these bootmakers and professional organizations, such as the Medical Association and the Legal Bar, in Massachusetts. He proved that the Medical Association was a combination for the improvement of its members and had regulations concerning fees, dues, and associating with nonsociety members. It even expelled a physician member for violating its rules.

Similarly, he drew a further analogy between the defendant society and the Boston Bar (Judge Thatcher, presiding at this trial, the district attorney, Daniel Webster, and other prominent lawyers were members thereof), which had rules fixing minimum fees "as to the lowest which we can reasonably and honorably receive." The rules also forbade members "to advise or consult or be in any manner associated with any non-member attorney." The main point that Rantoul tried to drive home was that combinations for improvement of conditions of members are not necessarily punishable conspiracies.

In brief, Rantoul's main points were:

1. The states did not adopt indiscriminately the whole mass of either common law or statute laws of England. "Had the States done that, they might as well be governed by England."

2. English laws grew out of her institutions and her state of society which differed greatly from the American institutions and society. The English laws were founded on property rights. Their laws sacrificed the rights of laborers to the ruling classes. "They were part of the English Tyranny from which we fled."

3. The decisions of English cases cited by the district attorney could not be a precedent in this case because in England at that time there existed a statute which prohibited workers from asking higher wages than that statute permitted. The defendants in those cases were charged with conspiracy to violate *that existing statute.* But in Massachusetts no such law limiting the right of workers to ask for higher wages existed. Therefore, the asking of such wages could not be deemed a conspiracy to violate a law.

4. The defendants were entitled to do by their combination what each one of them could lawfully do without a combination. While a combination may become a criminal conspiracy if it is for the purpose of doing an unlawful or criminal act, the purpose of these defendants was not shown to be either unlawful or criminal, and therefore their combination could not be a criminal conspiracy.

5. The indictment was defective in that it did not clearly set forth the alleged illegal purposes of the defendants. The provisions in the constitution of the society recited in the indictment did not clearly show any illegality, and therefore the indictment should be dismissed.

It is fair to assume that the learned and exhaustive arguments of the defense and the prosecution were far above the heads of the jurors. They were too technical and legalistic for any ordinary jury. But Judge Thatcher made the task of the jury much simpler. In his charge, he summed up the issues, but not without indicating quite forcefully his own opinion of the conduct of the defendants. In substance, not necessarily in these words or order, he charged the jury:

(a) The Massachusetts courts had held that conspiracy was an offense at common law in *that* state, so the question of what the English common law was was not material.

(b) Although it was lawful for these defendants *individually* to refuse to work for any master bootmakers who should employ a nonmember of their society, yet if the defendants combined together to prevent the employment of any other persons or to extort from anyone the payment of a sum of money not justly due, "I consider that both the means and the object were violations of law."

(c) The question was not whether the bootmakers had the power, but rather whether they *assumed* a power which in the hands of irresponsible persons was liable to great abuse. If the law permitted that, these bootmakers would probably make new and still more burdensome regulations. The jury must judge whether the defendants did not propose to have such control of the industry as to compel the people of the commonwealth to pay for their boots and shoes whatever price the Society of Bootmakers should set.

(d) The fines imposed by defendants for violation of their regulations amounted to an imposition of taxes, and only the legislature might lawfully tax its citizens.

(e) As a matter of law, this Society of Journeymen Bootmakers, organized for the purposes described in the indictment, was an unlawful conspiracy against the laws of this commonwealth.

In the face of this clear and concise charge to the jury, no other verdict than that of guilty could have been expected. The jury was not disappointing. It brought in a verdict of guilty. Rantoul filed exceptions to the judge's charge and to the verdict. The judge withheld sentence until the Supreme Judicial Court should rule upon Rantoul's exceptions.

V

More than a year passed between the time the jury rendered the verdict of guilty and the time the Supreme Judicial Court of Massachusetts rendered its decision on Rantoul's exceptions. During this time, several events occurred which could not have been unnoticed by the Appellate Court before rendering its decision. Among these events were the following:

In 1840, when the defendants were indicted and tried, the community experienced an economic revival. The textile interests, which were quite influential in state politics, enjoyed prosperity. Business was good and profits were high. These interests feared that if unionism got a strong foothold in the bootmaking industry, it would spread to others, including textiles. An acquittal of the defendants after an indictment which had received so much publicity, they feared, would stimulate organization of laborers in their mills.

But in 1842, when the Appellate Court rendered its decision, there was a depression in the textile industry. The time was not propitious for labor organization. There was no fear that in such times the worker who had a job would risk the loss of it by joining a union. The textile interests at this time had no fear that the acquittal of the defendants would lead to unionization in their plants. Moreover, they were greatly concerned to secure tariff protection for the textile industry. To incur labor enmity by an unfavorable legal decision in this case might have meant inviting labor's opposition to the tariff protection, thus jeopardizing the chances of carrying through the desired tariff legislation.

Moreover, at the time, considerable dissatisfaction with the attitude of the judiciary toward labor organizations was brewing among workingmen. There was a report that in New York State workers protested against Judge Savage and burned him in effigy for his decision in the case of *People* v. *Fisher,* in which he held that a combination of workers to raise wages was a criminal conspiracy. There were also reports of political activity of workers in support of the party that favored labor organizations and in opposition to those which sought to suppress them.

All these facts could not have escaped the attention of Chief Justice Lemuel Shaw when he rendered the decision in the appeal of *Commonwealth* v. *Hunt.*

VI

The history-making decision was rendered in 1842, almost a year after the appeal was argued. While the Appellate Court was to pass only upon the exceptions made by Rantoul, the decision rendered and the basic principles enunciated by Chief Justice Shaw went far to remove the taint of crime from labor organized for improvement of working conditions.

In substance, Chief Justice Lemuel Shaw held:

1. The common law of Massachusetts did adopt the English principle that it was criminal to combine to do that which was unlawful or criminal, but much that was unlawful or criminal in England was not necessarily criminal or unlawful in Massachusetts.

2. This case was distinguished from the English case, *Rex* v.

Journeyman Taylors of Cambridge, because that case was based upon the fact that the combination to raise wages was a conspiracy to violate a *then existing* law in England concerning wages and by reason thereof was an unlawful conspiracy. The facts in the present case were different, since no law fixing wages existed in Massachusetts. Therefore, the combination of the defendants to raise wages was not a combination to violate a law.

3. Similarly, the case at bar differed from the New York State case of *People* v. *Fisher.* In New York State there was a statute making restraint of trade a crime and that court found that the objective of the workers' combination was to restrain trade. It therefore found the defendants guilty. But there was no such statute in Massachusetts.

4. While not every combination was necessarily punishable as a conspiracy, a combination whose intended object was unlawful or where the means used were unlawful, although not criminal, might be a punishable conspiracy.

5. The indictment in this case did not recite facts which would show that either the intended object or the means used by the combination were unlawful. The mere fact that the defendants agreed not to work for any employer who did employ a nonmember of their society was not in itself unlawful or improper because the power of the society might be exerted for honorable purposes and not necessarily for injury to Society as a whole.

6. The means used by the defendants were not necessarily unlawful. The defendants were free to work or not to work for whom they pleased. They did not induce any breaches of contracts of employment; they did not use force, coercion, or duress to compel Waite to discharge Horne. Only the agreement of the defendants among themselves not to work with Horne prompted Waite to discharge him. Such means were not necessarily unlawful.

Chief Justice Shaw sustained one of the main exceptions made by Rantoul, namely, that the indictment did not set forth any agreement to do a *criminal* act or to do an unlawful act by any specified criminal means. Accordingly, he directed that the indictment against the defendants be dismissed.

VII

Chief Justice Shaw's decision was a masterpiece of legal diplomacy. He appeased the labor element by declaring that there was no objection legally to the formation of labor organizations, and at the same time retained the weapon of criminal conspiracy to be used against them as the occasion might present itself.

The chief justice was conscious that common law which had been developed and interpreted in a feudal era could not be literally applied to an industrial civilization. He used his ability to adapt the essential principles of the common law in a modified way to the industrial era. Since it was obvious that open suppression of labor unions by the judiciary would not endure for long, and that the prestige of the judiciary would greatly suffer in the eyes of organized labor, it was imperative to find a legal basis for tolerating the existence of labor unions. Diplomacy and practical appreciation of social conditions, fortified by skillful legal reasoning, enabled Justice Shaw to enunciate a formula which has been and still is being followed by the judiciary in labor disputes. He introduced the doctrine of *ends and means, motive and purpose.*

This doctrine of "ends and means" modernized the application of common-law conspiracy, reconciled it to some degree with precedent, and made it palatable to all classes of the community. Justice Shaw reasoned that, since it is natural for workers to seek improvement of their conditions under our industrial system, the *purpose* of the combination was a lawful one and a combination of workmen for a lawful purpose was not prohibited by law. By this reasoning he appeased the laboring class and removed the greatest factor of their dissatisfaction with the judiciary. His declaration that a combination of workers for the lawful purpose of improving their conditions must be legally tolerated by society, was greeted with joy by labor.

However, Justice Shaw had no intention of having the judiciary lose its control over the conduct of an effective labor combination. Shaw was conscious that the doctrine of criminal conspiracy, by its very nature, had always been a vague one. There was no concrete measure of testing the *motive* of a combination. Is the judge bound to consider only the *immediate* aim, or may he also consider the *ultimate* motive and purpose of a combination? Since *motive* is one of the main issues in any case of conspiracy, an individual judge may be influenced by his own bias as to what motives are socially desirable and what motives are socially objectionable.

The doctrine of "ends and means" in conspiracy cases had been used by another court prior to Justice Shaw's decision. But in that case it was used for the protection of employers. This occurred in the case of *Commonwealth* v. *Carlisle,* in Pennsylvania, where the workers sought to apply the doctrine of criminal conspiracy against their employers who combined to reduce the workers' wages. In that case the court held that a "combination to resist oppression, not merely supposed but real, would be perfectly innocent; for where the act to be done and the means of accomplishing it are lawful, and the object to be attained is meritorious, combination is not conspiracy." The defendant employers were declared not guilty because it was not shown that they were actuated in their acts by an improper motive. The judge reasoned that a businessman might, by competition, seriously injure a competitor, but as long as this was accomplished without malice and by fair means, there was no basis for a legal action because such an interference with a competitor's business was permissible. He treated the wage question as pure business and concluded that the employers could combine to reduce the workers' wages, as an ordinary business matter.

In the case of *Commonwealth* v. *Hunt,* Chief Justice Shaw applied the same legal reasoning, but for the protection of a labor organization. He reasoned that, since the motive or purpose of a labor union was the improvement of working conditions, its object was not an improper or unlawful purpose; and as long as the means used to accomplish it were not unlawful, the doctrine of criminal conspiracy did not apply to it.

The decision in *Commonwealth* v. *Hunt* is one of the most important in the history of evolution of union rights in the United States. Coming in the early period of union development and made by Chief Justice Shaw, who enjoyed great prestige in the legal profession, it has gone far to discourage the use of the criminal conspiracy doctrine in labor cases. It enabled workers to organize themselves into unions. It removed the fear that they would be subjected to criminal proceedings for merely joining a labor union. It also enabled other labor organizations to encourage membership in their unions and to get strength from their unity because their refusal to work with nonmembers was held by Justice Shaw not to be unlawful. Labor unions secured legal approval of the "closed shop" principle, which immeasurably strengthened their ranks and enhanced their prestige.

While this important decision discouraged the use of the criminal conspiracy doctrine in labor cases, it did not necessarily leave labor free from prosecution under this doctrine. There have been numerous instances where a court considered the conduct of a labor union as socially injurious or oppressive and therefore applied the theory of criminal conspiracy, although the conduct of the union was admittedly not legally criminal. The vagueness of the doctrine of criminal conspiracy enabled individual judges to exercise their own prejudices, in its application.

This doctrine of "virtuous ends pursued by virtuous means" inaugurated an era of what may be characterized as *reluctant tolerance* of labor unions. The unions were legally to be tolerated, but reluctantly. This reluctance enabled the judiciary to interfere with the growth of unions on many occasions. This doctrine of "ends and means" laid the basis for many an injunction in labor disputes. A labor union, under the conspiracy doctrine, could be held responsible for the acts of individuals, and the unlawful conduct of any member of a labor combination made the entire combination an unlawful one. Thus, after this decision, labor was confronted less with the charges of the criminal conspiracy doctrine but became confronted more with the use of a new legal weapon against it—the injunction.

-3-

Government by Injunction—The Pullman Strike

(1894–1895)

UNITED STATES V. DEBS

I

In the early history of American labor unions the nation's interest was aroused by a strike which occurred in 1894. The noble efforts of an idealistic union were smashed by the railroads, which enlisted the willing aid of the attorney general of the United States. This is the story of the Pullman strike.

One of the unforgettable leaders of that strike was Eugene V. Debs, or Gene Debs, as he was popularly called by thousands of his admirers. In his early days Debs was a locomotive fireman, and an active member of his union, the Brotherhood of Locomotive Firemen. He combined a militant zeal for organizing with the idealistic spirit of self-sacrifice for the benefit of the men on the roads. From the post of local secretary of the Terre Haute Lodge, he rose in 1880 to the office of grand secretary and treasurer of the brotherhood and editor in chief of its *Locomotive Firemen's Magazine*. His efforts and energies were devoted to organizing a powerful union which should command respect from the railroad magnates.

Debs felt that the lack of a central authority among the railroad workers prevented them from presenting a solid front to the railroad; that the railroad workers' organization, based on separate crafts was likely to bring about mutual distrust and dissension among them. The loss of the locomotive engineers' strike against the Chicago, Burlington & Quincy Railroad in 1888 convinced Debs that one big union for the railroad workers was essential for their welfare. George W. Howard, the ex-grand chief of the Order of

29

Railway Conductors, was of the same opinion. In fact, Howard worked out a comprehensive plan for a central organization which would include all railway workers. In 1891, he submitted this plan to Samuel Gompers, president of the American Federation of Labor, and asked him to head such an organization. Gompers, however, turned it down as impractical and also because he thought that this plan would undermine the existing railroad brotherhoods. Howard then took the plan to Debs.

In 1893, after the railroad brotherhoods had failed to support the switchmen's strike at Buffalo, Debs resigned from the Brotherhood of Locomotive Firemen, to devote his time to the building of a new organization among railroad workers along industrial lines. With the aid of George Howard and Sylvester Keliher of the Order of Railway Conductors, on June 20, 1893, Debs organized the American Railway Union, which admitted all railway workers to membership, regardless of occupation, and regardless of whether they were employed on the roads or in the roads' shops.

The success of this new union was instantaneous. Very early in its career it was compelled to test its strength when James J. Hill, president of the Great Northern Railroad, cut the wages of its laborers, members of the American Railway Union, and refused to arbitrate the issue with the workers. Debs met Hill's highhanded action with a strike by the members of the American Railway Union without the firemen and engineers, who belonged to the brotherhoods. An injunction was issued against the strike leaders. Debs's impassioned pleas for unity kept the men on strike. Finally, pressure from the business community in St. Paul and Minneapolis forced Hill to confer. In May, 1894, Hill yielded on several issues and some of the wage cuts were rescinded. Unity of action proved a success. The prestige of Debs and the American Railway Union enormously increased. By June, 1894, the American Railway Union claimed 150,000 members organized in 465 local lodges.

The General Managers' Association, a group of railroad executives formed in 1886, took note of this new organization as a force to reckon with. They were determined to defeat it at the first opportunity. Very shortly the opportunity presented itself.

II

The town of Pullman, outside of Chicago, Illinois, was founded by George Pullman, the originator of Pullman Palace Car Company,

builder of Pullman sleeping and dining cars. This was a so-called
"model company town." George Pullman reigned supreme. His
company owned the churches, the shops, the very homes of the
workers, as well as the hotel located there. Even the hotel was a
"model" hotel, run on the principle of temperance (drinks delivered
to gentlemen only in their rooms). Pullman fixed the wages of the
workers and Pullman fixed the rents the workers had to pay for
their housing accommodations. The company pamphlet boasted that
the town of Pullman "has illustrated the helpful combination of
Capital and Labor without strife or stultification, upon the lines of
mutual recognition." But the pamphlet did not say that George
Pullman would not recognize or tolerate any organization of workers
in his factory.

The panic and depression of 1893 adversely affected the Pullman
business. For the purpose of stimulating business the company
claimed it was selling its output for less than cost. It cut the wages
of the workers by more than 30 per cent, but did not cut the 8 per
cent dividend to its stockholders and refused to cut the rents charged
by the company to the workers for housing. As a result of the wage
cut, the winter of 1894 was a winter of misery for the Pullman
workers. They were aroused and decided to form a union. They
were unable to meet in the model town of Pullman, which had no
hall or even a saloon where the workers could meet and talk freely,
so some of them crossed over into the neighboring town of Kensing-
ton. There they formed a union and later affiliated with the American Railway Union.

On May 7, 1894, a grievance committee, representing the workers,
visited the Pullman Company and requested three things: (1) that
the wage cut be rescinded; (2) that the wages be restored to previous
levels; (3) that the rent for the housing be decreased. They were
advised to see Mr. Pullman himself. Two days later they met with
Mr. Pullman. He told them that the company was taking work even
at a loss, so that it might give them employment and therefore
would not rescind the wage cut. He refused to consider the rent
question because that to him was a landlord-tenant problem and
not an employer-employee issue. He induced the workers not to take
any action, and promised that the company would not discriminate
against any member of their grievance committee. He also promised
that shop abuses they complained of would be investigated.

But on the day following, three members of the grievance com-

mittee were fired. All that night and into next morning the representatives of the nineteen Pullman locals met. The discharge of the
three committeemen convinced them of Pullman's duplicity in his
dealings with them and they voted unanimously to strike. George
Pullman got wind of it and decided to lock out the workers but the
union beat him to it. Twenty-five hundred employees left the shops
immediately, while six hundred quit work at noon. They went out
on strike in support of the three requests their grievance committee
had made to Mr. Pullman.

The company posted a notice that the plant would be closed
indefinitely.

III

It appeared to be a peaceful and orderly strike. The strikers made
various attempts to negotiate a settlement but George Pullman
steadfastly refused to negotiate. After the strike had been going on
for a few weeks, the Pullman strikers appealed to the American
Railway Union, their parent organization, which was then holding
its convention in Chicago, to order a sympathy strike so that its
members should refuse to haul Pullman cars on any railroad. At
that time the American Railway Union was faced with other pressing problems—wage cuts on many railroads, blacklisting of its members, and the refusal of the General Managers' Association to deal
with it. Debs urged that the Pullman strikers first seek arbitration
of their dispute. The strikers did so, but met with absolute refusal:
George Pullman had "nothing to arbitrate." The strikers renewed
their appeal for a sympathy strike. Debs and the other American
Railway Union officers were reluctant to involve their young organization in a test of strength on such a broad scale, but the stirring
appeal from the Pullman delegates swayed the convention. On June
21, 1894, the convention gave Pullman an ultimatum: unless he
consented within four days to negotiate a settlement with his employees, a sympathy strike would be ordered. Pullman again had
"nothing to arbitrate."

Debs, not convinced but faithful to the convention decision, an-
nounced a boycott on Pullman Palace cars. The members of the
American Railway Union would not inspect, switch, or haul the
Pullman cars on any railroad.

George Pullman was not alone in his fight against the American

Railway Union. The day before the boycott was officially declared, Pullman enlisted the support of the unreluctant General Managers' Association. The association grasped this opportunity to crush industrial unionism on the railroads and destroy the American Railway Union. Their plans were well laid in advance. Though the union members were willing to haul all trains, refusing only to handle Pullman cars until the Pullman Company should consent to arbitration, the railroad officials determined that if the Pullman cars were not handled, the mail cars should not move. They ordered that cars carrying the mails be attached to the Pullman cars, so that when a switchman cut out a Pullman car, the car carrying the mail was automatically cut. They also ordered the discharge of all men who refused to haul the Pullman cars, compelling the union to strike for the protection of the discharged men. By these means they converted the boycott against Pullman cars into a general strike against the railroads, the nerve center of the industrial life of America, involved the union in legal battles in the federal courts, and prepared a pretext for interference by the federal government.

The General Managers' Association also called upon the United States marshal for special deputies to prevent the obstruction of the mails and to protect their property. On instructions from the United States attorney general, 3,600 deputies were hired. They were armed and paid by the railroads and the bills for the "services" in the long run amounted to $400,000. These deputies acted in the double capacity of railroad employees and United States officers, but were not under the direct control of any government official while exercising authority. They were hired indiscriminately, without regard to character or past activities. Many of them proved to have criminal records, and were characterized by the Chicago chief of police as "thugs, thieves and ex-convicts."

The General Managers' Association well knew that John P. Altgeld, then governor of Illinois, had alerted the state militia to maintain order, but they also knew that the governor was sympathetic to labor and, though he would use the militia to keep order, he would not use it for crushing the strike. So they enlisted the aid of Richard B. Olney, attorney general of the United States. It is not amiss to mention that Mr. Olney previously had been a director of the Chicago, Burlington & Quincy Railroad and had been a member of the General Managers' Association, the very group that was now engaged in fighting the union. It may also be pointed out that Olney previously had been the attorney for several railroads, so it is fair to assume that he was influenced by his personal association with them. At the request of the association, he designated Edwin Walker as special counsel to assist the federal attorney in Chicago. The railroads could well rely upon Walker to protect their interests. His biographical sketch in *Who's Who in America* was: "Walker, Edwin, lawyer . . . removed to Chicago in 1865; has represented several railroads as general solicitor since 1860. Illinois counsel for C., M. & St.P.R.R. since 1870. . ."

Immediately after Walker's appointment, plans were laid for federal government interference in this strike. It is reasonably certain that Olney himself sent a letter to Walker advising "vigorous action" and suggesting steps to lay a basis for federal action. Olney advised Walker to charge the union with *conspiracy* to restrain transportation and to obstruct the United States mails, and to apply for an injunction against all leaders of the strike.

Accordingly, on July 2, 1894, a complaint was filed on behalf of the federal government, charging the American Railway Union, Debs, and sixteen other named individuals and "others whose names are not known" with a conspiracy to interfere with and restrain regular transportation, obstruct the transportation of the mails, and by menaces, threats, and intimidation prevent the employment of persons.

On the basis of this complaint and some affidavits, the attorney general secured from Judge Peter S. Grosscup an injunction against all the defendants, restraining them "from in any way or manner interfering with, hindering, obstructing or stopping" any of the business of the railroads entering Chicago, or any trains carrying United States mails or engaged in interstate commerce.

Olney was determined to circumvent the state authorities and to crush the strike. Immediately upon the issuance of the injunction, he prevailed upon President Cleveland to dispatch to the scene federal troops and, on July 4, 1894, the federal government sent its soldiers—four companies of the 15th Infantry—to the Blue Island railroad yards near Chicago to enforce the injunction. In vain did Governor Altgeld, in a telegram to President Cleveland, vigorously protest that the sending of the troops was unconstitutional interference in the affairs of the state of Illinois and that, "if any assistance were needed, the State stood ready to furnish a hundred men for every one man required, and stood ready to do so at a moment's notice." Altgeld also charged that the sending of federal troops in this case was motivated by politics and was in violation of state rights. But Cleveland, on Olney's advice, disregarded the protest. The federal troops remained there.

The very arrival of the federal troops caused great resentment and disturbed the peaceful conduct of the strike. Their very presence irritated the strikers. The hired deputies, many of whom had criminal records, provoked and contributed to lawlessness. Riots followed. Finally, at the request of the mayor of Chicago, state militia was sent in by Governor Altgeld, and the militia restored order.

IV

The injunction and the sending of federal troops aroused the leaders of labor. They saw in it a new technique for effective hamstringing of legitimate activities of unions. They feared that this threat would hang over labor in any strike. They reasoned that if a judge without hearing any witnesses, merely on "information and belief" affidavits, could restrain a union from either calling a strike or conducting it—then the right to strike would be without substance. True, an injunction technically is supposed to keep things in *status quo*—to leave the situation where it was—but the very purpose of a strike is often to seek a change in a situation. If picketing, paying strike benefits, and appealing to the public could be banned by a temporary injunction issued on the request of an employer, then a strike would be crippled before it could be effective. Once it was crushed and the spirit of the strikers with it, even a dismissal of the injunction later would be useless to the union. The damage to the union would be irreparable, and the opportunity to secure collective bargaining in such a situation might not recur for a long time. In the Pullman strike the labor leaders became still more aroused because the federal government, under the excuse that there was interference with the mails, came to the help of private employers, the Pullman Company and the railroads, to assist them in crushing the strike. Debs tried to organize a sympathy strike of all labor in the entire country and a conference for this purpose was scheduled to be held in Chicago on July 12, 1894.

In the meantime, the office of the attorney general took steps to hasten and assure the defeat of the strike. Accordingly, Judge Gross-cup summoned a grand jury and charged it to the effect that the strike amounted to an *insurrection* against the state. Under such instructions, the grand jury on the same day, July 10, voted indictments against Debs, Howard, Keliher, and Rogers—the president, vice-president, secretary, and a director of the American Railway Union—charging them with criminal conspiracy (*a*) to obstruct the mails, (*b*) to interrupt interstate commerce, and (*c*) to intimidate citizens in the free exercise and enjoyment of their rights and privileges under the Constitution. The federal authorities broke into the offices of the union and seized all union papers and legal documents. All the indicted union officers were arrested, but released on bail of $10,000 each.

The attorney general's strategy proved effective. An attempted general strike in the city of Chicago proved a failure. The conference to consider a sympathy strike in the entire country under the guidance of Samuel Gompers, president of the American Federation of Labor, concluded that the vigorous action taken by the federal government against the strike, the hostility of the press, and the fact that this was a depression period, militated against plunging into such a sympathy strike.

Debs offered to call off the Pullman boycott on condition that all the railroad strikers, except those convicted of a crime, be rehired without discrimination. This plea for mere reinstatement of strikers practically admitted defeat of the strike. The General Managers' Association ignored the offer. Aware that victory was in the bag, it now wanted to destroy the union that preached and practiced industrial unionism on the railroads. More than that, it wanted to make an example of these union leaders. Within one week after the four union leaders had been arrested on the indictment, Debs and the three other leaders were again arrested, this time on the charge of contempt of court for violating the injunction. Their bail was set again at $10,000 for each. Within two days thereafter, the federal grand jury indicted 75 individuals on 23 indictments naming Debs, Howard, Keliher, and Rogers in nearly all of the indictments. More than seven hundred strikers were arrested. Some were charged with violation of federal statutes; others with violation of state laws.

The strikers were disillusioned, disheartened, and despondent. So was Debs. The railway strike was officially called off on August

5, 1894, by a special convention held in Chicago. The General Managers' Association was victorious. So was George Pullman. The strike against the Pullman Company also was called off officially on September 6, 1894.

V

The legal steps taken by the federal government against the strikers did not terminate with the calling off of the strike. It will be recalled that the government prosecuted the strike leaders in two ways: one by charging them with contempt of court for violating the temporary injunction; the other by indicting them for criminally conspiring. The criminal conspiracy charge that played such an important part in crushing the strike was never pressed to final prosecution and, in fact, was dismissed. The circumstances of the dismissal are rather interesting. It was reached for trial on February 9, 1895, about six months after the strike had been called off. It was to be tried before Judge Grosscup, the same judge who had issued the injunctions. The attorneys were Edwin Walker, the same attorney who had secured the injunctions, representing both the government and the railroads, and Clarence S. Darrow, appearing for the defendants. Darrow's policy was to emphasize the social issues involved. Accordingly, he subpoenaed George Pullman as a witness and announced that he intended to examine the members of the General Managers' Association and show that they conspired to destroy the American Railway Union and that their actions had brought about the railway strike and the interference with the mails. But Darrow was not given the opportunity. George Pullman left the state to avoid testifying. The General Managers testified that they did not remember what had taken place at the joint General Managers and Pullman meeting. Darrow demanded the production of the printed proceedings of their conference, but Darrow had no chance to examine these minutes because court adjourned for lunch and after lunch Judge Grosscup announced that one of the jurors had suddenly been taken ill. The judge adjourned the case in spite of the fact that Darrow was willing to proceed with the trial. The case, at the request of the government, was adjourned on several occasions and thereafter never prosecuted. Apparently, having achieved their main aim in defeating the strike and smashing the union, neither the government nor the railroads would risk failure to make the criminal conspiracy charge stick, nor would they risk exhibiting and placing in the public records the practices and means by which they had defeated the American Railway Union.

But the contempt charges for violating the temporary injunction were prosecuted with vigor, both by the government and by the railroads. Two petitions charging contempt of court were filed during the strike, one by the attorney general of the United States and the other by the receivers of the Atchison, Topeka & Santa Fe Railroad.

The two petitions, one in July and the other on August 1, 1894, in substance charged: that the defendants having knowledge of the injunction restraining the strike activities and also of the fact that there were receivers and that the court prohibited interference with the receivers' possession and management of the property, nevertheless violated it; that Debs and the other defendants had continued advising and directing the strike, thus violating both the injunction of July 20, 1894, and the court orders of December, 1893, and June 29, 1894, prohibiting interference with the receivers' possession and management of the Atchison, Topeka & Santa Fe Railroad; that the defendants knew that there had been violence and must have known that the continuation of the strike would result in further violence. It was further charged that the union was a monopoly and that the defendants conspired to interfere with interstate commerce in violation of the Sherman Antitrust Act.

The defendants in their answer denied the conspiracy charge and that they had any intention to interfere with interstate commerce and that the Sherman Act applied to labor unions. The union contended that the railroad companies with the Pullman Company formed a conspiracy to reduce wages and that it was this conspiracy which brought about blocking of interstate commerce. Alleging also that the strike had been peaceful and voluntary, the union interposed a technical defense contending that the federal courts had no jurisdiction in this case because even if there had been interference with the *highways*, the latter are not interstate commerce. If the court had no jurisdiction, disobedience of an invalid injunction would not be a punishable contempt.

The defendants were tried on the contempt charges in September before Judge William A. Woods and about three months later, on December 14, 1894, he announced his decision. He overruled the union's contentions that highways are not within interstate commerce and that labor organizations are exempt from the Sherman Act. He concluded that the United States had a property right in the mails, that the court had a right to issue the injunction, and that the injunction was violated by the defendants who knew, or should have known, that violence was likely to occur.

The judge further held that the right to strike was not absolute. There was no basis for the assertion by defense counsel that " in free America every man has a right to abandon his position, for a good or a bad reason, and that another, for good or bad reason, may advise or persuade him to do so." Concluding that the Pullman boycott committed the American Railway Union to an unlawful conspiracy and all members were criminally responsible therefor, Judge Woods found the defendants, with the exception of one, guilty of criminal contempt and sentenced them to jail—Debs to six months, the other defendants to three months each, to be served at Woodstock County jail.

The defendants petitioned the United States Supreme Court for (*a*) a writ of error and (*b*) a writ of habeas corpus. The petition for the writ of error was immediately denied on the technical ground that the order of the Circuit Court was not a *final* judgment or decree, and therefore not appealable.

VI

The procedure called a "writ of habeas corpus" was the ancient method of securing personal liberty, by getting a court order to "produce the body" of the detained person before the court, so that the latter might judge whether or not the person was properly jailed. The question as to whether the writ of habeas corpus should be issued by the Supreme Court in the case of these defendants was argued on March 25-26, 1895, before the United States Supreme Court.

Lyman Trumbull, associated in the defense with S. S. Gregory and Clarence S. Darrow, made the principal argument. He raised various technical objections in connection with the procedure in the injunction case, and then attacked the order on substantive grounds. Mr. Trumbull contended: (1) The activities of the American Railway Union could not be considered an unlawful conspiracy because they were directed merely to bringing about an adjustment of the differences between the Pullman Company and its employees. To gain that end, the union called upon its members to quit work. Such activities were not unlawful. (2) Even if the workers' refusal to work for the railroad company did interfere with interstate commerce, nevertheless, it was not a crime and therefore the defendants could not be held guilty of a criminal conspiracy. (3) The government's bill for injunction should have been dismissed because the complaint was aimed at preventing interference, not with government property, but with *private* property. (4) If the defendants were guilty of a crime—interference with United States mails—they should have been tried in a criminal court. Under our laws no injunctions are issued to stop crimes. (5) The defendants were sentenced by a court of equity for doing things forbidden by criminal statute, but courts of equity, under our laws, have no jurisdiction over crimes. In criminal matters defendants are entitled to a jury trial, but in this case a court of equity deprived persons of liberty without a jury trial. (6) The Sherman Act did not apply in this instance and if it did, then the act was unconstitutional and the complaint should be dismissed.

About two months after the argument, on May 27, 1895, Justice David Josiah Brewer delivered the opinion of the court. He said there were two main issues. First, under the Constitution, is the government authorized to directly intervene to prevent forcible obstruction of interstate commerce? Second, if the government has such legal authority, has a court of equity jurisdiction to issue an injunction to prevent such obstruction? He held, in substance:

One: The federal government had all the attributes of sovereignty within the limitations of the system; it acted directly on its citizens and had control over interstate commerce and the post office. The states might not obstruct interstate commerce by their laws. ". . . Can it be that any mere voluntary association of individuals within the limits of that state has a power which the state itself does not possess?"

Two: Since the national government had power over interstate commerce and the mails, it "may prevent any unlawful and forcible interference therewith."

Three: Legislation and punishment were not the only possible remedy for the evil. Criminal punishment was not practicable against a great body of the inhabitants of a state and might fail to achieve a desired end.

Four: The writ of injunction might be used to abate a public nuisance if the remedy at law be inadequate. The government had sufficient interest to appear as an equity plaintiff in this cause by reason of its property in the mails. By "express statute" the government had assumed jurisdiction over interstate commerce when carried upon railroads. It was charged, therefore, with the duty of keeping those highways of interstate commerce free from obstruction.

Five: A court of equity might properly assume jurisdiction. The injunction had been rarely used because it rarely had been necessary, but the special reason for the use of equity was evident in this instance.

Six: A court enforcing obedience by proceeding against a defendant for contempt was "not executing the criminal law of the land, but only securing to suitors the rights which it has adjudged them entitled to."

Seven: The Circuit Court had power to issue the injunction, to inquire as to disobedience of its orders, and to proceed to punish for contempt. Having full jurisdiction, the court's "finding of the fact of disobedience is not open to review or *habeas corpus* in this or any court."

The petition for a writ of habeas corpus was denied. The defendants Debs, Howard, Keliher, and Rogers were compelled to serve their sentences in the county jail of Woodstock.

VII

The collapse of the Pullman strike was charged by Eugene V. Debs directly to the actions of the federal government. Testifying before the United States Strike Commission, appointed to investigate the strike, he said "the ranks were broken, and the strike was broken up . . . not by the Army and not by any other power, but simply and solely by the action of the United States Courts in restraining us from discharging our duties as officers and representatives of the employees. . . ." Labor resented the government action in these cases as "government by injunction." The Supreme Court by its decision in this case not only put its stamp of approval upon the use of the injunction by the federal government in labor disputes, but also broadened the use of the injunction. Theretofore the injunction had been used to prevent irreparable injury to property, which had been interpreted to mean physical property. In this case there was no contention by the government that any injury to its *physical* property was threatened. However, Justice Brewer, by his legal reasoning, stretched "property" to mean not only physical property, but any *intangible right*. By his definition, the employer-employee relationship, the merchant-customer relationship, mail passage or shipment of goods in interstate commerce became a "property right." This broadening of the term "property" immeasurably broadened the possible use of the injunction in all strike cases since there hardly is a strike in which some kind of "property right" under this definition is not likely to be involved.

Danger to labor lurked not only in the court's reading new content into the concept of "property," but also in its reaffirmation of the application to labor unions of the Sherman Antitrust Act, which had been enacted only five years before for the purpose of curbing business monopoly. This reaffirmation gave early indication to organized labor of what it could expect from the courts by way of interpretation of legislation concerning labor's rights to better working conditions in modern industrial America.

The decision of the court confirmed the conviction of the labor leaders that workers must become politically conscious and use their votes to put into office friends of labor and to defeat its enemies, that labor must seek the "correction of industrial and economic ailment at the ballot box." The echo of this new labor policy reverberated in the platform of the Democratic Party of 1896, which repudiated President Cleveland and upheld Governor Altgeld in these words:

We denounce arbitrary interference by Federal authorities in local affairs as a violation of the Constitution of the United States and a crime against free institutions. . . . And we especially object to *government by injunction* as a new and highly dangerous form of oppression by which Federal judges, in contempt of the laws of the States and the rights of citizens, become at once legislators, judges and executioners.

The drama and tragedy of this Pullman strike had a significant influence on the development of the rights of unions. It high-lighted the need for social and legal recognition of labor unions by employers and the need for administrative procedures and techniques for the settlement of labor disputes. The United States Strike Commission, criticizing the Pullman Company for depriving its employees of the advantage of protection that a labor union might afford them, said in its report:

The policy of both the Pullman Company and the railway Managers' Association in reference to application to arbitrate, closed the door to all attempts at conciliation and settlement of differences . . . a different policy would have prevented the loss of life and great loss of property and wages occasioned by the strike.

Though the Pullman strike was definitely lost by the union, it propelled the development of union rights. The beginning of a public policy more tolerant toward labor may be traced to the investigation of this strike.

- 4 -

That "Freedom" to Hire and Fire

(1906–1908)

UNITED STATES V. ADAIR

I

The Pullman strike aroused the nation's interest in the railroad worker. President Cleveland, who, on the advice of his attorney general, had been instrumental in breaking the strike, appointed a special commission to investigate the causes of the strike and make recommendations for the prevention of similar occurrences in the future.

The commission found that the unrest of the railroad workers was to be attributed to the employers' conduct in preventing unionization by the employees and in their refusal to deal with labor organizations In its report of November, 1894, the commission made various recommendations for new legislation to be enacted with a view of preventing strikes on the railroads and protecting the workers' right to organize. The commission's report was sent by President Cleveland to Congress. In 1895, Representative Constantine Jacob Erdman of Pennsylvania introduced a bill based on the commission's recommendations. But the proposed legislation did not have smooth sailing. While the House passed it with modifications on two occasions, in 1895 and 1897, the Senate rejected it both times.

The railroad unions favored the bill, but the American Federation of Labor and the railroad owners opposed it. Their reasons and motives for the opposition were entirely different. Samuel Gompers and Andrew Furuseth for the AFL had opposed it because they regarded this legislation as a "step toward serfdom" since the bill prohibited workers from striking and quitting the job without

44

notice under certain circumstances. The railroad employers opposed it because they claimed that labor organizations were not really responsible, either financially or in their ability to control their members, and that, therefore, any arbitration award rendered would be one-sided, enforceable against the railroads but not enforceable against the unions. The AFL finally withdrew its opposition at the request of the railroad unions and in 1898, under the combined influence of the Interstate Commerce Commission, Labor Commissioner Wright, and the Railroad Brotherhoods, the Erdman Act was passed over strong opposition in the Senate. It became a law on June 1, 1898.

II

The main aim of the Erdman Act was to maintain industrial peace on the railroads of the nation. It set up a Railroad Labor Board with power to investigate industrial disputes on the railroads and recommend settlement terms. The act was an attempt to delay and if possible to prevent strikes on the nation's railroads, by the extensive use of mediation or arbitration machinery. Before strikes could legally take place, the parties were obliged to endeavor to mediate or possibly arbitrate their dispute. Arbitration was not compulsory. If both sides consented to arbitration, then the arbitration board would consist of three members, one member chosen by the railroad employer concerned, one by the union representing the employees (if the latter were unorganized, by a special selected committee), and the third arbitrator named by the other two. Pending the outcome of such arbitration, the employers were not to discharge or alter the terms of employment and the employees were not to strike. For a period of three months after the award, employees were not to quit their employment in groups without giving thirty days' notice in writing.

From the railroad unions' point of view, the most attractive provisions of the act were embodied in Section 10. It outlawed "yellow-dog" contracts. Under penalty of a fine, employers were prohibited from requiring that as a condition of employment the employee should agree not to be a member of a labor organization. Moreover, this section prohibited the blacklisting of employees on railroads and made it a misdemeanor to discharge an employee because of his membership in a labor organization.

It should be noted that in the past it had not been uncommon for railroads to discharge workers for joining a union and to blacklist workers who participated in strikes. In the light of these past experiences, it is small wonder that the Railroad Brotherhoods welcomed the Erdman Act and pinned great hope on the special protection extended to union members by Section 10. The unions expected that this would enable them to strengthen and extend unionization on the railroads. Their expectations did not materialize, however. True, two attempts were made to enforce this section. Hugh J. Hill, chief train dispatcher at Taunton, Massachusetts, employed by the New York, New Haven & Hartford Railroad Co., was indicted in 1899 for violation of this section and J. M. Scott, employee of the Louisville & Nashville Railroad, was indicted in 1906, but the indictment against Scott was dismissed on the ground that the law was unconstitutional and, though the indictment against Hill was upheld, he was not brought to trial until 1907. The jury, having disagreed at that trial, the case was dropped. Thus, Section 10 of the Erdman Act lay dormant on the statute books without benefiting the railroad unions.

During the beginning of the twentieth century there were fresh stirrings in American public opinion. Reformers like Robert M. La Follette were voicing progressive views in the United States Senate. Theodore Roosevelt was making progressiveness a popular and respectable idea. Unions sensed the changes in social attitude toward workers and initiated unionization campaigns to strengthen their position. In this atmosphere Section 10 of the Erdman Act was awakened from its sleep.

This was the background of the case of *United States* v. *Adair*.

III

The Louisville & Nashville Railroad, contrary to Section 10 of the Erdman Act, would not tolerate any union members in its employ and would have no dealings with unions. When William Adair, master mechanic for the railroad, learned that O. B. Coppage, a locomotive fireman in the railroad's employ, was a union member, he discharged him for belonging to a union. This happened on October 15, 1906. On the demands of the union that the Erdman Act be enforced, the United States attorney secured an indictment against Adair for violating Section 10 of the Erdman Act which made it a misdemeanor to discharge any employee for union membership. Adair's counsel demurred to the indictment on the ground that the section was unconstitutional. Justice Andrew M. Cochran of the United States District Court of the Eastern District of Kentucky, before whom the motion came up, handed down his decision in November, 1906. He said there were two constitutional issues: (1) Has the Congress the power to enact Section 10 of the Erdman Act under its "commerce" power under the Constitution? (2) If the Congress has such power, may the Congress do so without violating the "freedom of contract" guaranteed by the Fifth Amendment to the Constitution?

Justice Cochran observed that the Congressional power to regulate interstate commerce includes the power to regulate the *adjuncts of commerce,* and that railroads are such adjuncts. Since this legislation affects the relations between master and servant on railroads in interstate commerce, hence it affects the adjuncts of commerce *directly* and is within Congressional power to regulate such relation.

In passing on the second constitutional issue—"freedom of contract"—the justice observed that the position of a common carrier concerning regulation by the government was different from that of a private person engaged in an ordinary business. The carrier exercises a public function, to which it has no right unless it secures the consent of the national government, express or implied. The United States in giving its consent impliedly exacts some power of control. It undoubtedly has the power to require efficient performance of the public functions undertaken by the railroads. Similarly, it may prevent the railroad from acting in a manner which may cause an interruption in the performance of the public function of that railroad. Since Section 10 is aimed at preventing interruptions on interstate railroads by regulating the relations between master and servants on such railroads, the law has a direct relation to interstate commerce and is within the power of Congress. The justice concluded that the "freedom of contract" guaranteed by the Fifth Amendment to the Constitution was not intended to protect such individual "freedom" as will provoke strikes and cause the cessation of interstate commerce; that Congress in restricting the "freedom of contract" by prohibiting the discharging of a worker on interstate railroads for being a member of the union, acted within its constitutional powers.

Justice Cochran also passed on the claim of Adair's counsel that Section 10 was unconstitutional as *class legislation* because it protected only union members and not other workers. The justice pointed out that the law was aimed at preventing interruption of interstate commerce and observed that discriminatory discharge of union members was likely to cause such interruption while a similar discriminatory discharge against a nonmember was not likely to produce such interruption because there was nobody to back up such a nonmember. Hence, the public policy of preventing discriminatory action only against union members. The justice concluded that the law was not class legislation and not unconstitutional, overruled the demurrer of the defendant Adair, and ordered him to plead and stand trial.

Adair pleaded "Not guilty." At the trial the jury found that Adair did discharge Coppage, the locomotive fireman, for his membership in the union, in violation of Section 10 of the Erdman Act, and rendered a verdict of guilty. The court fined Adair $100.

On behalf of Adair the judgment was appealed to the Supreme Court of the United States.

IV

Under the title of *Adair* v. *The United States,* the case was argued before the Supreme Court on October 29, 1907. Adair's attorneys argued:

(*a*) Section 10 was unconstitutional. It dealt with matters which had only an *indirect* effect on interstate commerce, and, therefore, Congress had no constitutional power to enact this law. (*b*) This law attempted to regulate the ordinary relation of master and servant. *Such relation* was exclusively within *state*, and not federal, control. The Congress therefore had no power to legislate on matters that did not involve the question of interstate commerce. (*c*) This law destroyed, or at least impaired, the valuable property right of freedom of contract on the part of the employer to hire and fire his employees, which right was guaranteed by the Fifth Amendment, and, therefore, this law was unconstitutional. (*d*) Finally, Section 10 constituted *class legislation*. It conferred on union members privileges which were not conferred on others. It imposed limitations on the discharge of union members, but did not impose similar limitations on the discharge of nonunion workers. "Under our form of government which guarantees equal privileges to all before the law, it is not competent for Congress or state legislatures to make such an unreasonable classification as in the statute before us whereby union labor is preferred as against non-union labor."

The government attorneys, in support of the law, contended:

(1) Section 10 of the Erdman Act had a *direct,* not merely indirect relation to interstate commerce, and, therefore, it was within the power of Congress to enact such legislation. (2) The constitutionality of Section 10 was to be determined, in the light of the act's general purposes, not merely the separate sections. The purpose of the entire act was the protection of interstate and foreign commerce by the avoidance of strikes, lockouts, etc. Congress recognized that discrimination against employees by reason of their membership in labor organizations might bring on such disturbances. It had the power to adopt measures to avoid them, and Section 10 was merely a part of that general law. (3) In the judgment of Congress, the regulation of the railroads' relations with the employees embodied in Section 10 was necessary to safeguard interstate commerce, and Congress had the power so to regulate a common carrier as in its judgment was necessary adequately to protect and safeguard such commerce. (4) The right of "freedom of contract" guaranteed by the Fifth Amendment was *subordinate* to Congressional power under the Constitution to regulate interstate commerce. Moreover, common carriers, because of the nature of their business, were properly subject to greater control than ordinary enterprises, and must *subordinate* their "freedom of contract" to necessary regulations by Congress.

On January 27, 1908, the Supreme Court rendered its decision on this important legislation. Justice John Marshall Harlan (with Justices Fuller, Brewer, White, Peckham, and Day concurring), handed down the opinion of the court. He considered the real issue in the case to be: Has Congress the power to make a law that an interstate carrier or its agent, in discharging an employee for membership in a labor organization, is committing a criminal offense against the United States?

The justice answered the question in the negative and reasoned in substance:

One: Section 10 of the Erdman Act violated the Fifth Amendment. It was an evasion of the personal liberty, as well as the right of property, guaranteed by that amendment. The railroad had a right to fix the terms upon which it would accept the services of Coppage, and Coppage had the right to become or not to become an employee of the railroad company upon the railroad's terms.

Two: Although reasonable restraints on "freedom of contract" might be upheld by the court, it was not within the functions of government—at least in the absence of a contract between the parties —to compel any person in the course of his business, and against his will, to accept or retain the personal services of another.

Three: "The right of a person to sell his labor upon such terms as he deems proper is, in its essence, the same as the right of the purchaser of labor to prescribe the terms upon which he will accept such labor from the person offering to sell it."

Four: Adair had the legal right to fire Coppage for union membership. Coppage had the legal right to quit because nonunion men were hired. In all such particulars, the employer and employee had equality of right and any legislation that disturbed that equality was an arbitrary interference with the liberty of contract which no government could legally justify in a free land.

Five: If contracts existed, they could be enforced. Congress might make it a crime to ignore or refuse to perform the terms of such contract by employer or employee in interstate commerce, but this did not apply to this case because no such contracts existed in this case.

Six: While Congress had full authority over matters having "substantial connection" with commerce, there was no such legal or logical connection between an employee's membership in a labor organization and the carrying on of interstate commerce. Only by imputing to Congress a fear of illegal or violent measures by unions could this law be upheld. If Section 10 were upheld, Congress might pass laws requiring that only *union* or only *nonunion* men could be employed. Congress had no such power.

Seven: This Section 10 was enacted under the guise of regulating interstate commerce. It arbitrarily sanctioned an illegal evasion of personal liberty, as well as of the right of property of the defendant Adair. It was repugnant to the Fifth Amendment.

Eight: While Section 10 was unconstitutional, it was separable from the other provisions of the Erdman Act and, therefore, the arbitration and mediation provisions of the act might remain in force.

Two of the justices, Joseph McKenna and Oliver Wendell Holmes, dissented. The two dissenting opinions obviously had no effect on the decision but they are indicative of a current of progressive thinking in the high tribunal. In his dissenting opinion, Justice McKenna reasoned:

(*a*) The Supreme Court, in a previous decision concerning employers' liability, held that Congress, under its power to regulate interstate commerce, was entitled to establish new regulations of the master-servant relationship. Therefore, by the same process of reasoning, Congress had power to regulate the master-servant relationship on railroads. Through the scheme of arbitration provided for in Section 10 of the law, this obviously had an aim directly related to interstate commerce.

(*b*) Since the Supreme Court recognized the need of unions in our society, and since unions were legal organizations, might not the Congress take notice of their existence, and in legislating, recognize the power of the unions as a condition to be considered in connection with the particular legislation? ". . . Of what use would it be to attempt to bring bodies of men to agreement and compromise of controversies if you put out of view the influence which moves them or the fellowship which binds them—whether rightfully or wrongfully—to make the cause of one the cause of all?"

(*c*) In enacting Section 10 of the Erdman Act, Congress learned by its experience with the law of 1888. That law also contained arbitration provisions but gave no recognition to the labor organizations, with the result that the law was not effective. The Erdman Act, which was enacted ten years later, was intended by Congress to be an effective law and, therefore, the scheme of arbitration as visualized in this law required the recognition of labor unions. Hence Section 10 was an essential provision of the entire structure of the arbitration scheme under this law and as long as the majority did not invalidate the arbitration machinery it should not invalidate this essential part thereof.

(*d*) If the "freedom of contract" contended for by the railroads should enable them to discharge employees for merely joining a labor organization, and thus by their mere whim or caprice bring about an interruption of interstate commerce, then the intent of Congress to provide an effective arbitration machinery was thwarted and the law could not serve any useful purpose. "Liberty is an attractive thing, but the liberty which is exercised in sheer antipathy does not plead strongly for recognition."

(*e*) Section 10 had a *direct* effect on interstate commerce. The law must be judged as a whole. A provision of law which would prevent or tend to prevent the stoppage of every wheel of every car of the entire railroad system certainly had a *direct* influence on interstate commerce and, therefore, the law was within the power of Congress and was not unconstitutional.

Justice Oliver Wendell Holmes in his brief dissenting opinion concluded:

1. The position of unions in the railroad business had as "intimate and important" a connection with interstate commerce as safety couplers or the liability of master to servant. Legislation to prevent the exclusion of union members from service on the railroads was, therefore, justified under Congress's power to regulate commerce.

2. Section 10 was actually a limited interference with liberty of contract. The railroads were not required by this law to hire anyone. The section simply prohibited the more powerful party from threatening dismissal or exacting certain undertakings from its employees as a condition of employment. It was a reasonable restraint on "freedom of contract" and within Congressional power.

3. Congress was entitled to consider arbitration, as a means of checking railroad strikes, an important measure, and, therefore, Congress could reasonably think that Section 10 would help in that aim.

4. While differences as to the economic value of unions to the workers might well exist, "I could not pronounce it unwarranted if Congress should decide that to foster a strong union was for the best interest, not only of the men, but of the railroads and of the country at large."

In accordance with the majority opinion of the court, the verdict against Adair was reversed and the indictment against him was dismissed.

V

With all due respect to Justice Harlan, his decision in this case may justly be criticized. He based his decision on two premises, both of which were unrealistic and unsound. He justified his first premise, *legal equality of employer and employee*, by applying the abstract idealistic concept of equality to a situation in which, in reality, no equality existed. He paid high tribute to the ideal of equality, spoke eloquently of the equal right of the railroad to hire Coppage and of the equal right of Coppage to accept or reject employment but refused to acknowledge that the term "equality" in such a case has a hollow sound. The very concept of master and servant, employer and employee, suggests *inequality* in their relative bargaining positions. It is highly theoretical, merely illusory, if not plainly misleading, to reason that the worker has the same equal right to accept or not to accept a job as the employer has to give or not to give the job. There is this fundamental *inequality* between them: the employer in discharging an individual employee sacrifices little, if anything; either he will fill the job with another worker or he will get along with one worker less; but the individual employee in exercising his equal "inalienable right" not to accept employment may be depriving his family and himself of the essential necessities of life. The worker's equal "inalienable right" not to work is greatly curtailed by the law of nature, by the need to work in order to eat.

This premise of legal equality ran contrary to the Supreme Court's decision in *Holden* v. *Hardy* in which the court clearly commented on the inequality of the existing bargaining power of employer and employee. Because the court was convinced of such inequality, it affirmed state legislation restricting the hours of male workers engaged in dangerous employment in smelters and underground. If admittedly the individual worker has no equality in bargaining power, how could he enjoy equality of "freedom of contract" in bargaining with his employer? No amount of abstract logic could convince the unprejudiced that Coppage, the worker, could have enjoyed "freedom of contract" in bargaining with the Louisville & Nashville Railroad, his employer, concerning the terms upon which he, Coppage, would accept employment.

Equally unrealistic was Justice Harlan's second premise, that there was *no relation between the railroad workers and interstate commerce.* Experience had shown that the manpower in running the railroads is interwoven with the interstate commerce in which railroads are engaged. One does not need to stretch his imagination too far to realize that an effective labor organization on the railroads can effectively curtail their operations and thus directly interfere with interstate commerce. The country experienced several strikes on railroads caused by labor organization of the workers. This prompted Congress to enact the Erdman Act, which was under consideration in this case. Therefore, Justice Harlan's premise that there "is no connection between interstate commerce and membership in a labor organization" does not ring true. No wonder various legal writers, including Richard Olney, the attorney general in Cleveland's administration, who was instrumental in securing the injunction in the Pullman strike case, criticized this decision. Olney said, "The inability of the Supreme Court to find any connection between membership of a labor union and the carrying on of interstate commerce seems inexplicable."

Had the majority of the court been inclined to support the constitutionality of the Erdman Act, it could have easily done so on the basis that this was legislation to protect a weaker party against the unjust discriminatory practices of a powerful party, the railroad employer. The protection of the weak against the strong by means of antidiscrimination laws is in conformity with the idea of American democracy. It is not unreasonable to suggest that Justice Harlan attempted to exploit the policy of *reluctant tolerance* toward unions advanced in 1842. By that policy the judiciary tolerated unions, but reluctantly. It permitted their legal existence but would not advance their legal rights to enable them to become strong. Justice Harlan would not deprive a worker of the right to join a union but would not tolerate a law prohibiting the employer from penalizing the worker for joining a union. Again, the union is tolerated, but reluctantly, without a legal right to acquire additional strength.

The Adair decision obviously had an unfavorable effect on the railroad unions. It undermined the strength of the then existing unions and served to discourage further unionization. More than that, it in effect encouraged the railroads in their practice of blacklisting workers who were suspected of being active in unionization. This decision prompted the *Railroad Trainman* to observe sarcastically: "Just what law intended to take care of the people against the unfairness of their employers that is not repugnant to the Constitution, remains to be discovered."

While the abstract logic of Justice Harlan's reasoning might have appeared to be expedient, it was too narrow and too artificial to suit the industrial trends of the country or to be considered good law by the legal profession. Such an eminent authority as Professor

Roscoe Pound of Harvard was prompted to remark that such decisions are academic and artificial in their reasoning and likely to engender workers' distrust in the integrity of the courts. He expressed the view that "the evil of those cases will live after them in the impaired authority of the courts long after the decisions themselves are forgotten."

- 5 -

The Danbury Hatters Face the Sherman Act

(1902–1913)

LOEWE V. LAWLOR

I

To a man in the hat trade, the Mad Hatter in Alice in Wonderland did not appear comic, but was a grim and tragic reminder of the fate that might be his. Hatmaking at the end of the nineteenth century could well be considered a "hazardous" occupation. It involved dyeing, steaming, shaping, and finishing hat bodies in an atmosphere filled with steam and dust injurious to the lungs. The dyeing process then used, especially with the introduction of the early coal-tar dyes, ulcerated the hands and arms of the workers, and a great deal of the work was performed by hand. The prime hazard came from the acid, nitrate of mercury, in the "carroting" solution that was used to make the pelt-hair shavings sufficiently limp and rough for matting into felt. The finishing and pressing of the hat at high heat released mercury fumes, causing mercury poisoning. The early symptoms of the disease were swelling gums, loosening teeth, and an unpleasant dribbling of saliva. This was followed by palsy of hands and arms and acute irritability, often leading to insanity.

These trade hazards were an influential contributing factor which prompted the workers in the trade to seek protection through unions. As far back as 1830 union organization among hat workers started. At first it was only on a local level but subsequently the hat workers were among the first trades to organize on a national scale. In 1896, under the name of United Hatters of North America, they affiliated with the American Federation of Labor.

56

The hatters' union was among the first to urge the use of the union label. The union label in a hat indicated that it had been made under union working conditions and thus distinguished it from nonunion-made hats. This label device was designed to induce employers to recognize and bargain with the union. If an employer refused to deal with the union, he could not have the use of the union label and was deprived of customers patronizing union-made goods. Thus the label, and the appeal to the public to patronize union hats and to boycott the nonunion hat, enhanced the union's effectiveness in organizing workers, in settling strikes, and in bringing about collective bargaining.

II

The unorganized hat shop of Dietrich E. Loewe and Martin Fuchs, a copartnership, located at Danbury, Connecticut, was a sore spot for the United Hatters of North America. It pointed to union weakness. The union leaders decided to organize it. In March, 1901, they communicated with Mr. Loewe, requesting a conference to discuss a union agreement. In the course of their conversation, they pointed out to him that an unfavorable reply would prompt the union to use its "usual methods" to bring about unionization. This, apparently, meant a strike and an appeal to the public to boycott his hats.

The firm decided to fight. On April 22, 1901, Loewe replied in writing, that it refused to have its factory unionized. The union leaders realized that the answer was a direct challenge to their organization, but took no immediate action because they were then occupied with a strike in Philadelphia. More than a year later, with the Philadelphia strike settled, the union again communicated with Loewe, requesting him to negotiate a union agreement. Again he refused. This time the union was determined to fight it out. On July 25, 1902, the day following Loewe's refusal to "go union," the Loewe factory was declared on strike.

The union leaders did not know that Loewe was prepared for this. As a matter of fact, a group of antiunion hat manufacturers had previously agreed to finance Loewe to the extent of $20,000 in his fight against the union. The chief leader of this group was C. H. Merritt, a hat manufacturer, whose son, Walter Gordon Merritt, an attorney, later took a leading role in fighting many cases against labor unions. In reliance on the support and financial help of this group of manufacturers, Loewe undertook to fight the union.

Shortly thereafter the union declared Loewe's plant "unfair" and appealed to the public "not to patronize" its product. For a few months the shop was practically at a standstill, but in January, 1903, the plant reopened with nonunion workers. The majority of the new workers were not skilled at hatmaking. A shipping clerk whose sympathies were with the union, though in the employ of the firm, reported to the union the destination of shipments of hats made by Loewe. Using this information, the union dispatched organizers and "missionaries" to Loewe's customers, requesting them not to handle Loewe's hats and warning them that they might be boycotted if they did.

At the request of the United Hatters, the American Federation of Labor placed the Loewe firm on its "we don't patronize" list. Circulars were widely distributed by the union, describing the working conditions in Loewe's plant as inferior to others, and stating that Loewe maintained a 12-15 hour working day and that the wages of Loewe workers were $13 a week, while the "fair" shops maintained an 8-hour day and paid their workers $22-$24 weekly.

III

The boycott hit Loewe's business hard, but Loewe was urged by the newly formed American Anti-Boycott Association to continue his fight against the union. This association had been formed by a group of antiunion employers throughout the United States. The main objects of the association were to outlaw the boycott—the union appeal "not to patronize" a product—by judicial decision, to undermine the scope of union activities and thus weaken unionism. The leaders of the association persuaded Loewe to make a test case of this strike and the boycott against him. The case was to be carried, if necessary, to the highest court of the land. Financial support from other employers similarly minded was promised.

Their main object was to secure a court decision declaring such activities of unions illegal under the antitrust laws and holding workers *individually* responsible in damages for the actions of their unions. This one-two punch, they hoped, would lay unions low. The theory of the action was supplied by Daniel Davenport, a Connecticut attorney who organized the American Anti-Boycott Association.

Before instituting suit against the Hatters' Union, Walter Gordon Merritt, the young attorney, was given the task of searching the records to find which members of the union residing in Connecticut owned real estate and had bank accounts. With this task completed, two actions were filed by Loewe against the union and its members; one action in the Connecticut state courts, for common-law conspiracy, claiming damages in the sum of $100,000; the other in the United States District Court, for violations of the Sherman Antitrust Act, claiming damages in the sum of $240,000. Simultaneously with the institution of these actions, based on Merritt's search, the homes and bank accounts of 248 individual members of the union who resided in Connecticut were attached.

As calculated, this action caused great consternation in union ranks. It undermined the morale of union workers. The American Anti-Boycott Society demonstrated to the individual workman that he might run the risk of losing his accumulated property if he became a member of a union, it imbued workers with fear and anxiety for their security and future—and thus destroyed the effectiveness of the union appeal for organization. Several months passed before the union attorneys moved to vacate the attachments against the properties and bank accounts of the individuals. When they finally did move, the district judge, James P. Platt, denied the motion, and the properties and savings remained attached during the many long years of litigation that followed.

IV

The attorneys for the union first sought to defeat the action through legal procedure based on technicalities. When their motion was denied, they demurred to the complaint, contending that the union's appeal to the public to boycott Loewe's hats could not be interpreted as in violation of the Sherman Antitrust Act; therefore, the case should be dismissed.

The demurrer came before Judge James P. Platt, who announced his decision on December 7, 1906. In substance he held that the complaint did not show that there was interference either with the *means of transporting* the plaintiff's product or with the product itself while *being transported*. The interference was apparently with the *manufacturing* of the product, which, in itself, was not interstate commerce. He also pointed out that the complaint did not allege that the defendants were in interstate commerce. Therefore, there was nothing in the complaint to show interference with *interstate* commerce. Pointing this out, the court said: "The real legal question in this case was, whether a combination which undertakes to interfere simultaneously with both the manufacture of hats in one state and their sale in another is a conspiracy which *directly* affects the transportation of hats from the place of manufacture to the place of sale, the kind of combination which is prohibited by the Sherman Act." He concluded that, since the law was not certain, he would sustain the union's demurrer to the complaint. He dismissed the action, with costs.

With the aid of the American Anti-Boycott Association, the company appealed to the United States Circuit Court of Appeals for the Second District. Because the case involved a novel issue of law, that court asked instructions from the Supreme Court of the United States as to whether the plaintiffs on the facts in the complaint could maintain any action under Section 7 of the Sherman Antitrust Act. The plaintiffs and the defendants joined in requesting that the entire record be brought before the high tribunal for a decision.

V

On December 4-5, 1907, the case of *Dietrich E. Loewe and Martin Fuchs*, v. *Martin Lawlor, et al.*, already known as the *Danbury Hatters'* case, was argued before the Supreme Court of the United States. The American Federation of Labor, by permission of the court, also filed a brief *amicus curiae*.

Counsel for the plaintiffs bitterly assailed the union as a "vast combination called The United Hatters of America . . . one wheel in a still more intricate piece of machinery, the whole of which was dominated by the American Federation of Labor," and charged that in violation of the Sherman Antitrust Act it maintained a conspiracy to restrain interstate commerce. Eighty-two manufacturers of fur hats "had bent the knee to Baal . . . had surrendered their manhood and the right to run their factories as they pleased . . ."

The attorneys for the defendants stressed the technical legal side of the case. They contended that: (*a*) The Federal Court had no jurisdiction in the case because the controversy involved citizens of the same state and therefore the plaintiffs must bring their action in the state courts, and not in the federal courts. (*b*) Admittedly, the defendants did not interfere directly with transportation in interstate commerce. At best, their interference, if any, was *indirect* and therefore the Federal Court had no jurisdiction. (*c*) Since the defendants admittedly were not in interstate commerce, had no aim to restrain it, and had used no means which directly did so, the Sherman Antitrust Act was not applicable. (*d*) The Sherman Act did not apply to this case because there had been no lessening of the general flow of interstate commerce; at most there was merely a *diversion.* If such indirect influences as *interference with production* came under the Sherman Act, then all strikes would be contrary to law, since every strike might necessarily diminish the amount of such production in interstate commerce. (*e*) The activities of the defendants were lawful since the sole purpose of their activities was merely the improvement of working conditions by means of organization.

On February 3, 1908, Chief Justice Melville W. Fuller handed down the decision of the Supreme Court. After summarizing the contentions of the plaintiff briefly, and citing Sections 1, 2, and 7 of the Sherman Act, he stated the law applicable to this case briefly as follows:

One: The Sherman Act forbade *any* combination *whatsoever* to secure action which essentially obstructed the free flow of commerce between the states, or *restricted,* in that regard, the liberty of a trader to engage in business. The complaint in this case alleged sufficient interference with the free flow of interstate commerce to spell a cause of action.

Two: There was no need for the complaint to allege actual physical obstruction of interstate commerce.

Three: Innocent acts could not claim the shield of constitutional rights when they formed part of a plot. Since 70 of the 82 manufacturers of fur hats were organized, the United Hatters' acts must be considered as a whole and the plan was open to condemnation, notwithstanding that a negligible amount of interstate business might be affected in carrying it out.

Four: The contentions of the defendant that at best the interference with interstate commerce was *indirect* and that the defendants *were not in commerce* were invalid, because the Sherman Act declared *every* contract, combination, or conspiracy in restraint of trade illegal, whatever its form or nature or whoever the parties were.

Five: The Sherman Act was applicable to unions, organized for the improvement of working conditions. In a previous case the court had held that "the Congressional debates show that the law had its origin in the evils of massed capital, but when Congress produced its final Act the subject had so broadened in the minds of the legislators that the source of the evil was not regarded as material and the evil in its entirety is dealt with. It includes combinations of labor as well as of capital . . ."

The chief justice concluded that the complaint in this case stated a sufficient cause of action under the Sherman Act. Therefore, the judgment of the Connecticut District Court, dismissing the complaint, was reversed and the case was remanded to the United States Circuit Court for the District of Connecticut for further proceedings.

The American Anti-Boycott Association triumphed. It secured a powerful weapon with which to fight trade unions. The consequences of this decision were immediately felt by organized labor. More trouble was in store for it.

VI

About twenty months after the Supreme Court decided that the complaint was legally sufficient, the case was reached for trial in the Federal District Court.

As the trial proceeded, it appeared that Mr. Merritt for the plaintiffs attempted to broaden the issue so as to place responsibility for the acts complained of in this action upon the entire membership of the American Federation of Labor. He contended that the holding of the United States Supreme Court that the plaintiffs had a cause of action under the Sherman Act was substantially "a determination that every member of the United Hatters of North America . . . and every member of the American Federation of Labor . . . can be held liable for all things done by the officers of those organizations." Merritt oratorically declared "this Federation is a great engine of destruction."

The defense attorneys, faced with the legal decision of the highest court that the Sherman Act was applicable to the case, sought to arouse the sympathy of the jury by stressing that the entire suit was an iniquitous scheme to ruin the labor movement in general and the hatters' union in particular. As indicative of this scheme, they pointed their finger at the American Anti-Boycott Association and its active and aggressive interest in the case from its inception. The plaintiff company, they claimed, was only a pawn in the hands of this antilabor society.

In their summation, the defense attorneys appealed to the jury to absolve the *individual* union members of responsibility. They pointed out the injustice of holding the rank-and-file individual members liable for acts of their officers, acts over which the members could not reasonably have or be required to have effective control. The defense attorneys contended that the damages claimed were grossly exaggerated as shown by the fact that the year 1903 was a depression year and, therefore, the plaintiffs could not have earned the profits claimed as damages for that year. Moreover, they contended that a good share of plaintiffs' losses was sustained by plaintiffs' act in employing incompetent workers.

The judge's charge to the jury assured a verdict for the plaintiffs. He told them: "Having given you my positive conviction about a large part of the plaintiffs' case, I must impress it upon you that the defendants now remaining on the records of this court are parties to a combination which has been found by the Supreme Court to form a valid basis for this suit. The only question, therefore, with which you can properly concern yourselves is the matter of damages."

The trial had lasted almost four months. On February 4, 1910, the jury acted as told by the judge. They found for the plaintiffs against all remaining defendants and awarded them $74,000 in damages. Under the Sherman Antitrust Act, this amount was trebled by the court. Thus, the verdict, together with costs and attorneys' fees, resulted in a judgment in favor of the plaintiffs in the sum of $232,-240.12. The defendants appealed.

VII

The appeal was successful. On April 10, 1911, Justice E. Henry Lacombe, in delivering the opinion of the Circuit Court of Appeals, among other points held:

(*a*) The Supreme Court decision in *Loewe* v. *Lawlor* fixed the law. There was, therefore, no need to inquire into the legality of the boycott, for it was settled that if individuals combine to induce a manufacturer to conduct his business as they wish and, on refusal, combine to prevent him from manufacturing and to prevent his vendees from reselling, the combination interferes with the free flow of goods between the states and violates the Sherman Act. (*b*) The contention of the defendant that the trial judge had assumed the functions of the jury because by his charge he had decided all questions of fact but the amount of damages was well taken. (*c*) The Circuit Court, moreover, did not assent to the argument that membership in the United Hatters after 1903 made the individual member a principal of all union agents and made him responsible for any illegal acts or methods used by the union representatives. There must be proof that such individual members had given "express or tacit" assent to frequent use of unlawful means in the past. The 175 individual members, defendants in this case, denied they had knowledge of the use of unlawful means. The fact that the testimony was so voluminous and contradictory was good reason for its credibility to be decided by the jury and not by the trial judge.

On the basis of the reasons cited, the judgment was reversed and a new trial ordered.

VIII

The second trial of the Hatters' Union and 175 hatters began on August 26 and concluded on October 11, 1911. The jury again found for the plaintiffs. This time it awarded plaintiffs $80,000 damages, together with costs and attorneys' fees. This sum was trebled under the Sherman Act. On November 15, 1912, judgment in the amount of $252,130 was entered against the defendants.

Again the union took an appeal. Justice Alfred C. Coxe delivered the opinion of the Circuit Court of Appeals on December 18, 1913. The gist of the decision was: (1) The question of law stood disposed of, since the Sherman Act, by decision of the United States Supreme Court, applies to unions. (2) The jury was justified in accepting as true that the defendants who belonged to the United Hatters and paid dues were thus affiliated with the American Federation of Labor, and hence knew of the use of the boycott by their organization and of the damage done to the Loewe business by the boycott and their strike. The defendants who participated in or aided the conspiracy were liable for damages. Their mere knowing of the conspiracy's existence, without "direct and positive" proof of their participation in the conspiracy, was sufficient basis for liability.

(3) The defendants who were local residents and read the newspapers and the *United Hatters Journal*, thus had knowledge and were warned that they would be held responsible for unlawful acts by the organization and by the persons who were its, and their, agents. They therefore were individually liable. (4) The charge of the trial judge at the second trial contained no error. Nor had there been error in admitting testimony to show evidence of damage occurring after the original suit had begun. Plaintiffs were entitled to dispose of the controversy in a single action and were permitted to show damage from the beginning of their claim to the date of trial. The trial had been fair and impartial. There was no need for a third trial.

The judge affirmed the judgment, with costs, and the union took an appeal to the Supreme Court of the United States.

IX

The case, now under the title of *Lawlor* v. *Loewe*, was argued before the Supreme Court on December 10-11, 1914. The union attorneys, in substance, contended: (*a*) It was lawful to attempt to organize a plant, lawful to strike, and lawful to require an employer to use the union label; it was lawful to appeal to the public to buy only hats which had the union label. These lawful activities had produced an unusual demand for union label hats and Loewe, who had refused the opportunity to use the union label, had no cause of action if he suffered thereby. (*b*) The appeal by the union to the public to withhold patronage from unlabeled hats was not a boycott. (*c*) The individual defendants had not participated in the alleged unlawful acts charged in the complaint; membership and mere payment of dues by them were not sufficient to make them liable as members of a conspiracy. The case should be dismissed as against the individual members. (*d*) The court also erred in admitting as evidence articles from newspapers which the defendants were not shown to have read. Therefore, the judgment should be reversed. (*e*) There were other errors. The court admitted hearsay evidence by permitting witnesses to repeat what others—the retailers—had told them, by admitting in evidence depositions without an opportunity to the defendants to cross-examine such witnesses.

The attorneys for Loewe, on the other hand, argued (1) the court had charged the jury properly; (2) the testimony established the existence of an unlawful conspiracy and that, therefore, the strike and the union agitation against nonlabeled hats, used to further the conspiracy, became unlawful.

On January 5, 1915, Justice Oliver Wendell Holmes, in delivering the opinion of the court, in substance, held:

One: The circulation of an "unfair list" had been declared contrary to the Sherman Act if it restrained commerce. Since the boycott, the strike, and the label had been used in this case, combination and conspiracy were proved.

Two: The trial court committed no error in charging the jury that all members could be held jointly liable because they had continued to pay dues and delegate authority to their union officers in circumstances which they knew "or ought to have known" that the officers unlawfully interfered with interstate commerce. The jury could not do otherwise than to find that by union usage the acts complained of were authorized by the members and that the members, therefore, were responsible for the acts which interfered with commerce among the states.

Three: There had been no error in regard to the admissibility of evidence, no injustice or error in the trial.

The judgment of the District Court, for the reasons given, was affirmed, and the defendants were thus required to pay $252,130 in damages.

To round out the story of the Danbury Hatters, two items of human interest may well be added: one concerning the workers and the other concerning the employer. It will be recalled that at the time Mr. Loewe brought the action against the union he caused the attachment of various bank accounts and homes belonging to individual workers residing in the state of Connecticut. When the final decision of the Supreme Court was rendered in its favor, the company demanded payment of the judgment and subsequently started to foreclose the homes of 186 workers. The union did not have the money with which to pay the judgment. An appeal was issued by the American Federation of Labor to the entire labor movement, urging the workers to contribute an hour's pay on a specified day toward the payment of the judgment. The day on which the hour's work was to be contributed was designated as the *Hatters' Day.* Two such appeals were made, workers responded, funds were collected, and the judgment was paid. Thus, the homes of the 186 workers were saved.

The other item concerns Mr. Loewe himself. In spite of the huge sum of money he collected from the union, his business subsequently met with various reverses. According to Donald B. Robinson, in his book *Spotlight on a Union*, Loewe's "financial condition was so bad that the Manufacturers Association of Connecticut had to pass the hat for him in 1927 . . . A Dietrich E. Loewe Fund was established. So it was that Loewe, ill and almost blind, lived out his last years on charity. He died on September 12, 1935, tired and embittered. In 1947, his grandson, Matthias C. Loewe, Jr., was employed in a Wal-kill, New York, hat factory. He was a member of the Hatters Union."

X

The decision in this case was a terrific blow to unions. It affected fundamental union activities and deprived them of many opportunities for unionization. It deprived them of the use of the boycott as one of their effective economic weapons in industrial disputes. It instilled fear into the hearts of the individual union members who now could be sued for violations of the Sherman Act by their union or its officers. The mere potential threat of suit for damages would undermine the effectiveness of further unionization. It exposed labor to suits for damages in all effective strikes which threatened production of goods for interstate commerce.

According to Professor Edward Berman, the attorneys for the company misled the Supreme Court in an essential fact. In an attempt to show that Congress had *refused* to exempt labor unions from the provisions of the Sherman Act, the company lawyers asserted that an "amendment specifically exempting organization of farmers and laborers" was actually introduced but was "wholly omitted" from the final bill. This version of the legislative history of the Sherman Act is not borne out by the record. Professor Berman points out that what actually happened was that the Judiciary Committee discarded the original Sherman Bill with all its amendments and brought in its own version of an antitrust bill, *without making any mention* whatever of the possible application of the law to labor. It was, therefore, wholly inaccurate to assert that Congress by implication specifically *refused* to exempt labor unions from the act.

In his authoritative book *Labor and the Sherman Act*, Professor Berman concludes: "It is believed that no valid evidence can be found in the records of the legislative proceeding that Congress intended the Anti-trust Act to apply to labor organizations." He points out that Senator Sherman, the original author, in explaining to the Senate the purpose of the bill, said: "It does not interfere in the slightest degree with voluntary associations made to affect public opinion to advance the interests of a particular trade or occupation. . . . And so the combinations of workingmen to promote their interests . . . are not affected in the slightest degree. . ."

Another writer on this subject, Mr. Louis B. Boudin, in two very searching articles in the *Columbia Law Review,* also concludes that the Supreme Court grievously erred in applying the Sherman Act to labor. He points out that the phrase "combination in restraint of trade" at common law was not understood to apply to combinations of labor or labor activities; and that, since the Supreme Court had held that the Sherman Act merely embodies the common-law conception of prohibited combinations, it follows that labor could not have been included in the combinations referred to in the Sherman Act. Mr. Boudin concludes that neither the intention of the legislators nor the very language of the Sherman Act justified the Supreme Court in holding that labor was included in the combinations prohibited by that act.

The Supreme Court laid great stress upon the word "every" with which Section 1 of the act begins. It held that this word "every" preceding the word "contract" was intended to include in the prohibition of combinations every contract in every combination and therefore it must have intended to include also a labor combination. There was no need for the court to stretch its reasoning so far. There is no question that the law was originally prompted by the business monopolies and business evils existing at the time. Is it not logical to suggest that the word "every" used in the section was intended to apply to every *business* contract, to every *business* combination or conspiracy involving interstate commerce? In other words, the all-embracing word "every" meant to embrace only improper business combinations. Had the court adopted this logic, which flows naturally from the situation that prompted this legislation, there would have been no need for straining either logic or reason in this case. At any rate, the court's reasoning and the fact that it apparently did not check carefully the original debates concerning the law proved costly to labor rights in the United States.

It may not be amiss to mention that the Supreme Court in this case refused to apply the "Rule of Reason" which it had previously applied to business and industrial combinations. A few years before that, to wit, in 1911, the court had occasion to apply the Sherman Act to business concerns. This was in the cases of *United States* v. *American Tobacco Company* and *United States* v. *Standard Oil Company of New Jersey, et al.* In both of these cases the court found that the companies were combinations in restraint of trade. Nevertheless, by majority, the court applied the Rule of Reason. The court declared that *reasonableness* should be applied in interpreting the effect of the trade restraint by such combinations. Some restraints were to be expected, only "undue" or "unreasonable" restraints were in violation of the act and should be enjoined.

If the Supreme Court had applied the same Rule of Reason in the Danbury Hatters' case, the judgment of the lower court would have been reversed, since there was no showing that the restraint of trade occasioned by the strike or boycott of the hatters was "undue" or "unreasonable."

Similarly, if the Supreme Court had applied to the *Danbury Hatters'* case the reasoning or principle of "partial restraint" it applied to the *Dueber Watch Case Manufacturing Company* v. *E. Howard Watch and Clock Company, et al.*, the decision should have been in favor of the union. In the *Dueber* case, several watch companies combined apparently for the purpose of price fixing. The Dueber firm refused to join them. The companies in the combination then jointly refused to sell goods to any firm buying from Dueber Company. The combination was sued under the Sherman Act. The Supreme Court held that, since the combination did not include *all* watchmakers, their restraint was at most only a "partial restraint" of trade in an article not of prime necessity. Therefore, it was not illegal under the Sherman Act. Had the Supreme Court applied this mitigating doctrine of "partial restraint" of trade to the *Danbury Hatters* case, it would have had to reverse the judgment, since the union did not include *all* hat workers and the restraint was at most a "partial restraint" of trade, involving only one company in the entire industry manufacturing an article not of prime necessity.

Thus, the Sherman Act, which came into being as a result of the mounting resentment against business monopolies—the law that was designed as a protective measure for the small businessman against the destructive methods of the combinations of big business —was now applied by the courts against labor unions. The law that was designed primarily to curb the evils of massed capital and the accompanying concentration of economic power was now directed against organizations of workers who were not involved in business or commerce at all. If this application of the Sherman Act were to persist, it would constitute a standing threat and continuous menace to the very existence of labor unions.

Since the threat to organized labor's existence came from the application of laws regulating property rights, labor, for self-protection, was obliged to seek special legislation based upon the distinction between *human rights* and *property rights*. While the Danbury Hatters' case was wending its way through the courts, the American Federation of Labor, under the leadership of Samuel Gompers, exerted its utmost efforts to save labor from the threats of the Sherman Act. Gomper's slogan was: "The Sherman Law: Amend it or End it."

These efforts culminated in the passage of the Clayton Act in October, 1914. To what extent, if any, the Clayton Act shielded labor from the Sherman Act will be discussed in another chapter.

-6-

How Samuel Gompers Was Saved from Jail

(1906–1913)

Bucks Stove and Range Company v. Gompers

I

Two days before Christmas, 1908, Samuel Gompers, Frank Morrison, and John Mitchell, president, secretary, and vice-president of the American Federation of Labor, were sentenced to jail. Justice Daniel Theu Wright, of the Supreme Court of the District of Columbia, found the three labor leaders guilty of contempt of court and sentenced them to serve twelve months, nine months, and six months, respectively, in the District of Columbia jail. The very fact that the top leadership of the American Federation of Labor was threatened with imprisonment for supporting the struggle of one of its unions against an employer made the *Bucks Stove and Range Company* v. *Gompers, et al.* case spectacular.

The Bucks Stove and Range Company of St. Louis, Missouri, manufactured stoves and ranges. Mr. J. W. Van Cleave was its president. The company was a member of the Stove Founders' Defense Association, which had collective bargaining agreements with the Iron Molders' International and the Metal Polishers Union. The existing collective agreements contained provisions for settlement of disputes and maintenance of the status quo pending settlement.

According to the claim of the Metal Polishers in the company's Nickel Department, the 9-hour day had been in force in that department since June, 1904, but on January 1, 1906, the firm had announced a 10-hour day. The metal polishers requested that the 9-hour day be re-established, but pending an adjustment of the grievance continued to work ten hours. After waiting more than

71

seven months for the adjustment of the hours, three leaders of the Metal Polishers decided to force the issue. One day in August, 1906, they quit work at 5.00 P.M., after nine hours of work, instead of 6:00 P.M. The Bucks Stove Company promptly dismissed these three "ringleaders" and declared that its factory would maintain the 10-hour day. The polishers walked out on strike. Mr. Van Cleave replaced the strikers with nonunion polishers. The local union retaliated with a boycott and appealed to the public not to patronize Bucks Stove.

The strikers appealed for help to the other unions in St. Louis and to the American Federation of Labor. Both responded. The American Federation of Labor urged all workers not to patronize the company. The Bucks Stove and Range Company was put on the "We Don't Patronize" list, published in the *American Federationist,* the official organ of the AFL.

II

Mr. J. W. Van Cleave, the president of the Company, was at that time also the president of the National Association of Manufacturers, an organization known for its opposition to labor unions. There is little doubt that the association encouraged Mr. Van Cleave to take legal action against the unions. After the boycott had gone on for a year, the Bucks Stove and Range Company instituted an action in the Supreme Court of the District of Columbia for an injunction to restrain various defendants from carrying on the boycott against the plaintiff and its product. The suit was started and conducted with the aid and support of the American Anti-Boycott Association, a group of antiunion employers. The complaint named as defendants three labor organizations—the American Federation of Labor, the International Stereotypers and Electrotypers Union, and the Electrotype Molders and Finishers Union No. 17—the nine members of the Executive Council of the American Federation of Labor, and other individuals and officers and members of the defendant labor organizations.

The complaint enumerated twenty-five charges against the defendants. The essential charges were: (1) Defendants conspired to injure the business of the company by imposing a boycott. (2) The strike was to force the plaintiff against its will and business interest to run the Nickel and Polishing Department only 9 hours per day instead of 10 hours per day. (3) Circulars were distributed charging falsely that the employer increased the hours of labor from 9 to 10 and that J. W. Van Cleave was hostile to the labor movement and thus the defendants had interfered with the sale of Bucks stoves. (4) The American Federation of Labor had conspired with the Metal polishers to boycott Bucks stoves and the Federation put Bucks name on its "We Don't Patronize" list. (5) The Federation falsely stated that the company had blacklisted its members and had refused to adjust any dispute with the foundry employees' union.

The defendants alleged in their answer: (a) They denied any conspiracy. (b) The employer imposed a 10-hour day and the firm never intended submitting the matter to the Grievance Committee for adjustment. (c) They denied that the circulars contained false charges. (d) The Federation denied that it entered into any unlawful conspiracy but admitted publishing in the *Federationist* the name of the firm in its "We Don't Patronize" list. (e) The Federation contended that before listing the firm on its "We Don't Patronize" list it had made attempts to settle the dispute but in view of Van Cleave's hostile attitude toward labor organizations, it abandoned this effort as futile.

Hearings on the application for the injunction were held during November, 1907. About a month later, Justice Ashley M. Gould of the District of Columbia Supreme Court handed down his decision. The court stated there were two main issues: (a) Had the plaintiff shown the existence of an unlawful combination and conspiracy to destroy his business; and (b) were the defendants connected with that conspiracy? He answered both questions in the affirmative, namely, that an unlawful conspiracy did exist, that boycotts were unlawful as a combination of many to cause loss to one, and that the defendants participated in the conspiracy. He overruled the union's claim that under the constitutional guarantee of "freedom of the press" it might continue to publish the employer's name on the "unfair list" of its publication, by stating that the very publication of the name was part of the conspiracy that existed. The court also overruled the technical but essential contention of the union that since the union was a voluntary association it was not suable.

The court issued a broad preliminary injunction restraining the defendants, their attorneys, confederates, and "any and all persons acting in aid or in conjunction with them" from conspiring, agreeing, or combining to restrain, obstruct or destroy complainant's business or threatening a boycott. He also restrained the defendants from in any way publishing or distributing any copies of the *American Federationist* or other printed matter containing the name of the company or its product on a "We Don't Patronize" or "Unfair" list.

Mention must be made of a technicality in connection with this injunction. It contained a provision that the complainant should "first execute and file a bond" in legal form. The injunction was issued on December 18, but the bond was not filed until five days later. Technically, therefore, the injunction did not become effective until December 23, the date on which the bond was filed. This difference of five days—between the issuance of the injunction and the filing of the bond—became legally significant later when the defendants were charged with contempt of court for violation of the injunction.

An appeal from the injunction was taken by the defendants.

III

On March 11, 1909, the Court of Appeals of the District of Columbia handed down its decision on the appeal. It dismissed the action against the American Federation of Labor and the Electrotypers' Union on the ground that "there is no such legal entity as an unincorporated association." In so far as the individual defendants were concerned, however, this court affirmed the decision of the lower court but narrowed the injunction.

Justice Charles H. Robb, writing for the court, in upholding the injunction, reasoned that if boycotts were held to be legal the court would thus give support "to an engine of harm and oppression utterly at variance with the spirit and theory of our institutions, place the weak at the mercy of the strong, foster monopoly, permit an unwarranted interference of the natural course of trade and deprive the individual of the freedom guaranteed him by the Constitution."

As to the union's contention that under the constitutional guarantee of freedom of speech it might appeal to the public not to patronize Bucks Stove and Range Company, the court held that such appeal was part of the conspiracy and must be treated as such, that "Freedom of action is at least as sacred as an untrammeled tongue or pen, and those who conspire to defeat the former right are not to be permitted to interpose a plea based upon the latter." The court concluded, however, that the injunction went too far and that it should do no more than forbid the defendants individually and as representatives of the Federation from conspiring or combining to boycott complainant, or from aiding or abetting the boycott directly or indirectly.

In a concurring opinion Justice Van Orsdel observed that there was a point where "free speech and free press ends and unlawful interference with personal and property rights begins." However, this judge apparently was of the opinion that a boycott was not necessarily illegal. He considered a mere appeal to others to withhold patronage not to be unlawful, but that it became an unlawful boycott when threats or coercion were connected with such appeal.

Both the plaintiff and the defendants appealed from the decision to the Supreme Court of the United States.

In the meantime the company made a new strategic move. It will be recalled that five days elapsed between the granting of the injunction (December 18, 1907) and the filing of the necessary bond (December 23, 1907). The American Federation of Labor apparently made use of those few days by rushing through in advance the next issue of the *Federationist* which contained the name of Bucks Stove and Range Company on the "We Don't Patronize" list. The attorneys for the company saw in this a good opportunity for additional charges against the labor leaders. While the appeal from the original injunction was still pending before the Court of Appeals, the Bucks Stove Company filed charges of contempt of court against Samuel Gompers, Frank Morrison, and John Mitchell for "wilful and premeditated violation of the temporary and permanent injunction." In its charges for contempt the company, among other things, alleged: (1) To avoid the injunction, which was issued on December 18, and became effective December 23, 1907, the defendants rushed the printing of the *American Federationist* for January, 1908, and distributed the number with the Bucks Company's name on the "We Don't Patronize" list. (2) In February, 1908, the defendants Gompers and Morrison printed an editorial suggesting that only persons found in the District of Columbia could be punished for violation of the injunction. (3) John Mitchell presided over the miners' convention which put Bucks stoves on its "Unfair" list and imposed a

$5 fine on any United Mine worker who bought one. (4) On April 19, 1908, and on other occasions Gompers made a speech in which he said that workingmen would not boycott, if boycotting were illegal, but no one could make them buy Bucks stoves, thus furthering the boycott. (5) The defendants Gompers and Morrison had issued an "urgent appeal" for funds, after the injunction forbade it.

The sum and substance of the charges was that the defendants by their disregard of the injunction showed their contempt for the court, that their action lowered the dignity and prestige of the court, and that, therefore, the court should punish them. In other words, the aim of these contempt proceedings was to inflict punishment for injuring the prestige of the court. Such a contempt charge is known as "criminal contempt" as distinguished from a "civil contempt" in which the aim is to redress the injury suffered by the private party to the litigation.

The defendants in their answer claimed: (a) The defendants could not be held in contempt of the court's order for any acts committed by them before December 23, 1907, the date when the order became effective. (b) They denied that they had intended to treat the decree with contempt and claimed that they were not responsible for the adverse publicity the Bucks Stove and Range Company had received. (c) The defendants were within their rights in advising their followers concerning the effect of the injunction outside the District of Columbia. Such advice did not furnish a basis for the charge of contempt of court. (d) There was nothing improper in advising a man concerning his rights. Gompers's speech did not intend to violate the court's order but merely to advise the individuals of their rights in the matter.

On the first anniversary of the effective day of that injunction, namely, on December 23, 1908, Justice Daniel Theu Wright handed down his decision on the contempt charge. He lambasted the defendants and declared that the "uttermost speech of human kind is barren of term or synonym which measures to the task" of describing the iniquity of the defendants. He gave vent to his feelings about unions, saying in effect that there was not much benefit to workers in belonging to an organization whose leaders restrict their right to work and limit earnings, "thus exercising closer control over their membership than government over its citizens." Having such views about unions and their leaders, the judge found that the defendants were predetermined to violate the injunction. He also concluded that the penalty must be sufficient to "deter," "impose obedience," serve to "vindicate the orderly power of tribunals and establish over this litigation the supremacy of law."

He found the defendants guilty of contempt and sentenced Samuel Gompers to twelve months, Frank Morrison to nine months, and John Mitchell to six months, to be served in the District of Columbia jail.

IV

The severity of the sentences against the top leadership of the American labor movement shocked organized labor into realization of the extent of the power of the courts over the very existence of labor unions. It at once became a celebrated case. An immediate appeal was taken and on April 20, 1909, the appeal was heard before the Court of Appeals in the District of Columbia.

Alton B. Parker, of defense counsel, raised several technical objections to the sentence. Aside from the fact that the penalty was too severe and disproportionate to the act, he contended that since, as a matter of law, the injunction did not become effective until the bond was filed on December 23, 1907, Gompers and Morrison were not in contempt for what they had done between December 18 and December 23. They had a right to hasten the publication of the January number of the *American Federationist,* since they did that before December 23. He also argued that in considering the evidence in support of the contempt charge the judge had no right to consider the material circulated *before* the injunction became effective; that such material could not properly be made a basis for the contempt charge.

Mr. Parker also contended that the entire contempt order should be set aside because the original injunction upon which the contempt charges were based had been modified subsequently by the higher court and therefore voided at least in part, hence that injunction no longer existed. If the defendants were punished they would be punished for the void part of the injunction as well as the valid part thereof and the injustice of such punishment was obvious, since the two parts were inseparable and therefore the entire order was void.

On November 2, 1909, Justice Josiah Van Orsdel, for the Court of Appeals, delivered the majority opinion of the court. He held that the defendants violated the injunction by using the words "boycott," "unfair," "We Don't Patronize Bucks Stove and Range Company." He also held that the acts of the defendants encouraged AFL members to disregard and disobey the injunction and create "a lack of respect for the authority and dignity of the court"; that the resolution of the United Mine Workers' convention imposing a fine of $5 on any member who bought a Bucks stove or range was "a separate offence in an open and brazen disobedience" of the court's command.

Justice Van Orsdel overruled the contention of the defendants that the intertwining of the void and valid parts of the injunction prevented the punishment for the contempt thereof. He ruled that the valid counts in the injunction were sufficient to support the charge of contempt; and stated that since the defendants were men of high standing, the case was of peculiar significance and the dignity of the court was at stake.

Chief Justice Seth Shepard dissented. He believed that the order should be reversed because the contempt proceedings were criminal in nature and the charges of contempt in this case were too vague to permit punishment. Moreover, the defendants should not be punished for their alleged acts between December 18 and December 23 because the injunction could not be operative before the bond was filed. He pointed out that 31 of the 54 pages of the record of the lower court's opinion dealt with the conduct of the defendants prior to December 23, the effective date of the injunction, and, therefore, obviously the sentences were based on at least some parts of the injunction which were not valid. He concluded that the decree was in excess of the court's power, it was void and not merely erroneous, and hence the defendants should not be punished.

The jail sentences having been confirmed by the majority of the court, the defendants carried the case to the Supreme Court of the United States.

V

More than a year later, on January 27, 1911, this appeal by the defendants from the jail sentences reached the Supreme Court of the United States. At the same time the appeals by the company and by the union from the decision modifying the original boycott injunction also reached the Supreme Court. All these appeals were to be argued together. An interesting incident occurred. During the arguments, the Supreme Court learned the following facts that were not in the record: J. W. Van Cleave, who as president of the company instituted the action, died in 1910 and F. W. Gardner, the new president of the company, concluded a settlement with the Federation. There was a tacit understanding that the company would withdraw from the cases before the Supreme Court. But the American Anti-Boycott Association would have none of this. Gardner was charged with "the most flagrant duplicity" in dealing with Gompers because the association "had been paying the entire expenses of the suits" and the discontinuance of the suits would be keeping the association "and all the employers interested therein" from securing a decision on the boycott issue. There was apparently a veiled threat that unless the company continued the litigation it might be sued by the American Anti-Boycott Association for all the litigation expenses that the association had incurred. The company, therefore, authorized its attorneys to proceed with the appeals.

Since the strike itself had been settled, the Supreme Court dismissed the appeals from the order modifying the original injunction but proceeded to hear the appeal from the contempt order.

On May 15, 1911, the Supreme Court reversed the judgment of the Court of Appeals and on technical grounds dismissed the contempt proceedings. The reasoning of Justice Joseph Rucker Lamar, writing for the court, appears vulnerable, especially on the issue of "freedom of the press." In substance he held:

One: The Court's powers to issue an injunction covered every device whereby property is irreparably damaged or commerce is illegally restrained.

Two: In cases of unlawful conspiracy, the publication of words might be the signal for action thus giving them a force "exceeding any possible right of speech which a single individual might have. Under such circumstances they become what have been called 'verbal acts,' and as such subject to injunction as the use of any other force whereby property is unlawfully damaged."

Three: The trial court found the defendants guilty in violation of the injunction on nine counts, but since some part of the injunction had been subsequently voided by the Appellate Court, therefore, the judgment that had been based on all nine counts could not be affirmed. If it were, the defendants would be punished for acts charged in the counts which, in law and in fact, had been found not to constitute a disobedience of the injunction.

Four: The sentence imposed on the defendants was punitive. Such a sentence was appropriate only to charges based on criminal contempt. But the parties in this case behaved as if in a civil proceeding, as was evident from the fact that the petitioner in the contempt case was the company, a private party, and not the court. This made it necessary to set aside the imprisonment order.

Five: The power to punish for contempt was a necessary and integral part of the independence of the judiciary. If the defendants were guilty of contempt, the court itself might institute the necessary steps for punishment.

VI

Strange logic and strained reasoning prompted Justice Lamar to conclude that written words may become "verbal acts." Apparently, he did not want to go so far as to say that freedom of speech may in such cases be suppressed, so he converted the "writing" into *verbal* and the "speech" into *act* and created the "verbal acts" that may be suppressed without violating the Constitution. While Justice Lamar set aside the jailing order on technical grounds, he extended an opportunity for renewing the contempt charges against the defendants, provided the proceedings were initiated by the judge himself. Judge Wright took full advantage of this opportunity. On May 16, 1911, on the very next day after the Supreme Court handed down its decision, Justice Daniel Theu Wright appointed a committee to prepare contempt of court charges and prosecute them if there were reasonable grounds for such charges. The committee at first consisted only of the very attorneys who represented Bucks Stove and Range Company in the litigation, but later Clarence R. Wilson, the United States attorney for the District of Columbia, was added. It was a foregone conclusion that such a committee would find sufficient grounds for charging the defendants with contempt.

About five weeks later, the committee's report supported the original charges of contempt against Gompers, Morrison, and Mitchell, but recommended that an opportunity be extended to the defendants to acknowledge their guilt, apologize, and assure their future submission to the court in a manner which would "sufficiently answer the necessary purpose to vindicate its authority and that of the law." The defendants refused to acknowledge their guilt or to apologize for their action and pleaded not guilty.

At the hearing on these charges the defendants raised the additional defense of "statute of limitations," namely, that more than three years had passed since the alleged contempt was committed and, therefore, the charges at this time were barred. The court overruled the defendants, and not unexpectedly again found the defendants guilty. The court again imposed the sentences of twelve, nine, and six months' imprisonment for Gompers, Morrison, and Mitchell, respectively. Again an appeal was taken to the Court of Appeals of the District of Columbia.

VII

The new appeal was decided on May 5, 1913. The majority opinion was again delivered by Justice Josiah Van Orsdel. After observing that the record disclosed "loose practice" on the part of the prosecution, the judge, nevertheless, arrived at the same conclusion he had reached on the previous appeal. After castigating the defendants by saying: "We are confronted with a deep-laid conspiracy to trample under foot the law of the land and set in defiance the authority of the Government. . . . If law is to be supreme, if the authority of the Government is to be maintained, it is not for the Courts to treat lightly a conspiracy for their destruction, either because of the prominence and influence of the conspirators or in deference to the inspired clamor of their misguided followers . . ." he nevertheless concluded "that the punishment imposed is unusual and excessive."

The court pointed out that the extreme punishment in a criminal prosecution for the offense charged should not exceed a fine of $500 and/or three months' imprisonment. He therefore directed that the case be remanded with instructions to find the defendants guilty of contempt, that Morrison and Mitchell were to be fined $500 each and Gompers was to be sentenced to thirty days in jail.

Chief Justice Seth Shepard again dissented. He did not consider the refusal to apologize as contempt of court and held that the demand that the defendants promise to obey the law in the future was outside of the offense charged "and beyond the power of any Court." Besides, Justice Shepard held that the criminal contempt with which these defendants were charged was an offense subject to the three years' statute of limitations and, since the alleged contempt had been committed more than three years ago, action thereon was barred at this time.

VIII

The defendants petitioned for a writ of error in order that the case might be taken to the Supreme Court of the United States. Originally it was denied to them but about a month later Chief Justice Edward D. White of the Supreme Court allowed a writ of certiorari.

Thus, the litigation that started in 1907 reached its final stage before the Supreme Court of the United States seven years later. This last appeal was first argued in January, 1914, and then re-argued in April and May, 1914.

Justice Oliver Wendell Holmes delivered the opinion of the court. He held:

One: The evidence concerning the violation of the injunction which was subsequently modified "not only warranted but required a finding of guilty."

Two: However, the power to punish for contempt "must have some limit in time" and, by analogy with similar offenses, he concluded that the three-year statute of limitations was applicable.

Three: Since these charges of contempt were based on violations of the preliminary injunction, which expired on March 23, 1908, when the permanent injunction was granted, more than three years had passed before these proceedings for contempt were instituted and they were barred by the statute of limitations.

Four: The judgments of contempt and the jail sentences against these defendants must be reversed.

Justices Pitney and Van Devanter dissented without opinion.

IX

Time saved Gompers from jail, but labor received a setback by this case. The basic decision blunted, if it did not destroy, the boycott as a means of bringing an employer to terms through labor's economic pressure. It slackened organizational activities. The boycott having been outlawed and its use having been declared conspiratorial, employers acquired more courage to resist unionization of their plants. They could now look to the injunction for aid and comfort. Moreover, the decision in the case enhanced the prestige of the American Anti-Boycott Association and the National Association of Manufacturers. It engendered an atmosphere of antiunionism and cast disrepute on labor leaders.

The significance of this case lies not alone in its legalistic connotations but also in its social repercussions. It became a symbol of the ever-heightening tension between the National Association of Manufacturers, on one hand, and the trade-union movement on the other—a "class struggle" waged in the courts.

As a result of their experience in this case, the leaders of the American Federation of Labor became convinced that the courts harbored a hostile attitude toward organized labor and that it was essential for labor to secure legislation which would protect the rights of unions to engage in their normal activities and limit the power of the courts to issue injunctions in labor disputes.

- 7 -

The "Yellow-Dog" Contract

(1907–1917)

HITCHMAN COAL AND COKE COMPANY V. MITCHELL

I

By the turn of the twentieth century some employers in the United States had revived an old scheme for warding off unionization in their plants. This scheme consisted of exacting from employees a promise not to belong to a union and not to strike or participate in any collective action against the employer during the entire period of employment. Without such a promise a worker would not be given employment. In some cases the promise was merely oral; in others the promise was embodied in a so-called contract, which the worker had to sign on the dotted line if he wanted the job. The so-called "contract" promised nothing to the worker by way of either terms of employment or period of employment. The employer was free to discharge the worker at will. The worker, likewise, was free to quit his job, but he was not free to join a union and keep his job.

This strategy nipped unionization in the bud. A worker who declined to sign such a contract was not given the job and a worker who did sign was afraid to join the union and lose the job. This type of contract became known as the "yellow-dog" contract. For many years the yellow-dog contract was the theme song of the antilabor employer chorus and was used to block unionization. Labor's efforts to organize were seriously hampered. The United Mine Workers probably more than any other union, suffered from this contract scheme. The legality of the yellow-dog contract was tested in the *Hitchman Coal and Coke Company* v. *Mitchell* case.

II

The United Mine Workers by 1906 had established fairly regular contractual relations with the bituminous coal operators in Ohio, Indiana, Illinois, and much of Pennsylvania. The operators of southern bituminous fields, in West Virginia particularly, enjoyed competitive advantages over the other bituminous mineowners. Their coal was of coke quality, ran in heavier veins, was less mixed with slate and other noncombustible matter. Besides, the coal was nearer the surface so that the cost of production was less. In addition to these gifts of nature, the operators also paid lower wages to the miners. Enjoying all these advantages, the southern mines could easily undersell the northern operators and drive them out from a large part of the soft-coal market and thus throw the miners in the North out of work. Consequently, the United Mine Workers sought to organize the southern miners, especially in West Virginia, and equalize their wages with those of the North. The southern mine-owners offered furious resistance. They imported and armed mine guards, had them deputized as sheriffs, and imposed their own laws in the coal towns, which were largely operator controlled, and not even incorporated political units of the state.

In April, 1906, the United Mine Workers called a general strike in the soft-coal industry. The Hitchman Coal and Coke Company, which then had been mining coal in the West Virginia Panhandle as well as on the Ohio side of the Panhandle, had a contract to supply the Baltimore & Ohio Railroad with engine coal. The company asked the local union to continue mining engine coal at the old rate, with a retroactive adjustment if other operators raised their miners' pay. The United Mine Workers refused to permit the local to accept the Hitchman proposal, and the Hitchman mine was struck on April 16, 1906. About six weeks later the Hitchman miners, impoverished by the strike, asked Hitchman for a settlement. They were told that the company would re-employ only those who would return to work as individuals, without a union contract.

The workers as individuals returned to work. Events then moved fast. Within two weeks the Hitchman local union had surrendered its United Mine Workers charter and on June 25, 1906, the Independent Mine Workers of West Virginia was chartered, and the workers at the Hitchman mine became members of this company-dominated organization. On behalf of the United Mine Workers, William Green, then secretary-treasurer of the union (subsequently president of the AFL), with A. R. Watkins and John Zalenka, asked the Hitchman manager to renew relations with the United Mine Workers, but the Hitchman directors refused. In September, 1907, Thomas Hughes, a United Mine Workers organizer, came to Benwood, West Virginia, nearest town to the Hitchman mine, and again began organizing the miners.

III

The Hitchman Company took legal steps to prevent organization of its mines. On October 24, 1907, it applied to the Federal Circuit Court for the Northern District of West Virginia for an injunction against the union and its officers, John Mitchell, John L. Lewis, and William Green, against Districts 5 and 6 and their officers, as well as against Thomas Hughes, the organizer for the union.

The complaint essentially alleged that the union called a strike in the Hitchman coal mine on April 16, 1906, and that several weeks later the company made agreements with the individual workers that they would not join the union during their employment by the company; that the union and their officers knew this fact, but in spite of it, they conspired together to induce the workers to break their contracts with the company and prevent other workers from making similar contracts of employment with the company. The complaint also alleged that the union conspired to ruin the company's business so that it could maintain or secure union contracts from rival operators and that the union fraudulently was spreading circulars falsely stating that the company gave permission to the workers to join the union and would recognize the union. The complaint also claimed that the United Mine Workers union was an unlawful organization under the Sherman Act.

On the basis of this complaint, supported by 28 affidavits, the court granted the company a *preliminary* (before hearing) injunction, restraining the defendants from any kind of activity in connection with their organization drive or from communicating in any way or manner with present or potential employees of Hitchman.

It is significant to note that at the time the Hitchman Coal and Coke Company applied for the injunction it had no written agreement with the workers not to join the union but three months later, in January, 1908, the Hitchman Company was not satisfied with the workers' verbal promise and demanded that each employee, by signature or mark, sign the following pledge:

I am employed by and work for the Hitchman Coal and Coke Company with the express understanding that I am not a member of the United Mine Workers of America and will not become so while an employee of the Hitchman Coal and Coke Company, and that the Hitchman Coal and Coke Company is run non-union and agrees with me that it will run non-union while I am in its employ. If at any time while I am employed by the Hitchman Coal and Coke Company I want to become connected with the United Mine Workers of America, or any affiliated organization, I agree to withdraw from the employment of said company, and agree that while I am in the employ of that company I will not make any effort amongst its employees to bring about the unionizing of that mine against the company's wish. I have either read the above, or heard same read.

After several adjournments, a hearing on the preliminary injunction was held on May 26, 1908, resulting in the court's granting a temporary (pending the trial) injunction. The temporary injunction was sweeping. It not only prohibited the defendants from inducing breaches of so-called contracts between the Hitchman Company and its employees, but also restrained the defendants from using "argument, reason and persuasion" or "talking to" Hitchman employees "or persons about to enter" its employ, to induce them to become members of the union or to win them over to the union. In vain did the union attorneys move to strike from the injunction that portion which prohibited any *peaceful* communication with Hitchman employees or potential employees, for the purpose of winning them over to the union.

It took four months before the motion was argued before the court, then it took the judge an additional five months to decide the motion, and when he finally did decide it, he denied it. In deciding the motion, on September 21, 1909, Justice Alston G. Dayton held: (a) A conspiracy to persuade persons to quit service in violation of their contracts was enjoinable. Since a worker's joining the United Mine Workers necessarily meant breaking his contract with Hitchman, the very fact of asking him to join the union was not peaceful persuasion. (b) Besides, the United Mine Workers was as plain a conspiracy to injure and ruin the plaintiff as could well be conceived of. It called a strike, causing a 50-day stoppage of business and considerable damage. (c) And this "foul and injurious prostitution" of the United Mine Workers had been made because rival operators of the Hitchman company refused to grant union terms unless Hitchman was organized. (*d*) A conspiracy against the Hitchman business existed and had done damages for which the plaintiff might recover in an action at law. That conspiracy was continuing although the United Mine Workers had been "thwarted for the time being by the making of the contracts with the employees direct. . . ." (*e*) The United Mine Workers organizer won over 125 of the Hitchman miners to the United Mine Workers; therefore, the need of the injunction, restraining the defendants from injuring the company, continued.

An appeal from this decision was taken by the union, but it was dismissed on the technical ground that it was not brought within the 30-day period required for such appeals. Almost five years passed before the case was finally reached for trial. During all those years the injunction was in full force. The case was tried before the same judge who issued the injunction. Elaborate briefs were submitted and on December 23, 1912, two days before Christmas, Justice Dayton delivered his opinion.

After elaborating on the origins and legal standing of labor unionism in England and the United States, he emphasized that West Virginia was living under the common law as that had existed before 1776 and that under such laws, in the absence of special legislation, "it is just as unlawful for labor to combine to form a trust or monopoly, as it is for capital to do so." Without any hesitation the judge stated that the very principles and practices of the union proved it to be an unlawful organization. He condemned the union requirements that a member must obey the union rules and cease working when a strike was called by the union, because such union principles deprived the workers of their freedom to work when and for whom they pleased. Moreover, he held that the union requirement limiting the employer's right to hire and fire his workers destroyed the right of the employer to conduct his own business as he pleased. The judge also condemned the union's conduct in making agreements with the operators in the Central Field by declaring: "It has by express contract joined in a combination and conspiracy with a body of rival operators, residents in other states, to control, restrain, and, to an extent at least, destroy, the coal trade of the state of West Virginia."

He ruled that: (*a*) "It [the union] seeks to create a monopoly of mine labor such as to enable it, as an organization, to control the coal mining business of the country." (*b*) The United Mine Workers of America was "clearly a common law conspiracy, too far reaching to be reasonable, in restraint of trade, as well, in my judgment, a direct violation of the Sherman Anti-Trust Law." Justice Dayton concluded that the injunction was necessary and proper, because if the injunction were dissolved, the union would continue to try to organize the Hitchman mine, thereby depriving it of its competitive advantages. He made the injunction perpetual.

The union appealed from the decision.

IV

The appeal was heard by the United States Circuit Court of Appeals for the Fourth Circuit. On May 28, 1914, Justice Jeter C. Pritchard, reversing the lower court which had granted the injunction, delivered the opinion of the court. After reviewing the bill of complaint, the United Mine Workers' answer, the evidence in the case and the terms of the permanent injunction. Justice Pritchard criticized the principles enunciated by the lower court. In substance, he held and reasoned:

1. *The union was not an unlawful conspiracy*. The struggle between capital and labor was an existing condition, not a theory. Unions might use peaceable and persuasive methods to keep their organizations intact and work for higher wages, mine safety laws and other objectives. Workers' organizations were necessary to balance the otherwise absolute power of mineowners over conditions of employment.

2. *The West Virginia common law of 1776 did not apply*. Since it was now recognized by "all civilized countries that labor is the basis of all wealth. . ." it was necessary to take a more comprehensive view than was possible in 1776, even though the act complained of might be deemed illegal under that law.

3. *The union agreements with the operators in the Central Field were not conspiratorial*. Fair interpretation of the agreements and conference reports cited showed that the purpose of the organization was to get the miners of West Virginia to join the union and to secure the highest wages possible.

4. *Court's finding that under the Sherman Act the United Mine*

Workers was an unlawful organization was improper. The pleadings never made such a charge and therefore the court was not warranted in making such a finding. Moreover, under the Sherman Act only the government, not a private party, could sue to have an organization declared unlawful by the courts.

5. *There was no evidence of wrongful inducement of breach of employment contract by the defendants.* The Hitchman contracts with the individual employees did not run for any specific term. The employer could discharge them at any time and workers could quit at any time. Therefore, the workers could at any time join the union, if they so wished and leave the company's employ. Hence, inducement of a worker to join the union did not entail inducement of breach of contract and therefore no action for damages could lie against the union.

6. *Peaceful communication with the Hitchman workers by the union should not be prohibited.* In modern life, organization was necessary and practiced by all professions and many businesses. "It is just as essential and perhaps more important, that the laboring people should organize for their advancement and protection . . . In no instance should a union be restrained from using lawful and peaceable methods for the purpose of maintaining its organization."

7. *The record did not show that the union had used unlawful methods.* It was not unlawful to agree to strike when called upon; the union had no arbitrary power to enforce membership, nor was it a secret organization. It was no crime to force negotiation by winning over a majority of employees or to bring all miners into union membership by lawful means.

8. *Illegal means would justify an injunction.* In cases involving violence, coercion or intimidation, the mineowner would be entitled to an injunction protecting him in the right to use his property as he saw fit. No such means were found to have been used in this case.

Accordingly, the Circuit Court of Appeals set aside the injunction and instructed the District Court to dismiss the complaint, with costs. The Hitchman Company appealed from the decision of the Circuit Court of Appeals to the Supreme Court of the United States.

V

Sharply split, the Supreme Court upheld the lower court and reversed the Circuit Court. The majority, in an opinion delivered on

December 10, 1917, by Justice Mahlon Pitney, frowned on the social and economic principles sanctioned by the Circuit Court of Appeals. The minority, in an opinion delivered by Louis D. Brandeis, with whom Justices Holmes and Clarke concurred, strongly dissented.

Justice Pitney held:

One: A contract not to join a union during employment was valid. Hitchman had a right "to make non-membership in a union a condition of employment" just as the workers had a right to decline this as a condition of employment. A closed nonunion shop was the answer to a closed union shop. "This is a part of the constitutional right of personal liberty and private property. . . . Unionizing the miners is but a step in the process of unionizing the mine." The employer was as much entitled to prevent the first step as the second.

Two: Inducement to join the union was equivalent to inducing a breach of contract. The employer was entitled to the "good will" of his employees, as a merchant to that of his customers. This good-will was destroyed by the union when it induced a worker to join it, knowing that under the contract he would have to terminate his employment.

Three: Union was guilty of fraudulent practice. The union not only had induced a breach of contract, but also practiced fraud by inducing the workers to join the union but to conceal this fact from the employer, and thus remain at work, contrary to the terms of the employment contract.

Four: Right to strike was not a right to instigate a strike. "This case involves no question of the rights of individual employees. The right of the employees to strike would not give the *defendants* the right to instigate a strike. The difference is fundamental."

Five: The defendants were guilty of combining to injure the plaintiff. There was sufficient evidence in the case that there was a combination which injured Hitchman. This combination alienated a sufficient number of the employees to shut down the mine, so that fear of losses through a strike might coerce the plaintiff into recognizing the union. It was not necessary to prove by independent evidence that the combination was "criminal or otherwise unlawful."

Six: Injunctive relief was proper remedy. The injuries that plaintiff might suffer from the unlawful activities of the defendants might not be compensated for by a judgment in a civil suit for damages.

The relief that plaintiff might obtain in a civil suit for damages might be far from adequate. Therefore, injunctive relief was the proper remedy in such a case.

The majority opinion affirmed the injunction as originally granted, except that it eliminated that part which referred to picketing and physical violence, because such activities being criminal activities should be dealt with in criminal courts and not in equity.

Justice Brandeis, for the minority of the court, sharply disagreed with the majority. After pointing out that the injunction as granted included three defendants who were never served with process and that the District Court included findings on matters not in the original complaint, Justice Brandeis reached a conclusion diametrically opposed to the majority. He held:

(a) *Defendants were not guilty of inducing a breach of contract.* The Hitchman workers under their contract could leave their jobs and were free to join the union. By the terms of the very contract itself, they were not obliged to leave their employment until they actually became members of the union. Mere indication on their part of willingness to join was no breach of contract, and there was no proof of actual membership. *Preparation* to join the union in a body was not unlawful. Hence, the defendants could not be guilty of inducing a breach of contract.

(b) *Neither the union as such nor its activities were unlawful.* He criticized the District Court for its gratuitous finding that the United Mine Workers was an unlawful organization under the Sherman Act, since there was no such charge in the complaint and it was not supported by law.

(c) *Both the ends and means used by the union were legal.* The means were legal because the record did not show that there were any threats or violence or intimidation used by the defendants. Since it was recognized as legal that a union could strike for wages, or the establishment of grievance machinery, "why may it not strike or use equivalent economic pressure to secure an agreement to provide them?" Hence, the ends here also were legal.

Judge Brandeis concluded that the majority of the court was grossly in error and that the decision of the Circuit Court of Appeals, reversing Justice Dayton who granted the original injunction, should be sustained.

VI

By its majority decision, the high authority of the Supreme Court lent legal sanctity to the yellow-dog contract. Prior to the Hitchman decision, workers who were compelled to sign a yellow-dog contract might feel no *moral* compunction in disregarding it by joining a union; the deterrent then was merely *psychological*. With the Hitchman decision the breach of such contract became a violation of the law of the land.

In reality the yellow-dog contract should never have been given the sanctity of a contract because it was merely a scrap of paper obtained by economic coercion. The court should have been cognizant of the fact that workers were coerced into signing these papers. They had no choice in the matter because that was the only way they could get employment. To tell a man under such circumstances, as the Court reasoned, that "This is a part of the constitutional right of personal liberty," that he is free not to accept employment, is double-talk. It is tantamount to telling him that, under his "constitutional right of personal liberty," he is free not to live.

Furthermore, the yellow-dog contract, by the ordinary legal tests of contracts, is not the kind of contract that should justify a court of equity in granting injunctive relief against a threatened breach thereof. This "contract" could be terminated at will by either party: the employer could discharge the worker at any time and the worker could quit his job at any time. The employer assumes no obligation to the worker in exchange for the employee's sacrifice of his right to join the union. He is neither obliged to supply the worker with work nor obliged to pay a specific wage. The employer's benefit from the employee's work has not been affected by the employee's joining or not joining a union. Since the worker was under no duty to continue working for Hitchman, obviously no right of Hitchman was infringed when the worker was induced to discontinue working. What property right, then, did the employer have in this "scrap-of-paper" contract? The whole legal concept of the employer's property rights under the yellow-dog contract is highly artificial, unrealistic, and stems from an economic philosophy based on prejudice against organized labor.

Moreover, the majority of the court applied an early nineteenth-century concept of the rights of property to twentieth-century conditions. It ignored the tremendous changes that had taken place from the days of the master-servant relationship to the employer-employee relationship in an industrial economy. The court should have condemned the yellow-dog contract as against public policy because there could be no liberty of contract where there was no equality of bargaining position and where the worker was forced to accept what the employer imposed upon him. Had the court not ignored realities, it would have listened to the voice of the great dissenter, Justice Holmes, who two years previously, in a dissenting opinion, said: "In present conditions a workman not unnaturally may believe that only by belonging to a union can he secure a contract that shall be fair to him . . . If that belief, whether right or wrong, may be held by a reasonable man, it seems to me that it may be enforced by law in order to establish the equality of position between the parties in which liberty of contract begins."

This Hitchman decision not only strengthened the hand of employers against organized labor, but brought about the development of "company unions." In the language of William Green, president of the American Federation of Labor: "Ever since the Hitchman injunction case . . . employers of labor have been making what they term 'individual agreements' with their employees. These agreements usually provide that the employee will not join a labor union while in the employ of the corporation . . . Along with the individual contract there has developed the company union."

But there was more danger to organized labor in the Hitchman case than the mere validation of the yellow-dog contract. In this case a federal district court had held that the union in and of itself was an unlawful organization under the Sherman Act. True, the Supreme Court did not pass upon this specific issue but its failure to comment on this finding by the district court had made labor apprehensive of what might follow. If unions *as such* were unlawful organizations, then their very existence was threatened and they might be subjected to numerous actions for dissolution by antilabor forces.

This was also the first case in which the Sherman Act was applied by a court against an attempt to organize workers engaged in production *within* a state. Heretofore, it was thought that the Sherman Act, applicable only to interstate commerce, did not apply to production *within* a state; but in this case Judge Dayton widened its use and made it applicable also to any industrial dispute involving production destined for intrastate commerce; and the Supreme Court on appeal did not specifically overrule this interpretation. Thus, the danger to labor flowing from the Sherman Act became greater.

The Hitchman decision challenging the very existence of free and independent labor unions added to the already piled-up resentment of labor against the accumulating judicial decisions limiting its legitimate activities and development. It spurred labor to a widespread campaign for legislative help, which should provide an effective remedy against the yellow-dog contract, the plague of injunctions, and the rampaging of the Sherman Antitrust Act.

-8-

The Vanishing "Magna Carta"

(1913–1921)

Duplex Printing Press Company v. Deering

I

As a result of the clamor of the American public against the evils of business monopolies, Congress in 1890 enacted the Sherman Anti-trust Law. It was thought that this law would effectively end the monopolistic practices of stifling competition and of price fixing. This antitrust act, which was "obviously aimed to curb the menacing powers of concentrated capital," was immediately turned against labor unions. In vain did labor contend that this law was never intended to be applied against unions. Aroused by the potential danger lurking in this act, unions began an unrelenting campaign *specifically* to exempt labor from the Sherman Act.

As early as 1900 the American Federation of Labor succeeded in having the House of Representatives adopt an amendment to the Sherman Act exempting labor unions from penalties under the act, but that amendment never became law. The Federation brought political pressure to bear so that the platform of the Democratic Party in the presidential year of 1908 declared the party in favor of exempting unions from the Sherman Act, but that did not result in any relief. An indirect method of getting relief was tried by labor by having Representative William Hughes of New Jersey, in 1910, introduce an amendment to the appropriations bill denying the Justice Department funds for prosecuting labor unions under the Sherman Act. The House passed the amendment but the measure was lost in the Conference Committee of the House and the Senate. A similar "rider" was introduced to the Sundry Civic Bill. This rider passed both houses of Congress, but was vetoed by President Taft.

Finally in October, 1914, labor succeeded in having Congress enact the Clayton Antitrust Act, which Samuel Gompers, the president of the American Federation of Labor, characterized as the Industrial Magna Carta, "upon which the working people will rear the construction of industrial freedom." This act embodied the lofty declaration of the principle that "the labor of a human being is not a commodity or an article of commerce." Gompers jubilantly proclaimed that "those words . . . are sledge hammer blows to the wrongs and injustices so long inflicted upon the workers" by the courts' interpretation of the Sherman Act.

President Woodrow Wilson and others believed that the Clayton Act was a real measure of relief for labor. After affixing his signature to the act on October 15, 1914, President Wilson wrote to Representative Underwood: "Incidentally, justice has been done to the laborer. His labor is no longer to be regarded as if it were merely an inanimate object of commerce disconnected with the fortunes and happiness of a living human being to be dealt with as an object of sale and barter." On another occasion, at a dedication of the AFL office building, on July 4, 1916, President Wilson reiterated his belief that a man's labor is a part of his life and cannot be treated by the courts as a commodity, by saying: "I am sorry that there were any judges in the United States who had to be told that. It is so obvious that it seems to me that that section of the Clayton Act [Section 6] were a return to the primer of human liberty; but if the judges have to have the primer opened before them, I am willing to open it."

This Clayton Act was supposed to relieve labor in two ways: (1) To do away with the evils of the indiscriminate injunction by limiting the federal courts to the issuance of injunctions only in certain cases and prohibiting them from issuing broad, sweeping injunctions. (2) It was to protect unions from prosecution under the Sherman Act by specifically providing that they are not illegal combinations or conspiracies in restraint of trade under the antitrust laws. The act was so worded, or at least the labor leaders thought so, that the sad experiences unions had had in the Debs case, the Danbury Hatters case, the Bucks Stove case, and the yellow-dog contract cases would no longer be repeated.

In so far as labor is concerned the significant provisions were embodied in Sections 6 and 20 of the Clayton Act. These crucial sections in part provided:

Section 6:

The labor of a human being is not a commodity or article of commerce. Nothing contained in the anti-trust laws shall be construed to forbid the existence and operation of labor, agricultural, or horticultural organizations, interested for the purposes of mutual help and not having capital stock or conducted for profit, or to forbid or restrain individual members of such organizations from lawfully carrying out the legitimate objects thereof; nor shall such organizations, or the members thereof, be held or construed to be illegal combinations or conspiracies in restraint of trade, under the anti-trust laws.

Section 20:

That no restraining order or injunction shall be granted by any court of the United States, or a judge or the judges thereof, ... in any case between an employer and employees, or between employers and employees, or between persons employed and persons seeking employment, involving, or growing out of a dispute concerning terms or conditions of employment, unless necessary to prevent irreparable injury to property, or to a property right, of the party making the application, for which injury there is no adequate remedy at law, and such property or property right must be described with particularity in the application, ...

No such restraining order or injunction shall prohibit any person or persons, whether singly or in concert, from terminating any relation of employment, or from ceasing to perform any work or labor, or from recommending, advising, or persuading others by peaceful means so to do; or from attending at any place where any such person or persons may lawfully be, for the purpose of peacefully obtaining or communicating information, or from peacefully persuading any person to work or to abstain from working; or from ceasing to patronize or to employ any party to such dispute, or from recommending, advising, or persuading others by peaceful and lawful means so to do; or from paying or giving to or withholding from any person engaged in such dispute, any strike benefits or other moneys or things of value; or from peacefully assembling in a lawful manner, and for lawful purposes; or from doing any act or thing which might lawfully be done in the absence of such dispute by any party thereto; nor shall any of the acts specified in this paragraph be considered or held to be violations of any law of the United States.

While the leaders of labor were jubilant about the Clayton Act, others, seasoned observers of the operation of the judicial mind and fancy, were doubtful about the benefits that would redound to unions from this legislation. Their doubts were justified. In its very first test before the Supreme Court, the law failed labor, as we shall see from the facts of the case that follows—*Duplex Printing Press Company* v. *Deering*.

II

In 1913, the manufacturing of printing-press machinery in the United States was confined to four firms—Hoe of New York, Goss of Chicago, Walter Scott of Plainfield, New Jersey, and the Duplex Printing Press Company of Battle Creek, Michigan. The first three companies maintained union shops. Their collective agreements with the International Association of Machinists provided for union wages and an 8-hour workday. The Duplex Company was nonunion. It maintained a 10-hour workday, and its wage scale was lower than the one prevailing in the union shops. Although Duplex was the smallest of the four concerns, its competition, based on its low labor costs, was keenly felt by the others. Hoe, Goss, and Scott—the three unionized companies—informed the machinists' union that they would cease dealing with it unless it consented to a lowering of their labor standards to the level of Duplex or brought Duplex up to their union standards.

In August, 1913, after a futile interview with the representatives of Duplex, the union called a strike against the company. Of the 300 employees, only about 13 machinists responded. A picket line was thrown about the plant, but that did not hinder operations. The union then applied additional economic pressure against Duplex. The New York lodges of the International Association of Machinists refused to handle Duplex presses brought into New York City for installation. The union also secured the co-operation of their affiliated carting organization and this organization refused to cart Duplex presses. Emil J. Deering, the business agent of I.A.M. District No. 15, also attempted to prevent the exhibition of Duplex machines at a commercial fair then current in New York.

The Duplex company went to court. On April 13, 1914, on a complaint and affidavits, it obtained from the United States District Court for the Southern District of New York an *ex parte* injunction

—without a hearing—against the International Association of Machinists (I.A.M.), its District No. 15, New York Lodge No. 328, the New York Riggers' Protective Union, and the business agents of those organizations as individuals. The injunction restrained the unions from interfering with plaintiff's trade and goodwill and from interfering with the sale, carting, installation, use or operation of printing presses made by the plaintiff or from in any manner circulating plaintiff's name on an "Unfair" list. A couple of weeks later the *ex parte* injunction was made a temporary injunction to remain in effect until trial.

The complaint charged that the International Association of Machinists controlled nearly all the skilled machinists in New York City, and that it, together with the Riggers' Protective Union, both members of the New York City Building Trades Council, and the other defendants, engaged in a conspiracy against the Duplex Company contrary to the common law; that they conspired to keep the company from exhibiting at the National Exhibition Company's New York display.

On April 23, 1917, Justice Martin T. Manton rendered his decision. After pointing out that the defendants in the action were sued only in their individual capacities and that no process had been served on their organizations, the court found no evidence that the strike was undertaken for other than a lawful purpose, namely, the improvement of workers' conditions. Finding that the defendants did act in concert against the Duplex Company in accordance with a plan, he also found that they did so peacefully; the defendant Deering had urged employees to stand by the union but did so in a peaceable manner; the threat of withdrawing union cards from the disobedient union members was justified according to a union bylaw. The court found that a man refusing to abide by that bylaw had been assaulted, but there was no evidence connecting the defendants with the act. The court also found that the cartmen who had refused to carry Duplex presses were union affiliates and had been won over by peaceful persuasion. The evidence showed that the defendant Deering apparently said to the heads of two newspapers, the New York *Law Journal* and the *Italian Herald*, that they might have trouble if they installed Duplex presses, but since nothing actually happened the justice could see nothing wrong in this conduct. It was also brought out that Deering informed the manager of the newspaper publishers' exhibit that union machinists might refuse to work at the exhibit if Duplex machines were displayed, but that was interpreted by the justice as merely an exchange of views, without ensuing action.

Justice Manton concluded that, "There is nothing in this record which warrants my granting the injunction sought." A peaceful and orderly strike to improve working conditions was lawful; this strike was for a lawful purpose and conducted by lawful means, hence the mere hardships to the company were not sufficient to warrant the issue of an injunction.

The District Court then dismissed the company's bill of complaint, with costs, and the temporary injunction was vacated.

III

The case of the *Duplex Printing Press Company* v. *Deering, et al.*, was then carried by the company to the United States Circuit Court of Appeals for the Second Circuit. On May 25, 1918, Justice Charles M. Hough delivered the majority opinion, with Justice Learned Hand delivering a brief concurring opinion. They held:

(a) The plaintiff would have been entitled to injunctive relief against the unlawful acts, such as threatening to make trouble for users of its presses and threatening to break its contract with the Exposition Company, but the plaintiff asked to restrain the *peaceful* efforts to organize its factory. That it was not entitled to.

(b) The secondary boycott was not illegal in New York provided no fraud, malice, violence or force was involved, but since the acts complained of in this case affected interstate commerce, the federal law was applicable.

(c) Under the federal law, plaintiff would be entitled to an injunction unless prohibited by the Clayton Act. Section 20 of the Clayton Act was apparently meant to legalize the secondary boycott, but the statute was "blindly drawn." This Section 20 prohibited the issuance of an injunction in any case "between employers and employees, or between persons employed or seeking employment . . ." Was Section 20 meant to apply only to cases involving employer and the employees *directly* employed by him, or was it meant to apply to employers and employees *generally*?

(d) "Unless the words 'employers and employees' as ordinarily used, and used in this statute, are to be given a strained and unusual meaning, they must refer to the business clan or class to which the parties litigant respectively belong." Therefore, it must be concluded that the activities of the defendants were not deemed unlawful under the Clayton Act.

Justice Learned Hand agreed that Section 20 legalized the secondary boycott. "I do not think that the section applies only when the employer is plaintiff and his present or former employees are the defendants. Further, I think that the dispute here under any definition included the conditions of employment." Hence, Justice Hand agreed with the reasoning and the decision of his colleague, but not with "all the expressions in his opinion."

The decree of the lower court, denying the injunction, was affirmed.

IV

The company appealed to the United States Supreme Court. On January 20, 1920, the appeal was argued before the court. The respective contentions of the parties were centered on the meaning and the application of the Clayton Act to this case. The plaintiff contended: (1) The Clayton Act did not extend any additional rights to organized labor, but merely restated the law as it already existed in judicial decisions. (2) Section 20 of the Clayton Act extended immunity against prosecution only to the very employees of the employer *directly* involved in the labor dispute, but the defendants in this case were not employees of the plaintiff and hence were not entitled to immunity against prosecution. (3) Moreover, the prohibition in Section 20 of the Clayton Act against issuance of injunctions was limited only to the restraining of lawful acts of employees, but the acts of a criminal conspiracy were not thereby limited. The defendants in this case could not claim immunity under this section. (4) If Section 20 legalized the acts of a criminal conspiracy, it would be unconstitutional as "class legislation," violating the due process clause of the Constitution. (5) The defendants were engaged in a conspiracy to attack and ruin plaintiff's trade and commerce by means of a boycott.

The defense contended: (a) No injunction could be granted because the Clayton Act was intended to protect organized labor against the application of the Sherman Antitrust Act to it. (b) The acts of the defendants were lawful, since the Clayton Act recognized that the efforts of labor organizations to equalize wages and working hours in a trade were lawful, and that was exactly what the defendants were trying to do in this case. (c) The term "employees" as used in the Clayton Act was intended broadly to encompass *any* employees, whether or not they were employed directly by the particular company, party to the dispute. (d) There was no actionable wrong in striking against an employer and in securing the co-operation of others not to perform work which might benefit such employer. (e) The publicizing of the strike among plaintiff's customers was not unlawful. It was a legitimate activity of unions, and protected by law as an essential part of freedom of speech. (f) An injunction against the refusal to handle Duplex presses forced men to work against their will. Just as the plaintiff could hire whom he chose, the workingmen had the right to choose whom they would work for and under what conditions. (g) The right to solicit business was not a property right, and, moreover, no proof of injury to that right had been shown. (h) The Sherman Act did not apply because no unlawful interference with interstate commerce had been shown, since the refusal to handle the presses occurred after they reached their point of consignment within New York State. Even if the acts of the defendants did affect plaintiff's profits, a decrease of profits was not interference with interstate commerce. (i) Finally, since the Clayton Act declared that labor was not a commodity or an article of commerce, any interference by labor's representatives with production was not an interference with commerce, and hence labor representatives could not be enjoined.

For almost a year the effect of Section 20 of the Clayton Act on labor rights remained unknown. Finally, on January 3, 1921, by a court split six to three, in favor of the company, a decision was rendered. The majority opinion was delivered by Justice Mahlon Pitney, and the minority opinion by Justice Louis D. Brandeis.

Justice Pitney, after reviewing and interpreting the facts, held:

One: The defendants' acts would not be lawful unless made so by the Clayton Act, but the Clayton Act did no such thing.

Two: That act was a supplement to the Sherman Act and merely incorporated the previous judicial interpretation of what constituted lawful acts by organized labor.

Three: Business was a property right, entitled to protection against "unlawful injury or interference." The plaintiff's business required unrestrained access to commerce.

Four: A combination to hinder its business existed in this case. The plaintiff, therefore, had a clear right to an injunction if injured "due to violation of the Sherman Act as amended by the Clayton Act," because conspiracies in restraint of trade were unlawful. It was already held in *Loewe* v. *Lawlor* that "peaceable persuasion is as much within the prohibition as one accomplished by force or threats of force . . ." and was not justifiable by the fact that the conspirators might have intended to pursue an object of benefit to themselves.

Five: The heart of Section 6 of the Clayton Act lay not in what it authorized labor unions to do but in *what it failed to authorize.* Since this section failed specifically to exempt labor from liability in conspiracy cases, then it must be held that they were not in such cases exempted from the Sherman Act. Nor could it be construed to enable "a nominally lawful organization to become a cloak for an illegal combination or conspiracy in restraint of trade as defined by the anti-trust laws."

Six: The provisions of Section 20 of the Clayton Act were limited to those disputes concerning terms and conditions of employment where the parties to the dispute were in a *direct relationship* of employer and employee. The restrictions against the issuance of injunctions applied only to parties "in proximate relation to a controversy," but did not cover others, not direct parties to the dispute. The exceptional privilege of Section 20 must be confined only "to those who are proximately and substantially concerned as parties to an actual dispute respecting the terms or conditions of their own employment, past, present or prospective." Congress had in mind *particular* industrial controversies, not a general class war, not persons who were affected merely by "sentimental and sympathetic" sense to the cause of dispute.

Seven: Section 20 did not include all members of a single union in its exemptions, but only those members involved in the specific dispute with the particular employer.

Eight: Furthermore, the emphasis on lawful and peaceful means and acts in Section 20 did not justify instigating a sympathy strike; the law did not legalize the secondary boycott, except that parties to the dispute might cease to patronize and might ask others to cease to patronize a party to the dispute.

Nine: The complainant had a "clear right to an injunction under the Sherman Act as amended by the Clayton Act." That injunction should restrain the defendants from attempting to interfere with the sale, transport, or delivery of presses or their carting, installation, use, repair, or display by using any force, threat, command, direction or even persuasion or any "other threatened conduct" with the object or having the effect of causing any person to decline employment under any person "who buys from or handles the plaintiff's presses."

Thus, the majority reversed the judgment in favor of the defendants and directed that the case be returned to the District Court for the Southern District of New York for the injunction to issue.

Justice Brandeis (with Justices Holmes and Clarke concurring) wrote a vigorous dissenting opinion. He ridiculed the majority's view that the Clayton Act merely embodied previous judicial interpretations of the Sherman Act and extended no new rights to labor by asking, If no change was intended, then what purpose was served by such legislation?

He pointed out that Congress did not restrict the provisions of Section 20 to employers and working men *in their employ* but provided for employers and employees *in general.* This showed that Congress was not aiming merely at a legal relationship between a specific employer and his employees but was aiming at a *general* industrial relationship. Moreover, if the words "employers and employees" in the section were to be so narrowly construed as to apply only to those who maintained a direct employer-employee relationship, then the law became meaningless when applied to strikes, because the strike severed the continuity of the legal relationship between employer and employee. What, then, was the purpose of this very section, what protection did it extend and to which employees would it then apply?

Brandeis reasoned that: (*a*) There was a presumption underlying any piece of legislation, that it was designed to change the existing state of affairs. (*b*) In this particular instance Congress intended by the Clayton Act to enlarge the "allowable area of economic conflict" for labor unions. (*c*) Congress was conscious of the fact that unions had an interest in the working conditions existing in nonunion shops, since such conditions affect the terms and conditions of employment in the entire industry, including union shops. (*d*) The allowable area of economic conflict had been broadened by the act to include *all* employees thus economically affected. (*e*) "The conditions developed in industry may be such that those engaged in it cannot continue their struggle without danger to the community. But it is not for judges to determine whether such conditions exist. . . . This is the function of the legislature. . . ."

V

The decision of the Supreme Court of the United States in *Duplex Printing Press* v. *Deering* rocked organized labor back on its heels. Labor's "Magna Carta" vanished into thin air. Successful prosecution of unions under the Sherman Act could go on unabated. More than that, the Clayton Act left in its wake a new instrument for the undermining of organized labor. Heretofore under the Sherman Act only the government could apply for an injunction but under the Clayton Act private individuals were enabled to secure injunctions. While that right was again intended as a protection to the small businessman against monopolistic trusts, it was certain to be used also against labor. It was a foregone conclusion that as a result of this decision labor was likely to be confronted with many more injunctions than before the enactment of the Clayton Act. The act that was thought by labor to be an instrument for its emancipation was converted by this decision into an instrument of oppression. Labor's defensive weapon was turned by the court into an offensive weapon against labor.

By this decision employers were stimulated to greater opposition to unions and encouraged to apply for injunctions. The decision in the *Duplex Printing* case led to several other judicial decisions which completely emasculated the Clayton Act and destroyed its intended benefit for labor. The court blinded itself to the facts of our industrial economy and refused to recognize the interdependent character of modern industry and the consequent unity of interests of the workers employed in an industry. Brandeis's pertinent criticism that the majority opinion interpreted the Clayton Act as if it were never designed to change the existing state of affairs, and therefore meaningless legislation, was left unanswered. One jurist commented: "There is no reason that a just court can assign why American courts should not have as cheerfully obeyed the Clayton Act as the English courts obeyed the Trade Disputes Act of 1906."

Professor Charles O. Gregory, in his richly informative and refreshingly outspoken book *Labor and the Law*, explains the confusion concerning the Clayton Act as follows: "Ever since this first interpretation of Section 20 of the Clayton Act, almost all educated opinion in this country has been that the Supreme Court sold organized labor down the river when it construed this section. . . . Several astute lawyers thought that Congress was the body which had betrayed the labor unions when it enacted Section 20. They believed that Congress deliberately made this section ambiguous, with the surface appearance of going very far indeed, but nevertheless using restrictive words like 'employee' in close juxtaposition with the word 'employer' and craftily inserting words like 'lawful' and 'peaceful,' so that labor people would think, after a hasty reading, that they had achieved something substantial. . . .

"Evidence tending to support this belief was found in some of the Congressional committee reports on this section, indicating that Congress had no intention of going so far as to allow the secondary boycott. It is only fair to Congress, however, to remember that an understanding of concepts like the secondary boycott was even less clear in 1914 than it is today. Quite possibly none of the members of the committee knew what was being talked about when that group disclaimed all intention to legalize such a technique."

Labor was disappointed and disillusioned, but it became convinced more than ever that it needed some clear-cut labor legislation which would in unambiguous terms permit it to carry out its legitimate functions and aims. It directed its activities to securing a federal law which would limit the use of the injunction in labor disputes, extend protection to labor in all its disputes within the area of allowable economic conflict, and broaden the terms or conditions of employment regardless of whether or not the disputants stood in the proximate relation of employer and employee. To what extent labor succeeded will be discussed later.

- 9 -

"Pink-Tea Picketing"

(1914–1921)

American Steel Foundries v. Tri-City Central Trades Council

I

The plant of the American Steel Foundries Company at Granite City, Illinois, was shut down for almost six months, during which time most of the workers remained unemployed. Upon its reopening on April 6, 1914, only 350 of its usual 1,600 employees were recalled to work. Those re-employed were told that their wages would be cut from 2 to 10 cents an hour.

The Tri-City Central Trades Council, consisting of thirty-seven craft unions from the neighboring cities of Madison, Granite City, and Venice appointed a committee to interview the company's management and try to get the old wage restored. But the manager refused to take up the grievance with the committee because the company did not deal with labor organizations. He told the committee that the dissatisfied employees might call upon him as individuals. A week later, on April 22, the council called a strike and on the following day picketing began. In addition to a few direct employees who went on strike and picketed, the plant was also picketed by former employees who were not recalled to work, but who had hoped to be recalled, and by members of the Tri-City Council, workers who were not employees of the American Steel Foundries.

On May 18, the company secured an *ex parte* (without a hearing) injunction from the United States District Court for the southern division of the Southern District of Illinois. They charged the Tri-

City Council with calling a strike to get wages raised, with picketing and creating violence and disturbance so that prospective employees refused to take jobs. Pickets were accused of attacking strikebreakers, of kicking lunch baskets out of a porter's hand, and finally of engaging in a riot on May 13, 1914. The defendants denied the charges and claimed that the company witnesses had perjured themselves, that it was the strikebreakers who had used firearms and had fired on the pickets.

Justice Otto Humphreys of the Illinois Federal District Court issued a temporary injunction and within two weeks made it permanent. He also ordered that one hundred printed copies of the injunction be posted conspicuously about and in the vicinity of the American Steel Foundries plant. The injunction was sweeping. It perpetually enjoined the defendants and *all persons* in some way connected with them from threatening or intimidating or even persuading in "any way or manner whatsoever" the employees of the American Steel Foundries Company or any "person *desiring* to be employed," so as to refuse to perform any of their duties as employees. The injunction also prohibited "assembling . . . about or in proximity of" the company's plant, and picketing near the premises "or on streets leading to the premises." It prohibited any kind of interference with the company and its officers in the "free and unrestrained control and operation of its business."

The unions appealed.

II

The appeal was heard by Justices Julian W. Mack, Samuel Alschuler, and Evan A. Evans of the United States Circuit Court of Appeals for the Seventh Circuit.

In summary, the appellants' main contentions briefly were: (1) The decree when issued was too broad because it restrained the union from engaging even in lawful acts. (2) The Clayton Act, which was enacted subsequent to the issuance of the original injunction in this case, permitted the activities in which the defendants engaged and therefore this injunction must now be held invalid.

The company, on the other hand, contended: (a) The order did not restrain picketing as such, but restrained an unlawful conspiracy of which picketing was a part. (b) The District Court might properly restrain lawful acts if these were committed to carry out the purpose of an unlawful conspiracy. (*c*) The defendants were not *employees* but "trouble makers fomenting strife" and therefore did not come within the protection of the law. (*d*) At any rate the company's rights under the injunction decree were not affected by the Clayton Act, which had been subsequently passed, as the latter had no retroactive effect.

On December 6, 1916, Justice Evans, reversing the lower court, delivered the opinion of the Circuit Court of Appeals. Observing that the "obvious effect and purpose" of the decree was to prevent *all* picketing and "to prevent these parties from persuading their fellow employees to join them in their effort to secure what the strikers evidently considered the laborers' just demands," he held: (*a*) The lower court had erred in restraining *persuasion* and picketing as such. (*b*) The court had erred in declaring the Tri-City Council an illegal combination for its effort to get the company to pay the wage scale of November, 1913, because the right to strike for higher wages was firmly established as a legitimate activity of unions. The use of unlawful means could not make a lawful purpose unlawful. (*c*) In "the pursuit of a lawful purpose to secure a raise in wages, picketing may be employed" to find out whom the employer had hired and "persuasion may be used to induce them to refuse or quit the employment." The lawfulness of a strike was not to be judged by its interference with an employer's business. (*d*) The injunction issued by the lower court failed to distinguish between lawful and unlawful means used in the conduct of the strike. Since the injunction restrained *all* picketing, *all* persuasion, and *all* interference with the plaintiff's control of his plant and business, "it transcends the limit of proper restraint." (*e*) The injunction should be modified by eliminating the prohibition against "persuasion" and the prohibition against picketing should be limited only to picketing *"in a threatening or intimidating manner."* All peaceful picketing, whether done by employees or by outsiders, should be permitted.

The company appealed from this decision.

III

The case of *American Steel Foundries Company* v. *Tri-City Central Trades Council* first came for argument before the United States Supreme Court in January, 1919, and it was finally reargued in October, 1921.

The company's attorney argued:

1. The Trades Council, in declaring the strike, had acted without the vote or even a request by the company's employees. The two workers who went on strike had nothing to do with the calling of the strike. Under these circumstances, picketing was prohibited under the laws of the state of Illinois even if there was no physical violence.

2. Under the decision of the *Hitchman* case, it must be held that the Tri-City Council was in a conspiracy to force employees to leave their work, abandon their contracts, and force a new basis of employment. The fact that the company had no written contracts with its employees was immaterial because the company had a right to have its employment relations with its workers undisturbed by this conspiracy.

3. The Council and the defendants were both "strangers and interlopers" in a situation that was tranquil and in which they had no interest.

4. Since the Clayton Act was not law when the action began, the petitioner had a vested right in the final injunction and decree of which it could not be divested by subsequent legislation.

5. Furthermore, the Clayton Act was not applicable because (*a*) it could not be invoked, at this late date, upon the appeal, especially since at this time there was no strike, controversy, or dispute between the petitioner and its employees; (*b*) the injunction was needed to prevent an irreparable injury to property rights and Section 20 of the Clayton Act specifically permitted injunctive relief for such purpose; (*c*) Section 20 did not prohibit the issuance of an injunction against any kind of picketing, even if there was no violence, because the term "picketing" was not even mentioned in that section.

For the union, it was contended:

(*a*) There was no evidence of any conspiracy by either the Tri-City Council or the individuals named as defendants. A union organization was not necessarily an unlawful combination.

(*b*) Neither ordering a strike nor the picketing was unlawful. Hence, the injunction should not prohibit either persuasion or picketing.

(*c*) The pickets were neither interlopers nor strangers. Temporary layoffs did not sever the employment relationship. Besides, between 80 and 90 per cent of the company's workers were members of locals belonging to the Tri-City Council and obviously the council could not properly be termed an interloper.

(*d*) The Tri-City Council was within its rights in doing peaceful picketing, as a matter of general law and, moreover, Section 20 of the Clayton Act specifically sanctioned the activities attributed to picketing, and it was immaterial, therefore, whether the term "picketing" was or was not specifically mentioned in that section.

(*e*) The district court was not warranted in enjoining people from congregating on sidewalks, speaking about the business of the company, or distributing circulars. For to "prevent a workingman from exercising the right of persuasion would deprive him of the right of free speech guaranteed by the Constitution."

(*f*) No property right was involved here since the plant had not been injured, labor was not a commodity, and "an employer has no property right in his workmen;" therefore, the issuance of the injunction was contrary to Section 20 of the Clayton Act, which was retroactive and controlling.

(*g*) The *Hitchman* case could not be a precedent here because no contracts of employment were involved in this case.

(*h*) The decree of the district court was "fatally defective because it was vague and ambiguous—a dragnet."

Chief Justice Taft, delivering the majority opinion of the Supreme Court on December 5, 1921, reversed in part the Circuit Court of Appeals. After reviewing the testimony, he, in summary, declared:

One: Complainant had no vested right in the injunction. Since relief by injunction operated in the future, Section 20 was controlling as to the terms of decrees entered after the passage of the Clayton Act and the complainant had no vested right in the decree against which an appeal was pending.

Two: "Peaceful persuasion" by "employees" was not enjoinable. Congress wished to forbid the use by the federal courts of their equity arm to prevent peaceful persuasion by those who were actually employees, *discharged* or *expectant*, in promotion of their side of the dispute. This introduced no new principle into the equity jurisprudence of those courts. It was merely declaratory of what always was the best practice.

Three: But "peaceful persuasion" was subject to regulation by the court. If in their attempts at persuasion or communication with those whom they would enlist with them, the labor side adopted methods which, however lawful in their announced purpose, inevitably led to intimidation and obstruction, then it was the court's duty, which the terms of Section 20 did not modify, *so to limit* what the propagandists might do as to *time, manner, and place* as should prevent infractions of the law and violations of the rights of the employees, and of the employer for whom they wished to work.

Four: Picketing indicated a militant purpose, inconsistent with peaceable persuasion. "Persistence, importunity, following and dogging become unjustifiable annoyance and obstruction, which is likely soon to savor of intimidation. The pickets had congregated in three or four groups of 4 to 12 men in each group. Assaults and violence had taken place. All information tendered, all arguments advanced and all persuasion used under such circumstances were intimidation . . . It is idle to talk of peaceful communication in such a place and under such conditions." *The number of the pickets was the constituted intimidation.*

Five: "Pickets" prohibited. Picketing thus instituted was unlawful, could not be peaceable, and might be specifically enjoined. The Circuit Court of Appeals was in error in directing that only picketing "in a threatening or intimidating manner" should be enjoined. This Appellate Court decision would recognize as "legal that which bears the sinister name of 'picketing.'" It was to be observed that Congress did not include the term "picketing" in this Section 20 which enumerated various permissible activities of unions against which no injunctions were to be issued. Apparently Congress did not intend to prohibit injunctions against "picketing."

Six: Only "missionaries" permitted. Equity courts must use their "flexible remedial power" to "try one mode of restraint, and if it fails or proves to be too drastic," to change it. "We think that the strikers and their sympathizers engaged in the economic struggle should be limited to one representative for each point of ingress and egress in the plant or place of business." The strikers should thus have the right to communicate, observe, and persuade but "with special admonition" that their communications be not "abusive, libelous or threatening" nor made in groups, nor calculated to obstruct unwilling listeners by dogging importunity. Equity must prevent "the inevitable intimidation of groups of pickets," but may allow *"missionaries."*

Seven: Only "employees" not strangers to a labor dispute were entitled to protection under Section 20 of the act. It had already been determined in the *Duplex* v. *Deering* case that the exemptions under the Clayton Act did not apply to persons who are neither "employees nor seeking employment." Since two of the defendants fell into the category of "employees," the injunction decree of the District Court barring *them* from using persuasion anywhere should be modified by striking out the word "persuasion" from the order.

Eight: Tri-City case was distinguished from Hitchman and Duplex cases. The *Hitchman* case did not apply because that had been an attempt to get miners into the United Mine Workers "so that the Union could control, through the union employees, the production and sale of coal in West Virginia, in competition with mines in Ohio and other states." That plan had been carried out with deception, misrepresentation, and procurement of violation of contract. The court had held that the union was engaged in an unlawful conspiracy because *both means and purpose* were unlawful in view of the remoteness of benefit to the workers "and the formidable, country-wide and dangerous character of the control of interstate commerce sought." The present case also was distinguished from the *Duplex* case because in this case there was no secondary boycott involved. *The members of a local labor union and the union itself did have sufficient interest in the wages paid to the employees of any employer in the community to justify their use of lawful and peaceable persuasion to induce such employees not to accept reduced wages and to quit their employment.* Hence, the District Court properly restrained the Tri-City Council from picketing, but it improperly restrained it from the use of "persuasion" to keep men from working or taking employment with the American Steel Foundries Company.

Nine: Social justification for the existence of trade unions in our economic society. ". . . Labor unions are recognized by the Clayton Act as legal when instituted for mutual help and lawfully carrying out their legitimate objects. They have long been thus recognized by the courts. They were organized out of the necessities of the situation. A single employee was helpless in dealing with an employer. He was dependent ordinarily on his daily wage for the maintenance of himself and family. If the employer refused to pay him the wages that he thought fair he was nevertheless unable to leave the employ and to resist arbitrary and unfair treatment. Union was essential to give laborers opportunity to deal on equality with their employer. They united to exert influence upon him and to leave him in a body in order by this inconvenience to induce him to make better terms with them. They were withholding their labor of economic value to make him pay what they thought it was worth. The right to combine for such a lawful purpose has in many years not been denied by any court. The strike became a lawful instrument in a lawful economic struggle or competition between employer and employees as to the share or division between them of the joint product of labor and capital. To render this combination at all effective, employees must make their combination extend beyond one shop. It is helpful to have as many as may be in the same trade in the same community united, because in the competition between employers they are bound to be affected by the standard of wages of their trade in the neighborhood . . ."

Ten: The injunction was warranted to prevent injury to the business of the company. The result of the union campaign in this case was to put employees and would-be employees in such fear that many abandoned work, and this seriously interfered with the complainant in operating the plant. Therefore, the issuance of the restraining order was justified.

The Supreme Court reversed that part of the decree of the Circuit Court of Appeals which legalized "picketing" and upheld that part which permitted peaceful persuasion, and the district court was directed to modify its original decree accordingly.

IV

Unless one understands the aim and function of picketing in labor disputes, one is likely to underestimate the effect of the decision on the development of union rights. Generally speaking, picketing is a technique used by organized labor to inform employees and the public that a labor dispute is in progress. This is accomplished by having a person or persons (pickets) patrol the place of business with a sign proclaiming the dispute and attempt to dissuade workers from accepting employment or shoppers from patronizing such employer or his product. But a striker on the picket line is not likely to be overfriendly to a nonstriking employee, or especially a strikebreaker who takes his job, and clashes between pickets and nonstriking employees or strikebreakers occasionally occur.

At first, courts looked with great disfavor upon picketing and declared it altogether illegal. One court was certain that "there is and can be no such thing as peaceful picketing, any more than there can be chaste vulgarity, or peaceful mobbing, or lawful lynching." However, as the needs for labor unions in our economic system became more obvious, courts were looking for means of reconciling some form of picketing with the court's view of the right of employers not to have their businesses interfered with.

In this *Tri-City* case, Chief Justice Taft endeavored to resolve the picketing dilemma by legalizing "peaceful persuasion," not by the "sinister" picket, but by a "missionary"; and by limiting the term "missionary" only to employees, ex-employees, potential employees, and to those who might have an interest in the outcome of the dispute. Total strangers to the dispute were to be excluded from having the privilege of a "missionary." Furthermore, he reserved for a court of equity the power to regulate this limited "missionary" activity with regard to number, time, manner, and place. He further provided that the court under its "flexible remedial power" could place greater or lesser prohibitions on such "missionary" activity. Labor circles dubbed this "pink-tea picketing."

While the chief justice called picketing "sinister" and limited the number of "missionaries," nevertheless he enunciated a progressive view of the need for labor organizations in modern society and furnished an enlightened analysis of the social justification of trade unions. He recognized the unity of interest of *all organized labor in a community* concerning the working conditions of all the workers in the community. Though the court held that total strangers, nonstrikers, and nonemployees under the Clayton Act could not do "missionary" work in front of the plant in the dispute, nevertheless the court recognized that fellow workers in the community, because of their "unity of interest," had the right peacefully to persuade employees to quit their employment.

The decision apparently limited the extent of "unity of interest" to the workers in the *local community*. The Supreme Court was not yet ready to recognize that "unity of interest" of workers in our highly industrial economy is not limited to the local community. The court stopped short. It failed to admit openly or to give recognition to the fact that industrial competition knows no geographic community boundary line.

The chief justice's emphasis on the rights of the court to *regulate* "missionary" work as to number, time, manner, and place, and the characterization of the term "picket" as "sinister," led some legislatures and courts to take the position that picketing in all forms, at least by strangers, should be prohibited. Thus, the *Tri-City* decision, though unintended, supplied some state courts with an excuse for suppressing picketing altogether. A New Jersey court in 1926 was encouraged by the decision to declare: "A single sentinel constantly parading in front of a place of employment for an extended length of time may be just as effective in striking terror to the souls of the employees bound there by their duty as was the swinging pendulum in Poe's famous story *The Pit and the Pendulum* to victims chained in its ultimate band. In fact, silence is sometimes more striking and impressive than the loud mouthings of the mob."

It may be well to point up that while, on the one hand, the Supreme Court of the United States gave sympathetic expression to the broad social justification of the existence of labor unions, on the other hand, when it came to the actual application of a law which was intended to broaden the rights of unions, the court took a very narrow view. It prohibited picketing as "sinister," it permitted only "missionaries," limited "missionaries" to "time, manner and place" and narrowed the application of the Clayton Act by limiting the protection to labor granted therein to "employees," not to strangers to a labor dispute. This narrow interpretation does not seem to square with the implications that flow from the expressed social justification for the existence of labor unions in our economic society.

When Picketing Meets "Due Process"

(1916–1921)

Truax v. Corrigan

I

In the year 1911 the territory of Arizona applied for admission as a state of the United States. With the application for statehood it submitted its proposed constitution for approval as procedure required. It appeared that the proposed constitution contained some provisions which were considered radical, such as the initiative, the referendum, and the "recall of judges." William Howard Taft, then president of the United States, refused to sign the bill giving statehood to Arizona until the "recall" provision of its constitution was eliminated.

Arizona complied and removed that provision from the proposed constitution. However, in 1913, after Arizona had become a sovereign state, its legislature promptly adopted the "recall of judges" as its fundamental law. President Taft's original objection to the Arizona constitution was thus circumvented. There was nothing Taft could do about it, because he no longer was president, and, even if he had been, Arizona as a sovereign state had the right to enact such a provision in its law.

Eight years later, in 1921, one of the Arizona laws came for review before the Supreme Court. Taft was chief justice. The law in question had been enacted by the same Arizona legislature which had circumvented Taft's objection to the "recall" provision. Taft wrote the majority opinion of the Supreme Court in that case, and found the law unconstitutional.

A psychiatrist might trace the origin of Taft's reasoning in this case to his frustration in connection with the "recall" provision in the proposed Arizona constitution, and explain his action by the working of the unconscious. But let us proceed with the more direct facts concerning the background of the case of *Truax* v. *Corrigan*.

II

The progressive spirit of the West found expression in the new constitution of Arizona. The lawmakers of that state in revising the state code of 1913 took a much more favorable attitude toward labor. The Arizona legislature held the view that workers might combine to protect and raise their living standards and that the state courts should not interfere through injunctions with the workers' economic struggle with their employers. In revising its code the legislature enacted Paragraph 1464, which in substance prohibited the state courts from issuing injunctions in labor disputes "concerning terms and conditions of employment, unless necessary to prevent irreparable damage to property or to property right of the party making the application, for which injury there is no adequate remedy at law. . ." The law was broadly worded and it was obviously intended that in the absence of any disorders or violence peaceful picketing should in no case be prohibited.

Whether the state of Arizona had the right to practice such philosophy in regulating industrial relations was the essential point in the *Truax* v. *Corrigan* case.

III

The facts in this case briefly were:

William Truax and William A. Truax were the owners of a restaurant called the "English Kitchen." It was a fair-sized restaurant located on Bisbee's main street, employing about ten workers consisting of cooks and waiters. In April 1916, Truax informed his employees that their wages would be cut and their daily hours would be increased. The change was supposed to take place on April 9. The workers belonged to the Cooks and Waiters Union of Bisbee. The union communicated with Truax and urged him not to change the working conditions, but he refused. On April 10, the day following the lowering of the working standards, the cooks and waiters of the English Kitchen went out on strike. They were supported in their strike by the Warren District Trade Assembly.

The union waged a hot campaign against Truax. Donkeys, draped with banners publicizing the strike, were driven about the town for several days. Various handbills and circulars attacking Truax's methods of treating the workers were distributed. One circular charged Truax with chasing the employees down the street with a butcher knife. Another circular referred to him as "12-hours Bill Truax." Some circulars stated that Truax's prices were higher and his food worse than in the other Bisbee restaurants. Other circulars imaginatively speculated about Truax's ambitions and stated that he wanted to hasten the day when he would have made his pile and could return to that "dear Los Angeles, perhaps with a Japanese valet, a Chinese cook and an imported Jamaica chauffeur." During business hours pickets paraded up and down in front of the restaurant with large banners publicizing their strike against Truax. Often sympathizers gathered near the English Kitchen and discussed the strike situation in loud voices. On the whole, the strike had no violence, and the picketing was peaceful. But the picketing had its effect. Truax's business dropped by more than half, from a daily intake of $156 to $75.

Truax went to court. He instituted an action against the Cooks and Waiters Union of Bisbee, Local No. 5, and some individuals. He charged that the union and its officers were engaged in an unlawful and malicious conspiracy to harass his business. He claimed that the defendants were financially irresponsible, could not respond in damages, and therefore he requested that an injunction should be issued restraining the defendants from directly or indirectly interfering with his business through threats, coercion, picketing, boycotting, or from in any manner referring to plaintiff verbally or in writing as "unfair."

The defendants denied the allegations and asked that the case be dismissed. They argued that the strike was undertaken with the lawful purpose of maintaining the wage and hour standards and, therefore, the defendants' actions in support thereof could not be held to be a conspiracy. Furthermore, they contended, the Arizona code specifically prohibited the issuing of injunctions in such cases.

Judge Alfred C. Lockwood, of the Superior Court of Cochise County, before whom the case appeared, sustained the union's contention and dismissed the case. Truax appealed.

IV

The appeal came before the Arizona State Supreme Court. Justice D. L. Cunningham delivered the opinion of the court. After observing that Truax's own testimony admitted that the picketing had been entirely peaceful, the justice, in substance, held:

(a) Since the Arizona law granted the right to organize and to maintain working conditions by peaceful means, the strike in this case was for a lawful purpose and the defendants' agreement to act together was lawful and not an enjoinable conspiracy.

(b) The union publicity concerning the strike was factually correct. No right of the plaintiff was violated by publicizing the correct facts and, therefore, no ground for issuing an injunction had been presented on this basis.

(c) The state constitution allowed every person freely to speak and to publish on all subjects, responsibility being imposed only for the abuse of this right. If an equity court could restrain these defendants from publicizing their dispute, then these citizens would be deprived of a constitutional right enjoyed by all other citizens of the state.

(d) A court of equity could not suspend the constitutional rights of a citizen because such citizen happened to be insolvent and financially unable to respond in damages. If financial disability should be the basis of an injunction, then should the court be called upon to decide what degree of wealth is required to authorize a citizen to enjoy all his constitutional rights without interference by the court?

The Arizona State Supreme Court concluded that Judge Lockwood had properly dismissed the complaint and affirmed his judgment.

V

A few months after the State Supreme Court dismissed the case, Truax started a new action. This was in December, 1918. The essential facts of the new case were identical with those involved in the previous case, but the legal issues raised were different. This time the action was based on the contention that Paragraph 1464 of the Arizona code, which restricted injunctions in labor disputes, was unconstitutional, in violation of the Fourteenth Amendment of the United States Constitution, which forbade any state to take property without due process of law or to deny a citizen the equal protection of the law.

Truax's emphasis on the new legal angle did not impress the court very much. Chief Justice Cunningham of the Arizona court delivered the court's opinion disposing of the new contention. He held that in the absence of violence the existence of a local strike might be publicized in the most effective way possible because peaceful picketing is a means of peaceful communication, a fundamental civil right. He further held that no man has a vested property in the esteem of the public, and that in the absence of a duty owed by the defendants to the plaintiff to keep their labor dispute secret, they had a right to publicize it by means of peaceful picketing. The court concluded that Truax had no rights which were violated by the defendants and that the law was not in conflict with the Fourteenth Amendment and therefore Truax's application in the new case for an injunction was again denied.

Truax appealed to the Supreme Court of the United States.

VI

Under the title of *Truax* v. *Corrigan*, the case was argued before the Supreme Court on April 29 and 30, 1920, and then reargued on October 5 and 6, 1921.

Truax's counsel argued:

(*a*) The Arizona law forbidding injunctions in labor disputes was unconstitutional. It made *arbitrary and capricious* distinctions among persons and properties. (*b*) The law was "class legislation." It denied the plaintiffs equal protection of the law since the interpretation of the statute by the Arizona courts discriminated against the plaintiffs and their property as a class. (*c*) The union's conduct was unlawful. The mere fact of picketing was in itself coercive. Besides, the handbills distributed were scurrilous, abusive, and contained threats, proclaimed the plaintiffs "unfair" and invited retaliation by organized labor against plaintiffs. (*d*) The union's acts constituted an unlawful secondary boycott. (*e*) The Arizona law deprived plaintiffs of their property rights to the public's goodwill and of their right to exercise their calling in violation of the Fourteenth Amendment.

Counsel for defendants contended:

(1) The sole issue in this case was whether peaceful picketing permitted under the Arizona law was unlawful and deprived Truax

of property rights. Truax's good will was not a property right. (2) The picketing by the union was a means of communicating information to the public concerning the labor dispute. The union's statements were true and within its interests. Since there had been neither disorder nor libel, the defendants had an absolute right of free speech which extended likewise to freedom of publication. Such rights were as sacred as the plaintiffs' rights to conduct business. (3) The Arizona statute was not class legislation because it applied to a *whole* class of persons—employees, employers, and persons seeking employment—and deprived no one of the equal protection of the laws. (4) The Arizona law was not violative of the Fourteenth Amendment. It substantially resembled Section 20 of the Clayton Act, which forbade federal courts to issue injunctions in labor disputes and that section was not regarded by the court as depriving anyone of a property right. Hence, Paragraph 1464 of the Arizona code must similarly be held not to contravene the due process clause of the Constitution.

By a split court of five to four, the Supreme Court of the United States ruled in favor of Truax. Chief Justice Taft, delivering the majority opinion on December 19, 1921, held:

One: The means used by the defendants in the strike were illegal. The libelous attacks on the plaintiffs, their business, and their customers, and the abusive epithets applied to them, were palpable wrongs.

Two: The picketing and appeals "all linked together in a campaign" were an unlawful annoyance and hurtful nuisance in respect to free access to the plaintiffs' place of business, and *business was a property right.*

Three: The picketing was not a mere appeal to the sympathetic aid of would-be customers or a request to withhold patronage. It was a moral coercion by illegal annoyance and obstruction. It was thus plainly a conspiracy.

Four: The Fourteenth Amendment was intended to preserve the fundamental principles of right and justice by the guarantee of due process. No state had the power to pass legislation which would result in wrongful and injurious invasion of property rights. The Arizona statute deprived the plaintiffs of a real remedy against the wrongs inflicted upon them and, therefore, disregarded fundamental rights of liberty and property and deprived the plaintiffs of due process of law.

Five: The Arizona law denied the equal protection of the laws guaranteed by the United States Constitution. It allowed injunctive relief to one and denied it to another. If the employers had committed the acts charged in the complaint, an injunction would lie against them. But when these acts were committed by the employees of the injured persons, an injunction was denied them. "If this is not a denial of the equal protection of the laws," then it would be difficult to conceive what would be.

Six: There was no parallel between the Arizona statute as interpreted by the Arizona court and Section 20 of the Clayton Act as interpreted by the Supreme Court. The latter considered that peaceful picketing was a contradiction in terms and restricted it to one "picket," for the purpose of publicizing the strike. The Arizona court set no limits to the picketing under the broad statute.

Chief Justice Taft concluded that the defendants' demurrer should have been overruled and the injunction granted as requested.

The minority, consisting of four justices, vigorously dissented and filed three dissenting opinions.

Justice Oliver Wendell Holmes, in his dissent, criticized Taft's holding and observed that: (1) "Delusive exactness is a source of fallacy throughout the law" and particularly in the application of the Fourteenth Amendment; (2) the majority opinion was confusing by calling the right to do business a property right. This right to do business is delusive in that it may look like any other property right but is not. Business is a "course of conduct"—not a "thing"; (3) business conduct, like any other conduct, is subject to modification according to time and circumstances; (4) *legislation concerning business conduct may begin where an evil begins.* "If, as many intelligent people believe, there is more danger that the injunction will be abused in labor cases than elsewhere, I can feel no doubt of the power of the legislature to deny it in such cases"; (5) the Arizona legislature could select the case of employees and employers for special treatment, dealing with both sides alike, and deny the extraordinary relief by injunction without violating the Constitution.

Taking the broad view that made him famous, Justice Holmes concluded:

"I must add one general consideration. There is nothing that I more deprecate than the use of the Fourteenth Amendment, beyond the absolute compulsion of its words, to prevent the making of social experiments, that an important part of the community desires, in the insulated chambers afforded by the several states, even though the experiment may seem futile or even noxious to me and to those whose judgment I most respect."

Justices Mahlon Pitney and John H. Clarke, in their dissenting opinion, also criticized the majority opinion. They reasoned:

(a) The Supreme Court was bound by the construction of the Arizona court that Paragraph 1464 merely established a new rule of procedure. That rule did not deprive the plaintiff of rights under the Fourteenth Amendment because the state had as much right to prescribe rules under which business should be done as the plaintiff had the right to do business in the state.

(b) One state may ban picketing and another legalize it. In neither case is the action so "arbitrary and devoid of reasonable basis that it could be called a deprivation of liberty and property without due process of law in the constitutional sense."

(c) Restricting the use of the injunction did not hamper the exercise of a right essential to acquire, possess, and enjoy property.

(d) The law did not discriminate against the plaintiff in favor of others, since Truax got treatment not less favorable than that given to others similarly circumstanced. The Arizona legislature was entitled to single out types of controversies for particular treatment. It might put employer-employee disputes into a separate class without violating the Fourteenth Amendment.

Justice Louis D. Brandeis, in his dissent, stressed the sociological background of industrial relations and the need of flexibility in that respect. Pointing out that the rules of employer-employee relationship often change, he observed that it was socially dangerous for the court to close the door to possible change. He urged that the decision of the Arizona court be left undisturbed, because: (1) The state court had the right to construe the meaning of the statute in question. Since the Arizona court construed the meaning of the law to be that "peaceful picketing" was legal, that construction was binding upon the Supreme Court. (2) Even if the state could not constitutionally allow peaceful picketing, it was still free to limit the issuance of the injunction if it deemed that such injunctions would be detrimental to the public welfare. A state was not required to protect *all* property by injunction because it protected some. (3) The denial of the extraordinary remedy of injunction was not a denial of rights guaranteed by the "due process" or "equal protection" clauses of the Fourteenth Amendment. Therefore, the Arizona court should be upheld in its right to decline to issue the injunction.

In accordance with the decision of the majority, the Arizona Supreme Court was reversed in its interpretation of the statute, and the state law prohibiting the courts' interference with peaceful picketing was declared unconstitutional.

VII

In a larger sense this case reflected the conflicting attitudes of the justices of the Supreme Court toward social changes in our society. The majority steadfastly stood for the *status quo,* for adhering to the old doctrine of inviolability of property rights, as that term was traditionally understood and interpreted by them. On the other hand, the minority urged flexibility in the law and an extension of opportunity for social experiment, necessitated by the social changes in our expanding industrial economy.

The significance of this case to the development of rights of unions in the United States lies in the fact that the Supreme Court deprived states of the right to curb their courts in the abuse of injunctions in labor disputes, and thus influenced many state courts to interpret liberal picketing laws in the narrow spirit of this decision. Not without justification did labor feel that it could not look to the Supreme Court, as then constituted, for a proper appreciation of the place of organized labor in modern industrial society. The same court, in the same year, in the *Duplex* case, narrowly construed the Clayton Act so as to deprive unions of the protection intended by federal legislation, and by the decision in this *Truax* case it deprived unions of the benefits intended by state legislation. Labor became more and more convinced that judicial power was being used against unions to thwart the favorable legislative intentions toward labor.

- II -

The Compulsory Arbitration Cure

(1920–1925)

CHARLES WOLFF PACKING COMPANY v. COURT OF INDUSTRIAL RELATIONS OF THE STATE OF KANSAS

I

The first year after World War I, the year 1919, saw a great deal of industrial unrest in the United States. About 4,154,420 workers were involved in various strikes. That year also saw the dramatic struggle for unionization in the steel industry. During two years previous to that, the state of Kansas had experienced 364 stoppages in its coal fields.

Governor Henry J. Allen of the state of Kansas thought he had found a cure for all industrial strife. He called the Kansas legislature into special session and prepared the cure—compulsory arbitration. Both organized labor and employers opposed the measure, but in spite of this joint opposition, the governor succeeded in having the legislature enact the Kansas Industrial Relations Act of 1920.

This act aimed to prevent interruption of production in the food, clothing, and fuel industries. It provided that workers in these industries could not strike and that employers could not lock out workers or stop production. All industrial disputes in these three industries, if not settled between the employers and labor, should be submitted for adjudication to the newly established tribunal, the Kansas Court of Industrial Relations. This Industrial Court consisted of three judges appointed by the governor with the advice and consent of the Senate. The law had teeth in it and provided that anyone who violated it or the orders of this Industrial Court might be fined $1,000 or imprisoned for a year, or both. The penalty was greater against

127

corporation officials or union officers who violated the law or orders; they could be fined up to $5,000 or imprisoned for two years at hard labor.

Emphasizing that the law was neither prolabor nor antiemployer, it provided that any award made by the Industrial Court should be such that workers "shall receive at all times a fair wage and have healthful and model surroundings" and that "capital invested therein [these three industries] shall receive a fair return to the owners thereof." It also provided that individual workers might quit their employment but that they might not *conspire* with others to quit employment or to engage in picketing and similar activities. Further to emphasize its impartiality, the law, which prohibited workers from quitting work collectively, also provided that employers in these three industries had no right to limit or discontinue operations except by permission of the Industrial Court. If employers suspended operation without permission, then the Industrial Court had the right to operate their businesses on condition that a fair award to labor and a fair return to capital would be assured.

In order to prevent a possible legal attack on the constitutionality of the law on the ground that it deprived the owners of property rights without due process, this law was limited to only three industries—food, clothing, and fuel—industries essential to the health and welfare of the public. In addition, the law specifically stated that these industries were "affected with public interest" and that it was necessary for public welfare that they should be operated without interruption. The makers of this law considered that these three industries, in their relation to the public, occupied a position similar to that of public utilities; and since it was established that the state might regulate such utilities, they concluded that the state had the right to regulate these industries.

In short, the Kansas Industrial Relations Act of 1920 visualized the state of Kansas as a state without any interruption of production in these three essential industries "affected with public interest." It introduced the remedy of compulsory arbitration to prevent interruption of production which might follow industrial disputes. It went further. It made certain that the Industrial Court would, when necessary for the continuity of production, itself operate the affected industries—food, clothing, and mining of fuel—and thus assure peace and plenty for the citizens of the state of Kansas.

II

The law was soon put to test. The labor contract between the Charles Wolff Packing Company of Topeka and Local 176 of the AFL Amalgamated Meat Cutters, expired at the end of 1920. Two weeks later the company announced that the contract would not be renewed; wages were to be cut about 10 per cent, amounting to a reduction of from 7½ cents to 15 cents an hour; bonus payments, the guarantee of 40 hours of work per week, and time and a half for overtime were to be eliminated. The local union, which included a majority of the plant's 300 employees, voted to strike. Their district officer, however, instructed them not to strike but first to file a complaint with the Industrial Court, as required by the Kansas law. The local union followed the instructions given and filed such a complaint.

The complaint was filed on January 19 and the company answered it on January 28. For about two months no action was taken by the Industrial Court. On March 10, 1921, while the case was pending, the workers at the Wolff plant voted, by 225 to 1, to join in the strike called by their national union against the Big Five of the meat-packing industry. Upon learning of this contemplated action by the union, the Court of Industrial Relations proceeded to conduct hearings on the union complaint filed with it in January.

About ten days later the Industrial Court made a *temporary* award, directing the company to maintain the 8-hour basic day until a final determination, and a few weeks later, on May 2, 1921, the court issued its final order disposing of all the disputes. It promulgated a new wage scale; the wage reduction ordered by the company was rescinded in part, so that the wage cut was only about 2.8 per cent; the 8-hour basic workday was retained but, on 2 days of the week, an additional hour each day might be worked without overtime pay, provided the total weekly hours during such week did not exceed 48. The award also made several recommendations on sanitary conditions and regulations as to the work of women employed in the plant.

The company protested and declared that the tribunal's award imposed further losses on the business. It offered to open its books for examination. The Industrial Court rejected the company's protest, declined the company's offer to open its books for inspection, and let its award stand.

III

The company refused to comply with the award. Pursuant to the law, the Industrial Court then applied to the Kansas Supreme Court for a writ of mandamus to compel the company to carry out the terms of the award. By this time the Associated Industries of Kansas had become cognizant of the broad import of the case for business and appeared in the case as "a friend of the court."

The defense interposed technical and substantive objections. It contended that (1) the Court of Industrial Relations had no right to sue in its own name; only the Wolff employees, if the order was enforceable, could bring an action to compel the payment of wages; (2) such power as the tribunal had could be wielded only in an emergency and that no such emergency had been alleged; (3) the law was unconstitutional because it violated the Fourteenth Amendment of the Constitution; only employers could be held to the terms of the award, but workers were not obliged to remain on the job at that wage; (4) wages were not affected with a public interest and, therefore, the court had no right to issue the award; (5) the singling out of the three industries to which the act applied was arbitrary and unjust; and (6) the order deprived both the Company and its employees of freedom of contract guaranteed by the Constitution.

Justice John Marshall delivered the opinion of the Kansas Supreme Court on October 8, 1921. He held in substance:

(a) The Industrial Court had power to bring this suit in its own name, as it had power to act on complaint by either party, and that the petition of the Industrial Court sufficiently alleged emergency to warrant action. Since the defendant was not forced to operate at a loss or to abandon his business, he was deprived of no constitutional right.

(b) The legislature had declared the packing industry affected with a public interest. Therefore, the rules of public utility regulation might properly apply here. Since the state might control rates in businesses affected with a public interest, and since wages were a principal factor in rates, these rates "cannot be completely controlled unless wages are controlled, and wages cannot be controlled unless charges are controlled." The two were interdependent. The unquestioned power to control rates implied the power in such industries to control wages. Wages, moreover, were the "most fruitful cause of industrial unrest." The state could not be powerless in protecting enterprises needed by the people.

(c) Moreover, the United States Supreme Court held that a state had the power to limit working hours and fix minimum wages for *women*. "The state should, it does, have power to protect laboring men to the same extent that it protects working women." Furthermore, if Congress's power over interstate commerce authorized it to fix the basic workday for railroad employees, the state's authority under the police power extended at least as far. The Court of Industrial Relations was as much the outgrowth of an emergency as was the Adamson Act, which fixed the 8-hour standard on the railroads to avoid strikes.

(d) All regulatory laws interfered with freedom of contract, yet they must be imposed to prevent violence in industrial disputes.

(e) "The flow of food supply from producer to consumer should not be stopped by conditions produced by industrial unrest arising out of wage problems." Nor was food, fuel, cloth, and their transport an "arbitrary and unjust" classification of industries "affected with a public interest." The legislature had the power to pass the Industrial Relations Act and to make it apply to the industries specified and not to others.

While Justice Marshall declared the act as such constitutional, he held that the evidence in support of the specific award in this Wolff case was not sufficient. He appointed a commissioner to take additional evidence and submit the report directly to him instead of to the Industrial Court. In the meantime he withheld the final decision on the application to enforce the award until the receipt of the commissioner's report.

Some time later A. L. Noble, of Wichita, whom the court had appointed commissioner to take evidence, submitted his report. He found that the company employed only about 300 workers. But he held that, although the plant was small, the inconvenience that a strike in this plant would cause to the public gave the Industrial Court jurisdiction over this dispute. The commissioner, however, concluded that the Industrial Court by this award exceeded its authority in several respects: it had no right to order equal wages for women; it had no right to fix a 54-hour maximum workweek, or one day's rest in seven; and it had no right to order the company to give workers advance notice of nonoperation of the plant. The commissioner further reported that the company was operating at a loss because of the decline in the value of its stock on hand and he therefore recommended that the wage award should not be enforced at that time because it would increase the company's loss.

The Kansas Supreme Court did not accept all the recommendations of the commissioner. In passing on the commissioner's report, Justice Marshall, for the majority, based his decision on the following trenchant social doctrine: "An industry of any kind that cannot be operated except at the sacrifice of its employees ought to quit business. An industry ought not to be permitted to recoup its losses out of the wages of its employees, where those employees are in such a condition that they cannot prevent it." The justice pointed out that the workers could not always exercise economic mobility and seek work in another field; that in this case the company was trying to place its business loss on the shoulders of its employees, and that this should not be permitted if employees were thereby compelled to work for less than living wages.

The dissenting minority contended that the Industrial Relations Act of 1920 was an emergency measure to cope with the coal strike that began in November, 1919. It was enacted in the interests of the public, and not merely in the interests of the workers or employees. It authorized intervention only to "insure such efficiency and continuity in the production of the necessaries of life as will save the people from annoyance and distress." Only large controversies had been envisaged as requiring action under the law. The orders in this case were improper because no statutory emergency had arisen when the tribunal intervened. Moreover, the irregular delivery of cattle made the 8-hour day impracticable; longer hours had to be worked for which extra compensation was given, hence the hour limitation was merely a means of setting wages. The scale of wages in the Wolff Packing Company was not so low as to justify a conclusion that productivity had dropped and that labor had been degraded, to an extent warranting action by the Industrial Court.

The minority further claimed that, even if a strike had ensued, no public interest would be affected because there was an "abundant supply" of meat available to the defendant. Besides, even if a strike did occur, the law prohibited picketing and "other trouble-making incidents of a strike;" therefore, production could not be much interfered with. Since there was no emergency, nor any need for the tribunal's intervention, the mandamus should not issue.

In accordance with the decision of the majority, the Kansas Supreme Court granted the original petition of the Industrial Court for the enforcement of its award only to the extent that the defendant should be compelled to pay the wages and maintain the hours as ordered by the tribunal, but the court declined to enforce the other terms of the award.

The company appealed from the majority decision of the Kansas Supreme Court to the Supreme Court of the United States.

IV

In its argument before the Supreme Court of the United States, the company argued that the Kansas Industrial Relations Act was unconstitutional and pleaded that the order directing it to pay the wages and maintain the hours deprived it of property without due process of law, in violation of the Fourteenth Amendment. It dwelt on the losses it had sustained in operating its business and stressed the fact that the Kansas Supreme Court unjustifiably disregarded Commissioner Noble's findings.

The Industrial Court argued: The state's power extended to the promotion of the public convenience and general prosperity. Since the packing industry had become centralized, it had become affected with a public interest and was properly subject to regulation, regardless of the size of a given enterprise. The state had power to regulate wages and hours, just as, under its police power, it had the right to enact a workmen's compensation law. Both add to labor costs and constitute, indirectly, a wage increase. Such laws did not violate the due process clause of the Constitution. The Kansas Supreme Court had found that an emergency did exist, and its determination was binding on this court, unless it appeared palpably wrong. Mere loss of profits was not sufficient ground to make state regulation unconstitutional.

About six weeks after the case had been argued, Chief Justice Taft, reversing the Kansas Supreme Court, delivered the opinion of the court on June 11, 1923. In substance, he held:

One: The Kansas law of 1920 assumed that the state, representing the people, could "compel those engaged in the manufacture of food and cloth and the production of fuel, whether owners or workers, to continue in their business and employment on terms fixed by an agency of the State if they cannot agree." This curtailed freedom of contract.

Two: Businesses affected with a public interest fell into three categories: those operating by a public grant of privilege, like franchised public utilities; those regarded as such by long custom; and those made such by devotion to public use. *Legislative declaration was not conclusive in declaring a business "affected with a public interest."*

Three: Since the adoption of the Constitution, neither the butcher, the baker, nor the candlestick maker had been deemed to conduct businesses affected with a public interest.

Four: Even if the state had the right to regulate an industry, *regulation* of the food industry did not extend to fixing its wages and prices, because the field was adequately competitive.

Five: Moreover, even when a business was properly affected with a public interest, that in itself did not determine the permissible extent of regulation. *Such regulation was not a matter of legislative discretion solely.* If mere legislative declaration authorized this type of regulation, "there must be a revolution in the relation of government to general business."

Six: The provisions of the Kansas law conflicted with the freedom to contract and to work, assured by the Fourteenth Amendment. The terms of the act made both employer and employee yield rights. The employer had to employ the worker at the wages fixed and the worker was forbidden to strike against the wages fixed "and thus is compelled to give up the means of putting himself on a bargaining equality with his employer which action in concert with his fellows gives him." The court considered the act as compelling the employer to pay the adjudged wages, and as forbidding the employees to combine against working for such wages. The Kansas law sought to change the "conventional relationship" to that resembling a soldier's position.

Seven: In the *Wolff* case, the likelihood of an emergency had been determined by the Industrial Court, itself a *subordinate* agency of Kansas. Therefore it could not stand on the same ground with a law enacted by Congress, the Adamson Act, which had been upheld as a proper exercise of Congressional power to meet a temporary emergency. Nor could the regulation of railroads be taken as precedent for applying the doctrine to the Wolff plant, whose classification as "affected with public interest" was at best doubtful.

Eight: The Kansas Industrial Relations Act, in so far as it allowed "the fixing of wages" in the plaintiff's packing plant was "in conflict with the Fourteenth Amendment and deprives the Wolff Company of its property and liberty of contract without due process of law."

Accordingly, the judgment of the Kansas Supreme Court was reversed.

V

The opinion of Chief Justice Taft hardly added to the popularity of the Kansas industrial tribunal, which was already generally unpopular. It had met with opposition not only from employers but also from labor. Labor's hostility to the act was aggravated by the actions of the Industrial Court during the railway shopmen's strike of 1922. At that time this court used all its power to crush the strike, forbade picketing, prosecuted railroad men for visiting nonstrikers, and prosecuted merchants for putting in their windows posters reading: "We are for the striking railroad men 100 per cent." The behavior of the Industrial Court during that strike prompted William Allen White, famous editor of the Emporia Gazette, to take up the issue. He placed a poster in his office window reading: "We are for the striking railroad men 49 per cent" and pledged to raise the percentage a point for every day the Kansas authorities continued to violate the constitutional right to freedom of speech.

Deprived by the Supreme Court of the power to fix *wages*, the Industrial Court brought a new mandamus proceeding in the Kansas Supreme Court to get its original order of May 2, 1920, enforced at least as far as the *hours* of work provisions were concerned. The tribunal petitioned the Kansas Supreme Court to have the wage schedule stricken from its award but to enforce the provisions for the basic 8-hour day, the one day's rest in seven, and the equal pay for women.

Justice Marshall, for the majority, rendered a decision on October 6, 1923. He held that the United States Supreme Court had invalidated only the wage-fixing clauses of the law of 1920 and that, hence, the hours rulings might be put into effect. Therefore, he issued the mandamus order directing the Wolff Company to comply with the order of the Industrial Court concerning the working hours. For the minority, Justice Burch repeated the substance of the previous dissent. Justice W. W. Harvey, also for the minority, declared that the mandate of the United States Supreme Court required a reversal of the Industrial Court order in its entirety.

The Industrial Court then applied for another modification concerning overtime pay. As a result of a hearing held about a month later, Justice Marshall on behalf of the majority modified the writ of mandamus he had previously issued, so as to add that the company should pay overtime rates if more than eight hours were worked on more than two days of the week, even if the total number of hours worked during such week was less than forty-eight. Once again, Justices Burch and Harvey dissented. Justice Harvey declared that time and a half for overtime was an order respecting wages which was invalidated by the Supreme Court.

The Company appealed.

VI

The case of the *Charles Wolff Packing Company* v. *the Court of Industrial Relations* of the state of Kansas was brought again before the Supreme Court of the United States. It was argued on November 20, 1924.

The attorneys for the company argued: (1) The Supreme Court's decision of June 11, 1923, required the entire judgment to be vacated, not merely to be modified. (2) The Industrial Relations Act was a compulsory arbitration measure. (3) Its regulation of hours was not motivated by the public concern for the health of employees which may be permissible under state police power. (4) Furthermore, the law was contrary to the Fourteenth Amendment. The portions of the order sustained by the Kansas Supreme Court were void because they raised the company's operating expenses when its income was below its expenses, which constituted deprivation of property without due process of law.

The defense attorneys insisted: (*a*) Since the Supreme Court's original decision reversing the Kansas Court had been limited to the question of *wages*, the lower court was justified in merely modifying, rather than vacating, the Industrial Court's order and it had the power to issue its new order. (*b*) The invalidation by the court of one section of the act concerning wages did not invalidate the entire act, because this law contained a specific provision that the invalid sections were separable from the remainder. (*c*) Since the previous opinion of the Supreme Court had not specifically declared that meat packing was *not* an industry affected with public interest, then the legislature's finding that it was "affected with public interest" was binding. (*d*) The act was not discriminatory, because it uniformly applied to all without discrimination. (*e*) The Industrial Relations Act was valid as to hours, because hours of labor in packing plants were a proper subject for the exercise of the state's police power. (*f*) Furthermore, freedom of contract must yield to the police power in any event. (*g*) Finally, the company had not proved that its losses were due to the hours limitation in the tribunal's order.

On April 13, 1925, Justice Willis Van Devanter, reversing the Kansas Supreme Court, delivered the opinion of the Supreme Court. He set forth several pertinent principles:

One: The United States Supreme Court had found the wage clauses of the order of the Industrial Court invalid. By that decision it had neither declared the whole act invalid nor had it tacitly admitted the validity of the law's provisions concerning the power to regulate working hours.

Two: The Kansas Supreme Court's declaration that the provision concerning regulation of hours of work in the Industrial Relations Act was separable from its other provisions would be taken as conclusive by this court.

Three: The case before the Supreme Court in 1922 had pivoted on the question of whether wage-fixing orders could be applied to the Wolff Company consistent with the Fourteenth Amendment. The court answered that question in the negative, since such a provision curtailed liberty of contract on inadequate grounds.

Four: What constituted reasonable regulation was a "judicial question," not a matter for legislative determination.

Five: The act proceeded upon the assumption of a paramount public interest in businesses called essential industries. By the terms of the law of 1920, employers might discontinue such businesses only on proof of loss or with the approval of the board. The legislature had power to compel a business to continue in operation *only* when the obligation to render its public service had existed directly and from its beginning. The system of compulsory arbitration established by the Kansas law of 1920 "is intended to compel, and if sustained will compel, the owners and employees to continue the business on terms which are not of their making." Such a system infringed the liberty of contract and rights of property guaranteed by the due process of law clause of the Fourteenth Amendment.

Six: The tribunal's authority to fix hours was merely *incidental* to the system of compulsory arbitration; therefore, *as part of the system it shared in the invalidity of the whole.* Whether that power would be valid if conferred independently of the system need not be considered in this opinion.

. *Seven:* The Kansas Supreme Court should have refused to give effect to any part of the order of the Court of Industrial Relations in the *Wolff* case.

Accordingly, the Supreme Court reversed the Kansas Supreme Court and held the entire order of the Industrial Court in this case unenforceable.

VII

The essential story of the fate of this Kansas experiment would not be complete without inviting attention to the following:

The Industrial Relations Act, it will be recalled, prohibited an "individual employee or other persons to conspire with other persons to quit their employment or to induce others to quit their employment. . ." A violation of this provision was punishable by a fine or imprisonment, or both. The Industrial Court issued such orders to Alexander Howat, then the Kansas leader of the miners and a bitter opponent of John L. Lewis, prohibiting him from calling a strike, and in fact ordering him to direct the miners to return to work. Howat refused to comply with such orders. An action was instituted against Howat and he was sentenced to jail. After several appeals the case reached the Supreme Court of the United States. The Supreme Court upheld the Kansas Supreme Court's decision that the penal section was separable from the rest of the act and enforceable.

Thus, the most elaborate experiment in compulsory arbitration as a means of adjudication of industrial disputes made by a state of the Union was declared unconstitutional in so far as the powers of the Industrial Court went toward fixing wages, hours, and other conditions of work—conditions which largely might have caused the strikes—but the power of the Industrial Court was upheld concerning penalties imposed by it on union leaders for calling a strike against its order. This prompted the *American Federationist* to draw the following inference: "It now seems clear that our various state legislatures may declare strikes for certain objects to be unlawful and one urging such a strike may be deemed guilty of a felony and be subject to fine and imprisonment. This decision . . . will undoubtedly be the forerunner of several attempts to curtail the right of labor unions to strike." To labor it appeared that once more legislation which was ostensibly designed to control unions and employers alike turned out by the court's interpretation to be a law effective only against the labor unions and not against the employers.

The significance of this case lies in the fact that it raised the basic question of a public policy for the adjustment of industrial relations.

Both labor and employers have consistently opposed *compulsory* arbitration, whereby in case of an industrial dispute they are compelled to submit the dispute to a neutral person or agency, and are also compelled to accept the solution imposed on them by such neutral person or agency. However, both labor and employers, from time to time, have practiced *voluntary* arbitration. Indeed, there are many instances in which arbitration has been welcomed by both sides as the sole means of breaking a log jam in an industrial dispute. Samuel Gompers in his autobiography, *Seventy Years of Life and Labor*, expressed labor's opposition to compulsory arbitration in these words: "I saw in the proposal to establish arbitration carrying any degree of compulsion a blow at the fundamentals of voluntary institutions which to my thinking are the heart of freedom." Employers likewise have vigorously expressed their opposition.

This bilateral opposition to compulsory arbitration stems from fear that the outside "disinterested" party will, through ignorance, prejudice or "politics," render a decision which may have a disastrous economic effect on either or both parties to the dispute. While the public at large may look upon compulsory arbitration as a panacea for all strikes, the employers and the unions will have none of that. Only a real national emergency may make them acquiesce temporarily to arbitration instead of what they conceive to be their right to fight out their industrial disputes without interference.

The Kansas Industrial Relations Act bit off more than it could chew. It was all very well to seek industrial peace, but the law as drafted and applied by the Industrial Court ignored realities. The law simply gave a blank check to an agency to impose its views, rules, and judgment on what was right and wrong in certain industries. That kind of approach could inspire no confidence in labor, employers, or the general public. It brought not peace but the sword of Damocles to the parties involved.

This Kansas experiment was a colossal failure. But the problem it sought to solve is still with us, the more so because the contending forces are so much more powerful today. One may indulge in intellectual speculation as to the attitude of the Supreme Court these days toward the police power of a state to impose compulsory arbitration of industrial disputes in essential industries. The time appears not too far distant when this problem of "compulsory arbitration" will engage the attention not of partisan politicians but of the earnest leaders in labor, industry, and the social sciences. And it is not at all unlikely that the solution may lie in a well-thought-out system of arbitration which will zealously guard the interests of labor, industry, and the public and still leave room for spontaneous progressive development of industrial relations.

- 12 -

The Confusing Coronados

(1914–1925)

CORONADO COAL COMPANY V.
UNITED MINE WORKERS OF AMERICA
(two cases)

I

No one has ever claimed that law is an exact science. There is much room for an individual judge or court to reflect his or its personal sense of justice in the decision rendered. The *inexactness* of law as a science is illustrated in the two Coronado cases with which this chapter deals. On practically the same set of facts, the Supreme Court of the United States reached two widely different conclusions regarding the legal activities of unions.

Franklin Bache, an engineer and mine operator, had come into the southwestern coal fields about 1897, and operated mines in both Oklahoma and Arkansas. In 1910, after dealing with the United Mine Workers' Union for seven years, the members of this Southwestern Coal Operators' Association agreed among themselves to break off relations with the union. Their mines were shut down. Bache, a leader of the association, advised that none of the members of the association should negotiate with the union, but some of them did not follow his advice. A number of them did negotiate and actually entered into collective labor agreements with the union. Bache himself held back. He attempted to run his Mammoth Vein Mine with strikebreakers, but the union miners marched to the pit and held a demonstration which was sufficiently impressive to scare away strikebreakers. Unable to carry out his plans, and aware of the fact that the other mine operators had settled with the union and were working, Bache resigned from the association and an hour later signed a union contract.

In spite of the signed agreement, Bache and the union did not get along well. The miners, conscious of Bache's attitude toward their organization, were rigid in the enforcement of their contract, and did not yield an inch. Bache, on the other hand, resented the union in his mines and was determined to fight it out at the first opportunity. Three years of this uneasy relationship followed, during which the resentment of one against the other mounted. Trouble was brewing.

In March, 1914, Bache instructed his manager to notify his financial backers in the East that he had decided to break with the union. He outlined the reasons for his action. He wanted to abolish the 8-hour workday and wanted to pay for the loading of the coal, after it had been dug, only the wage for a common laborer, rather than the miner's union wage. What he mainly wanted was to run his coal mines without a union contract. He told his backers that he expected a hard fight because Sebastian County, where the mines were located, was a thoroughly unionized area, but he hoped that the end result would be worth the cost.

II

Bache followed up his letter with immediate action. He repudiated the union contract three months before the expiration date, and hired guards for the property. The mines at Prairie Creek, Arkansas, were shut down, the property roped off, and "No Trespassing" posters put up. Miners living in company houses were notified that they must leave unless they would work on Bache's terms. The miners evicted from these company houses went to live in the shack settlement of Frogtown.

Resentment against Bache ran high in the neighboring towns of Hartford and Huntington, and certainly Frogtown, but Bache went on in his own way. He was making preparations for reopening the mine known as Prairie Creek No. 4 and brought in a few professional armed guards and some strikebreaking coal diggers from Tennessee.

When it became known that the mine was scheduled to begin actual work, a large crowd of union miners gathered, milling about the flimsy stockade. From time to time the crowd shouted "scab" and "scaly" at Bache's new employees, only to disperse with the appearance of Constable James Slankart on the scene. On the very day of the opening of operations at this mine, Sunday, April 5, 1914, several union locals held meetings in the nearby towns and laid plans for a demonstration at Prairie Creek No. 4. On the day following, the stores in Midland, Hartford, and Huntington shut down. The miners at the neighboring mine, Central Coal & Coke Company, did not appear for work. Led by the Huntington town band, about 1,200 people gathered at the schoolhouse that also served as a union hall and heard speeches by union officers and others. The speakers outlined the miners' grievances against Bache and the need for the miners to stand firm. A committee was chosen to urge mine superintendent Cameron to shut down pending further discussions which might bring a settlement. Then all the assembled—band, speakers, audience, and dogs— marched toward Prairie Creek No. 4.

Upon arrival at the mine, the committee chosen at the meeting was admitted into the guarded enclosure, but the crowd remained outside. In the forefront of the crowd was a little old man, apparently a cripple, who continuously waved an American flag. Somehow, the hired armed guards interpreted the presence of the cripple and his flag waving as a sign of mocking them. Barnes, a Burns Agency man with strike breaking experience, started to assert his authority, ordered the crowd to back up, and displayed his rifle, apparently to reinforce his authority. The crowd pressed forward. Bailey, another Burns Agency man, exchanged rough words with persons in the crowd. Tempers sharpened. When the committee that had been admitted into the guarded enclosure did not return as soon as expected, the crowd became restless. The air was charged with challenge. Suddenly, the crowd broke through the rope separating them from the mine property, disarmed Barnes and Bailey, and beat them up. The crowd took over. It beat up two former union members who had gone to work, and forced the foreman of the mine to "draw the fires." Someone hoisted an American flag and underneath it tacked on a banner: "This is a Union Man's Country." Superintendent Cameron telephoned Bache at Fort Smith and received permission to shut down the mine. Work had stopped, and the crowd returned to their homes, led by the band playing "Dixie."

Two days later Bache secured an injunction from Federal Judge Trieber, restraining the union from interfering with work at the mine. A month later the injunction was made permanent.

But in spite of the injunction, disorder continued. Local union leaders rode the trains coming up to Prairie Creek and tried to frighten away strikebreakers. Union partisans threw rocks at Bache's men carting supplies to Prairie Creek No. 4. Some shipments of freight to the mine were damaged. Bache's hired professional guards contributed to the disorder. Although warned to be cautious, they bore themselves arrogantly, flaunted their guns, drove mine mules over farmers' crops, and defiantly patronized the lady bootlegger. Their presence and behavior and the presence of strikebreakers were hardly likely to foster a spirit of calm in a unionized county.

The Bache property was under the guard of about fifty or sixty United States deputy marshals who were instructed to maintain order. The community assumed a state of passive resistance. No storekeeper in the community except one would sell goods to Bache, his employees, or the deputy marshals. Nobody in the Prairie Creek area would accommodate the marshals with room and board. The community was in full sympathy with the miners and the miners were determined not to let Bache dig coal in Prairie Creek No. 4. A union leader, according to one of the marshals working under cover, summed up the community feeling by saying: "Damn the injunction; the national government is against us but the people are with us and we don't mean to let them dig coal." In spite of the prevalent ill feeling, there were no large-scale disorders. As time passed, the large staff of United States deputy marshals was reduced, and by July 15, 1914, the last of them had been withdrawn. Only Bache's hired guards were left in the roped-off enclosures at Prairie Creek.

After the marshals had left, rumors spread that the Bache guards had "shot up" the shacks at Frogtown and also that they were going to make a full-scale attack on Hartford. Miners were urged to protect themselves. The air was rife with rumors, adding to the pent-up excitement of the community. There was continuous talk that the Central Coal & Coke Company, in which union miners were employed, would follow Bache's example and run a nonunion mine which would mean longer hours and smaller wages for the men. The miners were grimly determined that this should not happen.

The pent-up excitement came to the surface. On the night of July 16, 1914, all the lights at Prairie Creek No. 4 suddenly went out. The early morning was pierced by shots fired at the stockade.

The shooting became more frequent. A group of Bache employees took to the hills. A crowd swooped down and dynamited No. 3 tipple. Bache's mine guards and some employees took shelter behind loaded coal cars and kept on firing at the crowd until their ammunition gave out. At noon No. 4 tipple was set on fire. Later the mob destroyed company houses and burned the loaded coal cars.

During the afternoon, while United States marshals were being rushed from Fort Smith, most of the Bache employees were fleeing the mine. A group of strikebreakers from Tennessee was caught by the mob, brought to Hartford, given some shelter, and at the town's or the union's expense, sent back home. Two others were seized and, in the presence of Constable Slankart, were deliberately shot down by an unidentified man. On the following day, July 18, the attack continued and the powerhouse was burned. Two days later two smaller mines—the Dallas and Coronado properties—were burned.

On July 25, the Bache-Denman properties applied for a receiver, and the court appointed Franklin Bache as such receiver. In his capacity as receiver, Bache made another attempt to reopen the mines. Again the United States marshals came out to protect the property and again they were boycotted by the townspeople and all the storekeepers, except one. The miners did not give up. In October, 1914, a second attack was made by them on the Bache property. One of the marshals attempted to arrest a man for violating the injunction which had been issued the previous May, but the prisoner was rescued by a crowd. On the receiver's claim that the United States marshals were ineffective in maintaining order, Federal troops, four companies of United States cavalry, took the Prairie Creek Valley under their protection. This occurred on November 14, 1914. Violence ceased, but the community continued to treat the troops with the same silent resistance shown by it against the marshals and Bache employees.

Bache realized that he was not likely to succeed in running his mines nonunion unless he could sufficiently weaken the miners' national organization and its districts and locals, so as to remove them as effective opponents. With this in view, he laid plans to institute actions against the United Mine Workers' Union, its districts and locals, for heavy damages under the Sherman Antitrust Act.

This is the background of the two Coronado cases.

III

The First Coronado Case

On September 1, 1914, Bache, as receiver, brought an action against the United Mine Workers' Union, its District 21, their locals,. and their officers in the United States District Court for the Western District of Arkansas. The action was under the Sherman Antitrust Act. The complaint was in the name of nine companies, but since the first one named was the Coronado Coal Company, the case is known as the *Coronado* case.

The complaint disclosed a complicated financial setup. Apparently for the purpose of avoiding liability under the union agreement, Bache had organized a holding company and this company was also one of the plaintiffs in the action. The nine plaintiffs were: the holding company known as the Mammoth Vein Coal Mining Corp.; four coal operating companies—the Coronado, Prairie Creek, Hartford, and Mammoth Vein; four others—Denman Coal, Bache-Denman Coal, Sebastian County Coal, and Mammoth Vein Royalty—which were *financially* interested in the operating companies.

The complaint alleged that the plaintiffs were engaged in interstate commerce because their business *as a whole* must be considered. While coal mining by itself may be local in character, it involves interstate commerce because it requires the loading and shipment of coal to various consignees in various states. The complaint charged that all the defendants—the United Mine Workers, District 21, the locals, and the officers—had conspired to restrain interstate commerce and by their violence of April 6 and July 17, 1914, had interfered with interstate commerce. The complaint also alleged that the defendants by their conspiracy and actions caused losses and damages amounting to $427,820.77 and requested that this amount should be tripled under the Sherman Antitrust Act.

The union and its officers demurred to the complaint on the grounds that: (1) The court had no jurisdiction because none of the plaintiff coal companies was engaged in interstate commerce within the meaning of the Sherman Act. (2) The acts charged against the defendants, even if they were in violation of state laws, did not constitute, as a matter of law, interference with *interstate* commerce and therefore the Federal Court had no jurisdiction. (3) The defendant unions were voluntary unincorporated associations. As such associations they could not sue or be sued in their own name. The action, if any, must be brought against the members themselves. (4) The complaint was defective because it did not allege that the defendants conspired to monopolize any part of interstate commerce and it did not allege that the defendants entered into a contract, combination, or conspiracy in restraint of trade within the meaning of the Sherman Act.

Judge Frank A. Youmans, before whom the case came up, sustained the union demurrer on the specific ground that the Federal Court lacked jurisdiction in this case. He held that the Sherman Act was not applicable to this case because the acts of the defendants complained of were not in interference with *interstate* commerce or in violation of the federal statute upon which the complaint was based. He therefore concluded that the companies would have to look for their remedies elsewhere, if they so chose, but not under this federal law. He dismissed the complaint.

Shortly thereafter A. S. Dowd replaced Bache as receiver for the plaintiff companies. The new receiver appealed from Judge Youman's decision.

IV

The appeal was heard by the United States Circuit Court of Appeals for the Eighth Circuit. On July 21, 1916, Judge John E. Garland reversing the District Court delivered the opinion of the Circuit Court. After reciting the essential facts, he stated that the appeal involved two legal questions: First—May the unions be sued in their own name? Second—Does the complaint state a cause of action under the Sherman Act?

As to the first question, Judge Garland held that:

(*a*) It was clearly not the intention of Congress to exempt anyone from liability for injuries caused by combination and conspiracy in restraint of interstate trade. Section 8 of the Sherman Act defined "persons" to include corporations *and* associations existing under or authorized by the laws of the United States. Since the unions, as associations, could legally exist under our laws, they came within the meaning of this act.

(*b*) Since such unincorporated associations were included in the act they could be sued in their own name. If that were not permitted, the law would fail as against such associations because a judgment merely against their agents and employees might not be collectible, as such agents are often financially irresponsible.

(c) While the question of the liability of unincorporated associations had not been previously discussed, the very fact that Congress had not exempted them from liability was conclusive evidence that Congress did not intend to exempt them.

As to the second question, Judge Garland held that:

(a) The complaint in this case sufficiently alleged a combination, conspiracy, and restraint of interstate commerce because when the acts cited in the complaint were committed, the operating coal companies were engaged not only in mining but also in shipping of coal.

(b) Furthermore, a conspiracy to prevent a producer from doing any business at all necessarily places restraint on commerce. The Sherman Act broadly condemns *all* combinations and conspiracies which restrain the free and natural flow of trade in the channels of interstate commerce. Since the complaint alleged interference with and destruction of loaded coal cars of common carriers, that fact alone would show an interference with interstate commerce.

Hence, the judgment of the District Court was reversed and the case was sent back with instructions to overrule the demurrer and allow the defendants to answer the complaint so that the parties might proceed to trial.

V

After the lower court had been reversed, the plaintiffs found it necessary to amend their complaint several times. The third amended complaint was filed on February 27, 1917, by the new receivers, C. H. Finley and H. P. Hilliard. This amended complaint named additional defendants, individual miners who supposedly had participated in the attacks on the mines in April and July of 1914. The new complaint also added new allegations apparently for the purpose of strengthening the legal basis of the action. This time the complaint alleged that the United Mine Workers was conspiring to acquire a monopoly of all coal-digging operators, and that this national organization with its 400,000 members, was engaged in a general combination and conspiracy in restraint of interstate commerce; that all the acts done in wrecking the Bache-Denman properties were in furtherance of a conspiracy with the intent, purpose, and effect of forcing corporations, formerly engaged in interstate commerce as nonunion mines, to "refrain therefrom until such times as they would carry on said business as union mines upon terms dictated by said combination and conspiracy." This time the plaintiffs claimed that they had suffered damages in the amount of $740,-689.42 and under the Sherman Act they asked for triple damages, amounting to $2,222,068.26, plus costs and lawyers' fees.

The answer of the unions was filed on July 7, 1917. In substance, the answer denied the charges of conspiracy and raised the issue that labor could not be a monopoly since the Clayton Act had declared that the labor of a human being was not a commodity. The defendants alleged that the main purpose of the union did not concern itself with any sale or transport of coal but with the improvement of working conditions. It also alleged that the individual defendants had no authority from the United Mine Workers to represent the national organization in the commission of any wrong, and that the national organization could not be held liable for it.

The case was reached for trial in October, 1917, before Judge Elliott of the Federal District Court of the Western District of Arkansas and a jury at Fort Smith. It was tried during the months of October and November. Apparently, the jury must have had a great deal of sympathy for the United Mine Workers, for it had been out for about forty-eight hours without reaching an agreement. The judge then called it in for further instructions and instructed it along the following lines:

"Now, Gentlemen of the Jury, this is a pretty serious situation and I want to say to you that the Court has no thought at all of discharging you. . . . You are advised that this Court is of the opinion that the facts in this case justify you in the conclusion, overwhelmingly, that it was the policy and therefore the agreement for years of this national organization to prevent mining of non-union coal for the unlawful purposes named in this complaint . . . and that there is no question in this Court's mind but that the strike was ordered down there for that purpose to prevent the mining of non-union coal in these plaintiff mines. . . . Why, this Court has not a thought that there would ever have been any trouble there if it had not been for the prevention of the mining of non-union coal. Now, that is the judgment of this Court and if it were my duty to decide it, I would decide it here. Now, you are not bound by my opinion . . ."

After giving the jury his opinion in no uncertain terms, the judge told the jury that he would not discharge it, that it should not waste the expense incurred in the trial by any disagreement, and urged it to bring in a verdict. The jury finally did. It found the defendants guilty and awarded the company damages of $200,000.

At the request of the plaintiffs, the court amended the judgment to include interest from the date of destruction of the properties. This amounted to $40,000. The entire verdict, including interest at 6 per cent, was tripled by the court under the Sherman Antitrust Act, and thus amounted to $720,000. The court also allowed $25,000 for counsel fees to the plaintiffs' attorneys.

The union appealed and filed the bond required by the court in the amount of $800,000.

VI

The appeal again came before the Circuit Court of Appeals for the Eighth Circuit. Judge Trieber delivered the majority opinion of the court on April 28, 1919. In the main he followed the reasoning of the same circuit court on the previous appeal, and upheld the lower court in practically every respect except one, the trebling of damages of the interest. But he held that such error could be corrected without a new trial and directed the lower court to correct the judgment.

Judge Hold dissented. He based his dissent merely on the action of the trial judge in his charge to the jury. He pointed out that the trial court on its own motion had recalled the jury after it had been deliberating for two days and then "charged them in a way that soon produced the verdict," and that the language of the charge was "so forcible that it actually coerced a verdict." For this reason the dissenting judge thought the charge constituted an error sufficient for a reversal of judgment.

The union appealed to the Supreme Court of the United States.

VII

The appeal in the case, now under the title of United Mine Workers of America, *et al.*, against the Coronado Coal Co., *et al.*, was first argued before the Supreme Court of the United States on October 15, 1920, and subsequently reargued on March 22 and 23, 1922. It may be of interest to note that among union counsel at this time was Charles Evans Hughes, formerly chief justice and some years later to become again chief justice of the Supreme Court of the United States.

The substance of the union arguments on appeal was:

1. The court below had erred in holding that an unincorporated labor union could be sued. Since the Sherman Act was a penal statute, it was not to be broadly construed, and since unions were not mentioned therein, the lower court was not justified in going beyond the specific terms of the act in search of "any supposed policy" so as to bring in unions under the definition of "persons."

2. The evidence did not warrant recovery of damages against the United Mine Workers, the national organization. The districts were not the agents of the national organization. Under the constitution they had autonomy to call strikes on their own responsibility, and since there was no evidence that the national organization had authorized or ratified the acts done in Arkansas, the national organization could not be held liable for such acts. Similarly, there was no evidence that District 21 and its locals were to be held responsible for the acts of their membership in which the organizations as such had not participated.

3. There was no proof of "any combination or conspiracy in restraint of *interstate* commerce." The destruction of a factory or mine producing goods for interstate markets could not come under federal jurisdiction. Such acts constituted trespass and damage to property by the individuals committing them and when each act was separately considered it became clear that it could not be brought under the Sherman Act. The mere fact that an article was manufactured for export to another state was insufficient to constitute it an article of interstate commerce within the meaning of the Constitution. Only such conduct as had a *direct* relation to interstate commerce came under the act. If construed otherwise, no activity important to the community would be exempt from federal regulation, and that was not the intention of the act. Furthermore, the individuals who committed the wrongs charged were concerned with production, not commerce. *Although strikes might affect production, they bore no such direct relation to interstate commerce as would bring them under the Sherman Act.*

4. The efforts to unionize mines and the refusal to work with nonunion miners were not enough to show the existence of a com-

bination in restraint of commerce. The evidence that had shown that there were conferences between miners and operators since 1898 could not be construed as evidence of a combination and conspiracy, for the acts of the conferences were legal and there had been no finding that the parties in their conferences conspired in restraint of trade.

5. The judge had committed several other errors which warranted a reversal of the judgment, such as: his charge to the jury was highly prejudicial to the defendants; he permitted, improperly, the nine plaintiffs to sue in the same action; he ordered the union to produce books and documents to prove the guilt of its members and officers in violation of the Fourth and Fifth Amendments to the Constitution protecting an individual against being forced to testify against himself.

The attorneys for the companies argued that (1) the unions came under the heading of "associations" in the antitrust laws; (2) the United Mine Workers, the national organization, should be held responsible for the destruction of the plaintiffs' property because it had encouraged the defendants in their actions by laudatory articles in the union's publication, it had paid strike benefits, and it had failed to discipline the responsible subordinates for their acts against the plaintiffs; (3) the national union should be held responsible because it had set in motion a machinery "which in the natural course of events and according to previous experience would lead to the injurious results;" and (4) there was no need to prove *specific* intent to restrain trade. The intent was proved by the fact that the combination to restrain such trade existed and the acts of such combination resulted in such restraint of trade.

On June 5, 1922, Chief Justice Taft, reversing the lower court, handed down the opinion of a unanimous court. Observing that there were five principal questions involved in that case, he proceeded to answer them:

First: Had there been a misjoinder of parties-plaintiff?

He held that, since the companies were united in interest and under single management and receivership, all the nine companies could sue in the same action.

Second: Could unincorporated labor unions be sued in their own name?

In answer to this, the justice pointed out that in many respects the

United Mine Workers acted as a unit. Its Executive Board had authority to call a general strike in the industry and it also controlled strikes in various localities, especially in unorganized areas. In dealing with banks and other persons the national organization acted as an entity. "It would be unfortunate if an organization with as great power as this International Union has in the raising of large funds and in directing the conduct of 400,000 members and in carrying on, in a wide territory, industrial controversies and strikes out of which so much unlawful injury to private rights is possible, could assemble its assets to be used therein free from liability for injuries by torts committed in course of such strikes." The chief justice concluded that unions were suable in federal courts for their acts.

Third: Had the United Mine Workers participated in or ratified the interference with the Bache-Denman Company's business which had taken place between April 6 and July 7, 1914?

Chief Justice Taft held that the national organization was not to be held responsible for the damages suffered by the plaintiff, since there was no evidence that it either ordered or approved the strike. The strike was local, authorized and maintained not by the national organization but by District 21. The articles in the miners' journal justifying the union men and blaming the Bache guards for the trouble did not constitute ratification of the acts. Since the national body was not charged with supervising all local strikes, it could not necessarily be held responsible for this one. It would not be just to enforce a stricter rule against labor unions than against corporations, which are responsible only for wrongs committed by agents in the course of the corporations', not the agents', business. On this issue, the court should have directed a verdict in favor of the national organization and its officers.

Fourth: Had District 21 and the individual defendants participated in a plot to deprive plaintiffs of their employees by intimidation and violence and in destruction of their properties?

The conflict apparently was provoked by Bache's acts in shutting down the mines and by his formation of a holding company to cover up the breach of the contract he had with the district union. The riot of April 6 made it evident that the union men meant to attack Prairie Creek No. 4 and that the action was planned by the district and the members. The district might well be held liable for the unlawful injuries caused to plaintiffs' property.

Fifth: Had the acts of the defendants been committed in pursuance of a conspiracy to restrain and monopolize interstate commerce?

In order to hold the district liable under the Sherman Act it was necessary to prove that the conspiracy to attack the Bache-Denman mine was with the *intent* to restrain interstate commerce. Coal mining by itself is not interstate commerce and obstructing coal mining is not a direct obstruction of interstate commerce in coal although it may affect that commerce by reducing the amount of coal carried in it. The proceedings of the conferences between the union and the union-mine operators which had been introduced in evidence merely proved that these conferences stimulated the union to organize the unorganized fields. If the United Mine Workers had used unlawful means to unionize mines whose product was important, actually or potentially, in *affecting prices* in interstate commerce, the evidence would clearly tend to show that this body was guilty of an actionable conspiracy under the antitrust act. But there was no justification in interpreting the evidence in question as though it tended to show that the motive of organizing the nonunion fields actuated every lawless strike of a local and sporadic character initiated by a subordinate division of the union.

Chief Justice Taft distinguished this case from the *Danbury Hatters* case by pointing out that in the latter case the *object* of the attack was interference with the plaintiffs' interstate commerce in the sale of hats. But in this case there was nothing to show that the defendants had in mind interference with interstate commerce or competition when they sought to break up Bache's plan to operate his mines with nonunion men. There was ample local reason and local bitterness provoked by Bache's actions. Elaborating further on the question of interstate commerce, the chief justice pointed out that the 4,000 tons of coal the Bache-Denman companies shipped each week could have had no appreciable effect upon the price of coal or the competition of union and nonunion mined coal. He therefore concluded that no evidence had been shown to the jury which would justify them to find that the outrages, felonies, and murders of District 21 and its companions in crime were committed by them in a conspiracy to restrain or monopolize interstate commerce. The chief justice said that because the case lacked federal jurisdiction, the court regretfully could not affirm the judgment.

Hence, the judgment was reversed and the case was remanded to the District Court for proceedings in conformity with the opinion of the Supreme Court.

VIII

The Second Coronado Case

More than a year later, in 1923, the *Coronado* case went to trial again. It became known as the *Second Coronado* case. It was tried before Judge John C. Pollock of the United States Circuit Court for the Western District of Arkansas. Taking a hint from the court's opinion concerning the importance of showing *intent* to interfere with interstate commerce, the attorneys for the company changed their trial strategy. They concentrated on proving that the destruction of the Bache-Denman properties was with the intent of crushing competition from nonunion coal.

Most of the testimony at this trial consisted in reading the record of the testimony that had been given six years before, in the 1917 trial. Obviously, the proceedings at the trial were monotonous and wearing on the judge and the jury. The company, however, did produce a few new witnesses whose testimony at the time was not deemed of importance but later proved to be a decisive factor in the case.

Hanraty, a former president of District 21, testified that the union was always concerned about the competition of coal mined in the unorganized fields. A Dr. Routh testified that while stopping in a local hotel he had overheard conversation between officers of District 21. These conversations were to the effect that if the Bache-Denman nonunion operations were to succeed, they would have a tendency to lower the union wage scales and drive out union miners; that other union operators, if they were not afraid of the costs of fighting the union, would follow Bache's tactics; that some prominent local union leaders were concerned with the effect that Bache's fight against the union might have on the union's relations with the Central Coal & Coke Company.

Another new witness was James K. McNamara, former check-weighman at a Central mine. He testified that he presided at some union meetings and that, though speakers did warn against committing violence, these warnings were just a pretense to preserve favorable public opinion. He further testified that he had had occasion to speak to John P. White, the national president of the United Mine Workers of America, who told him that if nonunion coal got into the market, the union mine operators would stop dealing with the union, and that he, White, urged McNamara to carry this word to Sebastian County, but not to make the statement as coming from the United Mine Workers because the union did not wish to become involved in the Arkansas situation. On cross-examination, McNamara admitted that he had demanded money from District 21 and threatened that otherwise he would testify as to what he knew about the riots.

Another new witness was Tharel, the only storekeeper in the community who was not sympathetic to the miners. He testified that union miners had asked him to pledge himself in writing not to sell goods to Bache's employees and that he had overheard some defendants say that unless the Bache-Denman Coal Company was prevented, it would ship coal into Wyoming, Minnesota, and other markets to take the place of union coal.

After counsel for both sides rested, Judge Pollock charged the jury and pointed out that under the established laws the jury had to be satisfied that the plaintiff proved the following: (a) that there was a conspiracy as charged in the complaint; (b) that the defendants had participated in said conspiracy; and (c) that the conspiracy had as its *direct purpose* the restraining or monopolizing of interstate commerce. In reviewing the facts for the jury, the judge called attention to the fact that the evidence showed that District 21 was ready to take any measures to halt nonunion mining, but coal mining itself was not interstate commerce although the coal, after it was mined, might be the object of that commerce. Furthermore, while it had been proved that if unmolested Bache might have increased his production and so sold more coal in interstate trade, the interference with production did not raise an issue of interstate trade. Moreover, the evidence in this case might show that a conspiracy did exist, but it was not with the *direct purpose* of interfering with or monopolizing interstate commerce, but was for a different purpose—the unionization of mines; the interference with interstate commerce was merely incidental to it. The judge therefore directed the jury to bring in a verdict for the defendants.

This time the company appealed.

IX

The appeal, now entitled *Finley, et al., v. United Mine Workers of America, et al.*, came before the Circuit Court of Appeals for the Eighth Circuit. On July 12, 1924, Judge William S. Kenyon, for the Circuit Court, handed down the opinion of the court. He noted that the case was now before this court for the third time and that the questions of law previously determined must be followed on this appeal unless the new testimony warranted different conclusions.

Observing that the Supreme Court had already held that the national organization of the miners had not been responsible for that strike and that the strike was local, and that the *main purpose* of District 21 was not the restraint of interstate commerce, the court would consider only the company's contention that at this trial it had supplied the missing links between the local situation and interstate commerce.

Judge Kenyon held that in reality the so-called new evidence did not add anything substantially new. He observed that McNamara, who testified on behalf of the company, admitted that White, the president of the national union, did not wish the national organization involved; so McNamara's testimony could not be deemed substantial evidence against the national organization. Hanraty's testimony added nothing new to the record, because the previous record had shown the miners' aroused feeling against Bache and his attempts to run the mine nonunion. Storekeeper Tharel's testimony concerning the possibility of Bache's sending his coal into other states added nothing essentially new to the record, because there was much discussion of this character in the previous record. The unions apparently were not concerned as to whether or not their strike interfered with interstate commerce; their *main* concern was that Bache should not operate nonunion mines.

As to the company's contention that the defendants' *direct intent* was to restrain interstate commerce, Judge Kenyon observed that the record did not bear out this contention. Besides, the high court had already held "that the making of goods and the mining of coal are not commerce, and that obstruction to coal mining is not a direct obstruction to interstate commerce." Judge Kenyon reasoned that even granting that the record at this trial concerning the intent of the defendants was stronger than in the previous trial, yet in the light of the Supreme Court's decision the present record failed to pin liability on the miners' national organization and failed to show that the *direct intent* of the conspiracy of District 21 and the other defendants was to restrain or monopolize interstate commerce. The judge was satisfied that the evidence in the second trial was not substantially different from that in the first and therefore dismissed the appeal.

The company appealed to the Supreme Court of the United States.

X

On January 7, 1925, the second *Coronado* case was argued before the Supreme Court of the United States. About five months later, on May 25, 1925, Justice Taft delivered the opinion of a unanimous court. After summarizing the holdings in the first *Coronado* case, the justice pointed out that the issues in this appeal might be reduced to two: (1) Did the United Mine Workers' Union, the national organization, participate in the conspiracy; and (2) did District 21 and its subordinates *intend* to restrain interstate commerce?

As to the first issue, Chief Justice Taft said that the new evidence did not tend to establish the participation of the national miners' union in the Prairie Creek strike disturbances. The Supreme Court could not regard the testimony of McNamara concerning statements made by Mr. White, the president, as evidence against the United Mine Workers. While White might himself be held liable for damages on such testimony, his actions could not bind the organization as a whole since he had moved without authority and expressly disclaimed any purpose of involving the organization. Hence, the trial court's direction of a verdict in favor of the United Mine Workers, which the Circuit Court of Appeals had upheld, was to be affirmed by the Supreme Court.

As to the second issue—the *intent* of District 21 and its locals to restrain interstate commerce—Chief Justice Taft held that the new evidence was material and should have been submitted to the jury instead of having the trial judge direct a verdict in favor of all the defendants. The chief justice thought that on the issue of the intent and purpose of the leaders to interfere with interstate commerce, the jury could have given weight to the following evidence in the record on this trial: that District 21, at its convention of February 19, 1914, discussed the competition of nonunion coal; that delegates from this convention had subsequently participated in the riots against the Bache mines; that Hanraty had made speeches concerning the threat of nonunion produced coal to the markets of union-mined coal; that McNamara's testimony if credited by the jury would support the inference that the purpose of the union miners in District 21 was to destroy the power of the Bache-Denman mines to send their coal into interstate commerce to compete with that of union mines.

Chief Justice Taft went much further, and held that the amount of production interfered with was an important consideration. Thus, he observed that the new evidence showed that the Bache mines could produce five thousand tons *daily*, rather than weekly, as assumed at the first trial, and that the potential production of these mines was "relevant evidence for the jury to consider and weigh as a circumstance with the rest of the testimony in proof of intent of the leaders of District No. 21 to prevent shipments to neighboring states of such an amount of non-union coal at non-union prices." The chief justice observed that while ordinarily the prevention of manufacture and production of articles reducing their supply in interstate commerce is an *indirect and remote* obstruction to that commerce, it may become a *direct* violation of the Antitrust Act if the *intent* is to restrain or control the supply moving in interstate commerce *or the price* of it in interstate markets.

The chief justice concluded that there was substantial evidence at the second trial tending to show that the purpose of the destruction of the mines was to stop production of nonunion coal in Arkansas and prevent its shipment in interstate trade, where it would, by competition, tend to reduce the price of the commodity and affect the standard of wages and union labor in competing mines. He therefore concluded that the district judge erred in directing a verdict for the defendants other than the United Mine Workers' Union, the national organization, and directed a new trial as to District 21, its locals, and other individual defendants.

XI

After the Supreme Court's decision reversing the Circuit Court of Appeals, a third trial took place. This time the jury disagreed. The parties, having been in litigation for almost thirteen years, were tired of their lawsuits. To avoid a fourth trial, the case was finally settled on October 17, 1927. District 21 agreed to pay the Bache-Denman interests the sum of $27,500 in damages. This was the finale of the two *Coronado* cases.

XII

To the layman, as well as to lawyers, the decisions of the Supreme Court in the two *Coronado* cases are rather confusing. Factually nothing happened during the three years intervening between the court's decision in the first *Coronado* case in 1922 and its decision in the second *Coronado* case in 1925. All the violence, destruction of property, arson, and murder with which the defendants were charged allegedly took place before the decision in the first case. Nevertheless, the legal effect of the decision in the second case was thoroughly different from the first. In the first decision, the Supreme Court held that the acts of the defendants, the strike and the violence, must be viewed as *local* in character and that such acts should not be deemed interference with interstate commerce. In the second case, the same court, by the same judge, on the same essential facts, held that the acts could have been considered as interference with interstate commerce, and that therefore the case could come under the Sherman Antitrust Act. What happened to justify this change in the court's view?

The official explanation for the change is that the second trial supplied "new evidence" of the *intent* of the defendants to restrain interstate commerce. This official explanation appears to be too artificial really to explain the change; there was nothing really new in the "new evidence." There could have been no doubt in the court's mind at the time of the first decision that the entire issue in this controversy was union-mined against nonunion-mined coal. Franklin Bache broke his union contract because he wanted to run his mines nonunion and to compete successfully with union coal and nonunion coal in other markets. The union fought against him because it wanted to preserve its union standards wherever it had union contracts. This very point was continuously emphasized by the plaintiffs in the first case. Plaintiffs subpoenaed the union records and the proceedings of the conferences between the union and the union operators to prove this very point, to show that it was the intent and purpose of the union to protect the union operators from the nonunion operators who, because of their lower labor standards, could undersell union-mined coal. There can be no question that the Supreme Court was fully aware of this factor. Chief Justice Taft himself, in his first decision, had stated: "What really is shown by the evidence in the case at bar, drawn from discussions and resolutions of conventions and conferences, is the stimulation of union leaders to press their unionization of non-union mines not only as a direct means of bettering the conditions and wages of their workers but *also as a means of lessening interstate competition for union operators* which in turn would lessen the pressure of those operators for reduction of the union scale or their resistance to an increase." (Italics supplied.)

The chief justice correctly interpreted the union motive, intent, and purpose in fighting Bache, namely, that it was to the self-interest of the union to prevent the nonunion coal from coming into competition with union-mined coal. Knowing the union intent, the chief justice nevertheless concluded that, since the *main* purpose of the union's action was the improvement of working conditions, the prevention of coal production still remained *local* in character. The chief justice expressed it in so many words: "The individuals who committed the wrongs were concerned with production, not commerce." Again, the chief justice laid stress upon what the *main* motive of the defendants was and concluded that, since the *main* motive was production and not commerce, the controversy did not come under the Sherman Act. In the face of this very conclusion in the first case, is it logical to suppose that the so-called "new evidence" prompted the same court to discover a *new main* motive of the defendants?

And what was the "new evidence"? It consisted of testimony to the effect that some of the leaders of the strikers intended by their action to restrain interstate commerce. But the chief justice himself concluded, in the first decision, that *lessening of interstate competition for union operators* stimulated union leaders to press unionization of the nonunion mines. If this motive of the union did not bring the case under the Sherman Antitrust Act in the first *Coronado* case, why did it bring it in the second *Coronado* case? Is it because of the additional "new evidence" concerning *intent*? The court already knew of this intent and purpose when it rendered its first decision. The answer must lie elsewhere than in the official explanation about the *intent* of the defendants.

In all likelihood, the court utilized this "new evidence" as the easiest way of getting away from a dilemma created by the implications of its first *Coronado* decision. It decided to leave the door open for possible future action by the court in similar cases. The court's dilemma was: On the one hand, organized labor ought to be permitted legitimately to seek the improvement of working conditions in industry; when nonunion employers undermine union standards, the union should not be deprived of an opportunity of spreading its influence and bringing about uniformity of labor standards. To the extent that such union activity affects interstate commerce, such interference in our economic society should be tolerated. On the other hand, organized labor may be so effective in a strike that, though the strike may be local in character, its effect may become national. The problem, then, was how to reconcile labor's conceded right to strike with the possible need of curbing that very right?

Chief Justice Taft apparently became conscious of this dilemma after he had rendered his opinion in the first *Coronado* case. He began to fear the consequences and the implications of that decision, which laid stress upon the *main* motive or purpose of the union in a strike and not necessarily on the consequences thereof. When the second *Coronado* case reached the Supreme Court, the chief justice concluded that the court should not lightly give up federal control of the Antitrust Act weapon which it might wield against strikes affecting interstate commerce. Hence, it used the excuse of "new evidence" to modify the doctrine that only the *main purpose* of the defendants is the determining factor of the issue of interstate commerce. In seeking to reconcile the decision with that in the first *Coronado* case, Chief Justice Taft introduced the principle that apparently *any intent* concerning interference with interstate commerce, depending upon circumstances, may be sufficient for the federal courts to assume jurisdiction under the Sherman Antitrust Act.

This was not the first time that Chief Justice Taft used the formula of "yes and no" in order to leave the court's hands free to use its discretion to assume or not to assume jurisdiction in strike cases. He used a similar formula in the case of *American Steel Foundries* v. *Tri-City Central Trades Council* (Chapter 10). He interpreted the right of picketing under Section 20 of the Clayton Act with a "yes and no." He allowed "missionaries" but not pickets.

He even applied the yes-and-no formula to outside missionaries. "Yes," if they were outsiders but belonged to a union whose standards might be competitively affected by the nonunion conditions in the striking shop; "no," if the missionaries were outsiders but not affected competitively by the outcome of the strike.

Chief Justice Taft's aim was to leave as much discretion as possible to the court. He preferred flexibility of power to a fixed rule of law. His view was: "Each case must turn on its own circumstances. It is a case for a flexible remedial power of a court of equity which may try one mode of restraint and if it fails or proves to be too drastic may change it."

On the fundamental question involved in this litigation—does a local strike having an *indirect* restraint on commerce although *affecting* interstate commerce, come under the Sherman Antitrust Act?—the court answered "no" in the first *Coronado* case and "yes" in the second.

For unions these answers presented a perplexing problem. Almost every important and effective strike might to some extent affect shipments in interstate commerce. Might not, then, the Sherman Antitrust Act be made use of in all such instances to break the strike? If the union weapon, the strike, could so easily be broken, what would happen to the labor movement and to the gains it had so carefully nurtured for the millions of workers in its ranks? These two *Coronado* cases pointed up the need for a new approach in industrial relations in an ever-widening industrial economy. A vague law which left the rights of the parties to the inconstant blessing of the court could not solve the industrial relations problem.

- 13 -

The Stonecutters' Union Strikes a Rock

(1925–1927)

BEDFORD CUT STONE COMPANY V. JOURNEYMEN STONE CUTTERS' ASSOCIATION, ET AL.

I

Stonecutting is one of man's oldest crafts. It has enabled man to rise from the cave to the skyscraper. Before the development of machinery, stone was cut by hand, but even though machinery has taken over part of man's burden, stonecutting has continued as a skilled and hazardous craft. The introduction of machinery has increased the output, but it has also increased the hazard to the workers' health by reason of the increased amount of dust inhaled during work. This dust causes peculiar muscular and nervous disorders, affecting especially the arms and hands.

The stonecutters were among the first groups to establish a labor organization in the United States. The work hazards and the fact that the craft was a skilled one were the essential factors that prompted the stonecutters to organize. Their union, known now as the Journeymen Stone Cutters' Association, dates back as far as 1830, and has always been organized along craft lines. It was one of the first unions to affiliate with the American Federation of Labor.

Until 1921 the union's relations with industry were reasonably amicable. The union pursued the traditional policy of maintaining trade agreements with employers' associations. It was not an aggressive or militant organization, but felt quite secure in its position in the industry. Its membership, however, remained small, consisting of about five thousand.

The center of limestone quarrying at that time was the Bedford-

Bloomington area of Indiana. For many years the stone producers located in that center had maintained friendly relations with the union. However, in 1921, twenty-four of these stone producers combined and refused to continue dealing with the union. They locked out all the union members, hired nonunion workers, organized them into a separate workers' organization, and refused to employ any union stonecutter unless he would become a member of their workers' organization.

The union became convinced that the employers' new policy would destroy it. After attempts to reach an understanding with these employers failed, the union called a strike against them. The strike proved futile, because the companies had enough nonunion men to go on with their work uninterrupted. The union then decided to appeal to all its members for sympathetic action and declared the product of the Associated Indiana Quarries as "unfair." At that time—in 1921—the union had about one hundred and fifty locals located in various states. Under the union constitution all the members were pledged not to finish stone partly cut by men working in opposition to the union.

The antiunion firms shipping rough stone products out of Indiana knew that union stonecutters employed on buildings in other states would very likely refuse to put hammer and chisel to the stone coming from the struck area.

II

One of the companies engaged in the lockout of the union stonecutters in Indiana was the Bedford Cut Stone Company. This company realized that the union boycott might seriously affect its business and decided to take legal action to enjoin the union from carrying on a boycott against its product. Under the Sherman Act, only the federal government could seek injunctions to restrain practices which threatened interference with interstate commerce. However, the Clayton Act, labor's so called "Magna Carta," contained a provision—Section 16—which permitted private persons to apply for injunctions against interference with interstate commerce. The company decided to take advantage of that section. Accordingly, the Bedford Company and twenty-three associated firms instituted an action in the United States District Court for the District of Indiana for an injunction barring the union, its officers, and its locals from carrying out its policy of refusing to work on stone cut in the plaintiffs' quarries.

Justice Albert B. Anderson, who heard the motion for the injunction, refused to issue a temporary restraining order. The company took an appeal from the justice's refusal to issue an injunction.

III

The appeal of the case, *Bedford Cut Stone Company, et al*, v. *Journeymen Stone Cutters of North America, et al.*, came before the United States Circuit Court of Appeals for the Seventh Circuit. It was heard by Justices Samuel Alschuler, Evan A. Evans, and George T. Page. On October 28, 1925, Justice Alschuler, sustaining the lower court, delivered the opinion of the court.

In reviewing the events leading up to the case, the justice observed that the companies had had relations with the union for quite a while, and that they were the ones who now refused to deal with the stonecutters' union and organized their own employees' group. He also observed that the record did not disclose that the union had interfered with the quarrying or the setting of Bedford stone; moreover, there had been no picketing or appeals to other trades for sympathetic action; there had been no appeals to boycott the product of the plaintiff as such; and the actions seemed to be based upon the fact that the union had instructed its own members not to work on stone rough-cut by nonunion workers.

Justice Alschuler was of the opinion that (*a*) the stonecutters were within their rights to refuse to work on nonunion-cut stone; (*b*) while the acts of the defendants might have had a tendency to restrain interstate commerce, so long as it did not appear that the defendants resorted or threatened to resort to unlawful acts or means to accomplish their purpose, there was no impropriety in the lower court's refusal to grant a temporary injunction; (*c*) the union's acts fell within the rule of the first *Coronado* case, which required evidence that the prime purpose of the acts complained of was interference with interstate commerce; and (*b*) since there was no such evidence in this case, therefore, regardless of the means employed, the Antitrust Act did not apply and the federal courts had no jurisdiction.

Accordingly, the lower court's decision denying the injunction was sustained. The company appealed to the Supreme Court of the United States.

IV

On October 18, 1927, the appeal was argued before the Supreme Court.

Briefly, the company's arguments ran as follows: (*a*) The common law forbade combinations in restraint of trade. Besides, our statutes condemned restraint of interstate commerce as an interference with the rights of the buying public. (*b*) In refusing to finish the Bedford stone, the defendants burdened and hampered the use of the company's product outside the state of Indiana and therefore restrained interstate commerce. (*c*) The sole purpose of the defendants in refusing to finish the stone cut by plaintiffs was so to restrain the companies' market that they would be forced to change their conditions of production, and this was an interference with interstate commerce. (*d*) The Sherman Act prohibited the restraint of interstate commerce *before or after as well as during* the arrival of the product. The defendants violated the act because they interfered with the plaintiffs' product after its arrival. The mere fact that the plaintiffs were operating a nonunion or antiunion plant did not give a license to the union to bar the plaintiffs' product from interstate commerce. (*e*) Under the facts in the case, if the government were the plaintiff, it could secure an injunction under the Sherman Act. Since Section 16 of the Clayton Act extended a similar right to private persons, the plaintiffs were entitled to the injunction.

In opposition, the union counsel contended: (1) The facts in the case showed no violation of the Sherman Act. The union was not a business concern nor was it in league with any business competitors of the company. (2) The union was not motivated by any desire to eliminate the company's participation in interstate commerce and thus lessen competition or raise prices to the public. On the contrary, the union's sole motive in refusing to work on Bedford stone was to organize cutters and carvers of stone at the quarries concerned. The union had no other motive or purpose. (3) The *direct* purpose of the union's action was not to reduce the amount of stone in interstate commerce, but rather only to maintain workers' standards through unionization. Any reduction of stone in interstate commerce as a result of union action was at most only *incidental*. (4) The companies did not prove that any real injury to their business resulted from the union's action in this case.

On April 11, 1927, reversing the lower court, Justice Sutherland (with Chief Justice Taft and Justices Van Devanter and McReynolds concurring, and two others concurring in the result with separate opinions) delivered the majority opinion of the Supreme Court. Justice Sutherland's opinion went to the heart of the question of labor's right under the Clayton Act. He held:

One: It was apparent that the purpose of the union's action was to keep local employers from buying Bedford stone. Strikes according to union counsel's admission, would be useless unless the company's trade were affected.

Two: The restraint imposed on the sale of the product was not imposed with a *local motive*. Therefore, it was immaterial that the interference with the sale of stones operated *after* the stone had already been transported, delivered, and had already physically been taken out of interstate commerce.

Three: Under these circumstances, the prevention of the use of the company's production, which ordinarily might have been a purely local matter, was only a part of the conspiracy. When the conspiracy was considered in its entirety, the local transactions became a part of the general plan and purpose, which plan and purpose was to destroy or lessen petitioner's interstate trade. In other words, strikes against the local use of a product were simply the means adopted to effect an unlawful restraint on that product in interstate commerce.

Four: While unionization might be a lawful purpose, that purpose did not justify restraint of interstate commerce. In other words, it was not lawful to accomplish the ends of the strike by means involving restraint on interstate commerce.

Five: The union's action, which directly and substantially curtailed and threatened to curtail the natural flow in interstate commerce of a large proportion of the building limestone production of the entire country to the disadvantage of producers, purchasers, and the public, must be held to be a combination in undue and unreasonable restraint of such commerce within the meaning of the Antitrust Act as interpreted by the Supreme Court.

Six: The fact that the record showed no actual injury to the company was not material to the plaintiffs' right to secure an injunction, since an *intent* to restrain interstate commerce was shown and there was a dangerous probability that damage would occur. This probability was enough to justify equity to interfere and issue an injunction.

Seven: The fact that the union was a lawful organization and that its objects were lawful was not important in the consideration of the injunction. "Where the means are unlawful, the innocent general character of the organizations adopting them or the lawfulness of the ultimate end sought to be attained, cannot serve as justification."

As already mentioned, the Supreme Court was far from unanimous on this question of labor's fundamental rights. Justice Edward T. Sanford agreed with the majority decision but disagreed with the reasoning. While Justice Harlan Fiske Stone concurred with the majority, he expressed serious doubt as to whether the Sherman Act prohibited a labor union from peaceably refusing to work on non-union material "even though interstate commerce were affected." He believed that under the Clayton Act the union action complained of in this case was not an unreasonable restraint of trade and therefore was not prohibited by the Sherman Act. However, he felt bound to concur with the decision of the majority in this case only because of the court's previous decision in *Duplex* v. *Deering*. But Justice Stone added that he had not been in agreement with the principles enunciated by the majority in that case either.

Justice Brandeis (with Justice Holmes concurring) entered a vigorous dissent. He laid particular stress upon the fact that the union was acting "in self protection against an opposing union installed by employers to destroy the regular union with which they had long had contracts." He also emphasized the fact that the stone-cutters in this case were guilty neither of any trespass nor of any breach of contract. They did not picket. They did not use violence. They did not, so far as the record showed, plan a boycott. No outsiders were involved, and no attempt had even been made by them to secure aid from other crafts. All that they did was to refuse to finish stone partly cut by men working in opposition to their organization. "The contest was not a class struggle, it was a struggle between particular employers and their employees." He therefore concluded that the actions of the union in this case, even if they in some respect restrained interstate commerce, were not "unreasonable" restraints and that the union could not be deemed a monopoly by reason thereof. They were acts dictated by self-protection.

Justice Brandeis pointed out that the Supreme Court assumed a much more conciliatory attitude toward business combinations than toward labor, in its application of the antitrust laws. In applying the law to business, the court held that only *unreasonable* restraints were prohibited. The court thus permitted the United States Steel Corporation to own 50 per cent of the nation's steel industries without being adjudged a monopoly; it allowed the United States Shoe Machinery Company to control the entire shoe machinery industry of the country without being adjudged an unlawful combination; but in this case the co-operation of individual workingmen for self-protection, to retain their labor standards, was declared by the majority of the court to be an unlawful monopoly. He concluded that "it would indeed be strange if Congress had by the same Act willed to deny to the members of a small craft of working men the right to co-operate in simply refraining from work, when that course was the only means of self protection against a combination of militant and powerful employers. I cannot believe that Congress did so."

Justice Brandeis's trenchant logic did not prevail. The majority opinion reversed the Circuit Court of Appeals, ordered the granting of the injunction, and in effect compelled union stonecutters to help employers undermine their own organization.

V

Labor's expectation that the Clayton Act would extend protection from the crushing effect of the Sherman Act, at least in strikes involving employees in direct relationship with the struck employer, was blasted by the majority decision in the *Bedford* case. This decision climaxed a series of decisions by the Supreme Court which had interpreted various laws intended by Congress for the curbing of business monopolies as legislation intended by Congress to curb labor activity. Labor loudly protested its accumulated resentment against this judicial attitude toward unions.

Aside from the fact that labor resented the application of the Sherman Antitrust Act to unions, it was embittered by the fact that the Supreme Court in applying that law treated industry far more favorably than labor. In applying it to business, the Supreme Court, as early as 1911, had decided that the restraint on interstate commerce prohibited by the Sherman Act meant to bar only such restraints as the court would find "unreasonable." But the same court made no such distinction in applying it to labor activities, thus exposing unions to prosecution under the Sherman Antitrust Act regardless of the "reasonableness" of the restraint on interstate commerce. Under the *Danbury Hatters* decision, the unions were prohibited from using their combined purchasing power to secure better terms of employment. Under the *Hitchman Coal* decision, unions were prohibited from so much as persuading men to resist the imposition of yellow-dog contracts. Under the *Duplex* v. *Deering* case, unions were not permitted to appeal to the sympathetic support of other crafts not to use the product of a firm which refused to deal with organized labor. And now, under the *Bedford Cut Stone* decision, a union was not permitted to get even the co-operation of its own members in its economic fight against employers who replaced union workers by nonunion workers and who had organized an employer-dominated workers' organization in opposition to the established union. By this *Bedford* decision union members were compelled to work on the product of the very employers who had combined to destroy their union.

Apparently, the Supreme Court still suffered from the fear that the principles enunciated by it in the first *Coronado* case would encourage labor to conduct effective strikes on a national scale. It will be recalled that in that case the court held that if the main purpose of the union was union organization, then a strike would not bring such union activities under the Sherman Antitrust Act. Not satisfied with modifying that principle in the second *Coronado* case, the court went much further in the *Bedford* case by even prohibiting members of the same union from co-operating with their national organization in refusing to work on struck products. By the decision in this case, the court removed possible favorable implications to labor implied in the decision of the first *Coronado* case.

Ironically, the Clayton Act, which had been hailed by the leaders of labor as the panacea for prosecution under the Sherman Act, instead of extending protection to labor became an additional weapon against labor. Under Section 16 of this act, private persons were given the right to injunctive relief, a right which under the Sherman Act was limited to the government alone. And while this injunctive relief was really intended for business concerns who suffered from the monopolistic abuses of big business, it was immediately made use of by business against labor unions.

Organized labor became acutely conscious that its rights had dropped to a new low, that it was effectively denied the power to advance organization, and that the means to defend its own existence were being curtailed. More than ever labor became convinced that it must seek effective legislation to curb the application of the anti-trust laws against it, legislation which in no uncertain terms would extend protection to labor and would withstand unintended inter-pretations by the judiciary.

- 14 -

Advertising for Customers: Merchants by Window Display, Union by Picketing

(1935–1937)

SENN V. TILE LAYERS' PROTECTIVE UNION

I

During the depression in the early 1930's, many people became convinced that the lot of labor had to be improved. The suffering during the depression pointed up the need of workers to seek protection of their economic condition through collective bargaining, and the need of a law not to interfere with the legitimate activities of unions to secure collective bargaining.

This sympathetic feeling created an atmosphere receptive to federal legislation favorable to labor. Thus, in 1932 Congress enacted the Norris-La Guardia Act, which was designed to counteract the effect of the court's decision in emasculating the protection intended for labor by the Clayton Act and to supply an effective protection for organized labor against the application of the Sherman Antitrust Act. About a year later, after the election of Franklin Delano Roosevelt, Congress further demonstrated its favorable attitude toward organized labor by including Section 7(a) in the National Industrial Recovery Act (NIRA), which was taken as an encouragement to workers to join labor unions. When three years later NIRA was declared unconstitutional by the Supreme Court, the Wagner Act was adopted, which specifically granted labor the right to organize and further provided that an employer was obligated to bargain collectively with the labor organization representing a majority of his workers.

The same social attitude that prompted favorable federal labor legislation also prompted similar favorable state legislation. A number of states passed "little Wagner Acts" of their own. Among such states was Wisconsin. The new Wisconsin Labor Code expressly legalized peaceful picketing and prohibited the state courts from issuing injunctions in labor disputes, unless disorder actually occurred or was imminent. Peaceful picketing was considered a form of publicizing a labor dispute.

Such was the background of the case of *Senn* v. *Tile Layers' Protective Union.*

II

During the depression years the Tile Layers' Protective Union in Milwaukee was especially hard hit. Many of its members were without jobs. Some of the individual members tried to help themselves by becoming independent contractors and undertaking small jobs on their own account. Since they themselves did the actual work, their contract price often was so cheap as to undermine the existing union scale. This condition not only endangered union standards but also threatened the union's ultimate existence. If labor standards should continue to fall as a result of the competition from these contractors, employers would not employ union labor.

One of the independent tile contractors in Milwaukee was a man by the name of Paul Senn. Apparently he never was a union member. In fact, he was a plasterer by trade, but when construction work in his own field declined he turned to the related craft of tile laying. About 1931 he formed a partnership with William Neider, a member of the Tile Layers' Protective Union who resigned as member to enter business. These two hired Arnold Holly, a suspended union tile layer, and set themselves up in the tile contracting business. The Senn Company secured jobs largely because the owners themselves were doing the actual work with the aid of the hired mechanic and therefore were in a position to underbid the other contractors in the field. It continued as a small contracting company.

As business improved and favorable labor laws were enacted in Wisconsin, the Tile Layers' Protective Union in Milwaukee, which during the depression had lost about two-thirds of its membership, thus being left with only 41 members, undertook an organization campaign to restore the union's position and to secure more work for its members. The union demanded that the contractors sign a collective agreement with it. One of the clauses in the proposed agreement required that contractors should have their work done by employees and that the owners refrain from using tools themselves. The Senn Company was willing to sign a union agreement to maintain union wages and hours but it refused to accept the condition that the owners themselves should not perform any journeyman's work. Senn claimed that his company could not continue in business without the owner also doing the actual manual labor.

By July, 1935, about half the tile contractors in Milwaukee had accepted the union's terms. Senn, however, still refused to sign the agreement if the disputed provision (Article III) were part of it. Involved in this dispute were the Tile Layers' Union, Local 5, and the Tile Layers' Helpers' Union, Local 47. After Senn's final refusal, these two unions informed the local contractors and architects that Senn was "unfair." This implied that the buildings that employed the Senn Company on tile jobs might be picketed. About five months later, in December, 1935, Senn's own place of business was picketed by the unions. The pickets patrolled with banners reading "P. Senn Tile Company is unfair to the Tile Layers' Protective Union" and "Let the union tile layers install your tile work." Picketing was maintained in an orderly fashion during the usual working hours, 8:00 to 12:00 and 1:00 to 4:00.

Fearing that the picketing might seriously interfere with his business, Senn instituted an action in the Circuit Court for Milwaukee County. He charged that the unions were trying to force him to stop working as a tile layer and requested that an injunction be issued restraining them and their officers from interfering with his business, from picketing his place of business or his places of work. The case came up on April 3, 1936, before Judge Otto H. Bredenbach. At the trial the unions agreed to stop following Senn to his jobs and to cease writing to his potential customers that his company was unfair to labor. Under these circumstances the court refused to issue an injunction prohibiting peaceful picketing. The company then appealed to the Wisconsin Supreme Court.

III

On June 29, 1936, Justice Edward T. Fairchild, for the majority of the Wisconsin Supreme Court, ruled on the appeal. He held:

(*a*) Though none of Senn's employees was a union member and Senn himself was not eligible for membership because he had not served his three years' apprenticeship, nevertheless, since Senn's business methods actually involved a threat to union scales, the dispute between the union and Senn was a "labor dispute" within the meaning of the Wisconsin Labor Code.

(*b*) The Wisconsin Labor Code allowed peaceful picketing to promote the welfare of members in the same craft.

(*c*) The union's picketing was entirely peaceful. Since they had stopped following Senn, the lower court had been correct in deciding that there was no need to issue a restraining order.

The minority of the court—Justices Chester A. Fowler and George B. Nelson—entered a vigorous dissent. They reasoned:

(1) The picketing was for the purpose of coercing the plaintiff into the illegal act of barring himself from a lawful calling and of depriving him of liberty and property without due process of law. This was contrary to the Fifth Amendment of the Constitution.
(2) The practice upheld by the majority of the court would prevent men from rising in the world by the sweat of their brow and was in fact "un-American, oppressive and intolerable."

In accordance with the decision of the majority, the appeal was denied, but the vigorous minority opinion encouraged Senn to request a rehearing of the appeal on the ground that the Wisconsin Labor Code was unconstitutional and that refusal to grant the injunction would deprive Senn of means of earning a living. Senn again was unsuccessful. On September 15, 1936, the Wisconsin Supreme Court denied a rehearing on the ground that the court had already held that the act was constitutional.

Senn then appealed to the United States Supreme Court.

IV

The issue of the case—the right to peaceful picketing—prompted the American Civil Liberties Union and the International Juridical Association to file briefs as *amici curiae* in support of the decision of the lower court.

The case was argued before the Supreme Court on March 31 and April 1, 1937. Senn's counsel argued:

1. The right to work at lawful occupations was inalienable and

could not be taken away by the union under the color of a state statute.

2. The denial of the injunction against picketing must result in depriving Senn of his right to do his own work. In this respect the Wisconsin Labor Code conflicted with the "due process" clause of the Fourteenth Amendment to the Constitution, which protects the individual in his right to engage in the common occupations of life, and was therefore unconstitutional.

3. The Wisconsin Labor Code was arbitrary, capricious, and unreasonable. It was class legislation because it prohibited the granting against unions of the same kind of relief that could be obtained against others.

4. Furthermore, even if the code was constitutional, no injunction could be issued in disputes concerning wages, hours, or working conditions. The code was not applicable to this case because none of the defendants was an employee of plaintiff, former employee, or a representative of an employee. Therefore, since none of them was directly concerned with wages, hours, and working conditions, the injunction against them was not prohibited by statute.

The issues raised by this case resulted in sharp division among the justices. The Supreme Court was divided five to four. On May 27, 1937, Mr. Justice Brandeis delivered the opinion of the majority. After observing that the Supreme Court would consider only whether Senn's rights under the Fourteenth Amendment were violated by the Wisconsin Labor Code or by the Wisconsin court's interpretation of the code, he held, in substance:

One: The Wisconsin Labor Code authorized only "peaceful picketing and patrolling," singly or in numbers. The law barred any physical obstruction or interference with plaintiff's business, or intimidation of customers. Similarly, the kind of strike publicity that the code permitted was publicity without misrepresentation. Hence, in permitting such picketing the law did not deprive one of rights.

Two: The Wisconsin Supreme Court considered Article III of the collective labor agreement proposed to Senn as a reasonable rule in view of the existing economic situation. Since the Wisconsin court had found that the end sought by the unions in this case was not unlawful and that the means used in enforcing their ends also was not unlawful, there was no basis for an injunction unless the union activity complained of was prohibited by the Constitution.

Three: Members of a union might, without the authority of special state laws, publicize a labor dispute, making the true facts known to the public as a matter of free speech, a right guaranteed by the Constitution. In a legal strike the state could permit peaceful picketing as a means of strike publicity.

Four: Nothing in the Federal Constitution forbids unions from competing with nonunion concerns for customers by picketing as freely as one merchant competes with another by means of advertising in the press or by window display.

Five: The fact that none of Senn's employees was a union member or had sought union aid was immaterial to the case. The union's members, as well as Senn, had the right to earn a living, and each had the right to seek public favor by legal means even if the publicizing of the issues in the labor dispute annoyed Senn and kept him from getting jobs. Such annoyance was not an invasion of the liberty guaranteed by the Constitution.

Six: A hoped-for job was not a property right guaranteed by the Constitution; and the diversion of a hoped-for job to a competitor was not an invasion of a constitutional right.

Seven: One has no constitutional right to the "remedy" of an injunction against the lawful conduct of another. The Wisconsin statute, as interpreted by the Wisconsin court, was constitutionally valid and was not in conflict with the Fourteenth Amendment.

Justice Pierce Butler (with Justices Van Devanter, McReynolds, and Sutherland concurring) dissented. They were of the opinion:

(*a*) The Fourteenth Amendment forbids state action that would take from the individual the right to engage in the common occupations of life, assuring equality of opportunity to all under like circumstances.

(*b*) Since the union's purpose in picketing was to bar Senn from the trade, the picketing had been for an unlawful purpose and should be enjoined.

(*c*) As the Wisconsin law permitted the kind of picketing that, as in this case, deprived Senn of the right to work, the statute denied equal protection of the laws and therefore such statute was repugnant to the due process clause of the Constitution.

Thus, the Supreme Court majority affirmed the decision of the Wisconsin Supreme Court and Senn's appeal was dismissed.

V

Labor was quick to sense the value of the court's decision as strengthening the right to peaceful picketing. The decision was interpreted as holding that peaceful picketing is protected as "freedom of speech" under the Constitution. Justice Brandeis, in speaking about picketing and publicity, used the expression "freedom of speech" in connection with the word "publicity" and not directly with the word "picketing." It is doubtful whether Justice Brandeis intended to say that peaceful picketing is constitutionally protected as "freedom of speech."

The significance of the decision in this case lies in the fact that the Supreme Court in effect gave the states wide latitude in regulating picketing, which apparently it was not inclined to do in the case of *Truax* v. *Corrigan*. In that case the court emphasized that the legislative power of a state must be subordinate to the guarantees of the Fourteenth Amendment and concluded that the state law granting a wide latitude in picketing was in violation of that amendment. But in this case the court clearly held that the "due process" and "equal protection" clauses of the Fourteenth Amendment are not violated by a state law which liberally permits peaceful picketing. The Supreme Court majority was satisfied that states, under their police power, were within their constitutional rights to regulate and hence to extend opportunities for peaceful picketing, a means of making the facts in the dispute known to the public. One may reasonably argue from these premises that, since the court referred to peaceful picketing as a means of publicity, and since publicity has constitutional protection, peaceful picketing gets reflected constitutional protection. However, there was no such direct holding by the court.

The principle enunciated by the court in this case is not necessarily an assurance to labor of complete liberal permission of picketing. If a state has the power by regulation to extend opportunities for peaceful picketing, it may also by *regulation* narrow opportunities for picketing. Labor should be aware that what a state may grant it may also take away. However, the limit to which a state may go in its regulation of picketing without interfering with the constitutional right of the parties involved was still left as an open question.

In this case the court viewed realistically the competitive elements involved in the labor dispute. It concluded that in the dog-eat-dog atmosphere of competition the right of men acting collectively to preserve their working standards was not inferior to the right of Senn to secure orders or jobs for himself. The right of the union to appeal to the public to patronize union employers instead of non-union employers, and thus secure additional opportunities for jobs for its members, was placed by the court in the same category as that of one merchant competing with another through the means of advertising. It reasoned that the peaceful picketing was the advertising means used by the union for publicizing the facts in the dispute and that as long as the advertising was not misleading and was truthful there was nothing unlawful about it.

Some may question the wisdom of a union's policy in picketing a small contractor like Senn, whose means of livelihood depended on his own manual labor. However, one should not overlook the fact that such small contractors may at times seriously undermine the working standards established in a trade. This is especially true in industries in which invested capital is small and manual labor instead of machinery is used in the making of the product, as in the performance of services. If small contractors who, because of their own manual labor and long working hours and their willingness to accept lower standards, should continually underbid employers who pay union scales, then the union members would have less employment and would also be obliged to accept lower standards. Still, from the point of view of public relations, one may question the wisdom of union policy in refusing to enter into an agreement with such a small contractor, where his living depended on plying his trade. Means should and can be found of imposing reasonable restrictions on such a contractor's work so that he may not undermine union standards but at the same time not be deprived of earning a livelihood.

- 15 -

The Supreme Court Sees the Industrial Facts of Life

(1936–1937)

NATIONAL LABOR RELATIONS BOARD V. JONES & LAUGHLIN STEEL CORPORATION

I

This is the story of the case that revolutionized labor relations in the United States and marked the turning point in our governmental policy toward industrial relations. With the Supreme Court's blessing, *positive* rights for labor unions were established.

The Constitution of the United States does not specifically provide that Congress has power to regulate such a vital factor in the economic life of the country as the relations between employers and employees. Possibly the framers of the Constitution at the time could not visualize the potential development of our industrial system and the role that industrial relations would play in it and their effect on the community as a whole; or possibly the framers did not visualize that our courts, in their power to interpret the law, would curb the power of Congress to pass such legislation, or possibly they were afraid to entrust the federal government with such power. Whatever the reason, the fact remains that the Constitution failed expressly to give power to Congress to regulate labor relations. Each state supposedly had such power, but not the federal government. On more than one occasion the Supreme Court held that the process of manufacturing was an intrastate process and hence regulation of the employer-employee relationship, if at all permitted, was within state and not federal power.

But when the need for Congressional power to regulate labor relations affecting interstate commerce became urgent, and Congress passed such legislation, the Supreme Court of the United States proved to be ingenious enough to find approval for it in the Constitution. The Supreme Court distilled the "commerce clause" of the Constitution and extracted from it power for Congress to deal with labor relations affecting interstate commerce. The significance of this decision was enhanced by the fact that it was rendered in a case directly affecting the citadel of antiunion sentiment and antiunion forces—the steel industry.

The saga of labor relations in the steel industry before the New Deal is one of bitter conflict, lingering defeat, and years of apathetic resignation by labor. The savage blow delivered by Henry C. Frick in behalf of the Carnegie Steel Company to the union in 1892 at Homestead drove the Amalgamated Association of Iron, Steel and Tin Workers from all but a limited and insignificant sector of the steel industry. It took more than a quarter of a century for the union again to attempt unionization in that industry.

The new attempt was made in 1919, but that great steel strike, led by William Z. Foster, with the backing of the American Federation of Labor, again resulted in a smashing defeat for the union. The steel magnates continued to "run their own business." As an additional protective measure against interference by "outsiders," the steel industry initiated a policy of maintaining company-dominated welfare schemes, employee-representation plans, and extensive use of its own private police force.

When, in 1933, in the midst of the greatest economic depression in the history of the United States, President Franklin D. Roosevelt took office, he saw the urgent necessity of increasing the purchasing power of the masses of the people as one of the means to industrial recovery. He envisaged the need for stabilization of industry, the need for restricting competition based on unfair trade practices, and the need for stabilization of industrial working conditions. The encouragement of collective bargaining was made part of this program, which became known as the "New Deal."

When the National Industrial Recovery Act was passed in 1933, industry was urged to set up Codes of Fair Competition. However, no code for an industry was to be approved unless it contained a provision conforming with Section 7(a) of the National Industrial

Recovery Act, which required that (1) employees should have the right to organize and bargain collectively through their freely chosen representatives; (2) no employee or prospective employee should be required to join any company union or to refrain from joining a labor organization of his own choosing; and (3) employers should comply with conditions of employment approved of or prescribed by the president.

Section 7(a) of the NIRA stimulated free unionism in the steel industry. The Amalgamated Association of Iron, Steel and Tin Workers showed signs of life again. Some "company unions" or "employee-representation plans" began sounding like regular unions, demanding to be heard on wage and hour questions, holding conferences with representatives of employees from other plants of the same company, and even conferring with free unions. The new union recruits within the Amalgamated assumed leadership. They demanded collective bargaining and, in disregard of the advice of the old leadership in the Amalgamated, they planned to call a strike unless their demands for union recognition were met.

The union representatives succeeded in having a conference with President Roosevelt, which was held on May 30, 1934, at the White House. At that conference the president promised them that elections would be held to determine the bargaining agency but that such elections would be held as the occasion might demand. The Iron and Steel Institute, voicing management opinion, continued to oppose dealing with the union. On the other hand, the union continued to make militant statements.

The government became concerned lest a strike in steel, a basic industry in the economy, interrupt production generally and interfere with the recovery program of the Administration. Therefore, the president appointed a special labor board for the steel industry to consider various problems arising out of the employer-employee relationship. This board was appointed on June 1, 1934. The Iron and Steel Institute interpreted Section 7(a) of the act as permitting company unions and claimed that the new special labor board appointed would be the impartial authority to regulate and supervise the company unions in this industry. The Amalgamated, fearing that the special labor board might be inclined to accept the interpretation of the Institute regarding its functions, refused to participate in any hearings called by this special labor board. A strike was threatened, but at the request of William Green, president of the American Federation of Labor, the call for the strike was suspended.

Soon after, pursuant to new statutory authority given him, President Roosevelt named a special board for the steel industry, with specific powers to investigate the disputes concerning representation under Section 7(a) of NIRA, to direct and hold elections in the steel plants where it deemed necessary, and to name a bargaining agent chosen by the majority, reserving the right of others in the minority, however, to present grievances to the employer.

Sometime later, in November, 1934, employers in the steel industry offered to deal with their workers on a "proportional representation" basis, that is, that company unions be represented in the bargaining agency in proportion to their membership in the plant. The Amalgamated saw danger in this proposal. It felt that this employers' plan would divide the steelworkers into two separate groups instead of uniting them in one union. Besides, it feared that the company unions, nurtured and dominated by the employers, would dominate the bargaining agency and that under these circumstances collective bargaining would be a mockery. The union insisted on the application of the democratic principle of majority rule, and demanded that the bargaining agency designated by the majority, as contemplated by the legislative policy, should be the sole and exclusive bargaining agency for the plant. The dispute between the union and the employers in the steel industry continued unabated.

But, the entire question of the election machinery for a bargaining representation in the steel industry under Section 7(a) of NIRA became moot because in June, 1935, the Supreme Court, in the famous case of *Schechter Poultry Corporation* v. *United States,* held the entire act unconstitutional. Since Section 7(a) passed out with the act, there was no legal basis for obligating employers to bargain with any representatives of workers. With the wiping out of the codes and the consequent disturbance of industrial conditions, there came a flood of wage cuts followed by industrial strife.

II

Even before the court's decision in the *Schechter* case was announced, the dubious legality and questionable efficacy of Section 7(a) of the National Industrial Recovery Act prompted Senator

Robert F. Wagner of New York to introduce in the Senate a bill specifically designed to make collective bargaining the law of the land. The Senate passed that bill about two weeks before the NIRA was declared unconstitutional, but no action was taken on a similar bill by the committee of the House of Representatives. After the *Schechter* decision, the bill was almost immediately reported favorably by the House committee, brought to the floor of the House, and passed on June 19, 1935. This bill, known as the National Labor Relations Act, and popularly referred to as the Wagner Act, was immediately signed by the president and became law on July 5, 1935.

The framers of this new law were conscious of the fact that the opponents to this progressive approach to labor legislation might attack the law on constitutional grounds. For the purpose of meeting such possible legal attack and for the purpose of supplying the Congress with the necessary jurisdiction for such legislation under the "commerce clause" of the Constitution, this law specifically declared that industrial relations may affect interstate commerce. It set forth findings showing the injury to interstate commerce resulting from the denial by employers of the right of employees to organize, and from the refusal of employers to accept the procedure of collective bargaining. The section of the act entitled "Findings and Policy" is as follows:

Section 1. The denial by employers of the right of employees to organize and the refusal by employers to accept the procedure of collective bargaining lead to strikes and other forms of industrial strife or unrest, which have the intent or the necessary effect of burdening or obstructing commerce by (a) impairing the efficiency, safety, or operation of the instrumentalities of commerce; (b) occurring in the current of commerce; (c) materially affecting, restraining, or controlling the flow of raw materials or manufactured or processed goods from or into the channels of commerce, or the prices of such materials or goods in commerce; or (d) causing diminution of employment and wages in such volume as substantially to impair or disrupt the market for goods flowing from or into the channels of commerce.

The inequality of bargaining power between employees who do not possess full freedom of association or actual liberty of contract, and employers who are organized in the corporate or other forms of ownership association substantially burdens and affects the flow of commerce, and tends to aggravate recurrent business depressions, by depressing wage rates and the purchasing power of wage earners in industry and by preventing the stabilization of competitive wage rates and working conditions within and between industries.

Experience has proved that protection by law of the right of employees to organize and bargain collectively safeguards commerce from injury, impairment, or interruption, and promotes the flow of commerce by removing certain recognized sources of industrial strife and unrest, by encouraging practices fundamental to the friendly adjustment of industrial disputes arising out of differences as to wages, hours, or other working conditions, and by restoring equality of bargaining power between employers and employees.

It is hereby declared to be the policy of the United States to eliminate the causes of certain substantial obstructions to the free flow of commerce and to mitigate and eliminate these obstructions when they have occurred by encouraging the practice and procedure of collective bargaining and by protecting the exercise by workers of full freedom of association, self-organization, and designation of representatives of their own choosing, for the purposes of negotiating the terms and conditions of their employment or other mutual aid or protection.

The act defined the "unfair labor practices" in which an employer might indulge to defeat the purposes of the Wagner Act. It created the National Labor Relations Board, which was charged with the duty of enforcing the law. This board was given the power to issue "cease and desist" orders against those violating the law and was authorized to petition the federal circuit courts for the enforcement of its orders.

No sooner was the law passed than it was attacked by various antilabor groups and especially the National Association of Manufacturers, as unconstitutional. Fifty-seven prominent lawyers, sponsored by the Liberty League, lent their joint authoritative opinion to this sentiment of employers. There was open encouragement to employers to disregard this new law as unconstitutional. It was predicted that this law would have the same fate as NIRA in the *Schechter* case. The constitutionality of this law was finally tested in the Supreme Court of the United States, in the case of *National Labor Relations Board* v. *Jones & Laughlin Steel Corporation*.

III

The Jones & Laughlin Steel Corporation had been known for many years as an iron-making concern. At the turn of the twentieth century, it shifted to steel production. It was a nonunion plant. As far back as 1897 it had driven the Amalgamated Iron, Steel and Tin Workers from its plants and in 1919 it had succeeded in averting a steel strike in its plants. Under the management of Tom Girdler, this company kept the site of its largest plant, Aliquippa, Pennsylvania, a completely "company town," where a stranger who could not give a satisfactory account of himself was subject to beating, arrest, fine, and expulsion.

Shortly after the inauguration of the new law, in August, 1934, the Amalgamated Association of Iron, Steel and Tin Workers chartered the Beaver Valley Lodge No. 200 for the purpose of organizing the Jones & Laughlin Aliquippa plant. Organizing this plant was a monumental task since a company-dominated union already was functioning there. It was rumored that the company paid the salaries of the officers of this company union and that its president had been paid as much as $14,000 a year. Obviously, the company union and the corporation resisted the unionization effort of Lodge No. 200. The lodge was confronted with systematic terror, shadowing, spying, beating, arrests, and the denial of meeting places, indoors or outdoors. The union appealed to Governor Gifford Pinchot for protection. In response to the appeal the Governor, in October, 1934, dispatched state police to Aliquippa to maintain order, which thus enabled union men to hold public meetings.

After NIRA was declared unconstitutional, and in spite of the enactment of the new Wagner law, the Jones & Laughlin Steel Corporation proceeded to crush free unionism in its plant. It followed the usual procedure in such cases by discharging thirteen workers known to have been active on behalf of the union. This was calculated to dampen the union spirit in the plant. The union countered by filing charges with the National Labor Relations Board, accusing Jones & Laughlin of violating the National Labor Relations Act in that it had discharged these thirteen employees for union activity, refused to reinstate them in their jobs, and discriminated against a union member by demoting him. After a preliminary investigation, the board issued a complaint based on these charges against the company.

The first hearing on the complaint was held on February 27, 1936. The company appeared at the hearings. Aside from the fact that it claimed that the workers were discharged for inefficiency and violation of company rules, it challenged the entire proceedings on the ground that the Wagner Act was unconstitutional. In addition thereto, the company claimed that neither its manufacturing operations nor its labor relations were in *interstate* commerce, that at best they were *intrastate* activities, and therefore the National Labor Relations Board, being limited to interstate commerce, had no jurisdiction in the matter. When its motion to dismiss the case on constitutional grounds was denied, the company refused to participate any further in the hearings.

The hearings established the following salient facts among others: (*a*) Jones & Laughlin Corporation was the fourth largest producer of steel in the United States and manufactured more than $47,000,000 worth of products annually. It also owned railroad facilities and ore steamers, iron mines in Minnesota, limestone quarries in West Virginia, and sales and warehouse facilities in other states. (*b*) The company employed 22,000 men at its two plants in Pittsburgh and Aliquippa. In so far as Aliquippa was concerned, the company not only employed 10,000 of the town's 30,000 inhabitants, but also owned the streetcar line, the buses, the water supply of the town, 774 houses, and maintained its private police force in the town. (*c*) The company plants got their raw materials from various states through arteries and by means controlled by the company, and then shipped the products to various states of the Union.

These facts prompted the board to conclude that all the operations of the company must be considered together, its plants could not be considered merely "local phenomena;" that the operations of the company formed one giant indivisible economic process involving commerce among the states; that the works in Pittsburgh and Aliquippa "might be likened to the heart of a self-contained, highly integrated body;" and that the company was in interstate commerce and as such subject to regulation under the National Labor Relations Act.

Concerning the charge of antiunion activity made against the company the board found: (*a*) Efforts of the Beaver Valley Lodge to organize the plant at Aliquippa were "countered by systematic terror" by the company, including the beating, arrest, and fining of one John S. Moyer, a union organizer, who was even denied a transcript of the record of his case for appeal. (*b*) Union officers were shadowed by the company police, who kept a record of their visitors and followed their movements. (*c*) The rental of halls or the use of even open lots for union meetings was denied and the union was forced to hold its meetings across the river in Ambridge. (*d*) The company had introduced an employee-representation plan in June, 1933, which permitted only company employees (no outsiders) to be named as representatives for the employees, and after the invalidation of NIRA in June, 1935, the company held elections on its own initiative and the company's foremen and supervisors actively participated in such elections and urged their subordinates to participate.

Considering the cases of the ten men discharged (the original charge of 13 had been reduced to ten), the board stressed the fact that it was not a mere accident that these discharges affected all ranking union officers. Thus, the union's financial secretary, employed for five years, was fired for alleged negligence because a nut dropped off a crane he had inspected, though other workers—not union men—for much greater offenses, such as drunkenness while on duty, were not dismissed by the company. Phillips, the union local president, was discharged for not answering a whistle signal, although other men were not fired for the same offense. It was also proved that when the company learned that an application for a union charter was filed, it offered Phillips a job with the company police at higher pay than he was receiving in the plant. But when he refused the offer, he was beaten up. Obviously the dropped-off nut was not the real reason for Phillips's discharge. Another union member, Angelo Volpe, who had been in the company's employ for about twenty years and had never been laid off for cause before, also was among the discharged. Ostensibly Volpe was dismissed for operating a crane on a signal by *head* instead of the signal by *hand*, but such infraction of rules was common in the plant and other men had not lost their jobs for such violations. Evidence showed that when he became active in the union, a department supervisor warned him, "This is a company town."

In addition to the chief union officers, the company fired Royal Boyer, an active union member, a Negro employee who had worked for the company for more than ten years and had been advanced to machine operator in 1932; Domenic Brandy, an active union member, a leader among Italian employees, who was fired though he had worked for the company for fourteen years (he had testified on behalf of the union before the Special Steel Labor Board); Ronald Cox, an active union member in the company's employ for three and a half years, who was threatened with eviction from a company-owned house and with the loss of company store credit if he persisted in union activity.

The board found that these discharges were directed at union officers and group leaders, most of them employees of long standing and good record, for comparatively trivial faults for which the company had not penalized others not conspicuous by union membership or activity; that the antiunion discrimination was evident and that similar action had been among the causes that previously brought about the great strike of 1919, and the stoppage of 1934 when 9,844 men walked out, and 264,810 man-days of work were lost.

Applying the law to the facts in the case, the board ordered Jones & Laughlin Steel Corporation to cease and desist from interfering with self-organization of its employees and from discouraging union membership by discrimination. The corporation was directed to offer reinstatement to the discharged men and to pay them the wage losses for the period between their discharge and their restoration to the jobs, less their earnings in the interval. In addition, the company was directed to post, for thirty days, a notice stating that there would be no firing or discrimination for joining the union.

IV

The company refused to comply with the board's cease and desist order. The board then petitioned the Federal Circuit Court of Appeals for the Fifth Circuit for the enforcement of its order.

The case was heard by Circuit Judges Rufus E. Porter, Samuel H. Sibley, and Joseph C. Hutcheson. In a *per curiam* opinion, on June 15, 1936, the court denied the board's petition. The Circuit Court, in substance, held:

1. The Board had no jurisdiction over labor disputes between employer and employee concerning the discharge of laborers in a manufacturing plant.

2. The Constitution of the United States did not vest in the federal government the power to regulate the labor relations of employer and employee in production or manufacture, the latter being purely local in character.

3. Production and manufacture were purely local business regard-

less of subsequent sale and shipping of the product in interstate commerce. *Production was not commerce, but a step in preparation for commerce.*

4. The fact that a company was so large that a strike against it might affect interstate commerce did not give Congress under the commerce clause the power to regulate the relation of employer and employee in such business. The possible effect of industrial relations on interstate commerce was *too remote* to warrant federal invasion of the state's right to regulate employer-employee relations.

5. The fact that the company's import of raw materials and subsequently the sale of its manufactured goods entered into interstate commerce and that such commerce would be affected by strikes was not sufficient ground for giving the federal government jurisdiction to regulate the manufacturing and production of such company's business. Similarly, the fact that the same employer was an importer, manufacturer, and seller of such goods, did not alter the respective constitutional sphere of federal and state governments. The making and fabrication of steel by Jones & Laughlin Steel Corporation was *production regulable by the state of Pennsylvania* and that state's jurisdiction was not lost by the fact that the corporation also engaged in bringing in and sending out raw materials and goods in interstate commerce, which was regulable by Congress.

6. Furthermore, the facts did not show any specific *present intent* to impede or destroy interstate commerce by means of a strike, therefore the board's order dealt only with theoretical, not actual, effects on commerce.

7. The board's order was beyond the authority of Congress and therefore its petition for enforcement of its order must be denied.

Having failed to secure a rehearing, the board petitioned the Supreme Court of the United States for a writ of certiorari to review the Circuit Court's decision.

V

The board's petition was granted on November 9, 1936, a few days after the presidential election of that year. While the case was pending before the Supreme Court, several events occurred which must have registered with the justices of the court.

The most important event was the victorious re-election of Franklin D. Roosevelt against the bitter attack on the social and economic policies of the New Deal. This political landslide, in which the president carried every state in the Union except Maine and Vermont, could be construed in no other way than as an enthusiastic endorsement of the New Deal philosophy, with its sponsorship of collective bargaining as the law of the land.

Armed with this mandate from the people, President Roosevelt, who had been nettled by the Supreme Court's voiding of various New Deal Legislation—NIRA, the Frazier-Lemke Farm Mortgage Act, the Railroad Retirement Act, and the Agricultural Adjustment Act—sent a special message to Congress in February, 1937, proposing a reorganization of the Supreme Court. This proposal would have made judges of the Supreme Court eligible for retirement at the age of seventy. If a judge chose to remain on the high court bench after attaining such retirement age, the president would have the power to appoint an additional judge to the Supreme Court for each such judge, not exceeding, however, a total of six. The proposal was aimed at permitting the president to inject new blood, or possibly New Deal blood, into the Supreme Court. It was denounced as "packing the tribunal," and the vigorous opposition to it cut across party lines and shattered political friendships.

Another event of significance occurred before the Supreme Court rendered its decision. The United States Steel Corporation, the stronghold of the open shop, entered into a collective labor agreement with the union. As a result of conferences between John L. Lewis for the union and Myron C. Taylor for the United States Steel Corporation, a collective labor agreement was entered into between Benjamin Fairless, of Carnegie-Illinois, the largest subsidiary of "Big Steel," and Philip Murray of the Steel Workers' Organizing Committee, by the terms of which the union became the bargaining agency for its own members employed by that company. There was no longer any doubt which way the wind concerning collective bargaining in this country was blowing.

Whether or not there is any truth in the saying "Judges, too, have their ears to the ground," or whether there is any basis for Dooley's "The Constitution may not follow the flag, but the Supreme Court follows the election returns," the overtones of the tremendous popularity of the New Deal, shown in the election of 1936, and of the events above recited, may be detected in the Supreme Court's decision in the *Jones & Laughlin* case.

VI

The case was argued before the Supreme Court in February, 1937. The heart of the case lay in the question as to whether Congress had power to enact the National Labor Relations Act regulating industrial relations between employer and employees. Since the power of the Congress as against states' rights could be exercised only if *interstate* commerce were involved, the government offered an elaborate brief, complete with sociological, economic, and historical data, in support of its contention that this law, seeking to prevent interruption of production caused by industrial disputes, was by reason of precedent and analogy within the constitutional powers of Congress. The government in its brief and its oral arguments endeavored to show that this act, which might appear to be a law for the regulation of industrial relations, was in reality a law designed for the protection of interstate commerce, and therefore unquestionably within the constitutional powers of Congress. The attorneys for the company, on the other hand, contended that the law was beyond the power of Congress and that it was in violation of various provisions of the Constitution guaranteeing "due process," "freedom of contract," and the "right to a jury trial." The company attorneys also charged that in enacting this law Congress used its jurisdiction over interstate commerce as a *pretext* for legislation which in reality was nothing more than regulation of labor relations, which was exclusively within the state, and not federal, power.

Since the case involved legal technical issues, it was to be expected that the arguments of the attorneys for both sides would be highly technical, and they were. Precedents were cited. The "wisdom of our forefathers" was heavily relied upon and the court was reminded in no uncertain terms of the sovereignty of the states of the Union and the dangerous implications of "bureaucratic interference" which might flow from this act. Because the court in its unprecedented decision covered the various contentions raised by the attorneys, we shall omit the long and involved argument of counsel for government and for the company.

The Decision of the Court

The momentous decision, affecting the entire legal structure of employer-employee relations in the United States and having a profound effect on the development of the labor movement, was handed down by the Supreme Court on April 12, 1937. Chief Justice Hughes (Justices Brandeis, Stone, Cardozo, and Roberts concurring) delivered the opinion of the court. The substance of the court's decision on the essential issues follows:

One: The Wagner Act by its terms imposed collective bargaining upon only those industries which may be deemed to burden or obstruct interstate commerce. It was a familiar principle that acts which directly burdened or obstructed interstate or foreign commerce or its free flow were within the reach of Congressional power. Acts having that effect were not rendered immune because they grew out of a labor dispute.

Two: It was the *effect* upon commerce, not the source of the injury, that was the criterion of Congressional power. The fundamental principle was that the power to regulate commerce was the power to enact all appropriate legislation for its protection and advancement. The Congressional power under the commerce clause was plenary and might be exerted to protect interstate commerce no matter what the source of danger threatening it may be.

Three: While industrial relations in themselves were not subject to federal regulation, *they might be* if they had such a close and substantial relation to interstate commerce that their control was essential and appropriate for the protection of that commerce from burdens or obstructions. While manufacturing in itself was not commerce, the business of Jones & Laughlin was described as a flow of commerce with the Aliquippa plant as its focus. The board termed the Pittsburgh and Aliquippa plants "the heart of an integrated body." "Although activities may be intrastate in character when separately considered, if they have such a close and substantial relation to interstate commerce that their control is essential and appropriate to protect that commerce from burdens and obstructions, Congress cannot be denied the power to exercise that control."

Four: The findings of fact by the National Labor Relations Board must be taken as conclusive if supported by evidence in the record. The board found that the employees discharged were active leaders in the labor union and they were discriminated against by reason of their union activity. The company did not avail itself of the opportunity to present evidence to refute these charges of discrimination. The record on appeal, therefore, presented no ground for setting aside the board's order based upon the findings pertaining to the circumstances and purposes of the discharge of the employees concerned. All the evidence supported the board's finding.

Five: The right of employees to organize was a fundamental right. Employees had as clear a right to organize and select their representatives for lawful purposes, as the respondent had the right to organize its business and select its own officers and agents. Discrimination and coercion to prevent the free exercise of the right of employees to self-organization and representation was an appropriate subject for condemnation by competent legislative authority. Hence, Congressional prohibition of employer interference was not in violation of freedom of contract or due process. It was not an invasion of the constitutional right of either but recognition of the rights of both.

Six: The distinction between national and local issues was one of degree. Whatever amounted to a constant practice and threatened to burden or obstruct interstate commerce was within the regulatory power of Congress under the commerce clause of the Constitution and it was primarily for Congress to consider the fact of the danger and meet it. The company claimed that the exercise of this power was proper when it concerned enterprises like railroads, which were instrumentalities of interstate commerce. *But the agency was not superior to the commerce that used it.* It was the Congressional power over interstate commerce that extended its power to the railroads. Likewise, in this case it was the Congressional power over commerce that extended its power to control activities and practices which might threaten or obstruct interstate commerce.

Seven: Although an industry, when separately viewed, might be local in character, the application of the antitrust laws to labor illustrated how local acts might have the intent to restrain or control interstate commerce and that such intent may be inferred from the effects of the local acts on commerce. Hence, the fact that the employees here concerned were engaged only in production was by itself not determinative of their close or remote effect on interstate commerce. The real issue was the "effect upon interstate commerce of the labor practice involved." This case differed from the *Schechter* and the *Carter* v. *Carter Coal Company* cases, upon which the respondent laid stress, because in those cases the effect on interstate commerce was remote and the regulation involved an improper delegation of power. However, that was not so in this case.

Eight: Interstate commerce and interference with it were practical conceptions to be judged in the light of actual experience. In view of respondent's far-flung activities, it was idle to say that the effect of interruption of production would be indirect or remote. It was obvious that it would be immediate and might be catastrophic. "We are asked to shut our eyes to the plainest facts of our national life and to deal with the question of direct and indirect effects in an intellectual vacuum . . . When industries organize themselves on a national scale, making the relation to interstate commerce the dominant factor of their activities, how can it be maintained that their industrial labor relations constitute a forbidden field into which Congress may not enter when it is necessary to protect interstate commerce from the paralyzing consequences of industrial war." Both interstate commerce and interference with it were practical conceptions which must be appraised by a judgment that did not ignore actual experience.

Nine: Recognition of unions was an essential condition of industrial peace without which interstate commerce might be burdened or obstructed. Experience showed that recognition of the right of employees to self-organization and their free choice of collective bargaining agents was often an essential condition of industrial peace. Refusal by employers to confer and negotiate with representatives of their workers had been one of the most prolific causes of industrial strife. The power of Congress to protect against that cause had been admitted in regard to railroad employers. The case of employees in industries which could place interstate commerce in jeopardy was not essentially different from the case of employees of transportation companies. What purpose would it serve to protect the facility of transportation if interstate commerce was throttled with respect to the commodities to be transported? It followed that it was within the power of Congress to protect interstate commerce from such causes as might burden or obstruct that commerce.

Ten: The history of industrial relations in the steel industry was pertinent to the case. Steel was a basic industry. In presenting its case, the government had aptly referred to the steel strike of 1919-1920 and its consequences. The fact that there had been no major disturbance, either in the steel industry or in the Jones & Laughlin plant, did not dispose of "possibilities of future and like dangers to interstate commerce" which Congress was entitled to foresee and to exercise its protective power to forestall. The Jones & Laughlin enterprise presents in a most striking way the close and intimate relation which a manufacturing industry might have to interstate commerce and "we have no doubt that Congress had constitutional authority to safeguard the right of respondent's employees to self-organization and freedom in the choice of representatives for collective bargaining."

Eleven: The majority rule requirement was not arbitrary nor unfair. The obligation of the employer to bargain exclusively with the representative of the employees designated by their majority "imposed the negative duty to treat with no other." This majority rule did not preclude individual contracts. It did not compel agreements. It did not prevent refusal to make collective contracts nor did it bar individuals or groups other than that in the majority from presenting grievances. The act assumed only that opportunity for negotiation with accredited representatives designated by the majority would promote industrial peace. There was nothing arbitrary in that requirement.

Twelve: The Wagner Act did not interfere with the right of employers to hire and fire normally. What the law did provide was that the employer might not, under cover of the right to hire and fire, intimidate or coerce his employees with respect to their self-organization or representation. On the other hand, the National Labor Relations Board could not make its authority a pretext for interference with the right of the employer normally to discharge an employee. It would seem that when employers freely recognized the right of their employees to join their own organizations and their unrestricted right of representation, there would be less occasion for controversy in respect to the free and appropriate exercise of the right of hiring and firing. The act was criticized as one-sided—as extending protection to employees without at the same time imposing obligations on labor. *Congress was not required to deal with all phases of a problem at the same time.* The courts, in dealing with the power of Congress to pass specific legislation, were not concerned with the question of the extent to which the Congressional policy on that specific problem went or should go. The question was whether Congress had power to legislate to the extent to which it did legislate.

Thirteen: The Wagner Act was not an improper delegation of power. The National Labor Relations Board's procedure did not offend against the constitutional requirements governing the creation and action of administrative bodies. The law provided adequate review and protection against arbitrary action. The rules of administrative procedure were met by the board. The fact that the company withdrew from the hearings and declined to use its opportunity to meet the charges of engaging in unfair labor practices on the merits was immaterial. The board's findings were based on the facts presented at the hearing.

Fourteen: The company's contention that it was deprived of its right to a jury trial because the board's order directing reinstatement of workers with back pay involved sums of over $20 was without merit. The proceedings before the board were not the common-law proceedings referred to in the Constitution, providing for the right to a jury. The reinstatement and the back pay directed by the board were penalties for violating the law and were appropriate in order to secure the enforcement of the order of the board.

The exhaustive and learned opinion of the majority concluded that the National Labor Relations Act was constitutional and that the National Labor Relations Board was within its power to issue the cease and desist order against the Jones & Laughlin Corporation. Accordingly, the judgment of the Circuit Court of Appeals was reversed and the cause was remanded for further proceedings in accordance with this opinion.

While the main opinion holding the Wagner Act constitutional was delivered by the court in the *Jones & Laughlin* case involving the steel industry, the court at the same time upheld the act in four other cases dealing with various other phases of our economic life. These cases were:

Associated Press v. *National Labor Relations Board*, in which the act was attacked on the ground that it abridged the freedom of the press guaranteed by the First Amendment to the Constitution; *National Labor Relations Board* v. *Fruehauf Trailer Co.*, *National Labor Relations Board* v. *Friedman-Harry Marks Clothing Company, Inc.*, and *Washington, Virginia & Maryland Coach Co.* v. *National Labor Relations Board.* In the last case the court was unanimous.

The minority of the Supreme Court, consisting of Justices McReynolds, Van Devanter, Sutherland, and Butler, dissented in four of the five cases. Mr. Justice McReynolds, writing for the minority, agreed with the lower court, which held that the commerce clause of the Constitution did not cover employer-employee relationships. He considered the economic data concerning the company's business to be of no value to the case because, in his opinion, the size and character of the enterprise was "merely fortuitous."

In Justice McReynolds' opinion, the discharge of the ten employees by Jones & Laughlin at best could have only a *remote and indirect* effect upon commerce, and even such remote effect could be shown by the government only by the piling on of hypotheses, and therefore the board had no jurisdiction in the matter. Likewise, a refusal by a manufacturer to bargain collectively with his employees could not be construed as directly affecting interstate commerce and it was wholly immaterial whether the raw materials of that employer came from other states or whether the products thereof were regularly carried to other states. According to Justice McReynolds, the argument of the majority, that industrial strife might interfere with the "flow of commerce," went far beyond constitutional limitations and the conclusions drawn by the majority from such argument would interfere with states' rights to control industrial relations.

The Wagner law itself, in Justice McReynolds' view, was unfair because, on the one hand, it barred antiunion discharges on the theory that such discharges might provoke strikes which would hamper interstate commerce and, on the other hand, it safeguarded the right of employees to engage in such strikes; on the one hand, the law forbade an employer to discharge men for union activity but, on the other hand, it permitted coercion of nonunionists into labor organizations.

Citing the Supreme Court decisions in previous cases, Justice McReynolds contended that the National Labor Relations Act violated the Fifth and Fourteenth Amendments to the Constitution, because the right to "freedom of contract" was fundamental and included the privilege to select those with whom one was willing to have contractual relations. He held that this right was unduly abridged by the Wagner Act and that under it a private owner was deprived of power to manage his own property by freely selecting those to whom his manufacturing operations were to be entrusted.

Thus, while the minority opinion adhered to legal precedents, to the traditional social views of the past, the majority took note of the industrial facts of life in modern economy and its economic and political changes. The majority opinion was part of the court's acquiescence in major New Deal legislation, which helped disarm the proponents of Supreme Court reforms.

VII

While the court's decision made no immediate change in the Jones & Laughlin Company's antiunion position, it did have a tremendous influence on the spirit of the workers employed by that company. It demonstrated to the workers the power of the Wagner Act to protect men from discharge by reason of their union membership or activity.

Philip Murray, president of the Steel Workers' Organizing Committee (SWOC) began negotiating with the company, but since no agreement was reached by May, 1937, the workers voted to strike. The company then offered (*a*) to sign a contract with the union as the bargaining agent *only for its members*, but reserving the right to deal with other groups of employees; or (*b*) in the alternative, if the union would postpone calling the strike until an NLRB election might be held and if such election resulted in a majority vote for the union, the company would recognize it as the *exclusive* bargaining agent. Convinced that the proposals were made with the aim of either strengthening the company-dominated union or to gain time to exert pressure on the workers to vote against the union, the latter rejected the company's proposal. The SWOC felt that a demonstration of union strength was essential for successful organization and issued a strike call for May 12, 1937. The workers responded, and the strength of the union was effectively demonstrated; the success of that walkout surprised even the SWOC leaders.

The demonstrated union strength won it a contract. Jones & Laughlin recognized the union as bargaining agent for its members and agreed to accept it as the *exclusive* bargaining agent if it carried an NLRB election. The company also agreed to refrain from interference with the freedom of choice of its employees. The election of a bargaining agent was held on May 20 and the SWOC won by a vote of 17,028 to 7,207. Later the company union that had existed in the plant merged with the SWOC.

At first there was considerable bitterness and friction between the company and the union, but after both sides learned to know each other, collective bargaining relations were established on a reasonably amicable level.

VIII

The validation of the Wagner Act unleashed the organized energies of both the CIO and the AFL. The walls of the citadels of antiunionism came tumbling down. The mass production industries, theretofore guided by the "authoritative opinion" of the attorneys for the Liberty League, began to obey the law, and while they were still belligerent they were no longer openly defiant. The trade-union movement grew in numbers, in social status, and in political strength. Hardly a town or hamlet remained unaffected. Company-dominated unions either went underground, or disappeared, or joined the ranks of bona fide unions. Many "company towns" became "union towns." However, under the leadership of the National Association of Manufacturers and the United States Chamber of Commerce, many employers, though accepting the Wagner Act generally bent their energies on restricting its application and on having Congress adopt crippling amendments to the act.

The antiunion activities of employers took a new form. They initiated legislation in many states hampering union activity. Most of this legislation followed one pattern, indicating a master sponsor. The arena of the struggle was now transferred from the courtroom to the legislatures and public opinion.

IX

Socially and legally, the Supreme Court's thin majority decision in this case revolutionized industrial relations in the United States and climaxed more than a century of labor history. The court placed its stamp of approval not only on the legal status of organized labor and the law to protect the workers' right to organize, but also on the *duty* of employers to deal in good faith with the authorized representatives of the workers concerning wages, hours, and other conditions of employment. There could no longer be any question of a union's right to exist. The very interference with its existence by an employer through unfair labor practices became outlawed.

The commerce clause of the constitution, which theretofore had been made use of only for the protection of property, was now for the first time made use of for the protection of labor organizations.

The age-old constitutional ramparts of "freedom of contract" and of "due process" were no longer adequate refuges against this New Deal measure seeking protection for organized masses of workers. The commerce clause was no longer a one-way street but a highway of roads; workers too might be benefited by it if Congress so desired. "Freedom of contract" and "due process" rights were balanced by workers' rights to freedom of organization, not to be interfered with by employers. Property rights were not to be used to undermine human rights. In the words of the prevailing opinion of the court, "Employees have as clear a right to organize and select their representatives for lawful purposes as the respondent employer has to organize its business and select its own officers and agents."

Organized labor had consistently contended that the Supreme Court had been prejudiced against labor, that favorable labor legislation had been systematically declared unconstitutional or so narrowly construed as to deprive labor of its benefits, that laws not intended by Congress against labor, such as the Sherman Antitrust Act, were broadened by the court's interpretation of them to include labor; in other words, that the Congressional intent was thwarted and that the court, in effect, supervised Congressional policy toward labor under pretext of constitutionality.

The *Jones & Laughlin* decision was hailed by labor as a sign that the court was ready to abandon judgment-made labor law. In this *Jones & Laughlin* case, the Supreme Court, as if conscious of the justice of labor's attack, reacknowledged that it must allow Congress full sway in the adoption of policy; that it was the court's task to decide on the *power* of Congress to act, *not on its wisdom* in acting in a specific fashion.

Another aspect of the *Jones & Laughlin* case is its important bearing on the ever-present conflict of states' rights against Congressional power. Theretofore, industrial relations had been considered within the exclusive responsibility of the states, but the decision in this case changed that, and held that industrial relations could come within Congressional power, that industrial relations may affect interstate commerce. The court specifically held that the criterion of Congressional power was "the effect upon commerce, not the source of the injury," and that activities were not to be judged in isolation, but in their interdependent economic setting, by saying: "Although activities may be intrastate in character when separately considered, if they have such a close and substantial relation to interstate commerce that their control is essential or appropriate to protect that commerce from burdens and obstructions, Congress cannot be denied the power to exercise that control . . ."

Once the court broke away from the traditional narrow definition of "commerce" and once the court accepted the Congressional power to regulate labor relations affecting interstate commerce as provided in the Wagner Act, the court liberally supported the NLRB in many of the cases brought before it to test the power of the board under the act. The spirit of the New Deal permeated the high court.

Labor had real cause to celebrate this new spirit of the Supreme Court. Its gains were phenomenal. It won many a collective agreement without a real struggle. Its ranks swelled, its place in our economic society seemed assured, and its social and political position and prestige enormously enhanced. In justly celebrating its new legal status, labor failed to realize that such extension of Congressional power over industrial relations was not necessarily an unmixed blessing. Under this interpretation Congress was no longer constitutionally estopped from enacting legislation concerning industrial relations even though the legislation might be repressive or punitive and might deprive unions of many of their hard-won gains. What a liberal Congress could give a conservative Congress could take away, and this was what actually happened ten years later.

- 16 -

The Sit-Down Strike Boomerangs

(1937–1939)

NATIONAL LABOR RELATIONS BOARD V. FANSTEEL METALLURGICAL CORPORATION

I

For many years the metal trades were a stronghold of antiunionism. The hostility to labor unions among employers in those trades is manifest in a number of court cases, of which the celebrated case of *Bucks Stove and Range Company* v. *Gompers* was one. The National Metal Trades Association fought unionism skillfully and with varied weapons. One of those weapons was the furnishing of experienced industrial spies. Those spies would join union ranks, often assume leading roles in the union and act as agent provocateurs. They would gather information on the progress of union organization in a plant and report regularly to their agency or employer.

The Fansteel Metallurgical Corporation, located in North Chicago, was comparatively small as enterprises in the metal industry go, but it was quite an important company in its specialized field of manufacture of contact points, battery chargers, and alloy wires for radio tubes. In the summer of 1936 the company launched an efficiency campaign. It hired efficiency experts and those experts proposed new wage and production policies. The workers, who had never been organized in any kind of labor organization, not even a company union, realized that the new wage policy would undermine their earnings and they became aroused. About the same time, the Amalgamated Association of Iron, Steel and Tin Workers of North America was engaged in organizing workers in the metal trades, and it urged the workers of the Fansteel Corporation to join the union.

Many workers responded and in August, 1936, formed Local 66. Within three days after the local charter had been granted, the Fansteel Company applied for membership in the National Metal Trades Association and asked its help in combating the union.

Even before accepting the application for membership, the National Metal Trades Association recommended to Fansteel that it hire one Alfred Johnston as a worker in the plant. The Fansteel Corporation was to pay the association $25 a month for its services and $200 a month for Johnston's services, less the wages paid to him directly as an employee in the plant. Johnston had the necessary special experience for this job. He had previously rendered services in a similar capacity for the Sherman Service and the Corporations Auxiliary Company, notorious agencies for labor spies and strike-breakers.

As a worker in the plant, Johnston immediately joined Local 66, attended union meetings regularly, energetically participated in union affairs, and always urged action. He favored an immediate strike. Simultaneously, Johnston had been making confidential reports to the National Metal Trades Association on what was going on in the Fansteel plant among the workers and in the union. The association transmitted the reports to his nominal employer, the Fansteel Metallurgical Corporation. In October, 1937, the procedure was slightly changed: Johnston's reports were delivered directly to the home of Fansteel's president, who burned them after reading. These precautions became necessary because the La Follette Civil Liberties Committee of the United States Senate was investigating industrial espionage and the National Metal Trades Association preferred not to have Johnston's reports among its records in case they were subpoenaed.

In September, 1936, the new local union decided to ask for collective bargaining and requested an interview with A. J. Anselm, the plant superintendent. He refused to see any committee unless it consisted of plant employees of at least five years' standing. In order to test the real issue—collective bargaining—John Kondrath, the president of the local, appeared with a committee, each of whom had been in the company's employ for at least five years, and presented a proposed contract for collective bargaining. This contract called for improvement of working conditions, recognition of the union, the granting of a closed shop, and checkoff of union dues.

Anselm immediately rejected the requests for the closed shop and checkoff and said that the company would recognize no union with "outside influences." He handed to the committee several copies of a printed booklet setting forth the details of an employee-representation plan acceptable to the company and told them to consider it. He did not raise the question of whether the union represented a majority. His objection was directed to the "outside" union. The committee got nowhere in its first effort at collective bargaining and left the office.

At the same time Anselm was preparing action against the union on another level. At his initiative a movement was started to petition the company to have an *inside* union. The petition was circulated in the plant during working hours, Anselm himself and a number of foremen participating. Some foremen plainly stated, "We are trying to form a company union . . . you might as well sign up . . . The company will never recognize the outside union anyway."

About ten days later the union committee again called on Anselm. This time it was accompanied by a representative from the Amalgamated. The conference was short lived. Upon seeing the union representative, Anselm said, "I have nothing to do with this gentleman here. He is not on my payroll . . . get out of here. We do not want you." After he left, Anselm denied that he had made any appointment to see the committee, so the committee also left.

II

A few days after the aborted second conference, each employee received an interoffice envelope containing two documents. One document was entitled "A Plan of Employee Representation Which Has Been Pronounced Successful in a Large Number of Plants;" the other document was a statement of Fansteel's labor policies, containing various assurances of the company's willingness to treat its employees well. This document contained the statement that ". . . management reserves its right to reward individual merit . . . to preserve the rights of its individual workers . . . to discontinue the services of any whose work, abilities or general conduct is not in keeping with the best interests of the business and its policies as a whole."

With this as a basis for winning over the workers as individuals, the attack against the union shifted to another front, the undermining of the prestige of the union. The first step along these lines was to get rid of the union president. John Kondrath, the president of the local union, was transferred from the toolroom, where he had been regularly employed, to a separate place near Anselm's office, where he could be under constant observation. The official excuse for this transfer was that the company was engaged in a "development plan" and that it was advisable to have Kondrath in "seclusion" during the period of such development. Kondrath was kept in such seclusion during the regular working hours and was ordered not to visit the plant during his lunch hour. If no work was available for him, Kondrath was directed to take it easy, spend his time reading magazines which the company supplied. Kondrath was given a much easier job than before, but such ease was not to his liking. He resented the "isolation ward." The petty bribery did not sway him and the enforced isolation did not scare him. He resigned neither his job in the plant nor his office in the union. Kondrath remained in seclusion for several weeks and then the "development plan" was dropped and Kondrath was sent back to the toolroom.

In the meantime, Local 66 grew in strength. A majority of the workers, 155 of the 229 employees in the bargaining unit, had signed membership cards. The union decided to take action. On the morning of February 17, 1937, the committee called on Anselm and asked for recognition as bargaining agent. Anselm replied that he would have to confer with the company president before giving an answer. The committee decided to press for an answer and called a membership meeting during lunchtime that very day. The hiring of spies by the company was by that time well known to the workers. Restless and tense and resentful of the company's delaying tactics and its hiring of spies, the workers determined to act.

The news of the then current sit-down strikes of the automobile workers in Detroit and Flint very likely influenced the committee and the Fansteel workers. The meeting unanimously authorized the committee to press for an immediate answer on union recognition and, if the answer was unfavorable, to take whatever steps it might deem necessary to preserve the union. As the lunch hour went by, the workers were speculating excitedly as to what the answer of the company's president would be.

At two o'clock in the afternoon the committee returned to Anselm's office to get the company's answer. Anselm informed the committee that Mr. Aitchison, the company president, had not changed his mind, that the company might consider bargaining with an employees' committee, but it would deal with no group which had outside leadership and Amalgamated affiliation. When the committee mentioned its rights under the Wagner Act, Anselm dismissed that by saying that the Wagner Act was unconstitutional. The committee left the office in a determined mood. After a hurried meeting among themselves, they scattered throughout the entire plant, spreading word that a strike was on. Immediately about 90 workers occupied strategic places in the two principal buildings of the plant and announced that they intended to remain there until the company agreed to bargain collectively, and urged those who did not want to stay in to leave. Work stopped. The workers who had chosen to remain locked the doors from the inside. A sit-down had begun in the Fansteel works.

The company apparently was prepared for this eventuality. That very afternoon Anselm, with two policemen and the company attorney, pounded on the locked doors and ordered the workers to give up possession. When they refused, the attorney for the company announced that all of them were discharged "for seizure and retention of the plant." After making the announcement they left. Later a representative returned and posted written notice of intention to seek an injunction against the sit-downers. Swift action followed. Shortly after the notice was served, a hearing on the injunction application was held in the County Court for Lake County, Illinois. The court immediately granted the application and ordered the strikers to vacate the building. On the very same day, February 18, 1937, the Lake County sheriff and his deputies tried to serve the injunction order on the employees in the plant. Not being able to enter the building, he shoved the injunction order under the door. The company quickly secured a writ of attachment, directing the sit-downers to show cause why they should not be held in contempt of court. The sheriff, with one hundred deputies, again went to the plant to serve the writ. Once again the strikers refused to open the door or to come out. The sheriff attempted to force an entrance, but was met with a barrage of fire extinguishing chemicals, nuts, bolts, and wire reels. After using tear gas, he retreated without serving the papers on the individual sit-downers.

The strikers held possession of the plant for about a week. During this time, they oiled the machinery and kept the plant in good order. Fellow unionists from the outside supplied them with food, stoves, cigarettes, and other necessities. On the 26th of February the sheriff returned to the attack. This time, he added vomiting gas to his arsenal and subdued the strikers. Thirty-seven of them were arrested, tried for contempt in the County Court, convicted and fined from $100 to $300 with terms of 10 to 180 days in jail. Their convictions were appealed but they were sustained by the higher court.

III

The strike, however, continued. About a week after the sit-down ended, the union again asked recognition as bargaining agent. The company again refused, saying that "it was not in the iron, steel or tin business," implying that it would not deal with the Association of Amalgamated Iron, Steel and Tin Workers and that, besides, the union did not represent the company's employees because the strikers were no longer its employees. The company was willing to re-employ the strikers but only as individuals. The company also favored thirty-five of the men who participated in the actual sit-down, and in fact reinstated them to their former jobs and even paid them back pay as of the beginning of the strike. With the aid of these workers and by recruiting new employees, the company resumed operations.

While this dispute was going on, the Supreme Court of the United States, on April 12, 1937, decided that the Wagner Act was constitutional and that, accordingly, an employer was obliged to bargain with the representative of the majority of his workers. Within a few days after this decision, a small group of the Fansteel workers asked the management whether it would bargain collectively with their group. This group was headed by one Berquist, who had not joined the local union during the strike, and by two others, Ted Sylvin and A. R. Johnson, who were hired during the strike. Apparently receiving a favorable reply, a meeting was called to consider the formation of a company union. The Fansteel Corporation cooperated. It permitted the use of its bulletin board for the announcement of the meeting and supplied the committee with mimeographed ballots. The meeting was a success. Two-hundred workers attended and 185 balloted favorably. The ballots were sealed and put into the company's vault and a few days later, on April 19, having received a state charter, the Rare Metals Workers' Union, Local 1, Inc., was born.

The constitution of this new organization forbade affiliation with outside organizations or the conduct of strikes unless directed by 75 per cent vote. It also provided that any worker might bargain with the employer as an individual. Election of officers took place by ballot and these ballots were likewise locked in the company's safe. Within a month after its creation, the Rare Metal Workers' Union, Local 1, Inc., officially requested Fansteel for recognition as the exclusive bargaining agent of its workers. This request, as expected, was granted. Shortly thereafter, on May 25, 1937, the National Labor Relations Board issued a complaint against the Fansteel Metallurgical Corporation, charging it with unfair labor practices under the Wagner Act.

IV

The hearing on the complaint before the National Labor Relations Board trial examiner started in June, 1937. The company denied the charge of unfair labor practices and asked that the case be dismissed. It also argued that, since the Lake County Court had granted the company an injunction against the union the previous February, obviously the court thereby had found that the company was not guilty of any wrongdoing and that, therefore, the board's complaint was without any foundation. The motion was denied by the examiner. About three months later, the trial examiner submitted his intermediate report and recommendations. He found that Fansteel had engaged in unfair labor practices; that the Rare Metal Workers' Union, Local 1, was company dominated; that the discharge of the sit-down strikers, with the exception of ten, was discriminatory and contrary to law. He recommended that an order be issued directing Fansteel to disestablish the company-dominated union, to reinstate the strikers with back pay, and to cease and desist from the practices complained of, and from refusing to bargain with Local 66. In arguing orally before the board, the company contended that it was within its rights in refusing re-employment because these sit-downers were lawbreakers, that they had been discharged and therefore were no longer employees of the company and, besides, that the company was in the process of reorganization and could not employ as many workers as it had previously.

After reargument, the board issued its final order and held, in substance: (a) The criminal conduct of employees who had already been punished by state authority did not make the company less guilty of its violations of the act. (b) The company's refusal to reinstate some participants in the sit-down, while at the same time it rehired other participants and gave them back pay from the beginning of the strike, indicated that the company had not been acting in good faith and that its refusal to rehire the strikers was not because they were lawbreakers, but rather because they were unionists. (c) The strikers were entitled to reinstatement upon request. (d) They were also entitled to loss of pay, from the date of refusal of reinstatement, but not from March 12, 1937, as recommended by the trial examiner. (e) The reorganization contemplated by the company should not be made an excuse for discriminatory discharges and therefore the strikers should be reinstated before the reorganization took place. The company might thereafter proceed with its reorganization without discrimination against union members. (f) The company, upon request, was to bargain with the union. (g) The company was to withdraw all recognition from the Rare Metal Workers' Union of America, Local 1, and disestablish it.

The company refused to comply with the board's order and petitioned for review.

V

Under the title *Fansteel Metallurgical Corporation* v. *National Labor Relations Board*, the company's petition for review came before the United States Circuit Court of Appeals, Seventh Circuit. On July 22, 1938, Judge William M. Sparks (with Judge Walter C. Lindley concurring) delivered the opinion of the court. He held: (1) Substantial evidence in the record supported the board's contention that the company had violated the Wagner Act. (2) However, the record did not show that Local 66 had a majority; hence, there was no evidence to support the charge that the company improperly refused to bargain with that local. (3) The discharges of the sit-downers on February 17, 1937, were justified because the employees by their sit-down had taken the law into their own hands and had rejected their legal remedy—proceedings under the Wagner Act. Since they were properly discharged, they were no longer employees and were not entitled to reinstatement and the union was not entitled to represent them.

Justice Walter E. Treanor dissented. He reasoned: (*a*) The Wagner Act provided for the continuance of the employer-employee relationship during a strike; hence, the sit-downers were employees of the company. (*b*) While in issuing its order the board might take into account the illegal conduct of employees, the board's main concern was with the violation of the Wagner Act by the employer and it was not concerned with the conduct of the employees. (*c*) Since there was substantial evidence of unfair practices by the company, such as refusal to bargain, discrimination against the union by reason of bargaining with individuals during the strike, and discriminatory reinstatements favoring thirty-five sit-downers and refusal to reinstate the others, the board's order was justified and should be upheld.

In accordance with the opinion of the majority, the Circuit Court of Appeals set aside the entire order of the board. The board secured a writ of certiorari from the Supreme Court of the United States for review of this decision.

VI

On February 27, 1939, Chief Justice Hughes, upholding in the main the Circuit Court, delivered the opinion of the Supreme Court on the writ of certiorari. Observing that the principal question before the court was whether the board had authority to order reinstatement of employees discharged because they had engaged in a sit-down strike, he, in substance, held:

One: The company had engaged in unfair practices and its refusal on February 17, 1937, to bargain with the union was an unfair practice.

Two: The discharges of the sit-down strikers on the very first day of the sit-down had been clearly proved. These discharges were justified because the employees, instead of using the remedy provided in the Wagner Act, had engaged in illegal practices. If the court were to confirm the reinstatement order of the board, it would justify the conduct of these sit-downers and would thus put a premium on violence.

Three: Illegal methods had been employed in the conduct of this strike and those who engaged in such methods ceased to be employees entitled to the protection of the Wagner Act.

Four: The company's reinstatement of *some* participants in the sit-down strike did not justify the board in ordering reinstatement of the other sit-downers.

Five: The order of the National Labor Relations Board should be modified so as to provide that the Fansteel Corporation cease and desist from its unfair practices and withdraw recognition from the Rare Metal Workers' Union, Local 1, Inc., as well as disestablish it, but the strikers need not be reinstated. The company need not bargain with Local 66, since there was no basis for the board's order issued March 14, 1938, and no proof that after the plant had resumed operation in March the union represented a majority of Fansteel's employees.

Justice Stone, in a separate opinion, concurred only in part with the majority. He concluded that the board's order directing reinstatement of all strikers was invalid, because the sit-downers had been properly discharged and were no longer employees, but, on the other hand, the fourteen workers who aided and abetted the sit-downers by the supply of food, etc., had not been properly discharged or indeed discharged at all. Therefore, they were employees within the meaning of the act and were entitled to reinstatement.

Justice Stanley Reed (with Justice Black concurring) filed a dissenting opinion. Observing that the real issue, aside from emotional fears of the consequences of giving the workers immunity from their unlawful conduct, was whether striking employees could be discharged during the dispute and thus made ineligible for reinstatement by a board order, he reasoned: (*a*) Under the Wagner Act, strikers continued to be employees, regardless of the lawfulness of their conduct during the strike. Lawlessness was to be taken care of by authorities other than the board. In fact, in this very Fansteel case, the state authorities dealt with the lawlessness of some strikers. (*b*) The majority's reasoning, if extended, would allow the discharge of strikers for any reason. In any strike, a situation might arise which necessarily might result in conduct of employees which normally, except for the strike, would justify a discharge. All strikers, then, under one excuse or another, could be discharged and thus lose their status as employees under the Wagner Act. The Congress did not intend this. (*c*) It was not wise for the Supreme Court to interfere with an administrative body like the National Labor Relations Board in its judgment as to the kind of remedy that is most likely to promote industrial peace in a given situation. (*d*) As both sides in this case had been guilty of wrong, restoration of the situation to what it had been before the wrong occurred on February 17 could not be considered unreasonable and, therefore, the board's order should be sustained as a whole, including the reinstatement of the Fansteel strikers as directed by the board.

While the minority opinions raised important issues, the majority opinion, naturally, prevailed and the board's order was directed to be modified accordingly.

VII

The sensational sit-down weapon boomeranged. The Fansteel strike proved a failure on the economic as well as the legal level. The sit-down failed to yield any benefits to the workers or to the union. In fact, it resulted not only in real immediate economic losses to the workers but also in loss of legal rights, since they lost their status as employees of Fansteel and hence protection under the Wagner Act.

Public opinion generally supported the majority opinion of the court. While a peaceful strike was accepted by the public as a legitimate union economic weapon, the public did not so consider the physical occupation of an employer's property by strikers. The view urged by some union spokesmen that workers have a right in their jobs and, therefore, may hold on to the tools or the factory necessary to preserve those jobs was far removed from the public's idea of employer-employee relationship. The union's position was vulnerable; the public could hardly condone the occupation of a plant to force recognition of the union when there was a legal remedy, the Wagner Act, available.

The decision of the Supreme Court in this case went far to discourage workers and unions from imitating the sensational sit-down strikes staged by the automobile workers during the winter of 1937. Since workers might be discharged for participating in such sit-down strikes and lose their status as employees, no advantages were likely to result from such tactics and the practice of the sit-down was discontinued by unions.

Without justifying the sit-down technique, one may question some phases of the majority's decision in this case. In depriving the sit-downers of their status as employees, the majority of the court applied the old familiar principle of equity that "no one should benefit by his own wrong." Since the sit-downers resorted to "high-handed procedure without shadow of legal right" and illegally took possession of the employer's property, the court would not aid them in benefiting from their wrongful acts. So far so good. The same reasoning apparently guided the majority of the court in concluding that the fourteen workers who had not been directly involved in the occupation of the employer's property, but who had aided and abetted the sit-downers by supplying them with food and other necessities, were participating in and furthering the wrongful acts of the sit-downers and they, too, were not to profit by their own wrong.

While the doctrine that "no one should benefit by his own wrong" is sound ethically, the majority of the Supreme Court did not apply that same doctrine with the same force to the Fansteel Corporation. The record before the court clearly showed that the main object of Fansteel in this case was to prevent collective bargaining with the Amalgamated. For that very purpose, it engaged in various unfair labor practices to undermine the Amalgamated and foster and maintain a company union. In fact, the court sustained the board's findings that Fansteel engaged in unfair labor practices, and upheld that part of the board's order which directed the company to disestablish the company-dominated union; but nevertheless helped the company in successfully carrying out its main unlawful objective —the prevention of collective bargaining. By relieving the company of the obligation of bargaining with the Amalgamated, the court did aid Fansteel to benefit by its own wrong, contrary to the principle it applied against the strikers. Since both sides, workers and employer, acted wrongfully, neither of them should have been enabled to profit by wrongdoing. If the participants in the sit-down strike were to pay the penalty for their wrongdoing, why should not the employer pay a penalty for his?

It might be argued that the order directing Fansteel to disestablish the company union was a sufficient penalty for the company. Those versed in industrial relations will take such reasoning with a grain of salt. Fansteel was interested in the company union only to the extent that it could use it as a tool for prevention of collective bargaining with any "outside" union. To that extent this tool had already served it well. The original union members having been got rid of as a result of the sit-down strike, and the remaining workers having been sufficiently frightened away from the union by the fate of the discharged workers, Fansteel no longer had a need for this tool as a buffer against an "outside" union. Hence, the disestablishment of the company union was no penalty to Fansteel.

It is fair to assume that in arriving at its decision, the court was influenced by the fact that the practice of the sit-down strike was spreading, very likely not without the acquiescence of the unions concerned. The court desired to check the sit-down. For this reason apparently, the court penalized not only the workers who directly participated in the sit-down but also the union, by depriving it of the right to act as the bargaining agency, though the board had found that the union had represented a majority of the workers prior to the sit-down. Thus, the union, too, was brought within the principle that "no one should benefit by his own wrong."

Were the same logic applied with the same force to the company, the decision of the court concerning the company's penalty would have been different. The record is quite clear that prior to the sit-down the company was obligated to bargain with the union in good faith, the union having represented a majority of the workers—155 out of 229. The company's wrong in refusing to bargain and in establishing a company union contributed to the sit-down. It was the company's wrong that helped to bring about the "altered conditions" that deprived the union of representation. All these wrongful acts were for the purpose of evading its duty to bargain collectively. Nevertheless, the court by its decision enabled the company to carry out its main purpose—to defeat collective bargaining. The court's decision was not aimed to discourage employers from maneuvers similar to those employed by Fansteel though the court's decision did aim directly to discourage unions from maneuvering sit-downs. It seems that greater justice would have been achieved if the board had been given wider latitude and permitted to apply a remedy which in its judgment would effectively carry out the purposes of the Wagner Act, and would not permit the company to benefit by its own wrong.

- 17 -

The "Free Speech" Umbrella for Peaceful Picketing

(1939–1940)

THE STATE OF ALABAMA V. BYRON THORNHILL

I

Byron Thornhill saw no significance in the incident. While on the picket line, he merely attempted to persuade a worker of Brown Wood Preserving Company in Brownsville, Alabama, not to return to work during the strike. He had done the same sort of thing on many other occasions. But this, to him insignificant, incident catapulted him to fame in the annals of the struggles of American labor to establish an important legal right. Byron Thornhill achieved the distinction of having the United States Supreme Court enunciate the principle that peaceful picketing by labor was a fundamental right, protected by the constitutional guarantee of freedom of speech.

The incident leading to this decision occurred in the state of Alabama, whose motto is "We dare defend our rights." This state is the leading heavy-industry state in the South. In the nation, it ranks third in iron mining, fourth in lumbering, and eighth in coal mining. While it has developed industrially, the influence of its plantation days may still be felt. Its employers in their industrial relations have transferred the traditional plantation owner's relations with tenants to the factory owner's relations with employees. For many years Alabama practiced the "convict lease" system, by which convicts were hired out to contractors and companies for their work. Since convicts are not free labor, they are easily exploited by employers who hire them from the state.

In many sections of Alabama the "company town" prevailed, particularly in mining and lumbering and also in the steel-making

217

industry. In such company towns the employers ruled with an iron hand. This attitude of the ruling group of Alabama toward labor was reflected in state laws which were designed to protect the employer against "interference by two or more persons to prevent an employer from carrying on his lawful business."

The Alabama Code of Laws, as revised in 1923, provided in Section 3448 that all persons who

without just cause or legal excuse go near or loiter about premises or place of business of any other person . . . with intent of influencing, or inducing other persons not to trade with . . . or who picket the works or place of business of such other persons, firms, corporations or associations of persons for the purpose of hindering, delaying, or interfering with or injuring any lawful business or enterprise of another, shall be guilty of a misdemeanor. . . .

The hangover of plantation days, the convict-lease system, the company-town practice, and the Alabama laws were hardly conducive to the organization of workers into unions. After the inauguration of the New Deal in 1933, labor organizations did come forward. The National Industrial Recovery Act, with its Section 7(a) "guarantee" of collective bargaining stimulated the United Mine Workers to organize the miners in the important Alabama bituminous fields. The workers in some other industries in Alabama also were stimulated to organization. Neither the employers nor the state of Alabama in the early stages of the New Deal invoked Section 3448 of the Alabama Code against organizing workers.

In the year 1936, however, Section 3448 prohibiting picketing was brought into play. A theater owner locked out the stage hands, members of the AFL. The locked-out workers picketed that theater. The picketing was peaceful. A single silent picket paraded in front of the theater bearing a placard reading "This theater does not employ stage hands affiliated with the American Federation of Labor." The picket was arrested and charged with violating Section 3448 of the state code. The picket contended that the law was unconstitutional, but he was found guilty. The Alabama Court of Appeals upheld the law and declared: "No intimation is offered as to what provision of the Constitution is thereby offended and we can think of none."

In spite of this decision, spurred on by the Wagner Act, the union organizational drive penetrated the Tennessee Coal & Iron Company, the Alabama bastion of the steel industry, the stronghold of anti-unionism in America. In 1937, the Steel Workers' Organizing Committee (SWOC) in Alabama contemplated calling a strike against the Tennessee Coal & Iron Company, but that proved unnecessary since a basic settlement was reached between the union and the United States Steel Corporation, parent company of Tennessee Coal & Iron Company. By August, 1937, shortly after the Wagner Act had been declared constitutional by the United States Supreme Court, Alabama had a resolute, growing labor movement.

II

The organizing spirit among the workers of Alabama reached the plant of the Brown Wood Preserving Company, Inc., located at Brownsville, Alabama. This company was engaged in the business of treating lumber with creosote and other solutions to keep it from rotting. It employed about one hundred workers. It maintained housing facilities for the workers, a company store, and other establishments for workers in the town. To all appearances Brownsville was a company town.

In spite of the company-town atmosphere, the workers organized themselves into a union and subsequently went out on strike. They maintained a 24-hour a day picket line at the employees' entrance. For a while the company suspended operations, but then it announced that it would reopen its plant. On the reopening date, Byron Thornhill, who was on the picket line, approached one of the employees who did not belong to the union and asked him not to return to work. Byron Thornhill was subsequently arrested and charged with violation of Section 3448—the antipicketing law—of the Alabama code.

It seemed to be a routine case. The clerk of the Inferior Court of Tuscaloosa County must have called out in his usual manner: "*The People of the State of Alabama* v. *Byron Thornhill*. The defendant is charged with violating Section 3448 of the Alabama Code of Laws. How do you plead—guilty or not guilty?" "Not guilty" was the answer of the attorney for the defendant.

The case then proceeded to trial. The facts were brief, the trial did not take long, and the defendant was found guilty. The sentence was $100 fine or 59 days in jail.

The Alabama State Federation of Labor then took up the fight.

The case was appealed to the Circuit Court of the county, which reversed the judgment but ordered a new trial. The second trial again resulted in a conviction. This time Thornhill was again sentenced to a fine of $100 and costs, but in default of payment of the fine, to 73 days in jail. Again an appeal was taken to the Circuit Court of the county.

III

The issue became the constitutional right to peaceable assemblage and free speech. For the purpose of testing this law, the attorneys for Thornhill demurred to the complaint and moved to exclude testimony concerning the violation of Section 3448 on the ground that this section was unconstitutional. Judge Henry B. Foster of the Circuit Court of Tuscaloosa County did not rule on the demurrer, but overruled the motion to exclude testimony concerning the violation of the section. In other words, he held that the section was not unconstitutional.

The case was then carried to the Alabama Court of Appeals. James J. Mayfield, attorney for the union, attacked the statute as in violation of the constitutional right of free speech. The state representatives defended the conviction and cited the precedents of previous decisions in Alabama which had held the law constitutional.

On January 17, 1939, Judge James Rice delivered the opinion of the court. He held that the evidence cited against the defendant was sufficient to bring his acts under the statute; that the statute must be held to be constitutional because the Alabama Supreme Court had so held it in two previous cases, and that that holding was binding upon his court. Hence the court must affirm the Thornhill conviction.

An application was then made for a rehearing but was denied on May 23, 1939. The defendant then applied to the Alabama Supreme Court for a writ of certiorari to have the judgment reviewed and revised, but the court denied this application. At this point, at the request of the Alabama State Federation of Labor, the American Federation of Labor entered the legal battle. The issue of free speech as it may affect the right of peaceful picketing was too important for the labor movement to let it go without challenge in the highest court of the land. An appeal was therefore taken to the Supreme Court of the United States.

IV

On December 11, 1939, the high court granted a petition for a writ of certiorari and on February 29, 1940, the case of *Thornhill* v. *Alabama* was argued before the Supreme Court of the United States. The union attorneys were Joseph A. Padway, general counsel for the AFL, and James J. Mayfield, attorney for the Alabama local unions. Their main contention was that Section 3448 of the Alabama code violates the rights of the individual to free speech guaranteed by the Constitution of the United States, and that therefore any conviction thereunder must be set aside.

The State of Alabama was represented by William H. Loeb and Thomas S. Lawson. They contended that:

(*a*) Freedom of speech and assembly were not absolute rights and that the state, as a matter of public policy, had the power to place restrictions on the use thereof; (*b*) the pickets were stationed to injure the company, not to advance their own interests. The intent to injure another by the exercise of lawful rights made that exercise an unlawful act, as appeared from the Supreme Court's decision in the case of *Gompers* v. *Bucks Stove and Range Company*; (*c*) Thornhill was a member of a relatively large picket line which was not peaceful "but an offensive and unjustifiable annoyance calculated to bring about public disturbance and breaches of peace;" (*d*) the petitioner could not assail as unconstitutional a statute which did not bar him from striking or presenting his case but merely from committing acts inherently wrong.

The Supreme Court squarely met the issue of free speech raised in the case and reversed the conviction in a decision rendered on April 22, 1940. The opinion was delivered by Justice Frank Murphy, who stated that the Supreme Court had granted a writ of certiorari "because of the importance of the question." He observed that the record in the case showed neither the nature of the dispute nor the events leading to the calling of the strike, nor whether efforts were made at conciliation, but did show that the picket Thornhill made no threats and did not "look mad" to the nonunion worker whom he had requested not to go to work.

In applying the law to the case, the court emphasized the following essential principles:

One: Freedom of speech and the press were fundamental rights secured by the First and Fourteenth Amendments. Their safeguarding was essential to free government.

Two: This Alabama statute lent itself to harsh and discriminatory enforcement by local prosecuting officials, against particular groups deemed to merit their displeasure. This fact in itself might result in a continuous and pervasive restraint on all freedom of discussion that might reasonably be regarded as within its purview.

Three: The freedom of speech and the press guaranteed by the Constitution embraced at least the liberty to discuss peacefully and truthfully all matters of public concern without previous restraint or fear of subsequent punishment. This statute was not less pernicious than the restraint on freedom of discussion imposed by the threat of censorship.

Four: In the circumstances of our times, the dissemination of information concerning the facts of a labor dispute must be regarded as within the area of free discussion guaranteed by the Constitution.

Five: Labor relations were not merely a local or private concern. While the state might set the limits of economic battle, it "does not follow that the State in dealing with the evils arising from industrial disputes may impair the effective right to discuss freely industrial relations which are matters of public concern."

Six: Safeguarding the means by which employees and others could inform the public of the "nature and causes of a labor dispute" was "essential to the securing of an informed and educated public opinion with respect to a matter which is of public concern." Every expression of opinion might cause action favorable to one rather than to another group. "But the group in power at any moment may not impose penal sanctions on peaceful and truthful discussion of public matters merely on a showing that others may be thereby persuaded to take action inconsistent with its interests."

Seven: The danger of injury to an industrial concern was not serious or imminent enough to warrant "the sweeping proscription of freedom of discussion embodied in Section 3448." A clear and present danger to the peace was not inherent in every picket's appearance.

Since the Alabama law was declared unconstitutional, the conviction of Byron Thornhill was set aside.

V

The insignificant incident of Thornhill's conversation with a worker urging him to join the strikers resulted in establishing one of the fundamental rights for organized labor, namely, peaceful picketing. The court held that peaceful picketing was a form of peaceful speech, freedom of which was guaranteed by the Constitution of the United States. Hence, no laws of a state could abridge it. The right to picket peacefully and publicize a labor dispute to win public support was established as a matter of *basic right* under the Constitution, without fear that a state law would prohibit it.

Until the decision in the Thornhill case, the legality of peaceful picketing depended upon the law in each state; it was not deemed to have been protected under the Constitution of the United States. Only three years before the Thornhill case, the Supreme Court of the United States, by a majority, had so held in the case of *Senn* v. *Tile Layers' Protective Union* (Chapter 14). In that case the court found that the state of Wisconsin was within its right to enact legislation permitting peaceful picketing. The minority of the court contended that the state had no right to legalize picketing just as it had no right to legalize libel or assault and battery because such law deprived property owners of their protection under the due process clause of the Fourteenth Amendment to the Constitution of the United States. Even the majority opinion by Justice Brandeis in the *Senn* case implied that the state possibly could prohibit, as it could legalize, peaceful picketing.

But in the Thornhill case, for the first time in the history of American jurisprudence, the highest court in the land clearly enunciated that peaceful picketing, publicizing labor's side of an industrial controversy, was a fundamental right, guaranteed to all individuals as part of the Bill of Rights.

As a result of the decision in the Thornhill case, California and Oregon laws similar to the Alabama statute were declared unconstitutional, and for the first time in forty years the Michigan Supreme Court, which had heretofore held that picketing was unlawful under common law, modified its view and declared peaceful picketing lawful.

While the Thornhill decision seemed definitely to hold that, under the Constitution, peaceful picketing could not be prohibited either by the states or by the courts thereof, subsequent decisions of the Supreme Court show that the court departed from its original holding.

Thus, the court sustained an injunction issued by the Illinois Supreme Court in the case of *Milk Wagon Drivers' Union* v. *Meadomoor Dairies, Inc.*, prohibiting *all* picketing, on the ground that the Illinois court concluded that the violence of the strike convinced it that future picketing if allowed was not likely to be peaceful. Similarly, in the case of *Bakery and Pastry Drivers Union* v. *Wohl*, though the court set aside the injunction issued against the union by the New York courts on the ground that there was a denial of free speech, Justice Jackson, writing for the majority, said: "A State is not required to tolerate in all places and all circumstances even peaceful picketing by an individual." This remark prompted Justice Douglas for the minority to say: "If the opinion in this case means that a state can prohibit picketing when it is effective, but may not prohibit it when it is ineffective, then I think we have made a basic departure from *Thornhill* v. *Alabama*." In another case, *Carpenters' and Joiners' Union* v. *Ritter's Cafe*, the Supreme Court, in a majority opinion, delivered by Justice Frankfurter, held that the Texas court was within its rights to limit the picketing to that "directly related to the dispute." Since the carpenters' dispute with Ritter concerned construction of a building having nothing to do with his restaurant, the Supreme Court held that the injunction issued by the Texas courts against peaceful picketing by these carpenters of Ritter's restaurant—which business was not involved in the dispute—was not in violation of the carpenters' rights to free speech.

The conclusion to be drawn from all these cases is that the Supreme Court has departed from its original decision in the *Thornhill* v. *Alabama* case. While peaceful picketing is still as a matter of law protected under the free speech doctrine, its application has been narrowed by the subsequent decisions of the court and consequently the opportunities of the states to place restrictions on picketing have been broadened.

- 18 -

The Sherman Act in Modern Dress

(1937–1940)

APEX HOSIERY COMPANY v. LEADER

I

For many years, union organization in the textile industry in the United States had been more spectacular than solid. There were strikes but little stable collective bargaining. The most stabilized local unions in the industry were in specific and rather specialized crafts, such as bleaching and dyeing and the production of full-fashioned hosiery.

In 1901 the United Textile Workers of America, the first national textile organization, was formed. Its achievements long remained meager. The great textile workers' uprising of 1912 in Lawrence, Massachusetts, and the later strikes of the Paterson silk workers were led by dissident and radical groups like the Industrial Workers of the World (IWW) rather than by the national union in the industry. In the period 1916-1919, the United Textile Workers of America showed strength. It actually won the 48-hour week in the northern mills of the industry and made some gains in the South. But during the deflation of 1920-1921, following World War I, it lost its few gains in the South and in 1922 it failed in its strikes in New England.

Labor conditions in textile mills again deteriorated, particularly in the South, where long hours, low wages, "the stretch-out system" (increasing the number of machines a worker was required to tend) were the rule by 1929-1930. A desperate outburst of strikes followed. Southern textile workers struck in Carolina cotton towns, notably Gastonia and Marion, and in rayon centers like Elizabethton, Tennessee. The strikes were crushed by the sweeping use of injunctions, militia, and physical force. After the defeat of these desperate depression strikes, the work week was lengthened, the stretch-out became more severe, and union organizations all but disappeared. Union defeats in the South adversely affected labor conditions in the North. Efforts of textile workers in New England, New Jersey, Pennsylvania, and New York to secure something approaching a living wage were defeated by the mere threat of moving the factories to the South.

II

The enactment of the National Industrial Recovery Act (NIRA) in 1933, with its "guarantee" of workers' rights to organize and have representatives of "their own choosing," stimulated unionism in the textile field. On August 30, 1934, 400,000 workers responded to the call of the United Textile Workers for an industry-wide strike. The strike lasted twenty-two days, with the result that the National Recovery Administration finally designated a special textile industrial relations board to inquire into labor conditions in textile manufacturing.

When the Supreme Court invalidated NIRA, the United Textile Workers lost members and a great deal of strength. However, the dyers and hosiery workers, who were affiliated with the United Textile Workers and had had their own autonomous organizations since 1913, continued to function effectively. Their crafts' superior skill and their longer experience in organization gave them an advantage over the newer recruits to unionism in the other branches of the textile industry.

During 1935-1937, a new organizational factor was making itself felt on the American economic scene. A number of unions formed the Committee for Industrial Organization for the ostensible purpose of organizing the workers engaged in the mass production industries on an industrial scale. Although these unions were expelled from the American Federation of Labor in November, 1936, this newly formed CIO achieved spectacular organization successes in the automobile and steel industries in 1937. The hosiery workers benefited markedly from both the new attitude toward unionism under the New Deal and the changed political climate in Pennsylvania, center of hosiery production. Thus, between September, 1936, and February, 1937, the Reading hosiery district was organized under the banner of the American Federation of Hosiery Workers. In

March, 1937, a Textile Workers' Organizing Committee (CIO) was formed. Various unions, like the Amalgamated Clothing Workers' Union, the International Ladies' Garment Workers' Union, and the Steel Workers' Organizing Committee contributed substantial sums of money for this organization campaign.

Most of the Philadelphia plants making full-fashioned hosiery were organized and had contracts with the American Federation of Hosiery Workers, but not the Apex Manufacturing Company, which employed about 2,500 workers. In April, 1937, William Leader, president of Local 706 of the Hosiery Workers, communicated with the Apex Company, requesting that it enter into a collective agreement with the union, but the firm ignored the request. The union then planned to stage a "demonstration" on May 6 in front of the Apex plant. The management got wind of it and sent the workers home at noon that day. However, that very afternoon a large crowd assembled before the Apex plant. Mr. Leader, the president of the local union, was with the crowd and requested to see Mr. Meyer, head of the Apex firm, but Meyer refused to see him at this time, though he offered to meet him later in the office of the company's attorney. When Inspector LaRue, of the Philadelphia police, conveyed this message to Leader, who was then on the front steps of the plant, Leader loudly said: "I declare a sit-down strike in Apex Hosiery Company."

His statement was followed by direct action. Bricks were tossed into the windows of the plant, doors were battered down, and the company offices were invaded. Meyer appealed to Leader to halt the disorder. Leader, in turn, asked him to sign an agreement. Meyer refused. Then a group of unionists, already gathered inside the plant, organized a sit-down strike. They brought in food and cots and announced their intention to hold possession until Apex concluded an agreement with the union. The strikers refused to admit maintenance workers or to allow the shipment of finished goods on hand. The police appear to have remained neutral. The strikers remained in the plant for about six weeks.

III

On June 5, 1937, the Apex Company brought suit and applied for a preliminary injunction to the Federal Court for the Eastern District of Pennsylvania. The motion for the injunction came up before Judge William G. Kirkpatrick. In denying the motion, the judge summarized the facts leading to the action:

Apex was engaged in the making of hosiery. On May 6, it had $600,000 worth of stockings ready for shipment in interstate commerce. On the day the trouble began "a mob of some 10,000 people" gathered in front of plaintiff's business, invaded the premises, damaged the office furniture and machinery, and threatened the "few unarmed and defenseless employees who were found on the premises." The defendants named in the complaint had entered with the mob and fetched in "cots and other equipment for a sit-down strike." However, it had not been proved that these defendants personally took any direct part in the violence. After the mob had finally drifted out, union members remained in the plant and "proceeded to occupy it." They excluded the plaintiff, its agents, and employees from entering the plant except as permitted by the defendants, and the result of the sit-down strike was a complete stoppage of production and a complete paralysis of all the plaintiff's business operations.

Although police officers had been present during the outbreak of May 6, they made no effort to interfere with the defendants. That conduct might have been the result of orders from superiors, or because of "the size and temper of the mob, they might have felt that such action would have been futile and dangerous to themselves." Later appeals to the police by the plaintiff received no response.

Judge Kirkpatrick declared that the occupation of the plant constituted a "continuing trespass and a flagrant violation of the law of the State of Pennsylvania." However, he denied the motion for the injunction on the ground that the Federal Court lacked jurisdiction in the case as no diversity of citizenship was shown, the plaintiff and the defendants being citizens of the same state. In rendering his opinion the judge considered various contentions of the plaintiff to the effect that jurisdiction was conferred by the Sherman Antitrust Act, but concluded that the evidence did not warrant a finding that it was the defendants' "purpose or intent to restrain or control" the supply of goods in interstate commerce; all the direct evidence as to the purpose of the defendants went to show that it was solely to compel the plaintiff by means of an indefinite suspension of manufacturing, and consequent financial loss, to accept the closed shop. Pointing out that "the Federal Court's jurisdiction is not enlarged by the illegality of the strike," the court not only denied the motion for a preliminary injunction but also dismissed the bill of complaint.

IV

This decision in the case of *Apex Hosiery Company* v. *Leader, et al.* was appealed by the company to the Circuit Court of Appeals for the Third Circuit.

Justice J. Warren Davis, on behalf of the Circuit Court, handed down the opinion on June 21, 1937. After recounting the facts, Judge Davis said that the underlying question was, may "a few lawless individuals," in defiance of law and order and in ruthless disregard of the rights of others, by assuming the name of a "union," deprive all others of their means of livelihood and compel them to contribute of their earnings, to self-styled leaders? The sole question to be decided, Judge Davis continued, was whether the acts of the defendants had so burdened or obstructed the plaintiff's materials and products from entering the stream of commerce as to constitute "restraint of trade" under the Sherman Act.

He held that the seizure of the plaintiff's factory did not merely burden the free flow of commerce but "absolutely stopped and dammed it up." He further held that, since there was a combination or conspiracy to restrain interstate commerce, that alone was sufficient to give jurisdiction to the federal courts, and that there had been a combination and conspiracy by the defendants, who had held back the shipment of finished goods. Taking up the defendants' argument that it was necessary to *prove intent* to restrain commerce, the judge held that such intent, "however, is necessarily to be *inferred* from the acts of the conspirators ... None of these defendants would have the temerity to deny that he was a member of a conspiracy."

Continuing with his decision, the judge said that the defendants argued that their aim was not to restrain commerce but to force acceptance of a closed shop; that the unlawful acts were only a means to an end and did not constitute a conspiracy in restraint of interstate commerce. To this the judge replied that the ultimate object of securing an agreement did not exculpate the defendants from violating the Sherman Act; the defendants knew that the company's raw materials came from outside Pennsylvania; they knew when they seized the factory and halted its operation and refused to allow

$600,000 worth of goods to be shipped that "they were restraining trade and the free flow of interstate commerce. This restraint of trade was a necessary and direct consequence of their acts and they must be held to have intended it." Judge Davis directed that the decree of the District Court be reversed, the bill of complaint be reinstated, and the injunction be granted; the defendants were to vacate the property and restore it to the plaintiff.

This decision was taken by the union to the Supreme Court of the United States on a petition for a writ of certiorari. An opinion *per curiam* was handed down by the court on December 13, 1937. It granted the petition for the writ and reversed the decree of the Circuit Court of Appeals. Since the sit-down had ended, there was no need for an injunction and the case was remanded to the District Court with instructions to vacate the injunction and dismiss the bill of complaint on the ground that the cause was "moot."

V

In the meantime, the Apex Company had brought an action for damages under the antitrust laws in the Federal District Court for the Eastern District of Pennsylvania. The suit named William Leader and the American Federation of Full-Fashioned Hosiery Workers (known as the American Federation of Hosiery Workers), Philadelphia Branch No. 1, Local 706, and others, as defendants.

The company was successful. The jury found that only the defendant union and Leader individually were guilty of violating the federal antitrust laws. Damages were set at $237,210.85 and trebled, under the Sherman law, to $711,932.55.

The judgment was appealed by the union and Leader to the Circuit Court of Appeals for the Third Circuit.

The importance of the case attracted the attention of many labor lawyers, especially because it provided the first opportunity since the New Deal to review the application of the Sherman Antitrust Act to labor unions.

On November 29, 1939, Judge Biggs delivered the opinion of the Circuit Court. In reviewing the facts he pointed out that during the sit-down, the company was not permitted to ship 134,000 dozen pairs of finished hosiery to its out-of-state customers, that machinery was damaged, that admission was refused to maintenance men, and that "judicial condemnation of such tactics cannot be too severe." However, he said, the fundamental question was: Did the defendants violate the federal antitrust laws and "was the damage suffered by the appellee the proximate result of such violation"?

After making references to the pertinent portions of the Sherman Act, that "every contract, combination or conspiracy in restraint of trade or commerce . . . is illegal . . ." to the fact that the Clayton Act declared that "labor was not a commodity," and to the fact that the antitrust laws were not to be construed as forbidding labor organizations, Judge Biggs declared that, according to established law, in cases of *conspiracy in restraint of trade*, unions might not escape by appealing to Section 6 of the Clayton Act.

He concluded, however, that in the *Apex* case there was no conspiracy to restrain commerce, the intent of the defendants was merely to unionize the plant, "an action local in motive and local in effect." He observed that the business of the Apex Company was less than 1 per cent of the industry's output. Therefore, "the combination was not such that by reason of the intent of the conspirators or the inherent nature of their acts public interest was prejudiced by unduly restricting competition or obstructing trade." Hence, the appellants were not guilty of violating the Sherman Act although they refused to let goods be shipped. Since the union did not *intend* "to restrain commerce or to affect prices within the industry" but merely intended to organize the Apex plant, the trial judge should have directed a verdict for the defendants.

Meeting the contention that the Circuit Court of Appeals had already held that the defendants were guilty of a conspiracy, Judge Biggs took the occasion to point out that the Circuit Court at the time had made two errors: (1) it had interpreted the term "commerce" in the Sherman Act as broadly as that term was used in the Wagner Act, overlooking the fact that the Wagner Act was applicable to all cases in which interstate commerce was *affected*, while the Sherman Act was limited and was applicable only to cases in which interstate commerce was actually *restrained to an unreasonable degree*; (2) it had concluded "that because the appellants committed unlawful acts they were therefore guilty of a conspiracy in restraint of trade," but such a conclusion was erroneous. The correct test was not whether the defendants committed unlawful acts, but rather "whether a combination or conspiracy was formed by them with the intent to restrain commerce." If such a conspiracy had been formed, the Sherman Act was violated, even though that conspiracy was carried out by legal and peaceful means. Since the decree in the injunction proceedings had been dismissed as moot, it was vacated and hence no longer the law of the case. In any event, in view of the errors pointed out, this Circuit Court as then constituted would have overruled the previous decision on the ground that the Sherman Act was not applicable to this case. Accordingly, the judgment of the lower court was reversed.

The company appealed to the Supreme Court of the United States.

VI

The case of *Apex Hosiery Company* v. *Leader, et al.*, was argued before the Supreme Court in April, 1940.

The attorney for Apex contended:

(*a*) The Sherman Act had been applied to labor unions for the past fifty years despite repeated contentions of their representatives that it was not applicable.

(*b*) In numerous cases, the Supreme Court had held that when, pursuant to a conspiracy, unions engaged in unlawful acts which restrained or obstructed the free flow of interstate commerce, they were subject to the penalties of the Sherman Act.

(*c*) In enacting and sustaining the National Labor Relations Act, Congress and the court recognized that a stoppage in a single plant might *directly* burden and restrain commerce.

(*d*) Even if the interference with manufacturing operations had only an *indirect* effect on commerce, the wrongful prevention of interstate *shipment* of goods on hand constituted a direct restraint.

(*e*) Besides, once the *intent* of the defendants to restrain commerce had been shown, it was not material whether the restraint on commerce was of a direct or an indirect character.

(*f*) The Circuit Court erred when it held that the law was not violated because no large portion of the hosiery trade was affected. Never before had the court applied the "rule of reason" to the "unlawful activities of a labor union." Even if the rule of reason were applied, the restraint on commerce in this case was not reasonable.

The attorneys for the union argued:

1. The Sherman Act did not apply to labor unions. The terms "contract, combination and conspiracy in restraint of trade" in the

Sherman Act were intended to be used in their common-law meaning, and that meaning did not include the relation of unions to employers.

2. The Congressional debates established the intent to exclude labor unions from the purview of the act. The court erred in its original decision in *Loewe* v. *Lawlor* [the *Danbury Hatters* case], when it applied the Sherman Act to labor unions. Besides, when one considered the history of the period preceding the enactment of the Clayton Act, the general trend of debate in Congress, and its legislative history, the conclusion must be that Congress meant to undo the verdict of the court in the *Danbury Hatters* case. Hence, the court should overrule its previous decisions in which it applied the Sherman Act to labor unions.

3. Moreover, even if the Sherman Act were applicable to labor unions, the respondents had not violated it. Theirs was a local strike, not part of a conspiracy aimed at interstate commerce, nor initiated with intent to monopolize supply or fix the price of an article moving in interstate commerce.

4. Intent to restrain commerce was neither alleged nor proved in this case. There had been concerted action to organize the Apex plant; the jury actually found only intent to conduct a sit-down strike, not intent to restrain interstate commerce. In so far as plaintiff's damages were concerned, the remedy must lie in an action in the state courts for trespass.

5. In upholding the power of Congress to enact the National Labor Relations Act, the Supreme Court did not broaden the definition of the term "commerce" in the Sherman Act, so as to bring labor unions further under its dominion. The Congress, by the National Labor Relations Act, wished labor to have an effective right to collective bargaining. Strikes and boycotts were often needed to secure such bargaining power. If, on the one hand, employees were given by Congress the right to organize and to strike—which meant interference with production—how could it be said that Congress, on the other hand, intended that the success of a strike in halting such production should bring the unions under the Sherman Act and thus deprive them of the opportunity of successful organization?

6. The Circuit Court of Appeals was not in error when it held that a *substantial* amount of commerce must be affected to constitute a violation of the Sherman Act.

7. The illegality of the means used was wholly immaterial in so far as the applicability of the Sherman Act was concerned.

On May 27, 1940, the court rendered its decision. The Supreme Court split wide open—six to three—on the scope and the applicability of the Sherman Act to this case. Justice Harlan Fiske Stone delivered the opinion for the majority and Chief Justice Charles Evans Hughes for the minority.

In a searching and painstaking opinion, Justice Stone considered various principles guiding the application of the Sherman Act to labor unions. He reviewed in some detail the decisions of the Supreme Court previously rendered, in which it held that the Sherman Act was applicable to labor unions, but he distinguished each of them from the *Apex* case. The court's efforts were bent on showing *consistency* between these previous decisions and the conclusion it reached that the Sherman law should not be applicable to the *Apex* case. Mr. Justice Stone reviewed the facts as found by the lower court. The pertinent points of Justice Stone's opinion were:

One: While the union's conduct in the *Apex* case was to be condemned as tortious and criminal under the laws of Pennsylvania, the only legal question to be decided on this appeal was whether the record "establishes a restraint of trade or commerce which the Sherman Act condemns."

Two: The court must regard the question whether labor unions were to some extent and in some circumstances subject to the Sherman Act as settled in the affirmative. It was equally plain that this court had never thought the act to apply to *all* labor union activities affecting interstate commerce. Under the Constitution, Congress, if it so wished, had power to pass legislation prohibiting such union activities as interfered with *production affecting* interstate commerce, but in enacting the Sherman Act it had not done so. The "critical" words of that law were "combination or conspiracy in restraint of trade or commerce." The precise question in this case was whether the restraint on commerce resulting from shutting down production because of the strike, maintained for the purpose of enforcing union demands, was the kind of "restraint of trade or commerce" that the Sherman Act condemned.

Three: The history and application of the act must be taken into account: (1) The law was not aimed at policing the interstate movement of goods and property. There was no lack of existing law to protect against evils ascribed to organized labor. The Sherman Act was the product of an era of trusts and combinations of business and capital organized and directed to control the market by suppression of competition *in the marketing* of goods and services, the monopolistic tendency of which had become a matter of public concern. (2) The end sought by the law was the prevention of such "restraints to free competition" as tended to restrict production, raise prices, or "otherwise *control the market* to the detriment of purchasers or consumers of goods and services." (3) The phrase "restraint of trade" used in the act was intended to prohibit activities which fell under the understood meaning of the term "trade" at common law. "This Court has . . . repeatedly recognized that the restraints, at which the Sherman law is aimed, and which are described by its terms, are only those which are comparable to restraints deemed illegal at common law . . ." Congress had embodied the common-law doctrine in relation to activities like suppression of competition, restriction of production, price fixing, division of customers—restraint of trade —in legislation.

Four: The court never applied the Sherman Act unless it believed there was some form of restraint upon commercial competition in the *marketing* of goods and services. The court refused to apply the Sherman Law in instances where the shipment of products in interstate commerce was prevented by a local strike conducted by illegal means but in which it was not shown that the restraint on shipments had operated to restrain commercial competition in some *substantial* way.

Five: The labor organization was not being used as a means of suppressing competition or fixing prices or restraining the market for the Apex Company's goods. The combination intended "to compel the petitioner to accede to the union demands" and an *effect* of that was "the prevention of the removal of the petitioner's product for interstate commerce." The delay of these shipments was not intended to have and had no effect on prices of hosiery *in the market* and so was in that respect not forbidden by the Sherman Act.

Six: Combinations of employees necessarily "restrain competition among themselves in the sale of their services to the employer," yet such a combination was not considered an illegal restraint when the Sherman Act was adopted. With the enactment of Section 6 of the Clayton Antitrust Act, "it would seem plain that restraints on the sale of the employee's services to the employer, however much they curtail the competition among employees, are not in themselves combinations or conspiracies in restraint of trade or commerce under the Sherman Act."

Seven: Strikes to compel employers to yield certain conditions of employment "may restrict to some extent the power of employers who are parties to the dispute to compete in the market with those not subject to such demands." But in other cases—nonlabor cases— this court had held that the "mere fact of such restrictions on competition does not in itself bring the parties to the agreement within the condemnation of the Sherman Act."

Eight: Successful union activity might have "some effect on price competition by eliminating that part of such competition which is based on differences in labor standards." Such was the objective of any national labor organization, but it was not considered the kind of curtailment of *price competition* prohibited by the Sherman Act. In any case, the restraint in this case had not been shown "to have any actual or intended effect on price or price competition."

Nine: Federal laws for labor standards and the protection of the right to organize "clearly recognize that combinations of workers eliminating competition among themselves and restricting competition among their employers based on wage cutting are not contrary to public policy."

Ten: Secondary boycotts were held to be restraints of trade within the meaning of the Sherman Act because the court viewed the activities directed against the use of goods by consumers offensive at common law by reason of its effect in curtailing a free market. The restraint operated to suppress competition *in the market.* A local factory strike, however, merely interfered with shipments, not necessarily with prices in the market. The court had previously declared that in order to interpret unlawful interference with manufacturing as a result of a local strike as restraint of trade, the interference must be such as to make those responsible for it able to monopolize the supply, control the price, or discriminate between purchasers of a commodity.

Eleven: The Sherman Act was not a means of policing interstate commerce or giving a remedy for wrongs actionable under state laws, but a means *to protect the market.* If, regardless of effect on the market, the court were to hold that a local strike halting production and interstate shipment violated this act, "practically every strike in modern industry would be brought within the jurisdiction of the federal courts, under the Sherman Act, to remedy local law violation." The act and Supreme Court decisions under it did not permit that.

Twelve: Moreover, it was important to maintain the federal-state balance "of police authority and of remedies, private and public, for public wrongs." Restraints not within the act, when achieved by peaceful means, were not brought within its sweep because, without other differences, they were attended by violence.

Justice Stone concluded his opinion by affirming the judgment of the Circuit Court of Appeals for the Third Circuit, and thus the award of triple damages against the union was reversed.

Chief Justice Charles Evans Hughes (with Justices Roberts and McReynolds concurring) vigorously dissented. He argued that the majority opinion in effect overruled previous decisions of the court regarding the application of the Sherman Act to labor cases. In substance he contended: (*a*) In the *Apex* case there was "direct and intentional prevention of interstate commerce in the furtherance of an illegal conspiracy." (*b*) The majority opinion made the Sherman Act more uncertain than ever and seemed to determine "definitely" that "a conspiracy of workers or others, to obstruct or prevent the shipment or delivery of goods in interstate commerce, does not violate" the antitrust law. (*c*) The Sherman Act applies to labor unions; Sections 6 and 20 of the Clayton Act exempted none but peaceful and lawful activities. (*d*) The rule of reason was to be tested by effects, not motives. The purpose of respondents to promote the interests of labor organization could not be deemed to justify the direct and intentional restraint they imposed upon interstate commerce. (*e*) The court had always held conspiracies to obstruct interstate commerce or which had such obstruction *as a result* to come under the ban of the Sherman Act. (*f*) Previous decisions in labor cases showed that the Supreme Court had not held "restraint of trade" limited to *market control* but comprehending all illegal means to restrain interstate commerce. (*g*) If the shipment of goods was not protected, it was useless to outlaw boycotts or assure a free market. In the second *Coronado* case, when the shipment of coal was obstructed, commerce was declared affected and the purpose of the strike was found not material. The untrammeled movement of goods was protected by the Sherman Act. (*h*) The National Labor Relations Act was passed to safeguard free movement of goods in interstate commerce. Since industrial strife caused by denial of collective bargaining rights hindered the flow of goods, Congress prohibited employers from denying it. It was "anomalous" for the court to bind employers by the NLRA because interstate commerce might be affected and not to call a "direct and intentional obstruction or prevention" of the shipment of goods by employees "a restraint of interstate commerce under the broad terms of the Sherman Act." (*i*) The right to quit work, to persuade others *peaceably*, "to proceed by lawful measures within the contemplation of the Clayton Act to attain the legitimate objects of labor organization, is to my mind quite a different matter from a conspiracy directly and intentionally to prevent the shipment of goods in interstate commerce either by their illegal seizure for that purpose, or by the direct and intentional obstruction of their transportation or by blocking the highways of interstate commerce."

VII

The majority decision in the *Apex* case gave organized labor its long-sought breathing spell after a half century of harassment by the Sherman Act. While this decision did not "amend it or end it" as called for by Samuel Gompers's slogan, the act was reinterpreted by the court in such a way as to lift the onus of "restraint of trade" from basic union activities.

Despite Justice Stone's admonition that labor unions were to some extent and in some circumstances subject to the Sherman Act, his opinion severely limited the extent to which the act might be applied to normal labor activities. Illegal means used in connection with a strike were no longer to serve as an excuse to widen the term "commerce among the several states" as used in the act. The phrase "restraint of trade" in the act was to be limited to its original meaning under common law, which was *restraint of market conditions* by those in a position to control the market through control of supply of goods and prices. There was no ambiguity in the court's pronouncement that the act was aimed at prohibiting combinations which sought to eliminate *market competition*—through control of supply of goods and prices—but not to prohibit labor unions from seeking to eliminate competition to themselves from nonunion-made goods. Such competition was not intended to be included in the term "market competition."

Justice Stone realized that, since collective bargaining had been declared to be the public policy of the land, it inevitably must follow that labor unions must not be deprived of the opportunity to exercise normal labor activities to bring about collective bargaining and that strikes were such normal labor activities. The court also realized that in the process of collective bargaining unions must seek uniform standards of labor conditions. The achievement of such leveling of labor conditions must mean the removal of price competition based on wages and other working conditions and would be a proper objective of any national labor organization. Standardization of *working conditions* was not rigging of prices nor standardization of *market prices*. Justice Stone concluded that "this effect on competition has not been considered to be the kind of curtailment of price competition prohibited by the Sherman Act" and curtailment of production as a result of labor disputes did not fall under the act.

Secondary boycotts, however, according to Justice Stone, must be viewed differently. They offend against the Sherman Act. He reasoned that such boycotts, being directed at consumers for the purpose of curtailment of the use of goods in the free market, were *market restraints*. He drew a delicate distinction between these two methods—the strike and the secondary boycott—though they might be aimed at accomplishing the same end. He conceded the right of unions to seek by strikes to eliminate competition from nonunion-made goods, based on the difference in labor standards, but prohibited the elimination of the same competition from nonunion-made goods based on the same difference in labor standards brought about by means of secondary boycotts.

This legalistic distinction made by the court is highly debatable. Since unions are within their rights to seek collective bargaining and, if necessary, to bring it about by means of a strike, why shouldn't these unions be within their rights to accomplish the same end—collective bargaining—by means of a peaceful appeal to other workers not to process a struck product? Since unions may strike for the purpose of achieving collective bargaining and the elimination of nonunion competition with their labor conditions, why shouldn't these unions have the right to achieve the same objectives by a peaceful appeal for cooperation to fellow unionists or to a sympathetic public not to patronize the struck product? Whether interstate commerce is affected as a result of an appeal to the public by strikers not to patronize a product or whether it is affected as a result of a strike which dries up the product at its production source is a distinction without a real difference.

The majority of the court apparently was desirous of remaining *consistent* and of preserving the court's previous decisions in applying the Sherman Act to labor cases while at the same time harmonizing the act with the spirit of the times as exemplified in the social legislation that characterized the New Deal. The latter compelled the majority of the court to dress up the Sherman Act in modern clothes and to declare that normal labor activities essential for securing collective bargaining were not to be deemed within the prohibition of the Sherman Act. The very underlying principles that logically led the majority of the court to free such normal labor activities from the Sherman Act would have justified the court in extending these principles to labor's peaceful appeals for co-operation of fellow workers and for public sympathy. Logically, these same principles would have justified the court in reversing its previous holding against labor unions outlawing peaceful secondary boycott activities. The court, however, declined to go that far, apparently fearing the consequences of the unbridled use by unions of such an economic weapon as the secondary boycott.

The majority decision, however, did cut away some of the artificial barriers imposed on labor theretofore by the unwarranted interpretations of the Sherman Act. The court did take cognizance of the social changes and of the industrial development in the past half century. It should be added that, although the court greatly reduced the applicability of the Sherman Act against labor, nevertheless the act, with all its uncertainties and vagueness, still remains a threat to labor. Admittedly, for half a century, it was prejudicially interpreted against labor. Its very susceptibility to the ebb and flow of judicial waves of opinion concerning labor makes it a questionable vehicle for the adjudication of labor rights in industrial disputes.

- 19 -

The Protective Wings of the Norris-La Guardia Act

(1940–1941)

United States v. Hutcheson

I

For more than half a century organized labor in the United States conducted a bitter campaign against the application of the Sherman Antitrust Act to labor unions. Many an injunction was issued against unions under that act. For example, approximately three hundred were issued in connection with the railway shopmen's strike of 1922. Labor demanded relief from "government by injunction," its rallying slogan against the act. When Congress enacted the Clayton Act in 1914, labor thought it would no longer be plagued by the Sherman Act. But when its Magna Carta vanished as a result of the decisions of the Supreme Court in the *Duplex* and *Bedford* cases, organized labor again turned to Congress for legislative help. Congress was sympathetic to labor's plea, especially because the Supreme Court's narrow construction of the Clayton Act was contrary to Congressional intent. Accordingly, in 1932, Congress enacted the Norris-La Guardia Act, designed to limit drastically the jurisdiction of the federal courts in issuing injunctions in cases involving or growing out of labor disputes. In this manner Congress counteracted the unfavorable decisions of the Supreme Court and restored to the unions immunity from the antitrust laws intended for them under the Clayton Act.

While the act curbed the power only of federal courts in the issuing of injunctions, it had a profound effect on labor rights in general. Many a state adopted similar legislation curbing the rights of the state courts to issue injunctions in labor disputes, except as specifically provided in the act. In addition to curbing the power of the court to issue injunctions, the act also prescribed the procedure to be followed and provided for hearings in open court with an opportunity for cross-examination, for the right of appeal, and for trial by jury. It assured employees the right to collective bargaining, and provided that neither a union nor its officers are responsible for unlawful acts of individuals in the absence of proof that the organization ratified or approved such acts.

The significance of the act may be observed from several of its sections. Section 2, setting forth the public policy of the act, states that:

. . . The individual unorganized worker is commonly helpless to exercise actual liberty of contract and to protect his freedom of labor . . . it is necessary that he have full freedom of association, self organization, and designation of representatives of his own choosing, to negotiate the terms and conditions of his employment and that he shall be free from the interference, restraint or coercion of employers of labor or their agents in the . . . concerted activities for the purpose of collective bargaining or other mutual aid and protection.

Section 4, specifically limiting the jurisdiction of federal courts to issue injunctions in "labor disputes," contains the following:

No court of the United States shall have jurisdiction to issue any restraining order or temporary or permanent injunction in any case involving or growing out of any labor dispute to prohibit any person or persons participating or interested in such dispute (as these terms are herein defined) from doing, whether singly or in concert, any of the following acts . . . [This is followed by enumeration of various lawful union activities in connection with maintaining the union, conducting organization campaigns and strikes.]

Section 13, defining broadly the term "labor dispute," contains the following:

When used in this act and for the purposes of this act—
(a) A case shall be held to involve or to grow out of a labor dispute when the case involves persons who are engaged in the same industry, trade, craft, or occupation; or have direct or indirect interests therein; or who are employees of the same employer; or who are members of the same or an affiliated organization of employers or employees . . . or when the case involves any conflicting or competing interests in a "labor dis-

pute" (as hereinafter defined) of "persons participating or interests" therein (as hereinafter defined).

(b) A person or association shall be held to be a person participating or interested in a labor dispute if relief is sought against him or it, and if he or it is engaged in the same industry, trade, craft or occupation in which such dispute occurs, or has a direct or indirect interest therein, or is a member, officer or agent of any association composed in whole or in part of employers or employees engaged in such industry, trade, craft or occupation.

(c) The term "labor dispute" includes any controversy concerning terms or conditions of employment, or concerning the association or representation of persons in negotiating, fixing, maintaining, changing, or seeking to arrange terms or conditions of employment, regardless of whether or not the disputants stand in the proximate relation of employer and employee. . . .

Section 15 provides that:

All Acts or parts of Acts in conflict with the provisions of this Act are hereby repealed.

II

For many years two powerful unions—the United Brotherhood of Carpenters and Joiners and the International Association of Machinists—had been engaged in a jurisdictional dispute as to whose members were entitled to be employed on certain jobs. From time to time their jurisdictional disputes would flare up. Not infrequently each of these two labor unions had separate collective agreements with the same employer for the work of its respective craft, but their crafts were overlapping and were not clearly defined. This intensified the disputes.

Both labor organizations were affiliated with the American Federation of Labor. The repeated efforts made by the parent organization to adjust the conflict between them produced at best only temporary adjustments.

Among the employers who had collective agreements with both organizations was the Anheuser-Busch Brewing Company of St. Louis. During the summer of 1939 the brewing company planned an expansion of facilities. The Borsari Tank Corporation, which was engaged to do the job, assigned the work to the members of the International Association of Machinists. The Carpenters' Union protested, claiming that the job should be done by its members. The brewing company rejected the union's claim and offered to arbitrate the dispute in accordance with the arbitration provision of its collective agreement. The carpenters refused and declared a strike.

The seventy-eight carpenters employed by Anheuser-Busch left their jobs and picketed the plant. At that time the Gaylord Container Corporation, a tenant of Anheuser-Busch in St. Louis, also was engaged in some construction work and its contractor was L. O. Stocker Company. The carpenters refused to work for that contractor as well as for the Borsari Tank Corporation, and picketed the Gaylord as well as the Anheuser-Busch Company. In addition, the union published in its official publication, the *Carpenter*, an appeal to laboring men and the friends of organized labor not to patronize Anheuser-Busch beer. This dispute led to the case of *United States* v. *Hutcheson*.

III

At the time that the carpenters' strike against Anheuser-Busch was going on, Thurman Arnold was assistant attorney general of the United States, in charge of prosecutions under the antitrust laws. Arnold declared that it was his purpose to remove all blocks which interfered with the free flow of commerce. He considered industrial monopoly and interruption of production of goods in interstate commerce caused by labor jurisdictional disputes as intolerable blocks. In conformity with these views, he initiated a series of prosecutions aimed at breaking up monopolistic practices in industry. The carpenters' strike against Anheuser-Busch, the sympathy strikes involving other firms, and the boycott prompted Arnold to use the criminal sections of the Sherman Antitrust Act against the union.

In his capacity as assistant attorney general, Thurman Arnold secured an indictment against William L. Hutcheson, president, and three other chief officers of the carpenters. They were charged with criminal conspiracy to restrain interstate commerce. The indictment charged that the defendants, by their boycott appeal, intended to keep Anheuser-Busch beer from moving out of Missouri; that the boycott of the Borsari Tank Corporation kept it from shipping material into Missouri; and that the acts of the defendants were calculated "to cut off manufacture and consequent shipping of beer and other products in interstate commerce."

The defendants pleaded not guilty. Each of them entered a separate demurrer to the indictment, asking for a dismissal of the indictment on the ground that the facts alleged in the indictment were insufficient, as a matter of law, to hold them criminally liable.

The demurrers came up before District Judge Charles B. Davis of the Federal District Court for the Eastern District of Missouri at St. Louis. The judge handed down his decision on March 29, 1940. In substance, he held:

1. An unlawful conspiracy had been defined as a combination to accomplish a criminal or unlawful purpose or a lawful purpose by unlawful means. However, under the Norris-La Guardia Act, the federal courts in labor disputes were prevented from issuing injunctions based on allegations that certain acts of unions involved in disputes amounted to an unlawful combination or conspiracy.

2. To sustain an indictment for criminal conspiracy under the Sherman Act it was necessary to show a *direct*, not an incidental or remote, restraint of trade; and it also was necessary to show that the defendants' activities were outside the scope of the legitimate objects and means that might be sought and employed by labor unions under the sanction of the Clayton Act.

3. The indictment in the case at bar showed only *incidental* restraints on commerce. The defendants' real purpose was not to restrain commerce but to win *in a local labor controversy*. Congress had not declared such disputes unlawful. Our courts had held previously that a local halting of operations in order to get union men hired should not be interpreted as affecting the sale of materials in interstate commerce.

4. While under certain state laws jurisdictional strikes were unlawful, under the Norris-La Guardia Act unions involved in such disputes were immune from suit in the federal courts. The Supreme Court had found that Congress, by the Norris-La Guardia Act, intended to legalize peaceful persuasion. The Supreme Court's interpretation of the Clayton Act in the *Duplex* case concerning peaceful picketing no longer applied. The fact that some of the strikes were sympathy strikes was immaterial because the Norris-La Guardia Act specifically extended the protection of Section 20 of the Clayton Act to "persons and organizations not immediate parties to the dispute."

5. The tendency of federal legislation had been to countenance conduct such as that set out in the indictment. Such union conduct did not furnish a basis for a civil action and this legislative policy was applicable to all relations between employer and employee. Since this conduct did not furnish a basis for a civil wrong, it certainly could not serve as a basis for a criminal action.

6. Since the indictment sought to charge a criminal offense, it should have set forth facts which, if proved, would constitute a crime. The indictment did not set forth such facts.

The court concluded that the indictment did not set forth a crime. It sustained the four defendants' demurrers. The case was dismissed.

Thurman Arnold, on behalf of the government, carried the case directly to the Supreme Court of the United States.

IV

The case was argued before the high court on December 10, 1940. The government contended:

(*a*) The object of the defendants was not the protection and advancement of the rights of labor; no question of collective bargaining, wages, or working conditions was involved, and the defendants' acts were merely an attempt to win by force a jurisdictional dispute with another union.

(*b*) This was not a local dispute between employer and employee but a jurisdictional struggle between national unions, resulting in various strikes in many different places, imposing *a direct and unreasonable* burden upon interstate trade.

(*c*) The defendants had tried to stop interstate trade of four companies with only one of which they had relations and against none of which they had a real grievance.

(*d*) They had attempted to make Anheuser-Busch their partisan in their dispute with the machinists or otherwise drive that company from the interstate market.

(*e*) There had been direct physical restraint in interstate commerce on the goods of Anheuser-Busch and the Gaylord Container Corporation by the interference with delivery of materials for both the construction companies and Anheuser-Busch, and the defendants had *intended* to restrain interstate commerce.

(*f*) The conduct of the defendants' interference with competition in every direction therefore came within the prohibitions of the Sherman Act.

(g) The present case was distinguished from the *Apex* case and other cases in which the court had held that the Sherman law was not applicable to unions because in those cases there was an actual industrial dispute between unions and employers. But in this case the defendants had no real dispute with the employers and nevertheless were trying to drive from the market an employer against whom the union had no real grievance. Such an exclusion from the market was a restraint of trade under both the common law and the Sherman Act.

(h) The action of the defendants could not be justified under the rule of reason since jurisdictional strikes directed against an employer were essentially unreasonable because the employer was powerless and had no control or means of settling such strikes.

(i) The Norris-La Guardia Act was not applicable to this indictment. That act merely limited the equity powers of the federal courts in the issuance of injunctions but it did not change the rules of civil or criminal law. If the defendants, as a matter of law, had committed a crime, the Norris-La Guardia Act did not extend them protection.

The attorneys for the defendants argued:

1. The Norris-La Guardia Act did not differentiate between strikes conducted for jurisdictional reasons and other strikes.

2. The *Apex* case held that strike activities could not be prosecuted under the Sherman Act and that unions under the Norris-La Guardia Act were given immunity for their lawful strike activities. That holding was applicable to the case at bar.

3. Even assuming that the Sherman Act, which was designed to curb business monopolistic practices, was also applicable to industrial disputes involving suppression of competition, nevertheless it was not applicable to the case at bar. In this case the competition, if any, was among the *labor unions themselves*, not involving any *business* monopolistic practices. A jurisdictional labor dispute could not be termed a "crime" under the Sherman Act.

4. The indictment in the case was contrary to the immunity given to labor in Section 20 of the Clayton Act and the Norris-La Guardia Act. The government's contention that the Norris-La Guardia Act was merely a regulation of equity procedure in federal courts was

erroneous. On the contrary, that act was a declaration of policy concerning the right of labor to strike, which right must be held to be a normal and legitimate act of labor unions. Since the indictment in this case sought to make the strike criminal, it was in violation of the specific rights granted by Section 20 of the Clayton Act and by the Norris-La Guardia Act.

5. The indictment did not cite any facts which would show that the defendants were engaged in a secondary boycott. There was nothing illegal in asking people not to patronize Anheuser-Busch beer; nor was the carpenters' refusal to work a crime, since the carpenters were not morally or legally bound to submit to the employers' choice giving the machinists the exclusive right to do the disputed work.

On February 3, 1941, the Supreme Court, by majority, dismissed the indictment. Justice Frankfurter delivered the majority opinion. He traced the history of the antitrust laws with respect to labor unions and pointed out:

(a) After the Supreme Court had held that the Antitrust laws were applicable to labor, the Congress in 1914 enacted the Clayton Act, which included Section 20 extending certain immunities to labor.

(b) After the Supreme Court had held that the immunities contained in Section 20 of the Clayton Act were intended to apply only to controversies between an employer and employee *directly* employed by said employer, the Congress in 1932 enacted the Norris-La Guardia Act.

(c) The Norris-La Guardia Act finally clarified the public policy of the United States in regard to industrial conflicts and broadened the allowable area of union activity to include all labor disputes and not merely those involving immediate employer-employee relationships.

After tracing the history of this legislation, Justice Frankfurter declared that the validity of the indictment in this case brought under the Sherman Act must be determined by reading the Sherman Act in the light of subsequent legislation, to wit, Section 20 of the Clayton Act and the Norris-La Guardia Act, and that taking this set of legislation as a whole, it must be concluded that:

One: There was no need for discussing those cases under the antitrust acts which had been decided by the court before the

Norris-La Guardia Act because by the latter act Congress meant "to restore the broad purpose which Congress thought it had formulated in the Clayton Act but which was frustrated, so Congress believed, by unduly restrictive judicial construction."

Two: The carpenters, in their dispute with the machinists, were not prohibited by law from stopping work, or picketing peacefully, or even asking people not to drink Anheuser-Busch beer. Congress did not exclude jurisdictional disputes from the immunities extended to labor by the Clayton Act.

Three: If the action were brought as a civil suit, no injunction could be issued regardless of whether or not the parties to the dispute were in an employer-employee relationship. If the facts did not warrant an injunction in a civil suit, there was so much more reason to conclude that there was no basis for a criminal charge. To argue otherwise would lead to the absurd conclusion that the kind of conduct which a court of equity considered allowable conduct "may, in a criminal proceeding, become the road to prison."

Four: As long as a union acted in self-interest and did not combine with nonlabor groups, the legality of its conduct was not determined by the right or wrong or lack of wisdom of its behavior. Since the unions in this case acted within the allowable area of conflict, the indictment against the four defendants was properly dismissed.

Justice Stone, in a concurring opinion, declared that there was no need to consider the effect of the Norris-La Guardia Act on the Clayton Act. The case could be decided on the issue that this was a *local* jurisdictional dispute and therefore presented no violation of the Sherman Act. He reasoned that the restraints of trade alleged in the indictment stemmed only from a local dispute, namely: the refusal to work for the construction companies, a local strike affecting buildings, the construction of which was not even begun. Moreover, the strike was not even directed against the use of any special material in interstate commerce; asking the public not to buy Anheuser-Busch beer stemmed from the local dispute and the restraint on commerce flowing therefrom was merely *incidental* to the local strike against a company doing interstate business. Justice Stone asserted that the charge that peaceful picketing of a *local plant* violated the Sherman Act was, to say the least, "novel," whatever consequences might have been intended by the strike; and if the crime charged in this indictment were sustained, then "every local strike aimed at closing a shop whose products or supplies move in interstate commerce, without more, would be a violation of the Sherman Act."

Justice Roberts (with Chief Justice Hughes concurring) dissented. He held that:

(*a*) The indictment was adequate because it alleged a secondary boycott affecting interstate commerce and since 1908 the secondary boycott had been unlawful under the Sherman Act.

(*b*) Section 20 of the Clayton Act did not increase the substantive rights of labor unions but merely regulated practice in granting equitable relief. Although the Norris-La Guardia Act broadened the scope of labor disputes and restricted the use of equity jurisdiction, it did not affect the Sherman Act as regarded either suits for damages or criminal prosecutions.

(*c*) The majority's opinion that the Norris-La Guardia Act modified the applicability of the Sherman Act to labor unions was equivalent to saying that Congress had repealed the applicability of the Sherman Act to labor; but that was wrong because Congress itself had consistently refused specifically to exempt labor from the antitrust laws.

In accordance with the decision of the majority, the indictment against Hutcheson and the other leaders of the carpenters was dismissed.

V

The basic and irreconcilable difference of opinion between the majority and the minority on the meaning and purpose of the Norris-La Guardia Act, in nontechnical language, was briefly this: The minority contended that the purpose of the act was a limited one, namely, to curb the power of the court to issue injunctions in "labor disputes" as the scope of the term was broadened under this act, and nothing more; this act, therefore, did not give immunity to labor from all provisions of the Sherman and Clayton Acts. The majority, however, ascribed a much broader scope to the Norris-La Guardia Act. Mr. Justice Frankfurter proceeded on the theory that the underlying aim of the Norris-La Guardia Act was to restore the broad purpose that Congress thought it had formulated in the Clayton Act, but which had been frustrated, so Congress believed, by unduly restrictive judicial construction. He therefore concluded that the Norris-La Guardia Act must be read together with the Clayton Act, because the former "reasserted the original purpose of the Clayton Act by infusing into it the immunized trade union activities as redefined." Since the facts in the indictment were lawful under Section 20 of the Clayton Act, there was no basis for the indictment.

The significance of this decision lies in the fact that by restoring the relief originally intended for labor by the Clayton Act, the unions finally secured effective relief from many attacks under the Sherman Act. The two original main purposes of the Clayton Act so far as labor was concerned were understood to be: (1) to exempt labor combinations from prosecution as conspiracies or monopolies under the Sherman Act; and (2) to limit the power of the federal courts in the issuing of injunctions in labor disputes. However, the Supreme Court in the *Duplex Printing* case and in the *Bedford Cut Stone* case so interpreted the Clayton Act that the intended protection for labor vanished. But in this case, in holding that the Norris-La Guardia Act restored to labor the immunized activities originally intended in the Clayton Act, labor not only received protection against the abuse of the injunction but could no longer be prosecuted as a conspiracy under the Sherman Act. While the court did not specifically overrule its former decisions in the *Bedford Cut Stone* case and in the *Duplex Printing* case, it did, to say the least, greatly undermine, if not actually destroy, the effect of these two decisions.

It should be borne in mind, however, that in making this decision Justice Frankfurter limited the immunities under Section 20 of the Clayton Act to "So long as a union acts in its self-interest and does not combine with non-labor groups. . . ." When this admonition is not observed by a union the fury of the Sherman Act may return to plague it.

- 20 -

"All Within the Union Are Brethren"

(1941–1944)

Steele v. Louisville & Nashville Railroad

I

The status of the free Negro in the United States immediately after emancipation still bore resemblance to that of the slave. The relations of the whites with the Negroes still reflected the former attitude of masters to slaves. The Negro's economic opportunities were limited and his social standing and political rights were curtailed by tradition and prejudice.

When in 1883 the second Civil Rights Bill giving the Negroes equality of treatment in theaters, railroads, hotels, and public places was declared unconstitutional by the Supreme Court, practically every southern state enacted Jim Crow laws. By such schemes as the "grandfather clause," which qualified practically all the whites to vote but not the Negroes, and the setting up of property and literacy tests and "white primaries," the Negroes in the South were in effect disfranchised. Discrimination against the Negroes was not limited merely to social and political life—it extended also to industrial life. In employment, only agriculture and domestic service were freely open to the Negro worker; other industrial occupations, except for certain unskilled jobs, were practically closed to him, in no small degree by the hostility of the white workers.

Organized labor's attitude toward the Negro worker in industry has not been without blemish. The white workers looked with suspicion on the attempt to add large numbers of Negro workers to the industrial force. They knew from experience that in strikes, employers made use of Negro against white and that generally

252

Negroes were used by employers to lower labor standards and prevent unionization. The white workers in unions of skilled crafts were particularly jealous of retaining their superiority and exclusiveness. This attitude of the white worker was evident even in crafts in which Negroes had been employed in large numbers before the emancipation, such as blacksmiths, cabinetmakers, plasterers, stone breakers, and masons.

With the development of mass production industries, the Negroes were more and more drawn into industrial life. They pressed for a remedy against the discrimination in employment practiced by employers as well as by labor. The leadership of the AFL opposed race discrimination. In fact, a great many of its affiliated unions did not tolerate race discrimination practices, whether in hiring, layoff, or promotion. The Congress of Industrial Organizations (CIO) prohibited race discrimination in unions. But still there were a number of AFL unions which did discriminate against Negroes, in admission into membership as well as in exercising rights of membership.

The situation of the Negro worker on the railroads especially was not a happy one. In fact, the brotherhood unions barred Negroes from membership. The Locomotive Firemen and Enginemen, for example, included among the qualifications for membership in their local lodges that the applicant "shall be white born, of good moral character, sober and industrious, sound in body and limbs . . . literate in English, of normal eyesight, have 30 days' service in handling engines, and be currently employed in the industry." The Negro railroad worker was limited at best to the hard and dirty work of a fireman. The fireman's job became a traditional "Negro job."

The southern roads have employed many Negro firemen not only because the work was a traditional Negro job, but also because Negro labor was cheap. During World War I the roads lost many Negro workers to war industries which offered them better wages than the railroads. For the purpose of making the railroad job attractive to the Negro so that he would not leave it to seek employment elsewhere, and as a matter of simple justice, William McAdoo, secretary of the treasury, who at the time as railroad administrator operated the railroads for the federal government during the war, ordered that Negroes were to receive the same wages as white men for the same work. This order indirectly had its repercussion on the attitude of the railroads as well as that of the white railroad workers toward the Negro firemen. Since the Negro fireman's wage had to be the same as the white fireman's, the southern railroads found no particular advantage in the employment of Negro firemen; they were perfectly willing to employ white firemen were it not for the tradition that a fireman's work was a Negro job. On the other hand, white workers were attracted by the opportunities that the fireman's job offered, especially since changes in the technique of a locomotive fireman's work tended to make the work less dirty and less backbreaking.

During the depression of 1921, workers were laid off, but the Negro fireman, with seniority in length of employment, possessed a prior claim to whatever employment was left for a fireman. The white workers resented seeing Negroes hold on to the jobs. The resentment and prejudice of the whites against Negroes, especially in Mississippi and Louisiana, went so far that in one instance, where unemployment was widespread, five Negro firemen were killed and eight wounded in an ambush. These brutal acts were perpetrated by individuals. In fact, the Brotherhood of Locomotive Firemen and Enginemen denounced the act, and the railroads, on whose property most of the shooting occurred, offered a reward for convictions. But the perpetrators of these brutal attacks went unpunished. The firemen who were indicted for these acts were found not guilty by a jury. At any rate, these ambushes bespeak the cruel racial discrimination that was practiced on the railroads by management, as well as by the individual union members.

II

Among the southern railroads which had been employing Negroes as firemen was the Louisville & Nashville Railroad. This is the same railroad that was involved in the case of *Adair* v. *United States* (see Chapter 4). While this railroad did not have any agreement with the railroad brotherhoods, it did have an agreement with its own company union, known as the Locomotive Firemen and Hostlers. This agreement was made in March, 1929, and established wage rates, seniority rights based upon length of service, and other working rules which were to continue subject to thirty days' written notice of change by either side. During the depression of the early 1930's workers on the road had to be laid off. This created a special problem for the white firemen. In order to qualify as engineers they were required to accumulate a certain amount of working time, but they could not do so because the Negro firemen had seniority rights and whatever employment there was for firemen was given first to the Negroes with seniority. Neither could the white firemen expect vacancies as a result of possible promotion of Negro firemen to engineers because the rules of the Locomotive Firemen and Enginemen excluded Negroes. Thus, because the Negro, outranking in seniority the white man, was nonpromotable by union rules, the white man, with lesser seniority, could not accumulate the necessary minimum working time to qualify as an engineer.

But something occurred in 1934 which these white firemen interpreted as a solution to their immediate problem. The Congress amended the Railway Labor Act, banned company unions on the railroads, and forbade company interference with the choice of collective bargaining representatives by the employees. The amended law required the roads to deal exclusively with the bargaining agent chosen by the majority vote of their employees.

In accordance with this law, elections were held on the railroads. In most instances the elections resulted in designating the railroad brotherhoods as the employees' bargaining agents. The Negro workers protested because they were excluded from membership in those unions. Under the law the dispute was submitted to the National Mediation Board. The Negro workers requested to be declared a separate bargaining unit and be entitled to choose their own bargaining agents. The Mediation Board decided that racial difference was not a proper basis for a separate bargaining unit and denied the request of the Negro organization. The National Federation of Railroad Workers, an unaffiliated organization of Negro employees, protested the decision of the Mediation Board. But its protest went unheard.

As on most of the nation's railroads, the elections of the bargaining agent for the firemen and engineers on the Louisville & Nashville resulted in the designation of the Brotherhood of Locomotive Firemen and Enginemen as the exclusive bargaining agent.

On March 28, 1940, the brotherhood, as the exclusive agent of all the workers, requested a change in the rules then governing the assignment of locomotive firemen. Since the parties could not agree, the dispute, in accordance with the law, was submitted to the National Mediation Board. However, in February, 1941, the roads and the brotherhood finally settled the dispute by an agreement which provided that (1) "promotable" (i.e., white) firemen were to receive preference in layoffs and work assignments and (2) only "promotable" firemen were to be hired by the roads in the future. The interest of the Negro fireman was sacrificed for the welfare of the white union man.

III

Among the Negro firemen employed by the Louisville & Nashville was Bester William Steele. He had been employed by the road since 1910, and was a competent and satisfactory worker. In April, 1941, after the changes in the working rules agreed upon in February between the brotherhood and the southern railroads, Steele was laid off for lack of work. A promotable fireman with less seniority was given Steele's job. As a result of this layoff Steele lost sixteen days' work.

Steele brought suit in the state court, the Circuit Court of Jefferson County, Alabama. He named as defendants the Louisville & Nashville Railroad and the Brotherhood of Locomotive Firemen and Enginemen. He requested that an injunction be issued restraining them from enforcing their agreement of February, 1941, in so far as it deprived him of his seniority rights, and that they pay him the damage caused him by his loss of wages.

Both defendants demurred to the complaint, claiming that Steele's complaint was insufficient as a matter of law. Judge E. M. Creel, before whom the demurrer came up, sustained the defendants' contentions and dismissed the case. Steele appealed.

IV

Steele's appeal came before the Alabama Supreme Court. Steele's counsel argued:

(a) The bargaining union could not enter into a modification of the working rules which discriminated in favor of the white majority group against the Negro minority. Under the Railway Labor Act, the brotherhood was to represent the *whole* craft of firemen and therefore, as agent, it had obligations to protect the Negro fireman.

(*b*) The brotherhood was guilty of fraud in that it failed to inform the Negro firemen that it was acting against their interests in concluding the agreement of February, 1941.

(*c*) Since Steele's right to his job and to his seniority was a property right, he was entitled to claim the benefits of a contract negotiated for the entire craft, but he was not bound by those provisions of the contract which discriminated against him in favor of other workers.

(*d*) If the Railway Labor Act forced minority workers, at the sacrifice of their seniority rights, to accept the collective bargaining agent chosen by the majority, then those provisions of the act deprived them of their property rights without due process of law and such law was in violation of the Fifth Amendment. Congress could not give the bargaining agent the unbridled power to destroy the minority's property right in their jobs.

(*e*) The brotherhood as such was liable for the wrong done and it was proper to issue an injunction against the brotherhood and the railroad to restrain them from committing the wrong.

The attorneys for the defendants contended:

(*a*) Since Steele relied upon seniority rights, which rights existed by reason of the contract between the union and the road, he was not at liberty to accept the seniority part of the contract that favored him and disaffirm the rest. The contract had to be treated as a whole.

(*b*) The custom of not promoting Negro firemen to engineer was "universal and accepted," "traditional and practiced," and was part of the contract between the union and the railroad.

(*c*) No injunction could be issued because Steele's services were not unique and extraordinary and the court would not enforce specific performances of contracts by injunctions unless the personal services involved were unique and extraordinary.

(*d*) The railroads did not conspire to damage the plaintiff in any right.

(*e*) The court had no jurisdiction in this matter. The board under the Railway Labor Act had exclusive jurisdiction to decide the issues involved. Plaintiff could resort only to the grievance machinery provided by that law and is barred from bringing the dispute before this court.

On February 13, 1944, Alabama's chief justice, Lucien D. Gardner, delivered the unanimous opinion of a seven-member court. After reviewing the facts, he observed:

1. Steele's claim to seniority did not rise out of an individual contract with the railroad but out of an agreement of March, 1929, with the organization known as Locomotive Firemen and Hostlers, not the brotherhood, the present bargaining agent. His seniority rights rested on a private contract.

2. The Railway Labor Act did not ban individual contracts. So far as the law was concerned, Steele could have made an individual agreement with the company to protect his seniority rights, but no such agreement existed in this instance; the road's agreement was with the brotherhood as the representative of the workers, and not with any specific individual.

3. Seniority right "was somewhat intangible and could not be denominated a vested property right." While improper interference with such right by a third person might be actionable, such seniority rights could be modified by the parties to the agreement.

4. Since Steele's complaint admitted that the brotherhood was his representative, the latter had a right to enter into the February, 1941, agreement, which had modified the 1929 agreement to complainant's detriment. Steele must be held to abide by the contract made by his recognized statutory representative.

5. While the brotherhood was Steele's representative, Congress had not meant to create the confidential relation of principal and agent between *each* union member and his collective bargaining representative. The duty of the agent for bargaining purposes was to bargain with reference to the *whole body* without any liability to the interests of particular individuals.

6. There was no basis for the charge that the defendant railroad conspired with the brotherhood to defraud Steele of his seniority. The railroads were bound as a matter of law to deal with the designated representative of their employees. The union's rule against Negro membership was within its rights as a voluntary organization. Steele knew that only white persons were made engineers, a custom so invariable that it became part of the contract. If the road considered it wiser to inaugurate a policy of hiring only white firemen, there was no law standing in its way in carrying out this policy just as there was no law limiting the brotherhood's freedom of choice in selecting its members.

7. The charge that the brotherhood had fraudulently disrupted seniority rights was unfounded. Even if it acted in favor of its own membership and against complainant's interests, its action was not fraudulent because it acted for the welfare of the majority. Complainant was in the minority group of his craft, and if he suffered any hardship it was due to the control of the majority. Such action could not be considered as fraud either in law or in fact.

The Alabama Circuit Court sustained the decision of the court below and dismissed Steele's case.

Steele's counsel secured a writ of certiorari to remove the case from the state to the federal courts on the ground that it involved the interpretation of a federal law and rights existing under it.

V

The very issues involved in the case, namely, racial discrimination and the duty of a majority in a labor union to its minority, attracted considerable attention. Although the United States was not a party to the action, the solicitor general filed a brief on behalf of the United States in support of Steele. Briefs were filed also by the National Association for the Advancement of Colored People and the American Civil Liberties Union, as *amici curiae*.

On November 14 and 15, 1944, the case was argued before the United States Supreme Court. About a month later, on December 18, 1944, Chief Justice Stone, reversing the Alabama Circuit Court, delivered the opinion of the Supreme Court. He summarized the main issues to be:

(*a*) Did the Railway Labor Act impose on a labor organization, acting by authority of the statute as the exclusive bargaining representative of a craft or class of railway employees, the duty to represent all the employees in the craft without discrimination because of their race?

(*b*) If so, did the courts have the jurisdiction to protect the minority against acts of the bargaining agent which were in violation of the agent's duties?

Chief Justice Stone, for the court, in substance, held:

One: Congress, in enacting the Railway Labor Act and authorizing a labor union chosen by a majority to represent a craft, imposed on the union the duty to protect the minority in that class. It did not extend to the union the plenary power to sacrifice the right of the minority for the benefit of the others.

Two: The labor organization chosen to be the representative of the craft or class had the obligation to represent *all* in the craft or class *regardless of their union affiliations or want of them.* While the majority of the craft chose the bargaining agent, that agent, when chosen, represented the entire craft or class, and not merely the majority.

Three: Since the brotherhood did not accept Steele and other Negroes as members, the brotherhood's power to represent them was derived only from the law. That law intended that such representative was to act for the benefit of *all* the employees in the craft it had undertaken to represent.

Four: The Railway Labor Act imposed upon the statutory representative of a craft as exacting a duty to protect *equally* the interests of the members of the craft as the Constitution imposed upon a legislature to give equal protection to the interests of those for whom it legislated.

Five: While a situation might justify certain differences in the treatment of the members of the craft, this did not justify the agent in practicing discrimination not based on relevant differences. The differences between the members in this case were based on race alone, and they were not such relevant differences as would justify different treatment. The agent's act in this case constituted unjustified discrimination.

Six: While the statute did not deny to a labor organization the right to determine the eligibility of its members, it did require the collective bargaining agent to represent the nonunion and the minority fairly, impartially, in good faith, and without hostile discrimination. So long as a labor union assumed to act as the statutory representative, it could not rightly refuse to perform that duty to represent *all* in the class *without discrimination.*

Seven: The Railway Labor Act provided no machinery for settling disputes between individual employees and the railroad. The adjustment machinery was between the road and the representative of the employees. Hence, Steele and the other Negro firemen must bring their case through the collective bargaining union, which apparently was hostile to their interests. Since the National Mediation Board had ruled against dividing crafts on race lines in representation elections, Steele and the other Negro firemen could not have their own chosen representative and were left without a means of remedying their wrong. Therefore, a judicial remedy was needed in this case.

Eight: The brotherhood, as the bargaining agent of the craft, breached its duty toward Steele, and the railroad as the employer failed to bargain as provided by law. Therefore, Steele was entitled to an injunction restraining the enforcement of the agreement of February, 1941, which modified the working rules against the interest of the Negro firemen, and Steele was entitled to damages suffered by him as a result of the wrong done to him.

In a separate concurring opinion, Justice Murphy, among other things, observed that the brotherhood's racial discrimination raised "a grave Constitutional issue that should be squarely faced." He held that "the utter disregard for the dignity and well-being of colored citizens shown by this record is so pronounced as to demand the invocation of Constitutional condemnation." Justice Murphy further added that the Constitution prohibited economic discrimination on racial grounds and warned that "a sound democracy cannot allow such discrimination to go unchallenged. Racism is far too virulent today to permit the slightest refusal, in the light of a Constitution that abhors it, to expose and condemn it wherever it appears in the course of a statutory interpretation."

In accordance with the court's decision, the judgment of the Alabama Supreme Court was reversed and the case remanded for further action. The railroads and the Brotherhood of Locomotive Firemen and Enginemen were thus enjoined from enforcing that part of their 1941 agreement which deprived Negro firemen of seniority rights. The white worker was reminded by the court that the Negro worker was his "brother" and should be treated in a brotherly fashion.

VI

The Supreme Court's attitude toward the Negro shown in the Steele case was miles away from its attitude in the original *Dred Scott* case in 1857. In the *Dred Scott* case the Supreme Court held, or at least implied, that Negro slaves were property, chattels, that they had no rights equal to those of white men. But in the *Steele* case the court asserted and applied the fundamental principle that the protective laws enacted by Congress must be applied equally, without discrimination as to race, creed, or color. With good reason, this decision has been characterized as the "Dred Scott decision in reverse."

While there is comfort in the knowledge that "all men are born free and equal," it is an open secret that discrimination has been practiced, openly and otherwise, contrary to this principle. Economic self-interest and emotional prejudice fortified by unreasoning tradition, motivate the continuation of discriminatory practices.

When the labor movement was comparatively weak, its race prejudices and its injustices toward minorities, while important as a matter of principle, did not play a significant part in the social structure of our economy. With the advent of the New Deal, however, this became important. The influence of unions was felt in every vein of our industrial life. The Wagner Act made it obligatory upon every employer to deal exclusively with the bargaining agent designated by the majority. The mass production system of industry attracted more and more unskilled workers who were entitled to be represented in collective bargaining and to have their interests protected. The traditional craft organization, consisting of skilled workers, could not be an adequate bargaining representative of all workers—skilled and unskilled—unless in good conscience it endeavored to protect the respective interests of *all*, both skilled and unskilled crafts. An organization which practices race discrimination or other prejudices in admission of members is not likely to discharge its duties as representative of the very workers whom it excludes from membership. It is almost paradoxical that an organization should seek to become the exclusive representative of all but that at the same time it should insist on the right to discriminate against some, not merely as a disciplinary measure but because of prejudice against race, color, or creed.

One would suppose that a group or class which itself has been suffering from suppression and injustice would be likely to be fully sympathetic, sensitive, and responsive to the needs of other minorities which similarly suffer from prejudice. But that is not necessarily the case. The labor movement in the United States, which had been seeking justice and fair play from employers, had to be reminded of the maxim that "he who seeks justice must do justice."

- 21 -

There Are No Rights Without Duties

(1942–1944)

<small>WALLACE CORPORATION v.
NATIONAL LABOR RELATIONS BOARD</small>

I

With the New Deal, organized labor grew in numbers and power. Unions came to many industries which had never been unionized before. Under the slogan of industrial unionism, in place of craft unionism, the Congress of Industrial Organizations (CIO) came to the forefront. The CIO at first concentrated on the mass production industries. Its unionization campaign had been successful in the steel industry and in the automobile industry and moderately effective in textiles and the utility fields. Gradually, the CIO extended its activities into other industrial areas. Before long it became embroiled in various jurisdictional disputes with the long-established AFL unions.

One of the new CIO unions was the United Construction Workers Organizing Committee (UCWOC). This union had no hesitation in invading the traditional jurisdiction of the AFL unions in the building trades. The UCWOC was bent on organizing whatever plant came its way. Raiding one another's jurisdiction became a common occurrence between the unions belonging to the competing parent organizations—the AFL and the CIO. Occasionally both such unions were confronted with the opposition of "company unions," which usually came into being at the behest or with the blessing of the company employer. These company unions usually were formed for the purpose of combating the activities of "outside" unions. As a rule company unions were limited to the plant or plants of a single employer and were dominated by the management, the company that employed these workers.

II

The Wallace Corporation was engaged in the making of clothespins, wooden dishes, and other small wooden objects. Its main office was in St. Louis, Missouri, but it had a plant in Richwood, West Virginia. The unionization trend prevalent in the country did not at first affect the Wallace workers. The company actively discouraged any organization among its workers, but in spite of this, in July, 1941, the workers did organize a union, and as Local 129 it became affiliated with the United Construction Workers Organizing Committee.

The Wallace Corporation took immediate steps to undermine that union. It did more. It discharged Harvey Dodrill, the president of the new local union, a few days after the union had been formed. It also threatened to shut down its plant rather than recognize a CIO union. When the union asked to be recognized as the bargaining agent, the company questioned its right on the ground that it did not represent a majority. When the union offered to submit its applications for membership and have them checked against the company payroll, the company representative refused this offer. He wanted to check the membership applications by a separate private interview with each applicant. The union became convinced that the company's suggested procedure of private interviews was a masked attempt to discourage union membership and therefore rejected the company's request. Neither of the parties would yield on the method of checking the union's majority status.

Not being able to make any progress in the negotiations, Local 129 went out on strike. This took place on September 25, 1941. Within a week a group of employees was invited to the home of an assistant foreman in the Wallace shop. In the foreman's home that evening a new organization came into being under the name of the Richwood Clothespin and Dishworkers' Union. This new organization chose as its business agent B. E. Thompson, the editor of the *St. Nicholas Republican*, a local paper, and was referred to as the Thompson group.

Upon learning these facts, Local 129 filed charges of unfair labor practices against the Wallace Corporation with the National Labor

Relations Board. The union charged that the company had interfered with the organization of its employees by fostering the Thompson group and by discouraging membership in Local 129. A few
days after this petition was filed, the Thompson group conferred
with the Wallace Corporation, ostensibly for the purpose of negotiating a collective agreement on behalf of all the workers. Shortly
after this conference the Thompson group, to counteract the union
petition, also filed a petition of its own with the NLRB asking that
it, the Thompson group, be certified as the bargaining agent for the
workers in the Wallace plant.

In the meantime the strike continued. Various conferences were
held between the board's representatives and the parties involved
in the dispute. The Wallace Corporation and the Thompson group
made several attempts to have the strikers return to work, but were
not successful.

Several months passed. On the 30th of December, 1941, the CIO
local proposed a settlement of all the issues. The suggestion was
that all parties should consent to the holding of an election to decide
the bargaining agency and that the Wallace Corporation should
agree in advance to conclude a closed-shop contract with the designated agent. While the company made no direct reply to the union
suggestion, Thompson's paper published a rejection of the union's
proposal, and shortly thereafter the Wallace Corporation made it
known that it intended to move its plant from Richwood. The
regional director of the National Labor Relations Board became
concerned and called an immediate conference of the parties. At that
conference an adjustment of the strike was reached on the following
basis: work should be resumed immediately and all the employees
should return to work without discrimination; the board should
hold an election to designate the bargaining agent; the company
should recognize the designated agent as the exclusive bargaining
agent and should consent to a provision for a closed union shop in
the contract to be negotiated. On January 19, 1942, the parties
entered into a stipulation containing the above terms. The election
of representatives was set for January 30.

All signs pointed to a peaceful solution of the dispute, but about
a week before the election Thompson's paper, in its office window,
displayed a copy of a telegram signed by Wallace which stated that
it was entirely feasible to move the plant machinery from Richwood,

and copies of this telegram were displayed in Wallace's plant near the time clock. Coupled with this, rumors were spread that if the CIO local won the election the company would shut down the plant and move elsewhere. These rumors were strengthened by statements made by some foremen to the workers that if the CIO local carried the election the main supplier of lumber would refuse to sell lumber to Wallace. The union considered all these maneuvers as an obvious attempt to influence the result of the election. When the board's representatives took up with Wallace the question of the telegram concerning removal of the plant the latter, to counteract the effect of that telegram, sent another telegram to the board stating that the first one had not been intended to influence the voting. This second telegram was not displayed in Thompson's newspaper office window. It was posted at the plant, but was removed by someone two hours after it was posted.

The election was held nonetheless. Of the 207 eligible voters, 186 cast ballots. The Thompson group received 98 votes, the CIO local 83, and no union, 5. Shortly thereafter the board certified the Thompson group as the exclusive bargaining agent for all the workers in the Wallace plant. The CIO local did not officially protest the election.

About a month after the Thompson group had been certified as the bargaining agent the company entered into a collective labor agreement with the Richwood Clothespin and Dishworkers' Union. The agreement was for a period of two years and was to be automatically renewed unless terminated upon thirty days' notice by either party. It provided for a closed shop so that all the workers employed at the time or in the future would be members of this union; it also provided that, should this union at any time become affiliated with a labor organization having membership outside of Richwood, the closed-shop provision in the agreement would become void. This agreement was entered into on March 7, 1942.

Nine days later, on March 16, notice was posted in the plant that all workers must become members of the Richwood Clothespin and Dishworkers' Union and two days later, 43 employees, all known partisans of the CIO local, were dismissed for not becoming members of the Thompson group. Among those dismissed were 31 who had applied for membership but had been rejected. When the company refused to reinstate the discharged workers, the CIO Local 129

filed charges of unfair labor practice against the Wallace Corporation and B. E. Thompson.

III

At the hearing of these charges, the trial examiner found that the
Richwood Clothespin and Dishworkers' Union was company dominated and was not a labor organization within the meaning of the
National Labor Relations Act. He concluded that the company was
guilty of unfair labor practices and recommended that the company
be ordered to disestablish this union, cease giving effect to its contract with it, and be directed to reinstate the 43 discharged workers
with back pay for the earnings lost by them as a result of their discharges. The company and the Thompson group filed objections to
the report.

After various delays and rearguments, on June 7, 1943, the NLRB
issued its final order. It found the collective labor agreement between
the company and the Thompson group to be an unfair labor practice; that the company had accepted the closed-shop provision knowing that it would be used as a means of discriminating against the
partisans of the CIO local; that the company need not alter the terms
of employment concerning wages, hours, seniority, and other working conditions provided for in the agreement, but that the 43
discharged employees were to be reinstated without prejudice to
their seniority rights and to their back pay for lost earnings.

The Wallace Corporation refused to abide by the board's order.
When the board applied to the Circuit Court for an order of enforcement, the company petitioned the court to review the board's decision.

IV

The case, under the title *Wallace Corporation* v. *the NLRB, et al.,*
came before the Federal Circuit Court of Appeals for the Fourth
Circuit. On February 3, 1944, Justice John J. Parker delivered the
opinion of the court. After reviewing the facts, he concluded that
(*a*) there was evidence to prove that the Thompson group was company dominated and supported; (*b*) since the discharges of the 43
workers constituted an unfair labor practice, the board had the
power to reopen the entire history of the case and it was not limited
by the stipulation of the parties concerning the election; (*c*) the

oppressive and highhanded conduct of the designated bargaining agent justified the board in disregarding its previous certification of the Thompson group as the bargaining agent; (d) while generally discharges of workers pursuant to the requirement of a closed-shop contract are legitimate, such discharges are not proper when union membership, to the knowledge of the company, is denied on the ground of activity in prior labor disputes. An employer may not enter into a closed-shop contract designed to discriminate "solely because of prior union activities." While the stipulation of February bound the company to accept a closed union shop, the company was not bound to acquiesce in a scheme to penalize the minority employees; (e) while the labor agreement required the employees to become members of the successful union, that agreement did not contemplate giving the union the right to get such employees fired by the simple device of denying them membership; and (f) the duty to prevent unfair labor practices permits the board to find an employees' organization company dominated even after it had previously certified that organization. While as a general rule settlements and orders made should be observed, they may be modified by the board "in the light of subsequent developments."

The court, accordingly, directed that the petition of the company should be denied and that the board's order should be enforced.

The Wallace Corporation and the Richwood Clothespin and Dishworkers' Union appealed to the Supreme Court of the United States.

V

The case was argued before the Supreme Court on November 16, 1944. The attorney for the company contended that the stipulation made between the parties on January 19, 1942, was binding and any acts occurring prior thereto should not have been considered by the board, and that the board's findings were not supported by evidence. The attorneys for the board, on the other hand, contended that as an administrative body it must have the freedom necessary in administrative proceedings and therefore it was not bound by the settlement of January 19, and further that the findings were supported by evidence.

On December 18, 1944, Judge Hugo L. Black delivered the thin majority's opinion of the court. He concluded that:

One: The settlement agreement of January 19, 1942, "plainly implies" that the old employees might retain their jobs by becoming members of whichever union had won the election, yet the company entered into a contract which resulted in the discharge of the CIO partisans and the man who had been the president of the CIO local.

Two: The agreement included a clause which made the union shop null and void if the Thompson group affiliated itself with an outside union. Before signing this agreement, the company had notice that the Thompson group claimed the right to refuse membership to employees formerly favoring the CIO affiliation. Thus, although the company had not conspired to oust the CIO partisans from employment, it had signed a contract with the Richwood Clothespin and Dishworkers' Union knowing it "proposed to refuse to admit them to membership and thus accomplish the very same purpose."

Three: The company had shown obvious hostility to recognition of a CIO union. This hostility extended to any employee who did or might affiliate himself with the CIO union. The court could not accept the argument of the company that, since Section 8(3) of the act permitted union-shop agreements, the company, having entered into such agreement, had no control over the union's conduct concerning admission to union membership and was therefore bound to discharge the nonunion members. The company was not compelled by law to enter into a contract under which it knew that discriminatory discharges of its employees were bound to occur. The record disclosed that there was more the company could and should have done to prevent these discriminatory discharges even after the contract was executed.

Four: The National Labor Relations Act was designed to wipe out discrimination in industrial relations. The court did not construe the provision authorizing a closed-shop contract as indicating an intention on the part of Congress to authorize a majority of workers and a company to penalize minority groups of workers which favored another bargaining agency. No employee could be deprived of his employment because of his prior affiliation with any particular union.

Five: The board was not estopped by the settlement of January 19, 1942, from considering events which had taken place prior to that time. The procedure of administrative bodies was quite different from other procedure, and the jurisdictional concept of *estoppel* might not be used to render the board powerless to prevent an obvious frustration of the act's purposes.

Justice Robert H. Jackson (with Chief Justice Stone and Justices Roberts and Frankfurter concurring), in a long opinion, dissented. He reasoned that there was no evidence that the employer had foreknowledge of which union would win or what that union's practices would be in regard to membership admission. Since all the parties, including the board, knew that the victorious union would exact a closed shop and all parties had consented thereto, the company was not guilty of an unfair labor practice in carrying out that agreement. Besides, only after it had been certified as bargaining agent did the Richwood Clothespin and Dishworkers' Union declare that its members would not work with those workers in the plant who were not favorable to their interests and that those workers would not be allowed to become members of their organization.

Justice Jackson believed that the efforts made by the company to have the bargaining agent consent to reinstatement of the 43 was not necessarily in bad faith; and that, since there had not been any unfair practices between the dates of the stipulation and the election, therefore, the only unfair labor practice charge against the company was the closed-shop agreement. But, since as a matter of law and in view of the previous arrangements among all parties, the company was bound to give the certified union a closed-shop contract, it was not guilty of an unfair labor practice. Justice Jackson said that the basic principle of the closed shop implied that acts "unfair when exercised by the employer in his own interest . . . are fair and lawful when enforced by him as an instrument of the Union itself." Furthermore, Justice Jackson argued, the Wagner Act did not give the board power to deal with union practices however "unfair they may be to members, to applicants, to minorities, to other unions, or to employers," and that therefore the board could not hold an employer responsible for the practices of a union which has enforced a closed-shop contract.

In accordance with the majority opinion, the Wallace Corporation was ordered to comply with the order of the NLRB, which directed the company to cease recognizing the Richwood Clothespin and Dishworkers' Union as the bargaining agency and to reinstate the discharged CIO partisans and make good their losses of pay.

VI

The Supreme Court decision in this Wallace case reemphasizes the maxim that wherever there is a right there is a corresponding duty; and that this maxim applies to labor unions as well. The right of the union to be the exclusive bargaining agent imposes the corresponding duty on the union to represent equally all workers whose bargaining agent it is, without discrimination and without favoritism.

Failure of unions to live up to this duty in good faith is likely to bring to the forefront the question of an *open union*. May a union by reason of becoming the exclusive bargaining agent of all the workers in a shop obtain higher working standards but limit these benefits to its own members and prevent other workers—nonmembers—from enjoying them by refusing to admit them as members? In the absence of special reasons, is it socially desirable that a union which obtained the right to be the exclusive bargaining agency should close its doors to new workers? Society is likely to raise the question whether such a union shall not, as a matter of social policy, be obligated to maintain an open union protected by a closed shop.

Some state courts, in considering these questions, have held that a union as a voluntary association has the right to limit its membership to persons acceptable to it; a union may legally enter into collective agreements providing for closed shops; but the union may not maintain both—the closed union and the closed shop. The reasoning is that where a union has "attained a monopoly of the supply of labor by means of closed shop agreements . . . such a union occupied a quasi-public position similar to that of a public service business and it has certain corresponding obligations." The court reached a conclusion that "an arbitrarily closed or partially closed union is incompatible with a closed shop." The American labor movement will do well to ponder this issue.

- 22 -

Let Unions Beware of the Company They Keep

(1935–1945)

ALLEN BRADLEY COMPANY, ET AL. V.
LOCAL UNION NO. 3, ET AL.

I

More than fifty years ago, in 1891, the New York City electrical workers engaged on outside construction work organized a federal union chartered by the American Federation of Labor. A year later this federal union affiliated itself with the International Brotherhood of Electrical Workers of America (IBEW) and became known as Local 3. Originally, the local limited its membership to electricians engaged on *outside* construction work but it later merged with Local 261, which consisted of workers doing such inside electrical work as fitting, wiring, and assembling of fixtures. The local worked in close co-operation with the other unions in the building industry, and with the support of these other unions succeeded in securing better conditions for its members and grew in strength and in influence in the construction field in New York City.

In 1932 the union's collective agreement with the electrical contractors in New York City expired. At the time the building industry in New York City was suffering acutely from the general economic depression in the country. There was a great deal of unemployment, but in spite of unfavorable economic conditions the union made new demands as a condition of the renewal of its agreement. As was to be expected, this met with great opposition. The employers resisted not only the new demands but the union itself. In fact, the members of the Electrical Contractors' Association locked out the Local 3 members, promoted an "independent" union, hired "detectives," and proclaimed a reduction in wages. The union had a fight on its hands. After the controversy had continued a while, a number of contractors reached individual agreements with the union; then the Brooklyn contractors as a group broke away from the Electrical Contractors' Association and made peace with the union. Finally, in November, 1934, a general settlement was made with the association.

In the meantime important political and economic developments, directly and indirectly affecting the fortunes of this union, were taking place in the country. The presidential election of 1932 resulted in a new administration. The Democrats, under the leadership of Franklin D. Roosevelt, assumed power. A new attitude toward labor was current in the country. In 1933 the National Industrial Recovery Act (NIRA) was passed. This act, it will be recalled, aimed to stimulate the economy of the country by securing more employment, by increasing the purchasing power of the masses, by encouraging collective bargaining, and by maintaining fair competition among businessmen through the adoption of Codes of Fair Competition in industries.

Local 3, as well as other unions in the country, made immediate use of the encouragement to organize extended to it by this new law. Under the leadership of its able and energetic business manager, Harry Van Arsdale, Jr., the union undertook a campaign to organize the electrical workers engaged not only in outside construction work but also in the manufacture of electrical equipment and its installation in New York City. A particularly active campaign for organization was conducted among the workers employed in shops manufacturing switchboards and panel boards.

The manufacturers of this type of equipment resisted union organization. They claimed that any rise in wages likely to be caused by unionization would so increase their labor cost as to make it impossible for them to compete with the manufacturers of this equipment outside of New York City, and that General Electric and Westinghouse might capture their business and drive local manufacturers out of this field of activity. The manufacturers wanted to know, assuming that they consented to unionization of their plants, whether the union would extend protection to them by keeping other manufacturers' products out of New York City. The record does not disclose what the union's direct reply was, but apparently some understanding on this subject was reached. The record does show that early in 1934 the union succeeded in getting agreements with New York City's principal switch and panel board manufacturers. Thus, Local 3 now included in its membership workers who manufactured equipment as well as the workers who installed it. The members engaged in the manufacture of equipment were treated by the union as a special class; they paid lower dues but had no right to vote, and were not given any voice in union affairs. As will be seen later, this expansion of membership led to events which were the basis of years of litigation and had a decided effect on the legal rights of unions throughout the country.

In spite of the fact that Local 3 had extended its organization to include both construction workers and manufacturing employees in the switchboard and panel board fields, its membership during 1934 and 1935 declined, mainly due to unemployment. Work had to be shared. Men were working in "rotation" in order to spread whatever work there was among as many members as possible. The local's big problem was how to secure more work for its members.

II

It will be recalled that in 1935 the Supreme Court of the United States declared the National Industrial Recovery Act (NIRA) unconstitutional. The employers were no longer bound by any fair trade practices embodied in the codes. But the effect of NIRA's existence was not lost on the manufacturers. Industry had greatly profited by the codes and was anxious to retain the trade practices stimulated by them. NIRA had demonstrated to small businessmen some of the advantages of combined action long known to large industrialists. The New York City electrical contractors, like other employers, also benefited greatly by NIRA and were anxious to retain the benefits. With this in view they held various conferences among themselves and with the union, and decided to adopt a voluntary code for the electrical industry in New York City.

The chief purpose of the voluntary code was ostensibly the exchange of information concerning bids to be made for contracts and the establishment of "standards" for bidding. According to these standards, every contractor, in submitting a bid, was obliged to calculate not only his estimated labor cost but also to add *as overhead* 35 per cent of his labor cost and 10 per cent of his cost of material. The bid also was to contain a condition that the contractor was to supply the material as well as labor and supervision. According to these standards, the builder apparently was not free to purchase his electrical equipment in the open market but was supposed to purchase it through the contractors. These "fair practice rules" were to be interpreted by a Voluntary Code Authority which could impose fines for violations of the code. Two representatives of the union were members of the authority's executive board.

During the construction of Radio City in New York, the union saw an opportunity of securing more work for its members. When the electric-power equipment was delivered to the Radio City job, it came "factory assembled" instead of "knocked down," for wiring on the job. Customarily, the assembly of such equipment was done by the construction electricians *on the job*. Obviously, factory-wired equipment further reduced the work of electricians in New York City. The union demanded that the electrical contractors order the equipment from the manufacturers to be delivered knocked down. The contractors conferred with the representatives of the equipment manufacturers. It seems that the manufacturers' representatives took the position that they were concerned only with the contractors' specifications for such equipment and would deliver the equipment in the manner the contractors specified. After some additional urging by the union, the contractors subsequently agreed among themselves to comply with the union's request and have the assembly of the power equipment done on the job. Accordingly, they notified the manufacturers to deliver the equipment knocked down.

This policy of the contractors not only satisfied the union but proved to be profitable to the contractors themselves. The contractors favored the union in another respect, by directing more and more of their business to the New York City manufacturers of electrical equipment. This policy too was pursued by them not without selfish motives, because under the voluntary code they charged 10 per cent commission on the cost of all purchases, and hence were not interested in seeking to obtain material at cheaper prices. On the contrary, they had an incentive to buy high-priced rather than low-priced goods. They were perfectly willing to favor union-labeled equipment made in New York City though it cost more than similar equipment could be purchased for elsewhere. It was not mere altruism that motivated the contractors in purchasing only union-labeled electrical equipment. It was "good business."

The union "policed" the industry and saw to it that no nonunion electrical equipment was used on any job where its members or members of other unions in the construction industry were employed. It enforced this policy by strikes and threats of strike. If the power equipment came to a job preassembled, the union insisted that such equipment be dismantled and then reassembled on the job. If it came from nonunion shops, the union members insisted on having it replaced by union-labeled equipment. A refusal to comply with this request meant a stoppage of work by Local 3 members and, possibly, also by members of other construction unions on the job. Such a stoppage would cause loss of time, waste of material and money, and obviously was unprofitable for the builder. Under these circumstances it was essential for the builder and the contractor to have all the electric equipment carry the union label and be assembled on the job.

Encouraged by the success in the switchboard and panel board fields, the union expanded its activities to include workers engaged in the making of electric fixtures, the installation and maintenance of electric signs, and even the installation of neon lighting signs. Since installation was in some way connected with electricity, Local 3 claimed the work for its members and picketed jobs where electric or neon signs were installed by others. If the work was not done by its members, the union continued picketing the store even after the installation of the sign until the store owner agreed to have the maintenance work on the sign done by union contractors.

This is the background of the case that subsequently became known as *Allen Bradley Company, et al. v. Local Union No. 3, et al.*

III

The out-of-town manufacturers of electrical equipment saw the sales of their products in New York City declining. They were receiving fewer and fewer orders from the city contractors. On the other hand, the New York City contractors and manufacturers of electrical equipment, and the union and its members, were benefiting by holding the city market for themselves. The out-of-town manufacturers decided to take legal steps to protect their interests.

On December 9, 1935, Allen Bradley Company and nine others

manufacturing electrical equipment outside of New York City instituted an action in the United States District Court for the Southern District of New York against Local Union 3, a number of its officers, and other individuals. The complaint, as subsequently amended, charged in substance:

(a) The union entered into a conspiracy to restrain interstate commerce in violation of the antitrust laws.

(b) For the purpose of carrying out the conspiracy it entered into collective agreements with contractors in New York City calling for a closed shop and compelling those contractors to use no equipment made by the plaintiff companies, by exacting promises from them to use no equipment other than that of local manufacture.

(c) The union enforced its policy by violence, strikes, and threats of strikes.

(d) The defendants engaged in an unlawful boycott by refusing to handle or work on goods manufactured by the plaintiff companies, and by threatening builders and contractors who would purchase goods from plaintiffs for use in New York City.

The plaintiffs requested the court to issue a broad injunction forbidding the defendants, and all persons working in conjunction with them, to enforce any regulation which would prevent the members of the union from handling plaintiffs' products or from inducing contractors to have material shipped knocked down if it normally was shipped assembled. The plaintiffs also asked that a declaratory judgment be granted to the effect that the union's actions violated the antitrust laws.

The defendants in their answer raised important issues of law. After denying all the essential charges of the complaint and specifically denying that they were boycotting the plaintiffs' products, they contended:

1. The union activities were directed toward the improvement of the workers' conditions. Such activities under the federal laws were immune from prosecutions under the antitrust laws.

2. The plaintiff employers refused to enter into collective agreements with the union, or the International Brotherhood of Electrical Workers, and therefore there was a labor dispute existing between the plaintiffs and the defendants.

3. The Norris-La Guardia Act prohibited the federal courts from issuing injunctions in labor disputes.

4. The controversy between plaintiffs and defendants arose from a *local dispute,* and therefore, the antitrust laws were not applicable and the federal courts lacked jurisdiction in this matter.

When the case appeared before Judge Vincent L. Leibell, the attorneys stipulated that the case be referred to a special master for the purpose of taking testimony and making findings "both as to facts and as to law" and reporting back to the court. The court then appointed John Kirkland Clark as the special master to hear and determine the facts and the law with his recommendations thereon.

IV

The hearings before the special master were long and protracted, lasting about two and one-half years. Four hundred witnesses testified, 1,700 exhibits were presented, and 24,000 pages of testimony taken.

Witnesses called by the plaintiffs painted the union in lurid colors, as an organization bent on suppressing competition by a highhanded action. One witness related an episode which was characterized as the "Tale of the Bomb and the Baby." He testified that he was *told by someone* that a stench bomb was flung through a recalcitrant contractor's bedroom window; that the bomb landed in a baby girl's crib, exploded, and blinded the baby's eye. Apparently the witness was highly imaginative. There was no evidence that a stench bomb had been thrown; testimony proved that the child referred to suffered from an eye condition which had existed long before the date of the alleged stench bomb incident, and furthermore that the child had not lost an eye at all. The witness's testimony was so grossly exaggerated that the special master directed that the story be excluded from the record. However, the story, having been given wide publicity at the time, naturally put the union in an unfavorable light before the public.

More than four years after his appointment as special master, and after reading the voluminous testimony and the attorneys' briefs, consisting of three thousand pages, John Kirkland Clark, on September 30, 1941, filed his report on the facts and the law. He made 374 findings of fact and 26 conclusions of law. Among his essential findings of fact were:

1. The membership of Local 3 increased from 4,500 in 1925 to

about 15,000 in 1938. Charter A members numbered about 7,000 and Charter B members, who had no right to vote, about 8,000.

2. The union membership covered virtually everyone working on or producing electrical equipment within the New York City area; a large part of the membership consisted of women employed in stores and factories which had nothing to do with installation of electrical equipment.

3. While the local had started out as a craft union, the inclusion of Charter B members made the local an industrial union with the added power that the possession of such control over an organized industry gave the union.

4. The business manager of the union, Harry Van Arsdale, Jr., was the all-powerful officer who, among other things, had complete power to select which members should fill existing job vacancies.

5. Typical of the local's activities was its conduct in connection with the electrical switchboard and panel board manufacturers. In return for a closed-shop agreement, higher wages, and shorter hours, Local 3 promised the manufacturers of switchboards and panel boards in New York City an exclusive market within the city.

6. The union fulfilled its promise by strikes, threatened strikes, and sympathy strikes by other unions in the building industry.

7. The contractors co-operated with the union, and so did the local manufacturers. This combination was designed to enable the manufacturers to name their own prices for the switchboards and panel boards manufactured by them. In addition thereto, the Voluntary Code of Fair Competition served as an additional instrument for maintaining high prices because every contractor was obliged to file every bid made by him and each bid had to include 35 per cent of the labor cost as overhead, 10 per cent of the material cost for commission, and 6 per cent of the total for management.

8. The Voluntary Code Authority imposed substantial fines on the violators. Two union officials were members of the code executive committee.

9. The union did not share in the fines imposed by the Code Authority and apparently did not take any direct action against a contractor for violation of the code.

10. Contrary to prevailing practice, the union did not permit lighting fixtures and control equipment to be wired at the factory but required the wiring to be done by its members on the construc-

tion job. Switchboards, for example, had to be delivered knocked down from the factory; if delivered assembled they had to be knocked down and reassembled at the job.

11. New York City was closed to nonunion manufacturers of electrical equipment. Plaintiffs' equipment was turned down by the New York electrical contractors even if the cost thereof was only one-third of the price charged for the same equipment by the New York City union manufacturers, because plaintiffs were boycotted by the powerful Local 3.

12. The union circulated a "fair list" of the manufacturers of electrical equipment, which in reality "constituted a black list of those not named upon it."

13. The local disregarded the no-strike pledge in its contracts and threatened strikes against the employment of nonunion contractors when they were low bidders and thus prevented the city of New York from securing federal grants in aid in connection with certain construction projects contemplated by the city.

The special master concluded that as a matter of law:

(a) The antitrust laws had been violated and the union contractors and manufacturers in New York City were engaged in a boycott which restrained interstate commerce in switchboards, panel boards, and other equipment.

(b) The union's defense that there was a labor dispute between it and the plaintiffs was without merit because no question concerning the terms and conditions of employment of the employees of the plaintiff companies was involved. Therefore there was no labor dispute within the meaning of the Norris-La Guardia Act and the issuance of an injunction was not prohibited.

(c) The combination and conspiracy in the case were clearly illegal and should be enjoined.

(d) Since the injunction itself would incorporate all findings of fact similar to those which would be embodied in a declaratory judgment, it was unnecessary to issue a separate declaratory judgment.

The motion to confirm the special master's report came before Judge Francis C. Caffrey. Various technical objections were raised as to whether the special master had a right to draw conclusions of law and as to whether a declaratory judgment aside from the injunction should be issued by the court. In view of the fact that the defendants' attorneys stipulated that the special master should hear and determine the "facts and the law," the judge overruled the union's objection and on June 10, 1943, he delivered his opinion in which, in reliance upon the special master's findings of fact, he concluded:

(a) Local 3 had a right to enter into closed-shop agreements and to decide with whom it would enter into such agreements, and the union had a right to determine whom it would accept or reject as members if their decision was reasonable and not arbitrary.

(b) Local 3's strikes against city projects for the purpose of getting employment for its construction members were unreasonable and unlawful.

(c) The plaintiffs were entitled to an injunction restraining the defendants from doing the acts charged in the complaint as recommended by the special master.

(d) The plaintiff companies were entitled to a judgment declaring that the acts of the union violated the Sherman Act.

(e) The plaintiffs were entitled to both an injunction under the Clayton Act and to a declaratory judgment.

The union appealed from the decision.

V

The appeal from Judge Caffrey's decision came before the Federal Circuit Court of Appeals for the Second Circuit. On October 12, 1944, Judge Charles E. Clark (with Augustus N. Hand concurring), reversing Judge Caffrey, delivered the opinion by the majority of the court. After commending the counsel in the case and the special master for their industriousness, as shown by the voluminous record and the 374 findings of fact and 26 conclusions of law, Judge Clark pointedly remarked that "the very verbosity and superfluity of the findings have not aided the decision as much as doubtless expected." The highlights of his decision were:

1. The defendants were entitled to a more direct and succinct statement of the illegal acts prohibited by the injunction. Since disobedience of the injunction might result in penalties of fines or imprisonment, the defendants were entitled to know more precisely what specific acts they were restrained from. The incorporation in the injunction of all the 374 findings of the special master's report made the injunction ambiguous.

2. The injunction was at best entirely too broad. It forbade some acts which the union officers legally might do, as, for instance, to induce *any* person, even by peaceful means, not to deal with the plaintiffs.

3. It was significant that neither the contractors nor the local manufacturers who supposedly were coconspirators with the union were named as defendants in this action. The injunction was directed against the union, and the unnamed "confederates" might not be reached at all.

4. The conditions of employment of Local 3 members by city manufacturers were "the matrix of the controversy." The special master, in fact, had found that the activities of the union were directed toward getting work for its members. It was a make-work campaign for the benefit of such members. It was now settled law that the members of a union, in order to improve their working conditions, could agree among themselves to refuse to work upon products of other manufacturers.

5. The immunities from prosecution under the Sherman Antitrust Act extended to unions by the Norris-La Guardia Act were interpreted by the Supreme Court in the *Hutcheson* case to be, for all practical purposes, a complete shield for the defendants' acts though said acts were injurious to the plaintiffs.

6. Unions did not necessarily forfeit the benefits of their statutory exemptions when they combined with nonlabor groups. Only when a union no longer acted in its self-interest and combined with nonlabor groups for the latter's selfish purposes might the union's immunity be questioned. In other words, the immunity was lost when the union named was used as a cloak for illegal activities.

7. The union's activities in this case were directed toward self-interest and protection of its members. Therefore, it had not lost the immunities extended to it by the Norris-La Guardia Act.

8. The union's policy and methods in relation to its own members were not at issue in this case. Since the policy and methods of union regulations were not the affair of the court, the judgment ought to be reversed and the action dismissed.

Judge Thomas W. Swan dissented. He held that no labor dispute existed because the union had made no effort to negotiate concerning the conditions of employment of the workers in the plaintiffs' plants and that Congress did not intend by the Norris-La Guardia

Act to allow unions to do what no state or city could do, namely, to exclude products from a market. Conceding that the language of the injunction was too broad, Judge Swan reasoned that the plaintiffs were nevertheless entitled to a declaratory judgment and to an injunction restraining Local 3 from agreeing with New York City employers to close the New York market to outside manufacturers of electrical equipment.

In accordance with the majority opinion, the judgment of the lower court was reversed and the case dismissed. The plaintiffs carried the case to the Supreme Court of the United States on a writ of certiorari.

VI

Under the title of *Allen Bradley Company, et al.* v. *Local Union No. 3, et al.,* the case was argued before the Supreme Court on March 8 and 9, 1945. About three months later, on June 18, 1945, Justice Hugo Black delivered the opinion of the majority of the court. He pointed out that the substantive issue of the case was: Could labor unions, prompted by a desire to get and hold jobs for their members at union standards, combine with employers and with manufacturers of goods to restrain competition in, and to monopolize, the marketing of such goods without violating the Sherman Antitrust Act? In answering this question Justice Black in the main reasoned:

One: The purpose of the Sherman Act was to protect consumers from monopoly prices brought about in the era of "trusts" and "combinations" of business which sought to control the market by suppression of competition.

Two: The combination of the contractors and manufacturers that was intended to and did restrain trade in and did monopolize the supply of electrical equipment in the New York City area was clearly unlawful unless this combination was entitled to immunity by reason of the fact that the union participated in such combination.

Three: There appeared to be two conflicting Congressional policies concerning the application of the antitrust laws. One policy sought to preserve a competitive business economy; the other sought to preserve the right of labor to organize to better workers' conditions through the agency of collective bargaining. The Supreme Court might reconcile these two conflicting policies.

Four: In enacting the Norris-La Guardia Act Congress had recognized the arguments made by labor continuously since 1890 that the Sherman Act was unfairly applied by courts to labor unions. However, while the Supreme Court recognized this Congressional policy, it held in the *Apex Hosiery* case that labor unions were still subject to the Sherman Act to "some extent not defined."

Five: In defining the "extent" to which labor unions were still subject to the antitrust laws, and in seeking to reconcile the two conflicting Congressional policies concerning the application of the antitrust laws, the following might be used as a guide:

(*a*) When the unions acted alone—without combining with nonlabor groups—their acts, even if similar to those committed by Local 3, were, under the Clayton and Norris-La Guardia Acts, immune from prosecution under the antitrust laws.

(*b*) However, when unions participated with a combination of nonlabor groups to control the market of goods and to eliminate competition, the unions no longer enjoyed the immunity extended to them by the exemptions of the Clayton and Norris-La Guardia Acts.

Six: If business groups, by combining with labor unions, could fix prices and divide up markets, the Congressional policy of preserving a competitive business economy would be a mere futile gesture. A business monopoly was no less such because a union participated.

Seven: Since in the case at bar Local 3 combined with contractors and manufacturers and aided these nonlabor groups in creating business monopolies and controlling the marketing of goods and services, the union was not entitled to immunity from the Sherman Antitrust Act.

Eight: In the case at bar, the declaratory judgment and the injunction issued by the lower court could not be sustained in the form in which they were entered because they were entirely too broad and because they prohibited the doing of the very things that the Clayton Act specifically permitted unions to do. The scope of the declaratory judgment was too vague and the commands of the injunction too sweeping and therefore they should be modified in accordance with this opinion.

Justice Roberts, agreeing that an injunction should be issued, disagreed with the reasoning of the majority of the court. He contended that the majority opinion would convey the wrong impression, namely, that the law would allow a union to halt interstate commerce and secure a monopoly of work through strikes and boycotts, as long as it did not co-operate with the employers. If that was permitted, Justice Roberts reasoned, then the unions could make a separate agreement with each employer, create a complete monopoly or a complete control of the market, and contend that each employer acted independently. Justice Roberts observed that the Supreme Court found itself in its present predicament because of its past decisions but he disagreed that the only remedy was new Congressional legislation. He apparently believed that the court might still interpret the law so as to prevent such practices by labor. For that reason he believed that the injunction should not be limited, as urged by the majority.

Justice Murphy dissented, stating that the Circuit Court should have been upheld in its dismissal of the case. He reasoned that if the acts of the union were to be held illegal because it used the aid of others, nonlabor groups, then such reasoning might lead to a holding that collective bargaining itself was illegal. In Justice Murphy's opinion, the reasoning of the majority might have been correct if the employers had used the union as a shield for their own interest; but since in this case the court found that the union had acted for self-interest and that the benefit to the employers was merely *incidental*, the union's acts were entitled to immunity under the Clayton and Norris-La Guardia Acts.

VII

The decision in this *Allen Bradley* case must be looked upon as an attempt by the Supreme Court to reconcile the conflicting public policies of (a) protection given to unions as combinations by the Clayton and Norris-LaGuardia Acts against prosecution under the Sherman Antitrust Act and (b) suppression of business combinations which seek to fix prices and maintain market controls in violation of the Sherman Act. The court's dilemma was how to make the same Sherman Act work simultaneously in two opposite directions.

The court was conscious that a labor union to be effective could legitimately seek to stabilize labor conditions in industry and to suppress competition from nonunion labor with established union conditions. The Clayton Act, as originally intended by Congress, was to extend immunity to labor for such activities, and this immunity extended to peaceful secondary boycotts which could be conducted by unions as a means of suppressing competition from nonunion made work. The Norris-La Guardia Act left no doubt that it was the intent of Congress to fortify labor's position in this respect. But in this *Allen Bradley* case the union's otherwise legitimate activity placed the employers in a position to fix prices and maintain market controls, in direct opposition to the public policy of suppressing such combination.

The court was thus faced with the troublesome problem of how to reconcile these two conflicting public policies without destroying either. The decision provided a "practical" solution, namely, labor's immunity under the Clayton and Norris-LaGuardia Acts against prosecution under the Sherman Act might remain in full force and effect but *only so long* as labor pursued its legitimate activities *alone*, without combining with employers; business monopolies were not shielded from prosecution under the Sherman Act by their combining with labor. Since the court became convinced that in this case there was connivance between the union and the employers, it concluded that the union was not shielded by the protective legislation of the Norris-La Guardia Act and directed the issuance of a limited injunction.

In evaluating the effect of this decision on rights of unions in the United States one must not overlook the particular conduct of the union in this case. It was this conduct that was condemned by the court. In so far as the rights of unions are concerned, the decision reasserted the *Hutcheson* doctrine that our laws do not prohibit a union from indulging in activities which may tend to bring about market control as long as the union does it *alone*, without combining with employers. Unions must beware of the company they keep.

- 23 -

The High Cost of Contempt

(1946–1947)

UNITED STATES V. JOHN L. LEWIS

I

The coal industry was for a long time a "sick industry." Competition was keen and employment irregular. In the 1920's the coal market, especially because of the use of oil as fuel, was shrinking. According to the leaders of the United Mine Workers, a miner at the time could not expect more than 215 days' work during a year and his earnings during the working period were far from sufficient to maintain his family during the entire year.

Help came to the United Mine Workers in the year 1932, when the Norris-La Guardia Act was passed by Congress. This act outlawing yellow-dog contracts opened many mine fields to union organization. But the union at the time did not have the wherewithal to engage in organizational campaigns. With the beginning of the New Deal, however, the picture changed. John L. Lewis, president of the union, immediately launched an intensive organization drive which swelled union membership and brought the union into areas previously barred by injunctions or by the activities of local police.

In the early fall of 1933 the miners employed in the "captive mines" (mines owned by the steel mills mining coal for their own use and not for the general coal market) went out on strike and by a large majority designated the miners' union as their bargaining agent. The owners of the captive mines refused to deal with the union, though they were willing to deal with the individuals chosen as the "elected representatives" of the employees. A face-saving compromise was contrived by the National Labor Relations Board,

287

under which the collective agreement was made not directly with the union but with the workers' elected representatives "who may be officers of the United Mine Workers of America."

From that time on, the United Mine Workers steadily gained in collective bargaining and in standing and prestige. With each renewal of the collective agreements the lot of the miner was improved. Thus, in 1934, the union secured the 7-hour day, 35-hour week, and a wage rise. In 1937 the union won payment at time and a half for overtime work. In 1939, as a result of a strike, the United Mine Workers finally penetrated the remaining unorganized fields, including those of the "dark and bloody ground" of Harlan County, Kentucky. The undisputed leader of the union, John L. Lewis, occupied a prominent place among the leaders of labor. He became a commanding figure in public life and front-page news.

The dramatic events of the miners' union thereafter cannot be told separately and apart from the dramatic personality of its leader. Under Lewis's leadership, an important group of AFL unions organized in 1935 a Committee for Industrial Organization (CIO). The announced purpose of this committee was to organize the workers in the mass production industries on an industrial instead of the traditional AFL craft basis. Lewis was in the news to stay. Later, when these unions were suspended by the AFL on the ground that they were fostering a dual trade-union movement, Lewis organized that committee into a separate national labor movement under the name of the Congress of Industrial Organizations. Naturally, John Llewellyn Lewis was its first president.

Lewis also became active in politics. Originally a Republican, he swung to Roosevelt in 1936 and organized Labor's Non-Partisan League, which actively supported Roosevelt. The miners' union contributed or lent a large sum of money to the Democratic Party in that campaign. When Roosevelt was victorious, Lewis's ambitions grew. He expected that his services in the campaign would be appreciated and that he would become an influential factor in Roosevelt's policies, but he was doomed to disappointment. Roosevelt did not seek or follow Lewis's recommendations, either in matters of policy or in government appointments. Neither was Lewis invited to major state dinners at the White House. Coolness set in between him and Roosevelt, but as late as 1939 Lewis was still hopeful. In her enlightening book, *The Roosevelt I Knew*, Frances Perkins, former secretary of labor, credits President Roosevelt with relating to her and Daniel Tobin the following:

"About two months ago, John Lewis came to see me one evening. He was in a most amiable mood, and he talked about the third term too then, just the way you have, only much smoother. . . . When I told him what I told you, that the people wouldn't like a third term and that it would be very hard going politically, what do you think he said, then? He said, 'Mr. President, I have thought of all of that and I have a suggestion to make for you to consider. If the Vice-Presidential candidate on your ticket should happen to be John L. Lewis, those objections would disappear. A strong labor man would insure full support not only of the labor people but of all the liberals who worry about such things as third terms'. . . . He didn't press me, he just asked me to think it over and give it consideration."

The Democratic convention of 1940, however, named Henry A. Wallace as the running mate for Roosevelt. In that year Lewis openly broke with Roosevelt. On the very eve of Election Day, in his characteristic dramatic fashion, John L. Lewis, over a national hookup, attacked Roosevelt and announced his support of Wendell Willkie. He also dramatically declared that should Roosevelt be re-elected for a third term, he, John L. Lewis, would resign as head of the CIO. Lewis kept his word. After Roosevelt was re-elected Lewis resigned as president of the CIO. He became embittered, and this expressed itself in the union's policy toward the government.

II

With the outbreak of World War II, the United States had entered a period of intensive nonbelligerent aid to Britain. The Lend-Lease bill was enacted. Uninterrupted production in the heavy industries became a basic need for the economy of the country, and production depended on a constant and uninterrupted supply of bituminous coal. John L. Lewis, conscious of the power of his union, was determined to take advantage of all opportunities.

Opportunities presented themselves. In the negotiations for the renewal of the collective agreement in 1941, the union demanded that the operators of the captive mines grant it full recognition and enter into agreement *directly* with the union as a party instead of merely with the "workers' elected representatives." When the operators refused, the miners walked out. A 30-day truce was arranged.

The majority of the National Defense Mediation Board, on November 10, recommended a settlement without a union shop clause. In protest, its CIO members resigned, and this Board was "done to death." (Subsequently a National War Labor Board was established.) Coal being the lifeblood of industry, President Roosevelt proposed that the miners return to work and that the issue of union security be either arbitrated or remain status quo for the duration of the war. At first Lewis turned it down, but when the President renewed it, Lewis, on November 22, accepted arbitration. The arbitrators, composed of John L. Lewis, Benjamin Fairless and John R. Steelman as chairman, as was to be expected, by a vote of two to one, awarded a *union shop*. Lewis won.

That very morning the treacherous Japanese attack on Pearl Harbor in December, 1941, brought the United States actively into the war. With the war boom, national income rose and the miners wanted a share in the new prosperity. When the collective agreement expired in 1943, the United Mine Workers made new demands, including "portal-to-portal" pay (pay from the time of entering the work gate—not the work spot—to the time of leaving the work gate). When the union and the coal operators failed to agree on the various new demands, the dispute was certified to the War Labor Board, but Lewis refused to appear at the board's hearings. He was continuing his fight against the public members of that board, especially against William H. Davis, its chairman. Scattered walkouts in mining areas occurred and were spreading to such an extent that on April 29, 1943, President Roosevelt directed the miners to resume work. He warned that, unless work was resumed by May 1, he would be obliged to use his power as commander in chief. In spite of this warning, the miners in the midwestern and eastern areas did not return to the mines, though they continued the maintenance work necessary to keep the mines in working condition. The president ordered the mines to be taken under government control. On May 4 Lewis directed the miners to return to work for a fifteen-day truce period, but his tilts with the government continued. He continued to refuse to appear before the War Labor Board, which was holding hearings on the miners' demands. He kept the threat of strike dangling before the government and the public eye.

While Lewis's desire to secure additional improvements for the miners was understandable and to a great extent justified, he went about it in a manner which gave the impression that he relished the idea of embarrassing the Roosevelt administration and that he was matching power with Roosevelt. This was resented by the public.

During the year 1943—a crucial year in the midst of the war—Lewis permitted or encouraged four union walkouts: May 1-4, June 1-5, June 15-19, and November 1-3. On two occasions—May 1 and November 1—the government had taken over control of the mines. Lewis stood his ground, government or no government, war or no war. Finally, the issue was terminated by the War Labor Board's making concessions on its Little Steel Formula. It allowed portal-to-portal pay to be figured at a flat forty-five minutes each day. Then it imposed a two-year agreement on the parties to remain in effect to April 30, 1945.

At the expiration of that agreement, new trouble began to brew in the coal industry. The union took a strike vote and filed a strike notice, as required by the Smith-Connally Act. The War Labor Board ordered the old contract extended without modification, but in spite of the board's order and in spite of the union's order to continue on the job for the next thirty days, widespread walkouts occurred. On April 10 the government took over 235 mines. On the very next day, the union and the operators of the soft-coal mines signed a contract for another year, which included provisions for full portal-to portal pay and increased vacation allowances. A similar contract was signed with the hard-coal operators in May. By June 23, 1945, the government returned the seized mines to private operation.

III

At the time of the expiration of this agreement in 1946, the shooting war was already over, but many new problems arose. The efforts to control the threatened inflation through OPA continued. All war legislation was still in effect. With the actual war over, many strikes broke out, especially in the automobile and steel industries. President Truman appointed unofficial fact-finding boards which recommended increases of 18½ cents an hour in those industries and these recommendations were finally used by President Truman as a basis of settlement of those strikes.

In this atmosphere John L. Lewis met with the mine operators to negotiate a new agreement. There were conferences but no settlement. The miners did not work on April 1, which is a traditional miners' holiday, and did not return to work on the following days either. The effort made by federal conciliators to bring about a settlement produced no results, and on April 10 the union representatives announced that further negotiations appeared to be useless. No conferences were held during the rest of April and no coal was produced in the mines. Freight and passenger train schedules on coal-burning railroads were sharply cut. Many cities imposed a "brown-out" to save coal. On May 4, 1946, President Truman declared the coal dispute a "national disaster" and suggested that both sides agree to submit the dispute to arbitration, but both parties rejected his suggestion.

On May 21, 1946, with the Smith-Connally Act still in force, President Truman ordered the mines seized, and on the following day Secretary of the Interior Krug took over the mines. Within a week, on May 29, 1946, Secretary Krug, as coal administrator, entered into an agreement with the miners' union, which agreement became known as the Krug-Lewis agreement. Under the terms of this agreement the miners received an 18½ cents an hour wage increase, the vacation payments were increased, and a Health and Welfare Fund was established to provide for "sickness, disability, death or retirement." The income of the fund was to be derived from the payment of 5 cents a ton royalty by the operators. The Krug-Lewis agreement was made subject to the previous National Bituminous Coal Wage Agreement of April 11, 1945, as amended and supplemented and was to cover "the terms and conditions of employment for the period of government possession." The last few words were destined to play an important legal role, as will soon be seen.

Peace reigned in the coal industry, but not for long. About five months later, in October, 1946, Lewis requested that a conference be held on October 21 to discuss wages, hours, and working rules. He claimed that under the National Bituminous Coal Wage Agreement the union had a right to reopen the contract upon notice and that, in view of the fact that the Krug-Lewis agreement was made subject to that agreement, the union still had that right.

The government took a different view. Navy Captain N. H.

Collison, in charge of the mines for the government during the seizure, took the position that the Krug-Lewis agreement was binding for the entire "period of government possession" of the mines and that, therefore, Lewis had no right to a reopening of the terms of the agreement. Lewis, however, insisted that unless a conference was held the union, under the terms of the original agreement, would consider the Krug-Lewis agreement void. In an effort to avoid this, Krug sent a telegram on October 27 requesting Lewis to meet with him on November 1, to which Lewis agreed. It was understood that the conferences were "without prejudice to the contention of the respective parties regarding the right" claimed by the union to terminate the Krug-Lewis agreement.

In pressing for a revision of the wage standard, the union contended that the increase in the cost of living during the war period amounted to 57 per cent, while the increase of wages to the miners aggregated only 34 per cent. In addition, the union feared that the earnings of the miners would be further reduced during the postwar period because it might not be necessary to work as long hours as during the war and therefore their earnings would shrink. Secretary Krug took the position that some of the union demands were fundamental and should be taken up directly with the owners of the mines rather than with the government "which is only the interim custodian of these properties." He outlined a proposal for negotiations between the operators and the union, but at the same time asserted that under the Krug-Lewis agreement Lewis had no right to terminate the contract that covered "the period of government operation." On November 15 Lewis notified Krug that since the negotiations had led to no agreement and that, since the union had given the necessary notice required under the original agreement with the operators, the Krug-Lewis agreement would be terminated by the union as of 12:00 o'clock midnight, Wednesday, November 20, 1946. On the same day Lewis forwarded a copy of his letter to Krug to all union locals "for your official information."

Three days later, on November 18, and two days before the termination date stated in Lewis's notice to Krug, the government served the union and John L. Lewis personally with a temporary injunction restraining them from breaking the Krug-Lewis agreement pending a hearing before the court.

IV

The temporary injunction was issued by Justice T. Alan Golds-borough of the United States District Court for the District of Columbia. The order directed the defendants, their agents, and all persons co-operating with them, to cease "continuing in effect" Lewis's notice of November 15 to Krug, and restrained them pending the hearing from breaching the union's obligations under the Krug-Lewis agreement. The injunction also restrained the defendants from issuing any publicity to the effect that the Krug-Lewis agreement had been or would be terminated or void during government possession of the bituminous coal mines. The injunction also forbade the defendants' taking any action which would interfere with the court's jurisdiction or would "impair, obstruct or render fruitless" the determination of this case by the court. The order was to expire on November 27.

While the order was served on the union and John L. Lewis on November 18, 1946, nothing was done by the union in connection with the order. Apparently the union preferred watchful waiting. Came November 20, the day set for termination of the contract in Lewis's notice, and the miners stayed away from the pits. On the following day Attorney General Clark filed a petition to punish the defendant union and John L. Lewis individually for contempt in willfully and deliberately disobeying the temporary injunction. Justice Goldsborough issued the order to show cause as requested.

On November 25 Lewis and the union appeared with their attorneys before Justice Goldsborough. Admitting that they had not taken any steps to withdraw the notice to Krug concerning the termination of the contract, they claimed that the court was without jurisdiction in the matter. They moved to dismiss the complaint and the injunction on the ground that under the Norris-La Guardia Act the court had no power to issue an injunction in this labor dispute. Two days later Justice Goldsborough extended the temporary injunction for an additional ten days, and later he denied the defendants' motion to dismiss the proceedings and directed that they stand trial for contempt of court for violating his injunction.

On November 29, 1946 the trial in the contempt proceedings took place. The miners continued to stay out. The eyes of the nation were upon Justice Goldsborough and he seemed well aware of the significance of the decision he was about to render.

Before stating his decision, a brief explanation about the meaning of "contempt of court" and the distinction between the technical terms "criminal contempt" and "civil contempt" is in order. "Contempt of court" generally means a willful disregard of the authority of a court. A person who acts in willful contravention of the court's authority or dignity, thus obstructing the administration of justice and lowering the prestige or dignity of the court, is likely to have committed contempt of court. If the person's act was not against the dignity of the court, but against the party in whose behalf the court order was issued, then such contempt is called *civil* contempt. If, as a result of the disobedience of a court order, the party in whose favor the order was issued suffers damage, the court may penalize the offender by a fine to indemnify the suffering party, the fine being commensurate with the damage suffered. A *criminal* contempt is an act which tends to bring the court's dignity into disrespect and injure the court's prestige. The court may penalize such an offender by a fine or imprisonment. The court, in criminal contempt, also may impose a fine or a prison term *conditioned* upon the offender's compliance with the court order. Such a fine or imprisonment is called *coercive*, the purpose being to coerce, to force the offender under the threat of the conditional fine or imprisonment to comply with the court mandate. The court lets the threat hang over the offender, warning him that unless he does what the court ordered he is likely to suffer the consequences of being fined or imprisoned.

To return to the story. Within a week after the trial in the contempt case—on December 6, 1946—Justice Goldsborough rendered his oral opinion. After asserting that he had been a member of Congress when the Norris-La Guardia Act was passed and that he had been friendly to its purpose, he held that the Norris-La Guardia Act's provisions were not meant to apply to the government. Since the Norris-La Guardia Act did not apply, the court had the power to issue an injunction against a labor union. Passing upon the technical question that the notice did not describe the contempt proceedings as criminal, the justice held that from the contents of the charges the defendants had sufficient notice of the nature of the proceedings. He therefore denied the defendants' motion to discharge the contempt proceedings.

Justice Goldsborough then considered the course of events from May 21 to November 15, 1946, leading to the contempt proceedings. He stressed the point that the declaration of "no contract" by the union did in fact amount to the calling of a strike because it was well known that miners, as a matter of policy, would not work in the absence of a contract. Since Mr. Lewis, in spite of the injunction served on him on November 18, took no steps to withdraw the contract-termination notice, his failure to do so amounted to encouraging a strike, interfering with the operation of government-held mines, and interfering with the court's jurisdiction. Justice Goldsborough concluded that the union and Lewis personally were guilty of civil and criminal contempt.

Emphasizing that he did not wish to hurt labor and that he could not "conceive labor's having a greater friend in this country" than him, nevertheless Justice Goldsborough concluded that the defendants must be punished. He thought that a prison sentence would be a proper penalty for the individuals involved, but since the government recommended otherwise he did not want to "disregard its recommendations." The sentence he did impose for the civil and criminal contempts committed and as damages for the harm done were fines: $3,500,000 on the United Mine Workers and $10,000 on John L. Lewis individually.

An immediate appeal was taken by the defendants from Justice Goldsborough's decision to the United States Circuit Court for the District of Columbia. At the request of the government, the Supreme Court consented that the appeal be taken directly to it. Lewis immediately ordered the miners to go back to work so that the high court should not be distracted in its deliberation by an atmosphere of economic crisis.

V

The case was argued before the Supreme Court on January 14, 1947. The contentions of the government indirectly appear in the opinion rendered by the court.

The union's contentions briefly were:

(1) The court had no right to issue the injunction because the controversy was a *labor dispute* and therefore, under the Norris-La Guardia Act, no injunction should be issued even if the government were the employer of the miners. (2) In reality, the government

was not the employer of the miners. At best, it was merely the custodian of the mines. (3) The action against the defendants was based upon alleged violation of the Smith-Connally Act. That act made a violation thereof a crime. It was well established that a court of equity would not issue injunctions to prevent a crime. Hence, this injunction was improperly issued. (4) The notice did not specify as required that the proceedings were for *criminal* contempt, and therefore the entire proceedings were fatally defective. (5) The defendants were tried for civil and criminal contempt in one proceeding. The mingling of the two kinds of contempt in one proceeding was a substantial error warranting a reversal of Justice Goldsborough's decision. (6) The United States did not prove that it suffered any damages and therefore no fine for the alleged civil contempt could have been imposed by the court. (7) The fines imposed by the court were arbitrary, excessive, and in no way related to the evidence adduced at the hearing, and therefore the decision should be reversed.

About two months later, on March 6, 1947, the Supreme Court rendered its decision. Four different opinions were written in this case. Chief Justice Vinson spoke for the majority. Justice Robert A. Jackson and Justice Frankfurter each wrote a separate opinion concurring in the result, but not in the basic reasoning. Justices Black and Douglas concurred in part and dissented in part. Justices Rutledge and Murphy dissented in separate opinions.

Passing on the issues raised by the union, Chief Justice Vinson, for the majority, in substance, held:

One: The Norris-La Guardia Act was intended to protect workers in their right to organize and strike. It prohibited the issuance of injunctions in labor disputes involving "persons," in their relationship as employers and employees. The government in its relation to its employees could not be considered in the same position as private "persons" or "employers" in relation to their employees. In common usage the term "persons" or "employers" did not include the sovereign, and unless a statute specifically included it, the word "persons" or "employers" would ordinarily not be construed to include the sovereign government. Hence, the Norris-La Guardia Act, which prohibited the issuance of injunctions in labor disputes between an employer and his employees, did not apply in cases where the government was the employer.

Two: The government must be considered as the employer of the miners in this case. The mines were seized in accordance with the Smith-Connally Act and under that act the operation of the mines became a government function. Hence, the government had "substituted itself for the private employer." This brought about the Krug-Lewis agreement. The defendants themselves recognized the government as the employer. They refused to deal with the operators of the mines as "strangers" to the Krug-Lewis agreement and referred to the "400,000 men who now serve the government of the United States in the bituminous coal mines."

Three: This was not a case where the question of the court's jurisdiction over the controversy and the defendants was frivolous. The defendants acted at their peril in making their private determination of the law applicable to this case. This disobedience of the court order was punishable as criminal contempt.

Four: The defendants were aware of the true character of these contempt charges. They, themselves, referred to it as a charge of criminal contempt. In view of their awareness that the charge was criminal contempt the error in the notice was not such as to require a reversal of the judgment.

Five: The defendants failed to show that the mingling of these two charges—civil and criminal contempt—in one proceeding resulted in substantial prejudices to them. In this hearing all the rights and privileges of the defendants were fully respected and therefore the mingling of the two contempts in one proceeding was not the kind of error that would warrant a reversal of the judgment.

Six: The United States was fully entitled to bring the present action. As a party to the civil proceedings it was entitled to benefit from the orders entered into in its behalf.

Seven: The penalty in this case was intended to have a double purpose: (*a*) Punishment for past acts—defendants' wilful disregard of the court order of November 18; and (*b*) punishment which intended to have a *coercive* power upon the defendants so as to compel obedience to the court's outstanding order.

Eight: The fine of $10,000 against Lewis personally for his contempt of court was clearly warranted. The fine against the union for its past disobedience should be reduced to $700,000, with the difference between that amount and the $3,500,000 penalty imposed by the lower court made "conditional on failure to purge itself from contempt within a reasonable time." The union could purge itself of this conditional fine for contempt by unconditionally withdrawing the notice of termination of contract within five days.

Justices Black and Douglas concurred only in part. They agreed with the majority that the Norris-La Guardia Act was not applicable to the government as employer, that the miners in this case were deemed to be government employees, and because of that they concluded that the court had the power to issue the injunction. They emphasized, however, that had they thought that the government's possession and operation of the mines was not genuine but merely pretended, they would hold that the Norris-La Guardia Act barred these proceedings. However, they disagreed with the imposition of the heavy fines as punishment for the criminal contempt for past disobedience to the court. Calling attention to the fact that under the Smith-Connally Act fines for the violation thereof are limited to $5,000, the justices believed that the punishment for contempt of court should not be higher than the punishment under the statute. They therefore urged that the fines in this case should be made entirely *conditional* upon the defendants' complete withdrawal of the contract-termination notice of November 15.

Although Justices Jackson and Frankfurter concurred in the result with the majority, their partial dissent involved a serious principle. Justice Frankfurter, in a long opinion, pointed out why he concurred in the result but not in the reasoning of the majority. He, in substance, held:

(*a*) The Norris-La Guardia Act barred injunctions in labor disputes even if the government was the employer, because that act limited the power of the courts to issue injunctions in *such subject matter*, namely, labor disputes, regardless of who the parties to the controversy were. Since the issue in this case was a labor dispute, the court was limited and it had no power to issue the injunction.

(*b*) Even if this act did not apply to the government as an employer, the government's relation to the miners in this instance could best be described as "hybrid" and not that of a real employer to its employees.

(*c*) Further, the Smith-Connally Act, under which the mines were taken over by the government, did not provide for the granting of injunctive relief to the government. In fact, the Senate defeated a Taft amendment permitting the issuance of injunctions in such cases at the request of the attorney general, and a House provision incorporating permission to secure an injunction was omitted in the conference between House and Senate reporting this legislation to Congress.

(d) Nevertheless, the defendants were guilty of contempt because they wilfully disobeyed a court order. Since the defendants flouted the authority of the court they must stand the consequences. A court order must be obeyed, for "ours is a government of laws, not of men."

Justice Murphy, in dissenting, observed:

1. The miners were private employees "despite the temporary gloss of government possession and operation of the mines." The government itself had recognized that it was not the real employer by advising the union to negotiate this very dispute with the real owners, the mine operators.

2. The *nature of the dispute*, not the status of the parties, was the "touchstone" of the applicability of the Norris-La Guardia Act. The dispute in this case was a labor dispute of the very nature concerning which Congress said that the courts were to refrain from issuing injunctions. If seizure justified injunctions, it could be used as a strikebreaking subterfuge, and after the strike was broken the properties be handed back to private employers.

3. Since this injunction was not properly issued by the court, disobedience to such a court order might have been bad union policy, but was not contemptuous and did not warrant any penalties.

4. The stoppage in soft-coal mines had indeed created a serious situation but that was no excuse for "misapplying the statutes according to the grave exigencies of the moment." The cause of orderly constitutional government was ill served by misapplying the law as it was written for the purpose of meeting an emergency situation.

Justice Rutledge's dissent (in which Justice Murphy concurred) was based also on these additional considerations:

(a) It was contrary to the American tradition in law to mix civil remedies and criminal punishment "in one lumped form of relief." The idea that "criminal prosecution and a civil suit for damages or equitable relief could be hashed together in a criminal-civil hodgepodge would be shocking to every American lawyer and to most citizens."

(*b*) The failure to specify in the notice the criminal nature of the charge made the proceeding fatally defective. A person charged with contempt had a right to know at the *beginning*, not the end, whether he was charged with civil or criminal contempt. This had not been done in this case and therefore this was reversible error.

(*c*) The penalty as well as the procedure had been prejudicial. The fine against the union was not only excessive in amount, but it was imposed in a lump sum without allocating the amount of the civil damage, the amount for criminal contempt, and the amount contingent upon future disobedience, as should be done in such cases. "When hybrid proceedings can produce penalties concealing what is for punishment and what is remedial, what criminal and what civil and in the process can discard constitutional procedure or protections . . . the courts are following not American, but Continental law." When courts failed to make the proper allocations they acted as "purely discretionary arbitrators of controversies. This cannot be done under our system."

Thus, on the important issue of the applicability of the Norris-La Guardia Act to the government as employer the court was divided five to four, but seven of the Supreme Court's nine judges agreed that Lewis and the United Mine Workers should be punished for disobedience of Justice Goldsborough's order.

VI

The significance of this case does not lie in the sensational fine imposed upon the union and upon John L. Lewis personally, nor even in the fact that the majority held that the Norris-La Guardia Act did not apply to the government when genuinely acting as an employer. Its real significance lies in the fact that the Supreme Court demonstrated once more that in all emergencies affecting the nation the court will find a way to interpret the statutes according to the need of the times as the court sees it. In this very decision Chief Justice Vinson was not satisfied to let the decision rest on the specific applicability of the Norris-La Guardia Act, but asserted that there are *alternative grounds* which support the power of the District Court to punish violations of its orders as criminal contempt. The vagueness of the phrase "alternative grounds" lacks that certainty which is essential to good law. In an emergency, the vagueness of this phrase may clothe a judge with unintended broad powers, because judges then make law and *emergency-made law is rarely, if ever, good law.* This attitude of the court must have prompted Justice Murphy in his dissent to comment that the judicial process became "a weapon for misapplying statutes according to the grave exigencies of the moment."

Labor must learn from its experience that laws on the statute books, without support from the general public, are not insurmountable by judges who genuinely seek to protect public interest in emergencies. Occasionally in interpreting a statute a court will stamp its personal philosophy or personal prejudice upon it, especially in passing on the controversial issues affecting labor laws. Such instances occurred in connection with the original interpretations of the Sherman Act and the Clayton Act. Nevertheless, when public opinion supports the purpose of the law, Congress by new legislation may force the court to correct its erroneous views. Congress did so in enacting the very Norris-La Guardia Act involved in this case. However, when labor arouses public opinion against it, labor is likely to lose the greatest source of its protection.

The labor movement in America was conscious of the accumulation of unfavorable public opinion against it, aggravated by the tactics of John L. Lewis. While labor was in sympathy with many of the objectives sought by the miners, it was not in favor of Lewis's dramatic defiance of government. But there was no one in the labor movement sufficiently influential with Lewis to make him change his mind or whose opinion or judgment Lewis deeply respected. Lewis was convinced of his superiority to his peers in the labor movement, he enjoyed and would not relinquish the reputation of being its strong man.

No one can take away from John L. Lewis his monumental achievements in freeing the coal miners from poverty and the "company town," in leading the movement for unionization in the mass production industries, and in infusing into organized labor a sense of its role in society. But history is likely to record that John L. Lewis, who made such great contributions to the advancement of the American labor movement, also contributed to the public sentiment that made it easier for antilabor forces to carry through antilabor laws, and which found expression in the Taft-Hartley Act.

With Malice Toward Labor

(1947–1948)

THE TAFT-HARTLEY ACT

I

This is the story not of a court case but of a law—the Taft-Hartley Act—which was intended to affect profoundly the rights of unions in the United States. Like the first recorded labor case—the *Philadelphia Cordwainers*—this law reflects the clash between the social philosophies of the two dominant political parties of the day. The backdrop for this law is the New Deal.

The elections of 1932, held in the midst of the depression, brought a Democratic administration to Washington after twelve years of Republican rule. President Franklin D. Roosevelt, directing his energies to restoring confidence in the future, warned the country that there was "nothing to fear but fear itself." At that time our industries were almost prostrated from the severe depression that started in 1929. The industrial wheels were turning slowly and irregularly. There was frightening unemployment and the air was filled with uncertainty and fear. The public lost confidence in the captains of industry and in the bankers, the captains of capital.

Roosevelt promised action, and action followed. Several laws were introduced heralding the New Deal, and the Blue Eagle became its symbol. The first law was the National Industrial Recovery Act (NIRA), which was designed to get the wheels of industry turning. When the Blue Eagle appeared on the horizon it was welcomed by both labor and capital. The industrialists were encouraged and permitted to set up their own rules of the game in the form of Codes of Fair Competition, and each code had to incorporate Section 7(a) of NIRA, which encouraged unionization. Employers who wanted a code for their industry were required to subscribe to the principle that workers had a right to organize and to choose their own bargaining agent.

The industrialists of the country were not in love with unionism. They were not particularly happy with the "union bride" offered to them by the president, but in their impoverished circumstances they were ready to compromise and resignedly accepted the prescribed match between industry and labor as a "marriage of convenience."

Shortly after the codes began to function, things brightened up. Numerous employers whose accountants had been using red ink to enter deficits on their books, now started to use black ink to show profits. Prosperity finally turned the corner, fear disappeared, confidence was restored, and the industrialists' self-assurance returned.

With the effective functioning of the New Deal came the gathering of the forces of the Old Deal. The industrialists started to grumble. They welcomed recovery but opposed reform. Employers resented the marriage with labor under the New Deal, claimed they had never wanted it, that it had been forced on them against their better judgment, and that it was a *shotgun wedding*. Many of them became openly unfaithful and clamored for a divorce on the ground of incompatibility.

The divorce was finally granted. NIRA was declared unconstitutional, the Blue Eagle was struck down, the Codes consequently nullified, and Section 7(a) was without any legal effect. Most industrialists greeted the divorce decree with a mixed feeling of joy and fear, joy at getting rid of the bonds of "matrimony" and government control and fear of the uncertainty of business prospects. Labor was despondent.

Deprived of the effective instrument of NIRA, the administration looked for other means by which to revive the economy of the country. The New Deal pushed on. President Roosevelt was convinced that the prosperity of the country required that the purchasing power of the masses be increased and that unhampered opportunity for labor to organize was essential for increasing workers' purchasing power. New legislation was necessary. Immediately after NIRA had been declared unconstitutional, the National Labor Relations Act (Wagner Act) was enacted by Congress and became law. Under the Wagner Act the rights of labor to organize became more definite and certain and their rights to collective bargaining were made legally enforceable.

The industrialists resented the Wagner Act and their resentment was not concealed. They fought it openly and challenged it at every opportunity. The National Association of Manufacturers and the United States Chamber of Commerce led the fight. Employers were advised that this law, like its predecessor NIRA, would be declared unconstitutional and that therefore there was no need to comply with it. Many injunctions were secured restraining the National Labor Relations Board from proceeding against employers charged with violations of the act. Numerous decisions made by the board were ignored by employers. The fight against the act continued even after the Supreme Court in April, 1937, declared it constitutional. But the tactics of the opposition changed. The new tactics called for undermining the act and many amendments were offered to nullify its essential provisions. In addition, effective antilabor legislation was put through various states of the Union. Thus, in 1939, Wisconsin replaced its "Little Wagner Act" with an Employment Peace Act which curbed the "union shop," listed certain acts by unions as unfair labor practices, and emphasized the rights of individual workers not to join a union. By 1943 the Christian American Association with headquarters at Houston, Texas, energetically pressed for antilabor legislation in many states.

This state legislation was aimed at slowing down and hampering union organization activities and at weakening existent labor organizations by the prohibition of union security clauses in labor agreements. Some of this legislation also required union organizers to be licensed and unions to file financial and other data. The general pattern of this antilabor legislation in the various states was the same, pointing to the same authorship and laying the groundwork for similar federal legislation.

II

World War II, as was to be expected, profoundly affected the economy of the country. Before the United States had been at war a year, it was faced with a manpower shortage. The demand for the tools of war made on the "arsenal of democracy" was tremendous. There were more jobs than workers to fill them. There was an imperative need for production. At the same time the mounting cost of living, despite price controls, prompted demands for wage increases. The Roosevelt administration was aware of the inflationary pressures on our economy and was conscious of the need for taking steps to control them.

In July, 1942, the War Labor Board designated by the president under the War Powers Act concluded that, in order to control inflation, control of wages was necessary. The board's policy was that wages were to be increased commensurate with the increase in the cost of living; this the board found to be 15 per cent as of January, 1941. This formula was enunciated in a decision involving the Little Steel companies and became known as the Little Steel Formula. The board relied on the OPA price regulations to hold the cost of living down to the then-existing level and reasoned that the 15 per cent increase in wages as of January, 1941, under this formula would be sufficient to meet the increase in the cost of living.

The formula fell short of expectations. The OPA was not altogether effective; the cost of living continued to rise. Low-priced merchandise gradually disappeared from the market, thus compelling the consumer to buy higher priced merchandise or go without. As employment increased, purchasing power accumulated, and as the supply of consumers' goods greatly diminished, the competition for the available goods became keen. Price was no object and "black market" operations were widespread. Many businessmen found various ways of either circumventing the OPA's regulations or delaying their enforcement. But the workers' frozen pay, limited to an increase not exceeding 15 per cent, did not lend itself to many legalistic interpretations or manipulations. Workers pressed for increases but were blocked by the rigidity of the Little Steel Formula. Though the formula at times was circumvented by the so-called "fringe" increases, workers were discontented and strikes occasionally broke out.

The antilabor forces used this opportunity for arousing public opinion against organized labor. Every strike was publicized far beyond its importance. Unions were blamed for manpower shortages, for lags in production, for absenteeism which these antilabor forces attributed to "weekend hangovers." The behavior of a *few* labor leaders reflected on the many in the labor movement. In spite of the fact that only less than 1/5 of 1 per cent of total man-days was lost by strikes, and that the labor movement as a whole generally lived up to its no-strike pledge in good faith and co-operated with the government in all war efforts, subtle propaganda reflecting on the patriotism of unions was poured out against labor as a whole.

It was against this background that the United Mine Workers made a demand in 1943 for a $2-a-day wage increase. Ignoring the public sentiment against interruption of production, the leaders of the coal miners authorized a strike. This strike in the midst of the war and in defiance of the War Labor Board decision strengthened the antilabor forces in Congress and precipitated the consideration of restrictive labor laws. The Smith-Connally Act was introduced. This act was a war measure to remain in effect only until six months after the proclaimed end of hostilities. It was designed ostensibly for keeping production going; it provided for a "cooling-off" period of sixty days; for taking a formal strike vote under government supervision before any strike could be legally declared; and for governmental seizure of struck plants or facilities essential to the war effort. It made it a criminal offense to instigate or aid in a strike in a seized plant. When the walkout in coal—the indispensible fuel and source of power—threatened to curtail production throughout war industry, Congress enacted the law in June, 1943, over the president's veto. Even the prestige of a wartime president could not check the antilabor sentiment. An influential bloc in Congress was determined to "put the unions in their place."

On April 12, 1945, President Roosevelt died suddenly. His death, which was deeply felt and mourned the world over, was particularly felt by labor. Shortly thereafter, in May, Germany capitulated, followed by the surrender of Japan in August, 1945. A world torn by war was suddenly faced with the problems of peace. Three months after V-J Day, in November, 1945, President Truman called a Labor-Management Conference for the purpose of solving the problem of postwar labor relations. But the conference solved nothing. It adopted a charter expressing belief that this will be "a new era based upon a vastly expanding economy and unlimited opportunities for every American," but it was unable to agree on concrete recommendations as to how to solve the pressing labor relations problem. The economy of the country after this devastating war, as in case of all wars, was faced with the tremendous task of readjustment from a war economy to a peace economy. In some instances a retooling period followed, causing a layoff of workers. In other industries, with the war over, there was no need for overtime, resulting in a substantial reduction of take-home pay.

There was a great deal of industrial unrest during the fall and early winter of 1945-1946. Workers in the steel, automobile, electrical, packing-house, and other industries went out on strike, demanding higher hourly pay. Labor contended that the profits of employers would enable them to absorb increases in wages without raising prices, but the employers resented consideration of their profits as the base for wage increases. President Truman appointed fact-finding boards to investigate the issues in the strikes. The boards lacked any legal authority to get the necessary data from the employers' books and were thus handicapped in the investigation. However, the steel strike was settled by President Truman on the basis of an increase of $18\frac{1}{2}\cancel{c}$ per hour. Other strikes were settled on a similar formula. The OPA ceiling price of steel was raised $5.00 per ton.

Some companies, for tax reasons, found it profitable not to continue for a while with production even after the strike was settled. Under the then-existing tax laws, operating losses sustained during the year could be carried back, to be charged off against the tax payments for the two years immediately previous. Under the "carry-back" tax provision of the law, some of the struck companies which had paid large taxes during the previous years stood to gain rather than to lose by not operating their plants. Since large tax refunds could be secured by them, the companies continued the suspension of work and used the time to retool, practically at government expense.

These shut-downs in the steel and automobile industries, because they were initially caused by strikes, though prolonged by the employers, served to animate the active drive against labor. The short railroad strike of May, 1946, heightened this feeling, President Truman appeared in person before Congress to seek special legislation authorizing him if need be to induct strikers into the army. Congress applauded his demand. The strike was called off, but the antilabor sentiment in Congress continued.

Such was the background and atmosphere in which the Congressional elections of 1946 were held.

III

The Republican campaign of 1946 was an outright anti-New Deal campaign with the Wagner Act as the focal point of attack. The Democratic Party, having had control of the administration for fourteen consecutive years, was on the defensive. It marshaled neither compact forces nor ideas to counteract the onslaught on the New Deal. Deprived of the inspiring leadership of President Roosevelt, the father of the New Deal, the Democratic Party seemed to be forlorn. It was fatalistic about the outcome, waiting for the ax to fall, anticipating that it would be injured, and only hoping that the injuries would not be fatal.

Organized labor remained divided. The AFL and CIO seemed to be expending their energies on fighting each other, rather than combining their efforts to ward off the blow that was likely to be delivered to both of them. The labor movement displayed its internal squabbles for all to see. The leaders of labor permitted labor's shortcomings to be painted in loud, unattractive colors—without making a joint, sustained effort to present their side of the story to the public. The initiative in exposing the few dishonest labor leaders was left to labor's enemies instead of prominent labor spokesmen themselves taking such initiative; the many honorable leaders were lumped with the few corrupt ones in the eyes of the public; the arrogance and stubbornness of a few union heads was imputed to the labor movement as a whole. The top labor leaders were either timid or felt bound by a mistaken theory of labor ethics not to dissociate themselves from those who meant well but were bad mannered, or from those who were within the "family" but should have been disowned.

In 1946 even persons who were considered liberal minded were ready to suggest checks on some union activities. The *bigness* of the unions and the potential use of their vast power by righteous but arrogant leaders, or by unscrupulous ones frightened them. The leaders of the Republican Party taking advantage of the antilabor sentiment, made abuse of power by unions one of the chief issues in the 1946 Congressional campaign. A great many of the returned soldiers, aroused by the widely publicized strikes in war production industries during the war and stimulated by antilabor propaganda, sided with those who were agitating for control of unions. A good part of the electorate was in a protest mood. It resented the wartime controls, it resented the meat shortage, the housing shortage, the scarcity of consumers' goods, and blamed the administration for all its discomfort. The protesting electorate in the 1946 elections, coupled with the fact that there was not a large turnout at the polls, gave the Republican Party a clear victory. The Democratic Party received a smashing blow, the roster standing 249 Republicans to 185 Democrats in the House and 51 to 45 in the Senate. The Republicans were in full control of the legislative branch of the government. They could now carry practically any legislation they chose.

IV

Immediately after the election results became known, the Republican leaders declared that the election was a "mandate" to revise the Wagner Act and to check organized labor. As soon as Congress convened, the Republican leaders went at it with a vengeance. They laid plans to uproot the New Deal.

The new Republican Congress saw the introduction of an avalanche of antilabor measures. In the House of Representatives Fred A. Hartley and Clare E. Hoffman were pushing an antilabor bill inspired by the National Association of Manufacturers. In the Senate Robert A. Taft was sponsoring legislation to replace the Wagner Act. The law that finally was enacted became known as the Taft-Hartley Act.

Labor opposition to these bills was delayed too long and was too vague to be effective. During the hearings on these bills, labor made a poor showing and an unfavorable impression. Neither the AFL nor the CIO was willing to offer any concrete amendments to the Wagner Act or to admit that there was room for improvement. Both limited themselves to the negative, to a "do-nothing" policy. They might have feared that once they consented to some minor revisions the Wagner Act would be ripped wide open by those who had always been hostile to it. Possibly both believed that, no matter what suggestions might be made by labor, the Republican leaders would disregard them just the same and carry out their own predetermined program. It is also possible that both factions of labor believed that even this new Republican Congress would not dare destroy the Wagner Act. It may also be that the do-nothing policy was due to the fact that neither the AFL nor the CIO really had any constructive suggestions to offer. Whatever the real reason or reasons of labor were, the policy of do-nothing resulted as usual in getting nothing.

Moreover, the behavior of some unions supplied additional ammunition for antilabor legislation. John L. Lewis contributed his share. Almost immediately after the Republican victory in November, 1946, the miners walked out on strike declaring the Krug-Lewis agreement at an end. The temporary injunction issued by Justice Goldsborough was not obeyed. The nation's newspapers carried the news on the front pages. Their editorial comments reflected on the arrogance and abuse of labor's power. The contempt proceedings against the union and against Lewis personally kept the news hot and up front. When, after the imposition of a staggering fine and a threat of further coercive penalties for disobeying the injunction, Lewis was compelled to direct the miners back to work, the evil of the injunction in the eyes of the public did not loom so large as before. The public was emotionally more aroused by the potential abuse of power by labor than by the principle involved in the government's use of the injunction in labor disputes.

The Republican-controlled Congress was in no mood to conciliate labor. Its leaders were quite aware that the electorate was psychologically ready for some changes in the Wagner Act. The legislation that finally emerged from the Eightieth Congress was a law blended from the Hartley measure in the House and the Taft measure in the Senate, the Labor-Management Relations Act, 1947, or more popularly known as the Taft-Hartley Act.

President Truman vetoed the bill on June 20, 1947. In a strongly worded message supported by a careful analysis he criticized it as "a menace to successful democratic society." The House received the veto message at 12:05 P.M. One minute later the clerk began reading it and three minutes after he had finished reading, without a word of debate, the roll call was started. The vote was 331 (including 106 Democrats) to 83 for overriding the veto. In the Senate the opposition succeeded in delaying the vote. However, three days later when the Senate vote was finally taken, the president's veto was overriden by a vote of 68 to 25. Thus the Taft-Hartley Act became law on June 23, 1947.

The moving spirit behind this legislation can be judged from the attitude of Congressman Hartley, one of the acknowledged authors of the act. In making his report to the House on the necessity for this legislation, he said:

For the last 14 years as a result of labor laws ill-conceived and disastrously executed, the American workingman has been . . . cajoled, coerced, intimidated, and on many occasions beaten up, in the name of the splendid aims set forth in Section 1 of the National Labor Relations Act. . . . His whole economic life has been subject to the complete domination and control of unregulated monopolists . . . His mind, his soul, and his very life have been subject to a tyranny more despotic than one would think possible in a free country.

The employer's plight has likewise not been happy . . . He has had to stand mute while irresponsible detractors slandered, abused, and vilified him.

V

The sponsors of the Taft-Hartley Act claimed that the new law was necessary because the Wagner Act was "one-sided" in favor of labor; that unions had grown big and powerful under the Wagner Act and had abused their newly acquired power just as employers previously had abused their industrial power; that the welfare of the country required that abuses by labor be done away with; and that the new act would merely redress the "balance of power" in collective bargaining between industry and labor.

Labor spokesmen, on the other hand, labeled the act a "slave-labor law." They charged that it was designed in the interests of employers, with the aim and purpose of weakening the fundamental collective bargaining power of labor, hindering its activities, and gradually sapping its strength. Some also asserted that the act was conceived in hatred of John L. Lewis so that whatever made Lewis and his union powerful was now forbidden to all unions, thus preventing them from becoming strong.

As partisans in the controversy, the proponents and opponents of the law were likely to emphasize only one side, the good or the bad aspects of the act. How does the act appear on an objective analysis?

The Taft-Hartley Act is the most complex and detailed labor legislation in the entire history of the country. Its title, "Labor-Management Relations Act, 1947," conveys the impression that its sole concern is with labor-management relations, but in reality it is more than that. It also seeks to regulate unions in many respects, not only in their relations to their members but even in their political activities. A summary of the substance of some essential provisions of this Act will prove enlightening.

Section 1, entitled *Findings and Policies*, sets forth the basic philosophy of the law. It recognizes that collective bargaining is necessary to safeguard commerce from injury and should be encouraged; that protection by law of the right of employees to organize and bargain collectively safeguards commerce from injury and promotes the flow of commerce by encouraging practices fundamental to adjustment of industrial disputes and by restoring equality of bargaining power between employers and employees; it also states that strikes are caused by the actions and attitudes of some employers toward collective bargaining. It adds that certain practices by some labor organizations *have the intent or necessary effect of burdening or obstructing commerce . . .*

Section 7 provides, as in the former law, that employees shall have the right to belong to unions and participate in concerted activities, but adds that they shall also have the right to refrain from any or all such activities.

Section 8, one of the most important sections of the law, deals with *unfair labor practices.* As in the Wagner Act, it prohibits certain acts of employers as unfair labor practices but reduces the liabilities of employers in several respects. It also prohibits various acts of unions as unfair labor practices, among which are: (*a*) to coerce or restrain employees or employers; (*b*) to encourage or engage in certain strikes or in secondary boycotts; (*c*) to charge excessive or discriminatory initiation fees in certain circumstances; (*d*) to refuse to bargain in good faith; (*e*) to coerce discrimination under union-shop contracts for any reason other than nonpayment of uniform dues or initiation fees.

Some of the essential provisions of the act affect union policies, their internal affairs, and the process of collective bargaining. In substance they provide the following:

(*a*) The closed shop is completely outlawed. (*b*) A provision for a union shop in a collective labor agreement is permissible provided (1) the employer agrees to it and (2) a special election is held on the issue and the board certifies that a majority of *all workers eligible* to vote have authorized such a clause in the agreement. (*c*) Not more than one valid election shall be held within one year. (*d*) The expression of *any* views or opinions on labor matters, unless they contain coercion or promise of benefit, shall not constitute evidence of unfair labor practice. (*e*) Not only are *all* secondary boycotts prohibited, but they are also made the grounds for injunctions on application by the board and also for damage suits by employers and by other persons damaged. (*f*) In cases of existing collective agreements, notice of termination must be given sixty days before expiration, during which period a strike or a lockout is prohibited ("cooling-off period"). (*g*) Before a union is entitled to invoke board process, it must file with the secretary of labor certain data, including its constitution and bylaws, rules and regulations concerning elections, negotiation and ratification of contracts, salaries of officers, and annually a complete financial report, a copy of which must also be furnished to union members. The union must also file with the National Labor Relations Board affidavits by its officers disavowing Communist affiliations.

Some other essential provisions are:

(1) The board may seek injunctions to stop unfair labor practice by a union or employer and *must* seek injunctions against *all* secondary boycotts and some jurisdictional disputes. The court may grant such injunctions without regard to any anti-injunction statutes (the Clayton and Norris-La Guardia Acts). (2) Employees on strike who are not entitled to reinstatement shall not be eligible to vote for a bargaining agent. (3) A union may be sued by an employer for damages in any court having jurisdiction of the parties for breach of contract and by private parties injured as a result of activities considered under the act as unlawful strikes or secondary boycotts. (4) The union is also made responsible for acts of "agents," although their acts may not have been authorized or ratified by the union. (5) In cases of strikes affecting an entire industry or a substantial part thereof, which would imperil the national health or safety, the president is empowered to apply for an injunction, which would require an 80-day delay before a strike could be legally conducted. (6) Unions are prohibited from making a "contribution or expenditure" in connection with an election to federal office, which includes primary elections, political conventions, or campaigns in connection with elections for president, senators, or representatives. (7) Any state laws prohibiting membership in a labor organization

as a condition of employment shall not be deemed superseded by the Taft-Hartley Act.

Among other provisions of the act are the following: (*a*) Checkoff of union dues is prohibited unless the individual worker authorizes the employer, in writing, to do so. (*b*) Supervisors are not "employees" under the act and an employer has no obligation to them as employees for the purpose of any law, national or local, relating to collective bargaining. (*c*) Strikes by government employees are prohibited. (*d*) The board may not designate its own general counsel. Instead, the general counsel, like the board members themselves, is appointed by the president with the advice and consent of the Senate. His office is an independent and separately functioning body within the same agency and he considers himself "not as counselor to the Board, any more than the District Attorney is a counselor" to the court. In some instances he has final authority "in respect of the investigation of charges and issuance of complaints."

This is a brief summary of the essential provisions of the Taft-Hartley Act. Single provisions of the act, when read separately, may not disclose the over-all aim of its authors, but when the law as a whole is examined the cumulative effect of the various provisions discloses the pattern. What is this pattern?

VI

"You are going to find that there is more in this bill than may meet the eye," boasted Congressman Fred A. Hartley, one of its authors, on the floor of the House of Representatives. This was no idle boast, for the law contains many hidden antilabor traps calculated to have far-reaching effects on the rights and strength of labor unions in the United States. The plan was well designed. Let us evaluate its basic aims and philosophy.

The fundamental aim of the act professes to be the encouragement of the collective bargaining process, which is basic for labor-management relations. But does the act unqualifiedly and genuinely accept collective bargaining as an essential and basic need in our industrial economy? That is doubtful, for the act provides too many opportunities for an employer to delay, avoid, hinder, and defeat collective bargaining. This is accomplished, directly and indirectly, in several ways by a change in the substance and in the procedure of the law. A few illustrations may be in order.

The act provides that whenever a petition shall have been filed by an employee or labor organization alleging that a *substantial number* of employees wish collective bargaining, or by an employer alleging that *one or more individuals* claim representation, the board upon finding that there is a reasonable question of representation, should hold a hearing and direct an election.

Experience has shown that in the initial stages of a unionization campaign in a plant a union may not have the majority necessary to win an election and thus become the bargaining agent. Should an employer at the beginning of a unionization campaign file a petition to determine the bargaining agent—and he can always manage to have *one or more individuals* claim representation—the union would very likely lose the election. Once the union is defeated, no new election can be held under the act within one year and thus the employer could successfully block collective bargaining for at least a year. Moreover, this blocking process may be successfully repeated in the following year and in addition thereto the workers will already have been discouraged with the union. Was it intended to make it easy for an employer to petition for such an election at the early stages of a union campaign and by these means avoid collective bargaining?

Coupled with this, the act enables an employer to agitate freely against unions. It specifically provides that speeches made or literature disseminated "shall not constitute or be evidence of an unfair labor practice" unless they contain a "threat of reprisal or force, or promise of benefit." Persons familiar with industrial relations know that an employer has many ways short of expressed "threats or promises" to restrain nonunion workers from affiliating with a union. Heretofore the board had developed the "totality-of-conduct" doctrine under which speeches or communications of an employer were evaluated as part of the *total* conduct of the employer. Under the new law, the Board must judge speeches and dissemination of views in isolation, separate and apart from the total conduct of the employer. The characterization of a union as "outlaw," "wild-cat," and "off-breed" was held to be permissible under this new law. What coercive effect such a speech by an employer is likely to have on nonunionized employees' joining a union is not difficult to imagine. Greater opportunities are extended to an employer to agitate openly against a union, thus affording him greater chances of defeating collective bargaining without violating the law. Moreover, the new law also provides that the board must apply stricter rules of evidence than formerly and must base its conclusions of law on the *preponderance* of the testimony, rather than upon "all the testimony taken." It is reasonable to conclude that the act intended to make it easier for an employer to defeat a union petition for a bargaining representative and to make it much more difficult for a union to prove an unfair labor practice against an employer.

In addition, under the new law unions are required to file with the secretary of labor various data concerning their internal affairs, including a complete financial statement, a copy of which must be furnished to all union members. They also must file with the board affidavits by their officers disavowing Communist affiliations. The filing of these affidavits and data was made a condition for the use by the unions of the board machinery. In other words, if unions do not supply the data to the government agencies, the board will not process any charge or petition of theirs and the employer will not be required to bargain with such unions unless and until they are in compliance.

One may properly ask why an employer should be relieved of his obligation to bargain collectively with the representative of his workers simply because a union fails to supply the government agency with the required data. Assuming that the data are essential for public welfare, should not the union be required to supply them regardless of whether or not it wishes to use the board machinery? And, at any rate, why should the employer be the beneficiary of the penalty imposed upon the union? Assuming that a citizen failed to file required reports or failed to pay his income tax, would he be deprived of using our courts to adjudicate his rights or claims against another citizen? The very fact that employers are made the beneficiaries of unions' failure to file the required information with the government agency is a further indication of the desire of the authors of the Taft-Hartley Act to lessen employers' obligations concerning collective bargaining.

Although the Taft-Hartley Act purports to recognize the need of collective action for workers, it stresses the rights of the *individual* worker at the expense of the *collective* bargaining power. While the union designated by a majority is entitled to be the exclusive representative of the workers, the law makes specific provision for *in-*

dividual conference concerning grievances. In various other ways the law emphasizes that it is its aim to protect the *individual* against the union, as if it set out to alienate the individual from the union. This is not accidental. The strengthening of bargaining by individuals must, in the long run, be at the expense of collective bargaining. Even antiunion die-hards in the days of the open shop were not opposed to "bargaining" with *individual* employees. Their opposition was directed to bargaining with the *collective* power of the workers, the union. The Taft-Hartley Act in effect favors a similar philosophy. It emphasizes and re-emphasizes the right of the individual *not* to belong to the union, *not* to join in concerted activities, *not* to be subject to any union discipline, and to be protected *from* the union. Obviously, when the *collective* power is split up among the individuals, there may be no need under the law for the employer to bargain.

With the high-sounding rights of individuals as the leading theme of this law, the next step in the authors' design was to weaken union power from within. Since the strength of a union usually comes from the numbers it represents in the plant or industry, from its cohesiveness, and from its financial position, the act provides a basis for undermining that strength. Under the slogan of protecting the rights of individuals, the act generally outlaws the closed shop in collective labor agreements. This obviously was intended to reduce union membership and weaken the union within the plant and industry. In line with the same policy, the act also lays several obstacles to a union shop. In spite of the fact that nearly one-hundred thousand collective labor agreements covering far more than eleven million workers provide for some form of union security, the Taft-Hartley Act did away with the custom and procedure concerning union security established during many years. This prompted President Truman in his veto message to say:

The bill disregards the voluntary development in the field of industrial relations in the United States over the past 150 years. Today over 11,000,000 workers are employed under some type of union-security contract. The great majority of the plants which have such union security provisions have had few strikes.

The act prohibits employers and unions from entering into union-security agreements unless (1) the employer consents to it and (2) a majority of *all workers eligible* to vote authorized such a clause at a special election held for such purpose under the supervision of the board. It should be noted that a majority of those participating in the vote is not sufficient. It must be a majority of *all eligible*. In other words, according to the authors' philosophy, an absentee vote must be counted as an antiunion-security clause vote. Obviously, without a union-security clause in collective agreements, a union is not in as favorable a position to protect its members, and will thus lose a considerable part of its strength.

The authors justified this requirement of the law on the assumption that large masses of workers had been forced into unions against their will, and that under the principle of "rights of individuals" these masses should be "liberated" from this yoke. That this assumption was based on the authors' prejudice against unions can be seen from the following fact: up to March 31, 1949, 31,795 elections involving 3,428,941 members had been held by the board on the issue of union security. More than 94 per cent of the participating workers voted in favor of a union-security clause in their collective labor agreements. This overwhelming vote emphatically demonstrates that there was no factual basis for this provision of the law and that it was dictated by prejudice against labor.

Other provisions likely to weaken unions internally and externally are contained in the act. It provides that certain discharged strikers, if they are not entitled to reinstatement, lose their right to vote for a bargaining agent. From this provision several opportunities for weakening a union may flow. In case of a strike called for economic demands (not involving an employer's unfair labor practice), strikers who have been replaced are not entitled to reinstatement and hence would not be entitled to vote for a bargaining agent. Should the employer during such a strike petition for an election to determine the bargaining agent, not the strikers but their replacements—in union parlance, the "strikebreakers"—would be entitled to vote for the bargaining agent or no agent. The result obviously would be that the union would be defeated, the employer would not be obligated to bargain collectively, and the union's position in all respects would be weakened. This policy may even encourage some employers to provoke strikes at advantageous moments and thus get rid of "undesirable" unions.

This provision of the law would also affect workers who have been discharged for participating in a strike considered under the act as unlawful, or for going out on strike without the 60-day notice, or during the cooling-off period. In all these cases workers so discharged would not be entitled to reinstatement and therefore would have no vote. This would result in weakening unions in several respects. Not only would a union lose its standing as a bargaining agent, but it would also lose the confidence, especially of the members who had lost their jobs. It would be blocked in its efforts to improve the condition of the workers. The confidence of many non-union members in the ability of the union to improve their conditions would be lessened, organizational activities would slacken, the morale of the general membership would suffer, and thus union strength would gradually diminish. The framers of the act did or should have visualized this long-range effect on labor unions.

VII

Unbiased observation of our industrial scene would disclose that the conduct and tactics of some unions made amendments to the Wagner Act inevitable. No amount of protestation on the part of labor leaders can wipe out the fact that at the end of World War II there was a growing resentment among a substantial portion of the electorate against labor for what the electorate interpreted to be labor's callous attitude toward the rights of others and the welfare of the innocent public. This resentment was directed especially against labor's activities in connection with jurisdictional strikes, some secondary boycotts, and strikes affecting national health and safety. No labor leader succeeded in convincing the public that a strike against an employer merely for jurisdictional reasons was justified. The public could not sympathize with a strike called for the purpose of compelling an employer to give his work to members of one union, rather than to the members of another, or for the purpose of compelling him to bargain with one union instead of another, especially when the employer was genuinely neutral in the dispute and willing to abide by the wishes of the majority of his workers.

Similarly, a large segment of the general public strongly disapproved of unrestrained secondary boycotts, by means of which a union brought economic pressure on one employer who had no interest in the dispute or its outcome to compel him to bring pressure on another employer to adjust the grievance the union had against the second employer. Especially was this resented when the first employer had no direct or indirect connection with the second employer and had no direct or indirect interest in the outcome of such a dispute.

The public was most bitter against some acts of labor unions which threatened the national health and safety. As a matter of self-protection the public at large welcomed a change in the Wagner Act so as to make it impossible for a union without fair warning and sufficient cause to stop vital industries which affect public interest and may involve a grave national emergency.

Had the sponsors of the Taft-Hartley Act addressed themselves to seeking a fair solution to these problems and curbing union activities in that direction only to the extent necessary, they would have been supported by a large public. But, capitalizing on the prevailing public sentiment, the sponsors took advantage of it and, instead of limiting themselves to the restriction of unions' objectionable activities along these lines, forged a legislative instrument for effectively undermining basic legitimate union activities. Under the pretense of curbing objectionable secondary boycotts, they prohibited *all* secondary boycotts. Thus, the authors intended that if employer Jones, against whom a legitimate strike is in progress has his work performed by employer Brown, a strike against Brown in an effort to prevent him doing Jones's struck work be prohibited as a secondary boycott activity. The workers in Brown's shop, though they and Jones's strikers be members of the same union, must not refuse to perform Jones's work. Thus they are compelled to help break the strike of their co-union workers in Jones's shop. Furthermore, the board would be compelled to seek an injunction against the union for encouraging such a strike and Jones and Brown could sue and recover damages from the union. President Truman assigned this as one of the reasons for vetoing the bill and said: "It would give employers the means to engage in endless litigation, draining the energy and resources of unions in court actions, even though the particular charges were groundless."

Moreover, the sweeping prohibition against *any and all* secondary boycotts may be converted into a device for suppressing even lawful primary action on the part of unions. A specific illustration is the case of Local 346 of the CIO Oil Workers' International Union. Its members went out on strike against Standard Oil Company in Toledo, Ohio, and picketed the dock. At this dock the Standard normally loaded products for its customer, the Pure Oil Company. The latter requested its own employees, who were members of the same striking union, to load products for Pure Oil from the struck dock. They refused. The board's general counsel held that picketing of the dock violated the Taft-Hartley Law's ban on secondary boy-cotts because it induced the employees of Pure Oil to engage in a concerted refusal to handle its products in order to force the Pure Oil Company to stop doing business with Standard.

That kind of reasoning might well outlaw virtually every effective strike, for all strikes may in some way interfere with business relationships between the struck employer and others. While the general counsel was subsequently overruled by the board in this specific case, the very fact that the secondary boycott provision lends itself to the interpretation given by the general counsel shows the potential danger of it to all lawful union activities and to the development of labor unions in the future. A slight difference in the factual situation may prompt the board, or for that matter the court, to give the wording of the act the same construction that the general counsel gave it. It is inconceivable that this result was not visualized by the sponsors of the Taft-Hartley Act in their design of it. There is more to it than "may meet the eye."

Many other provisions of the act also point to the fact that its authors intended to impose hardships upon unions and hinder their activities. In addition to establishing several "unfair labor practices" by unions, the act made serious inroads on the immunities obtained by unions under the Clayton Act and under the Norris-La Guardia Act. In some instances the board was empowered in its discretion to apply for injunctions; in other instances the board was *mandated* to seek an injunction against unfair labor practices by unions. Safeguards against "government by injunction," which the Norris-La Guardia Act erected, were undermined. Unions were again made responsible for acts of "agents" although the acts were not authorized or ratified by the union. By reimposing these responsibilities on the union the sponsors of the Taft-Hartley Act intended to reimpose the previous restrictions on concerted activities of workers. They thus removed the immunities extended to unions by Section 6 of the Norris-La Guardia Act, which required actual authorization or ratification of acts of alleged agents to impute liability to the union. The new law also encourages damage suits against unions for breaches of contract, for strikes contrary to the act and for boycotts by unions or "agents," as the term was broadly defined in the new act. The threats of such suits for damages were calculated to have a deterrent effect on union activities. Besides, unions might be called upon to pay damages for overstepping some of the restrictions in the act and thus their financial position could be seriously undermined. The very fact that the law provides so many opportunities for legal action by employers against unions in itself is a deterrent against union organization campaigns. One wonders whether this was not one of the concealed effects of the law to which Congressman Hartley referred in his statement that "there is more in this bill than may meet the eye."

VIII

There are various bits of evidence indicating that many provisions of the act were dictated by political expediency.

It has already been pointed out that key provisions in the act nominally took the form of an "amendment" to the Wagner Act. Why call it an "amendment" when it is a radically different law? The answer is that it was politically wise to do so, because the sponsors knew that large masses of workers would bitterly resent a repeal of the Wagner Act, hence the misleading designation of "amendment" to the Wagner Act, implying that the Wagner Act essentially was retained.

With the same eye on politics, the act was not to become effective at one time, but various sections of it were to go into effect on several different dates. Some major provisions were to go into effect sixty days after enactment; the checkoff provision was to remain in effect in the *existing* agreements until their expiration, or July 1, 1948, whichever was earlier. With regard to the administration of welfare funds, three different rules, again conditioned upon dates, were made applicable. Funds established after June 23, 1947, must have joint administration; union administration of funds established prior to January 1, 1946, was left undisturbed; but union administration of funds established between January 1, 1946, and June 23, 1947, could continue until their agreements expired but not later than July 1, 1948.

The outlawing of the closed shop and the limitation on the union shop again have different effective dates. Thus, in the collective agreements in effect on June 23, 1947, the union-security clauses were to remain in effect until their expiration dates, no matter how distant those dates might be. In contracts entered into after August 23, 1947, the union-security clause had to be in strict agreement with the new law. But contracts entered into between June 23 and August 22, 1947 (the enactment date and the effective date of the law), could provide for union shops, or even closed shops, as long as said agreements were not for a period in excess of one year, hence expiring not later than August 22, 1948.

Why so many varying effective dates in the same act? What prompted the sponsors of the act to enable the unions to extend the "objectionable" closed shop or union shop until August 22, 1948? What strange magic was there in the number 1948?

Is it too farfetched to suggest that the sponsors were not unmindful that there was going to be a presidential election in 1948? Politically minded men must be credited with being aware that by enabling unions to extend their collective agreements for a year with the closed shop and various other provisions, they would be appeased in 1947 and would express their resentment, if any, a year later, during 1948. If the unions acquiesced in these provisions, the sponsors of the act could point to their accomplishment of the reduction of strikes by this act. On the other hand, if the unions, at the expiration of the renewed agreements in 1948, resented the act by the calling of many strikes, the authors could point to the essential need for harnessing and curbing labor power. Thus, by the expediency of providing different effective dates for different sections of the act, the authors took no chances and practiced "Heads I Win —Tails You Lose."

Neither is it unreasonable to suggest that political motives also prompted the sponsors of the act to deal with the question of communism in this legislation. These sponsors knew that anticommunism had been a powerful issue in politics and that any law which included anticommunism provisions was likely to gain additional support. By requiring union officers to disavow Communist affiliations before the cases of their union could be processed, the sponsors aimed (1) to reflect subtly that many unions are Communist-led and (2) to make communism an issue in labor-management relations. Thus, everybody who wanted to be accredited as an anti-Communist would be irresistibly drawn onto the Taft-Hartley bandwagon.

That politics was much on the minds of the sponsors of the act is evident from the very fact that they deemed it necessary to prohibit unions from making any kind of political "contributions or expenditures" in connection with primaries, political conventions, or campaigns for the election of president, senator, or congressman. What place has unions' political activity in an act which is supposed to deal only with labor-management relations?

A close analysis of the act inescapably leads to the conclusion that the act was intended by its sponsors to benefit the employers by increasing their rights and reducing their liabilities and making it easier for them to block collective bargaining and get effective remedies against unions with the aid of the government agencies. In so far as unions are concerned, the act intended immeasurably to reduce their rights and increase their liabilities and was drafted with malice toward labor.

In so far as the federal government is concerned, the act, contrary to the assertion of its sponsors, compels the government to participate far more actively in labor-management relations than it had ever been called upon to do in the history of our country. Under this act there is hardly an industrial dispute of any significance in which the government agency is not compelled to intercede. Thus, while in theory the sponsors of the law insisted on "less government in business," in practice they stood for "more government in labor disputes."

Many strikes were the direct result of the new legislation, which supposedly aimed to curtail strikes. The nation-wide bituminous-coal strike of 1948 lasting forty days was directly the result of a dispute concerning the welfare-fund provisions of this law. The 9-day strike of 40,000 workers in the captive coal mines involved the union-security clause and the non-Communist affidavit requirements under the new act. In the 93-day strike in the West Coast maritime industry one of the major issues was the union hiring halls long in existence but apparently prohibited by the new law. The strike of 1,600 International Typographical Union members against the Chicago newspapers grew out of the union-security restrictions contained in the Taft-Hartley Act. In the light of these and other strikes and general tension caused by this legislation, it can hardly be said that the Taft-Hartley Act inaugurated a new era of harmonious labor-management relations.

IX

The key provisions of the Taft-Hartley Act have not as yet been fully tested in our courts. On general principles it is fair to assume that the basic key provisions of the act are within Congressional power. The provision prohibiting any and all political contributions and *expenditures* by unions resulted in an indictment against CIO and Philip Murray, its president, for publishing a statement in the union's *CIO News* of July 14, 1947, urging all members to vote for Judge Ed Garmatz, then a candidate for Congress in Maryland. The dismissal of the indictment was sustained by the Supreme Court of the United States without, however, passing on the constitutionality of that section. The requirements of non-Communist affidavits by the officers of the union as a condition for using the machinery of the board has been upheld by several lower federal courts.

Originally, almost all segments of the trade-union movement criticized the requirement of non-Communist affidavits, but only a few non-Communist led unions vigorously opposed it and, as a matter of principle, declined to file such affidavits. Outstanding among these were the known anti-Communists, Philip Murray, president of the CIO, and John L. Lewis, of the United Mine Workers of America. A number of other unions, while theoretically opposed to the filing of such affidavits, in practice took advantage of this requirement in their jurisdictional fights with some Communist-led organizations.

One must not fail to observe that this requirement penalizes many workers and sacrifices the rights of individuals through no fault of their own. For illustration, let us assume that one-hundred employees of a plant, none of whom is a member or sympathizer of the Communist Party, are represented by a union which has an officer who is a member of the Communist Party. The union, under the circumstances, is unable to comply with the requirement of the filing of a non-Communist affidavit. These hundred workers would be deprived of their right to collective bargaining. Does this policy harmonize with the theme of the rights of individuals enunciated and emphasized in the act?

Mindful of the fact that Communist-led unions could be a menace to the institutions of our country, nevertheless, the requirement of the non-Communist affidavit may be seriously questioned on legal and social policy grounds. As long as the Communist Party may legally function, why should its individual members be deprived of rights which may be enjoyed by members of other political parties? If the electorate is not penalized for electing a declared Communist to public office, why should the membership of a union be penalized for electing an undeclared Communist to a union office? What is becoming to the halls of Congress should not be legally declared as unbecoming to the meeting halls of a union. The dislike of communism does not lessen the danger of making political affiliation a *condition* for the enjoyment of a civil or statutory right. The right to seek redress before the National Labor Relations Board is a civil right. If Congress, because one union officer happens to belong to the Communist Party, may deprive such union of the right to seek redress before a governmental agency, then Congress might in principle make similar prohibition against any organization, an officer of which is a member of the Socialist, Liberal, Democratic, or Republican Party. If Congress has the power to do it in one case, it would seem that in principle it could do it in the others. Is such a policy socially desirable and should such a law get constitutional sanction?

X

The end of World War II found industry at a peak of prosperity, labor stronger than ever, and both experienced in collective bargaining. A constructive social policy would have dictated that legislation concerning labor-management relations should be approached with statesmanship and fairness, in a genuine desire to elicit the co-operation of organized labor and management. Had such legislation been limited to the specific problem directly affecting labor-management relations, it would have been possible in a statesmanlike manner to make a real contribution to the solution of the problem. But the sponsors of the Taft-Hartley Act chose an entirely different policy. Taking advantage of the Congressional majority achieved by their political party, they preferred to go far afield from this specific problem. In so far as labor-management relations are concerned, they wanted to achieve industrial peace by the method of repression, by a law which could progressively weaken labor unions. Instead of accepting collective bargaining as part of the warp and woof of American industrial democracy, the sponsors of the Taft-Hartley Act were only halfhearted about it. Their philosphy seemed to be that unions may be useful and socially desirable provided they are not strong. Based on this kind of philosophy, the act, instead of widening the area of collective bargaining, preferred to leave many loopholes for defeating and evading it. Instead of contributing to the solution of the labor-management relations problem, the act contributed to the confusion of the issues, beclouded the social principles involved, resurrected old prejudices and animosities, and revived mistrust.

Politically, the act proved to be a boomerang. The sponsors had intended to suppress labor's political activities, but instead labor was more than ever brought actively into politics. There had been other instances in which labor leaders called for political action. Samuel Gompers's policy of "rewarding friends and punishing enemies" was an expression of such an instance. However, in the past, labor's participation in politics had been sporadic at best, with the exception of the Political Action Committee (PAC), which has been maintained by the CIO for several years. But the enactment of the Taft-Hartley Act also catapulted the AFL into political action. At first its Executive Council, sparked by its vice-presidents John L. Lewis and David Dubinsky, formed an agency to combat the Congressional supporters of the act. With the threat of the Taft-Hartley Act continuing to hang over labor, this agency was subsequently set up by the Federation as its political arm under the name Labor's League for Political Education (LLPE). The establishment of this league prompted a seasoned Federation vice-president to comment: "The AFL may not know it but it is in politics for keeps. No retreat now."

The significance of this comment can be judged from a recent public statement by Joseph D. Keenan, the director of LLPE. Said he: "We are going to keep Labor's League for Political Education going on a permanent basis. We are going to set up organizations in every central body and in every local union." He was confirmed in this determination by George Meany, secretary-treasurer of the AFL, who publicly stated: "Under no circumstances is this league going to be the political tail to the kite of any other political party. . . .

Under no circumstances is it going to align with either one of the major political parties."

While the Taft-Hartley Act was designed to curb effectively the power and growth of labor unions, its real significance may prove to be in the political arena. It became a rallying point in American politics. It was a major issue in the presidential campaign of 1948, and promises to be similarly a major issue in the Congressional campaign of 1950.

A great opportunity presented itself for laying a lasting legal foundation for labor-management relations in an advanced industrial economy, but the Republican leadership muffed the ball. Instead of contributing to a solution, the law generated acrimonious debate and ill-will, and turned the problem into a political football to be kicked around at each election. What a pity!

- 25 -

The Open Gates of the Closed Shop

(1947–1949)

(a) Lincoln Federal Labor Union No. 19129 v. Northwestern
Iron and Metal Company
(b) George Whitaker v. State of North Carolina
(c) American Federation of Labor v. American Sash & Door
Company

I

From days immemorial employers considered themselves free to
deal with their employees as they deemed best. They considered it
their "natural right" to set wages, to hire and fire, and to decide
upon the terms of employment for each of their workers as their
conscience dictated or as their best interests prompted them. They
knew from experience that they could get the best of the bargain
when they dealt with workers as individuals.

With the development of the industrial system the individual
worker became an insignificant cog in the wheel of production. The
bargaining power of the individual worker dropped with the corresponding development of machinery. The value of human skill was
greatly diminished by the efficiency of the machine. Mass production
became the dominant cry of industry. But with the development of
mass production came mass organization of workers. Unions appeared
on the industrial horizon.

Employers resented any encroachment on their natural rights.
They resented the collective voice of the labor union and preferred
the barely audible voice of the individual worker. When the unions
claimed a right to organize, to strike, and to bargain collectively,
there developed a struggle between two clashing rights—the em-

ployer's claim to his *natural rights* and the union's claim to workers' *human rights* of collective action in a modern industrial society. Union workers claimed it as a human right to choose their own company at work, and they enforced this right by refusing to work with workers who refused to join their society.

The struggle between these two clashing rights inevitably landed in the courts of our land. At first the courts declared labor's attack on the employers' "natural" rights as a criminal conspiracy, but gradually the courts grudgingly yielded concessions to human rights. And so did society. It assumed an attitude of reluctant tolerance toward the existence of unions. However, employers as a class consistently resented unions and opposed them at every step. Unions had to fight for their existence, and their struggle for survival was a continuous battle. Unions would appear from time to time, disappear with every economic depression, only to reappear with economic improvement. The weakness of unions lay in the lack of a solid foundation, of a steady membership of those employed in the trade. Their ever-present fear was the loss of membership. This fear led the members of the union to fortify themselves, wherever they could, by insisting on working only with their own members. They insisted that employers maintain a "union shop."

The terms "closed shop" and "open shop," contrary to the prevailing impression, were not originated by unions, but were coined by the National Association of Manufacturers, at its convention in 1903. At that convention the association took formal cognizance of the increased activities of organized labor and proclaimed the open shop as one of the essential principles in its labor policy. The term "open shop" was intended to convey the impression that it was *open* to all workers, union or nonunion; while the term "closed shop" was intended to denote a shop *closed* to all except those who were already union members. These terms "closed" and "open" were good propaganda. The word "closed" conveys a feeling of prohibition and arouses resentment, while the word "open" conveys a feeling of freedom and is inviting. In reality, the open shop was *closed to union members*, because an employer with the unrestrained freedom of "hiring and firing" would not tolerate a union member in his open shop.

These terms subsequently came into general use: the closed shop indicating a shop in which workers at the time of hiring were *already* members of the union and the open shop a shop in which no collective bargaining with a labor organization existed.

During the first few years of the Wagner Act, the issue of union membership as a condition of employment was the chief controversy in a large percentage of the strikes that occurred in the United States. While open opposition to unions began to disappear, opposition to a union-security clause and especially to the closed shop continued. During World War II this issue threatened production. The imperative need for uninterrupted production was so great that the War Labor Board imposed upon labor and employers a compromise formula for the disposition of the union-security issue. This formula became known as the "maintenance of membership" clause. In simple language it meant that in any controversy concerning the union-security issue the employer should agree that those workers who at the time of the agreement were members of the union would maintain their membership in good standing during the entire period of the collective agreement while the union should agree that any worker who desired to "escape" membership might send in his resignation within the first fifteen days of the contract, and the employer would not be obligated to dispense with the services of such a worker for becoming nonunion. Any member who did not escape during the first fifteen days and others who joined the union subsequently would be obliged to continue their membership as a condition of employment, and the employer, on the other hand, could hire freely whomever he chose.

This compromise formula between open shop and union shop was tolerated as a war emergency by many employers, but reluctantly. They did not relish the idea of having the unions in their plants increase their strength. They realized that a large union membership was likely to become a force to be reckoned with in the postwar economic period. As the unions became stronger, the drive against them took on new vigor.

But even before the war—in fact, immediately after the Wagner Act was declared constitutional—a group of Houston businessmen, under cover of the virtuous name of Christian American Association, financed by antiunion forces, sparked the drive against the union shop—on the local level. Under the attractive slogan of the "American Way," it inaugurated campaigns in various states for antilabor legislation "to protect the workingman in his God-given right of earning a living." The association did not disclose what motives of their own the employers had in protecting such rights of employees.

The association was not beyond using high-powered publicity stunts. In Nebraska, for instance, a petition, anonymously printed and circulated and asking that a proposition be submitted to the voters forbidding union-security agreements, was carried from Omaha to the Capitol in Lincoln in armored cars, with armed guards, with sirens screaming. This sensational method was used to suggest to the voters that such elaborate armed protection was necessary against possible attempts by unions to highjack the petition on its way to the state capital. The effect of such a stunt on naïve voters is not difficult to imagine.

The appeal for the American Way was often supported by such catchy slogans with a noble ring as "right to work." Who in good conscience could really say that a man should not be protected in the right to work? Such a slogan was supplemented by propaganda that a union-security clause deprived a man of the right to work. The unions were placed on the defensive. In vain did they argue that a union shop did not deprive a man of work, and that in fact the unions extended greater right to workers by protecting and improving their working conditions, which is very essential to the right to work. The virtuous slogans "American Way" and "Right to Work" drowned out the union arguments.

The strikes of 1943, which occurred during the war, strengthened antiunion agitation. Thus, in 1944, Arkansas and Florida incorporated in their state constitutions the bans on union-security provisions in collective agreements. The large-scale strikes in the steel and automobile industries in 1945-1946, the railway walkout in the spring of 1946, and the miners' declaration of "no contract—no work" coming at about the same time intensified the antiunion-shop campaigns. By 1946 two more states—Arizona and Nebraska—incorporated so-called "right to work" amendments into their constitutions. By June, 1947, at least fourteen states had laws prohibiting the union-security clause and curbing various other union activities.

Such was the general background of the following three cases involving the constitutionality of state laws prohibiting union-security clauses in collective labor agreements.

II

During the fall elections of 1946 the citizens of Arizona voted on a so-called Right to Work amendment to their state constitution couched in the following language:

No person shall be denied the opportunity to obtain or retain employment because of non-membership in a labor organization, nor shall the State or any subdivision thereof, or any corporation, individual or association of any kind, enter into any agreement, written or oral, which excludes any person from employment or continuation of employment because of non-membership in a labor organization.

By a vote of 61,875 to 49,557, the amendment was adopted, and by proclamation of the governor it became effective in November, 1946. Shortly thereafter, the legislature enacted laws implementing the amendment. Under these laws contracts contrary to the terms of the amendment were declared void, injunctions could be secured against such contracts, and persons suffering from such outlawed contracts were entitled to damages.

It did not take long for the legality of the amendment and the implementing laws to be tested. The following incident occurred. At the time the amendment was passed there was in existence a closed-shop contract between the American Sash and Door Company and the AFL Carpenters' Union, Local 2093. After the new laws became effective, an employee defaulted in dues and lost his union membership. The union requested the employer to discharge the worker, but the employer refused on the basis of the new law. The union decided to test the law.

About the same time an employer, Ralph Henley, doing business as Ralph Henley Millwork, entered into a closed-shop agreement with the union *after* the amendment had become effective. He was perfectly satisfied with the agreement but was warned by the state authorities that civil and criminal proceedings might be instituted against him for entering into such agreement with the union. So he, too, joined with the union in a test of the law. Some local unions and the AFL likewise joined in this litigation. On February 12, 1947, a civil action was filed by them against the American Sash and Door Company and the attorney general of the state of Arizona, requesting an injunction restraining the attorney general from enforcing the law and requesting that the antiunion-shop amendment be declared unconstitutional.

Judge M. T. Phelps of the Superior Court dismissed the complaint on the ground that the amendment was constitutional. The unions and Henley appealed to the Arizona Supreme Court.

On February 4, 1948, Judge Levi S. Udall for the majority of the Arizona Supreme Court affirmed the judgment dismissing the complaint. He reasoned that this amendment was merely the logical counterpart of the right of states to curb yellow-dog contracts. Since the Supreme Court upheld the right of the state to prohibit contracts which discriminate against union men, it followed that a state had the right to regulate union-security clauses in contracts which discriminated against nonunion workers.

Chief Justice Stanford dissented in part. He was of the opinion that that part of the amendment which barred a union-shop provision in contracts which had been entered into prior to enactment of the law was unconstitutional, as depriving parties of property without due process of law.

The unions appealed the case to the Supreme Court of the United States.

III

In the meantime another case, from the state of Nebraska, was wending its way to the United States Supreme Court.

The facts in the Nebraska case briefly were:

During World War II new industries were brought to the state of Nebraska, which had always been mainly an agricultural state. The agricultural interests feared that the prevailing trend of unionism among the industrial workers might spread to agricultural labor. This fear prompted them to seek legislation curbing union activity. With this in view, under the guiding spirit of an organization which incorporated itself under the name of Nebraska Small Businessmen's Association, an amendment to the state constitution was proposed. This amendment, publicized as the Right to Work amendment, read in part: "No person shall be denied employment because of membership in or affiliation with or resignation or expulsion from a labor organization or because of refusal to join or affiliate with a labor organization." The amendment was carried in the November, 1946, election and became effective on December 11, 1946. Shortly thereafter, one Dan Giebelhouse, who worked for the Northwestern Iron and Metal Company was suspended from the union for non-payment of dues. The union, under its collective agreement, requested his discharge but the company refused on the ground that the adoption of the amendment had invalidated the union-shop clause of the contract. For the purpose of testing the law, the Lincoln Federal Labor Union, No. 19129, brought suit, in which other AFL unions joined, against the Northwestern Iron and Metal Company for specific performance of the union-security clause in the collective labor agreement and for an injunction restraining the enforcement of the amendment.

The District Court of Lancaster County, in which the action was brought, dismissed the union complaint on the ground that the amendment was constitutional. The union appealed to the Nebraska Supreme Court, but was not successful. On March 19, 1948, by a unanimous opinion, this court, reasoning as the Arizona Supreme Court had, held that the law was not unconstitutional and that the state under its police power could regulate the union-shop clauses of a collective labor agreement.

The union took an appeal to the Supreme Court of the United States.

IV

A third case, involving a state antiunion security law—this time from North Carolina—was shaping up for a test before the Supreme Court of the United States. The facts leading to this case briefly were:

The wages of the workers in North Carolina's chief industries—tobacco and textiles—were very low. At the same time the state was prosperous, twelfth in the nation in manufacturing, among the top leaders in agriculture, and producing more than half the cigarettes annually smoked in the country. The first noticeable improvement in workers' wages came with the New Deal minimum-wage laws. World War II brought about further improvement because the demand for workers was great and employers were obliged to offer higher wages to attract them. With the increase in wage standards, the textile industry became apprehensive of what would happen to it after the termination of war and the slackening of industrial activity. This apprehension became stronger when, after V-J day, both the CIO and AFL announced plans for intensive drives to extend unionism below the Mason-Dixon line.

The business leaders of North Carolina decided to undertake a campaign against unions. In 1947 an anticlosed-shop law was introduced and adopted by the North Carolina state legislature. This law declared the public policy of North Carolina to be that the "right of persons to work shall not be denied or abridged on account of membership or non-membership in any labor union and . . . the right to live includes the right to work . . ." It also provided that any person who might be denied employment in violation of the law would be entitled to damages, which he could recover from the employer or from any other person acting in concert with him.

On May 20, 1947, George Whitaker, a building contractor in Asheville, North Carolina, entered into a collective agreement with local craft unions of the AFL, in which he agreed to employ only members of the unions, parties to the contract. This contract on its face was contrary to the new antiunion-shop law. On July 15, 1947, a warrant was issued against Whitaker and several officers of the various unions, charging them with having violated the law by making membership in a union a condition of employment. They were also charged with having created by this contract a combination in restraint of trade. Such restraint, under the General Statutes of North Carolina, was punishable as a misdemeanor. The defendants moved to quash the warrant, alleging that the new law was unconstitutional and that it arbitrarily and unreasonably deprived the defendants of fundamental rights, liberties, and freedom protected under the federal Constitution.

Judge Zeb V. Nettles, of Buncombe County Court, overruled the motion to quash. The case went before a jury, and the defendants were convicted. Each was fined $50 and required to pay one-seventh of the costs. Whitaker and the other defendants appealed to the Supreme Court of North Carolina, but that court upheld the conviction.

An appeal was taken to the Supreme Court of the United States.

V

Thus, three cases, from the states of Arizona, Nebraska, and North Carolina, reached the Supreme Court during the October term, 1948. Since the basic legal issues involved, with minor exceptions, were the same in all three cases, the high court decided all of them at the same time.

The basic contentions of the unions before the Supreme Court briefly were:

(*a*) The right to form unions and maintain essential union activity was an exercise of the right of association or assembly guaranteed by the First Amendment to the Constitution. That right of "assembly" implied that a union member had a constitutional right to choose his company at work. These state laws in effect sought to deprive a worker of such constitutional rights and therefore they were unconstitutional.

(*b*) These state laws and amendments deprived the unions and their members of their fundamental rights to enter into contracts for their protection, and they also deprived them of such rights under previously existing contracts. Therefore, the unions were being deprived of contractual property rights *without due process,* contrary to the Fourteenth Amendment to the Constitution.

(*c*) The union-security clause in an agreement did not absolutely deny anyone the right to work. Hence, there was no public necessity for the creation of this so-called new right, not to join a union.

(*d*) The union-security clause in a collective agreement was indispensable for the effective existence of the union. These state laws or amendments creating a so-called new right—not to join a union— would destroy the effectiveness of the union. A state could not create a new right and thereby destroy the existing recognized right of the union—to contract for a union-security clause—essential for its existence.

(*e*) These laws, absolutely prohibiting instead of merely *regulating* a union-security clause in collective agreements, were arbitrary, discriminatory, without rational basis, and unconstitutional.

The contentions of the unions did not sway the Supreme Court. Holding that the states had the legal right to pass the legislation they did, Justice Black, for the majority, on January 3, 1949, delivered two opinions, one in the Nebraska and North Carolina cases and the other in the Arizona case. He held, in substance:

One: Freedom of speech and assembly. These state laws merely forbade employers acting alone or in concert with labor unions deliberately to restrict employment only to union members. They were not in violation of the First Amendment, because nothing in the language of the laws indicated a purpose to prohibit speech, assembly, or petition.

Two: Effect on existing contracts. These laws did not impair the obligations of contracts made prior to their enactment, and therefore were not in conflict with Section 10 of Article I of the United States Constitution.

Three: Equal protection of the laws. It was contended that the North Carolina and Nebraska laws denied unions and their members equal protection by weakening their bargaining power and correspondingly strengthening the power of employers. While that might be true, it did not necessarily make the laws unconstitutional. The unions' contention logically amounted to saying that the state law giving equal protection to union and nonunion members was unconstitutional because the federal Constitution required that union members were to be in some way favored. Such contention was not supported by the federal Constitution. These state laws protected the employment opportunities of members of other unions which were not parties to the collective labor agreement with the particular employer. This circumstance alone, even if there were no others, would be sufficient to negate the charge that these laws were in violation of the Fourteenth Amendment guaranteeing equal protection of the laws.

Four: Due process of law. The unions' contention was that under these laws persons were deprived of their (1) "liberty" and (2) of the right to make contracts for a union-security clause, *without due process of law* in violation of the Fourteenth Amendment. This contention was not sound. It had taken the Supreme Court many years to discard the due process philosophy it originally enunciated in the *Adair* case, in which it had held that under the due process clause the employer had the constitutional right to discriminate against union members. Now, the unions contended for a construction under the same clause which would give an employer a right to discriminate against nonunion workers. Since 1934 the court had steadily rejected such a construction, and it was now of the firm conviction that the due process clause could not be construed so broadly that Congress and state legislatures were put in a strait jacket when they attempted to legislate concerning conditions which they regarded as obstructive to the public welfare. "Just as we have held that the due process clause erects no obstacle to block legislative protection of union members, we now hold that legislative protection can be afforded to non-union workers."

Accordingly, Justice Black concluded that the Nebraska and North Carolina laws were constitutional. By the same reasoning he upheld the Arizona law, but in view of the additional issue involved in the latter case he rendered a separate opinion, saying in substance:

It was argued that the Arizona amendment was discriminatory because the language of the amendment specifically prohibited employment discrimination against nonunion workers but *did not* specifically prohibit discrimination *against union workers.* The failure to use the same language prohibiting discrimination did not violate the equal protection of the laws' requirement, because: (*a*) the state of Arizona had similar protection for union members. It had a law which made it a misdemeanor to coerce a person to make a yellow-dog contract as a condition of employment; and (*b*) even if this law did not extend the full measure of protection, the general rule was that "legislative authority exerted within its proper field need not embrace all the evils within its reach." The relative needs of different groups for protection was a matter for legislative judgment.

With the exception of Justice Murphy, who dissented in the Arizona case, all the justices concurred with the result of the decision, although separate opinions were filed by Justices Frankfurter and Rutledge.

Justice Frankfurter wrote a long concurring opinion, dwelling upon the social philosophy and the historical need for labor unions in a modern economic society. In the course of his opinion, he enumerated principles to be applied by the courts concerning legislation, and observed: (*a*) "In the day-to-day working of our democracy it is vital that the power of the non-democratic organ of our government be exercised with rigorous restraint . . . The court is not saved from being oligarchic because it professes to act in service of humane ends." (*b*) "Most laws dealing with economic and social problems are matters of trial and error . . . but even if a law is found wanting in trial it is better that its defects should be demonstrated and removed by new legislation than that the state law should be aborted by judicial fiat." (*c*) It would be arbitrary for this court to deny the states the right to experiment with such laws. In recent years there had been a large increase of union membership. The railroad brotherhoods had held their own despite Congressional prohibition of union-security clauses. In Great Britain and Sweden, countries which had advanced in industrial democracy, the lack of contractually guaranteed union-security clauses had not necessarily disturbed the growth of unions. "Whether it is preferable in the public interest that trade unions should be subjected to State intervention or left to the free play of social forces . . . and whether legislative correction is more appropriate than self-discipline and the pressure of public opinion—these are questions on which it is not for us to express views."

Justice Rutledge, in a concurring opinion, agreed that the states had a right to prohibit the making of contracts which required union membership as a condition of employment. However, he made the following reservation: The right to prohibit contracts for union security was one thing, but the right to force union members to work with nonunion workers was entirely different. . . . "If today's decision should be construed to permit a state to foreclose that right by making illegal the concerted refusal of union members to work with nonunion workers, and more especially if the decision should be taken as going so far as to permit a state to enjoin such a strike, I should want a complete and thorough re-argument of these cases before deciding so momentous a question."

Thus, a unanimous court (except for Justice Murphy's dissent in the Arizona case) concluded that the Constitution does not prohibit states from enacting laws which prohibit union-security clauses in collective labor agreements.

VI

Union security played a significant role in the development of labor unions in the United States. From their very inception, unions looked upon the union shop as a source of security for their existence. The strength of a union could almost be judged from the degree of unionization it exacted in its collective labor agreements with employers. Labor reasons that since the union as the bargaining agent for all the workers helps to determine the wages, hours, and working conditions that apply equally to all employees in the shop or plant, it is only fair and reasonable that all workers who share in the benefits should also share in the burdens and, hence, the justification for insisting that union membership be made a condition of employment in such shop or plant. It is the view of unions that "the rights of the individual workers under collective bargaining become analogous to those of a citizen in a political unit. The worker becomes a member of an economic society when he takes employment." Thus, unions consider the requirement of union membership as a condition of employment indispensable to their security and to their ability to discharge their functions as unions. State legislation prohibiting union-security clauses has been looked upon by the unions as an attack on their security and as an effort to undermine the very foundation of unions. In this respect the decision of the Supreme Court must be considered as a setback to labor rights.

But the decision of the Supreme Court came as no surprise to those versed in the Supreme Court's recent attitude toward states' rights in the exercise of their police power. As far back as 1921, the progressive minority of the Supreme Court in the case of *Truax* v. *Corrigan,* urged that states should not be hampered in their experiments of regulating industrial relations. Later in 1937, in the case of *Senn* v. *Tile Layers' Protective Union,* Justice Brandeis, writing this time for the majority of the court, held that the United States Constitution does not prevent states from passing laws permitting unions to engage in lawful picketing. He reasoned, "Whether it was wise for the state to permit the unions to do so is a question of its public policy—not our concern," thus emphasizing that the Constitution did not prohibit a state from passing legislation concerning regulation of industrial relations. In these three cases concerning union security, Justice Black properly emphasized that in the past the unions themselves had suffered from the interpretations given by the court to the due process clause, as a result of which the Supreme Court had held that a law which prohibited an employer from discriminating against a union member by reason of his membership was unconstitutional. This interpretation led to the invalidation of state legislation favorable to labor. Since the court had changed its position and concluded that the Constitution did not prohibit a state from extending protection to union members against discrimination by reason of union membership, it followed that the state also had the right to extend similar protection to nonunion workers.

In so far as the power of a state to pass favorable or unfavorable labor laws is concerned, labor was forcefully reminded by the court of the old adage: What is sauce for the goose is sauce for the gander. Labor was thus indirectly told that any relief it desired against prohibition of union-security agreements must come not from the courts but from the legislatures.

- 26 -

Looking Both Ways

Looking backward at the distant past, American labor unions will find little good in the "good old days." Looking forward to the not too distant future, they are likely to face the problem of assuming social responsibilities.

In the early history of organized labor in the United States, one glaring fact boldly protrudes: organizations of workers had no rights in society and employers as a matter of law had no duties toward them. This was a direct outgrowth of the colonial days. It was not uncommon at that time to sell servants at auction, especially immigrants to the New World. In *Labor in America*, Foster Rhea Dulles relates that colonial newspapers often carried notices of such prospective sales, as exemplified by the *Virginia Gazette*, of March 28, 1771, which carried the following announcement:

Just arrived at Leedstown, the Ship Justitia, with about one Hundred Healthy Servants . . . The sale will commence on Tuesday, the 2nd. of April, at Leeds Town on Rappahanock River. A reasonable Credit will be allowed, giving Bond with approved Security to

THOMAS HODGE

Since the servant was bought and paid for, the master's attitude toward the servant was that of an owner toward property. In a society in which the selling of human beings as servants was in order, rights for labor obviously were out of order.

This psychology of master and servant was reflected in the interpretation of the common law, which in turn reflected the views of the dominant social group. The prevailing view was that laws were for the protection of property and that there was neither the need nor the basis for laws for the protection of servants. When the

344

employer-employee relationship later took the place of the master-servant relationship, there were no legal doctrines by which to measure employer-employee rights except the doctrines that had been formulated in the preindustrial era, when no laboring class existed. The courts, in adjudicating employer-employee relationship rights, were greatly influenced by analogy to the master-servant era. They were influenced by the concept of property rights, and those rights at all times favored the employer.

When the industrial revolution and the factory system brought many workers under one roof, the foundation for labor unions was laid. The power machine began to compete with the power of man, and man resented it. Workers as individuals, being helpless in their relations with employers, sought protection in organization. The employers, however, being part of the dominant group in society, were the ones to set the code of conduct for the employer-employee relationship. This code was designed to suppress mass action by workers though piously permitting action by individual workers. The common law was interpreted so as to perpetuate this code of conduct. Thus, in the first stage of evolution of labor rights in the United States, the attitude of society and of the judiciary toward labor organizations may be characterized as that of *Open Suppression*.

It was in this period that the first recorded labor case took place in the United States, the case of the *Philadelphia Cordwainers*, in 1805. The presiding judge aligned himself with the aspirations of the then-dominant class in society. Seeking to impose on workers a standard of conduct prescribed by the interests of that class, the judge found the *combined* action of the Philadelphia bootmakers to increase their wages to be a criminal conspiracy under the English common law, which we presumably inherited. The judiciary came to the aid of the dominant group to maintain the status quo. According-ing to Professor Charles O. Gregory, in *Labor and the Law*, this doctrine of criminal conspiracy "was an arbitrary statement of a result, and depended for its existence on the economic views of the judges using it. Indeed, it is clear in retrospect that these economic views were really the law, while the doctrine of criminal conspiracy was merely the form in which it was presented for public consumption."

It took close to forty years for the judiciary to realize that the historic development of social forces within society demanded a change in attitude toward labor organizations. The rapid strides in the industrial development of the United States made it necessary to tolerate the existence of labor unions. It dawned upon the judiciary that workers should not be prohibited from having a vehicle for the improvement of their working conditions. The dilemma was how to reconcile the existence of labor unions with the "natural" rights of employers to go about their business as they pleased. The first sign of judicial tolerance toward labor unions appeared in the case of *Commonwealth* v. *Hunt,* in 1842. Chief Justice Shaw of Massachusetts, in deciding the appeal in that case, legally justified the existence of labor unions. At the same time he reserved the court's unabridged power to protect the interests of employers against aggressive combinations of workers. He accomplished this by the enunciation of the doctrine of "Ends and Means." Under this doctrine, the legality of the action of a union was to be judged by the *ends* it sought and by the *means* it used to accomplish such ends. If either was illegal, then the court could properly prohibit the union from engaging in the activities objected to.

The doctrine of "Ends and Means" gave great latitude to individual judges to interpret the motives underlying the union's conduct in each industrial dispute. Many judges, being products, in the words of the late Justice Cardozo, of their "inherited instincts, traditional beliefs, acquired convictions," were influenced by their own intellectual and social backgrounds. Consciously or not, they did not want to see any changes in the workers' status in society. Though in theory they would tolerate the existence of unions, at heart they were reluctant to aid their growth and in practice often restrained them from exercising their functions. They issued injunctions to block the activities of unions on the ground that either the ends sought or the means used in a particular strike were unlawful. This second stage in the evolution of labor rights in the United States may be characterized as that of *Reluctant Tolerance* toward labor unions by the judiciary and by society.

With the enactment of the Sherman Antitrust Act, in 1890, the setting was prepared for the third stage in the evolution of labor rights. This may be called the stage of *Judicial Prejudice.* Here the judiciary, more than society, showed its prejudice toward organized labor. Although the primary purpose of the Sherman Act was the curbing of business monopolies, shortly after its enactment it became, by the judiciary's interpretation, a law for curbing activities of labor unions. If the ends or means in a particular strike were interpreted by the judge to be unlawful interference with interstate commerce, the strike was restrained as a monopolistic practice prohibited by the antitrust laws. The charge of conspiracy under common law could now be replaced by the charge of conspiracy and monopoly under the Sherman Act.

It was during this stage of Judicial Prejudice that the Supreme Court decided the *Danbury Hatters* case holding that the Sherman Act was applicable to labor unions. It was also during this period that the Supreme Court decided the cases of *Duplex Printing Press* and *Bedford Cut Stone*, holding that the Clayton Act with its declaration that "labor is not a commodity" did not give labor immunity from persecution under the Sherman Act. This antitrust law became the basis for many protracted suits against unions. But in spite of the fact that the antitrust laws were used to curb their activities, unions continued to grow with the rapid growth of industry in the United States.

The fourth stage in the evolution of labor rights began with the New Deal. It may be characterized as the stage of *Social Recognition*. This was the first time that labor unions as organizations acquired *positive* rights in the United States. Theretofore only their economic power guided their activities; now legal status implemented their economic power. Employers became obligated to recognize and to bargain in good faith with labor unions representing a majority of their workers concerning conditions of employment. The National Labor Relations Act officially took cognizance of the fact that workers as individuals had no equality of bargaining power with their employers and that public welfare demanded that such equality should exist. The law now recognized that labor unions were necessary in our economy and, by implication, asserted that labor unions were indispensable to the general social welfare.

During this stage the judiciary, too, recognized the social need of labor unions in our economy and favorably responded to the new public policy toward labor unions. The majority of the Supreme Court of the United States, squarely facing the industrial facts of life, recognized the need of Congressional power to deal with labor relations. And this time the court found the same Constitution

elastic enough to grant such power to Congress. When the constitutionality of the Wagner Act was challenged, the majority of
the Supreme Court at the very first opportunity, in the case of
National Labor Relations Board v. *Jones & Laughlin Steel Corporation,* said: "Experience has abundantly demonstrated that the recognition of the rights of employees to self-organization and to have
representatives of their own choosing for the purpose of collective
bargaining is often an essential condition of industrial peace." This
new spirit of the court was evidenced in the support it gave to the
National Labor Relations Board in many decisions.

The employer class, however, never acquiesced in the public
policy of social recognition of labor unions. A substantial part of
the employer class resented being compelled by law to recognize
labor unions. A substantial group of businessmen feared the growing economic force of labor and its potential political power. These
opponents of the policy of social recognition of unions awaited an
opportunity to tip the social scales of public opinion against labor.

During the stage of Social Recognition, with the blessing of the
New Deal, the labor movement in the United States received tremendous impetus. The spirit of unionism spread over the entire
country. It penetrated all basic industries, including steel, automobile, and rubber; and there was hardly an industry in which
workers did not join union ranks. With the growth of unions in
numbers and strength, they also grew in social standing and prestige.
The awakening of labor was felt not only in industry but also in
politics. Labor's active support greatly contributed to the re-election
of Franklin D. Roosevelt for his second, third, and fourth terms of
office. Labor also became active on behalf of and in support of social
legislation; it became a power to be reckoned with in all walks of
life.

But though it has grown in strength and prestige, labor has not
acquired *full* equality in society. In his stimulating and provocative
book, *The New Men of Power,* Professor C. Wright Mills points out:
"Historically, labor organizations and their leaders have been in a
minority position. Their strategy has been shaped in an environment
of continuous hostility. Their official tribulations have been many,
and unofficial animosity towards them has been widespread. 'Labor,'
says one leader, 'has to overcome certain traditions . . . Labor in
America has not acquired emotional equality . . . The public is

more incensed about abuses by labor than it is about abuses by business.' " The emotional reaction of the community to acts of labor is different than to acts of businessmen. Abuse of power or wrong done by one industry or one businessman is not charged to all industry or to all businessmen, but abuse of power or wrong done by one union or one labor leader is charged to the *entire* labor movement. There is lack of equality in the emotional reaction. Labor is held to be its "brother's keeper," but not industry or business.

Though unions have acquired positive rights under the law and though the judiciary has supported them in their newly acquired legal status, they still feel insecure in their position in society. Professor Mills points out that "in each block [AFL and CIO] a majority feels that the unions are merely being tolerated . . . A sizable group of leaders go further. They believe that business intends to fight to the finish, that the policy makers of the larger business are working to break the unions altogether." This feeling on the part of sincere labor leaders is not without foundation. Agitation against the rising power of labor has been proceeding since the inauguration of the New Deal. Various states have enacted laws curbing the activities of labor unions. The Taft-Hartley Act of 1947 may be cited as a clear manifestation of the power and hostility of the industrial group and of some businessmen toward labor unions. Nevertheless, in this stage of Social Recognition labor has made its greatest strides. Unions have become big and powerful, capable of seriously challenging the traditionally dominant industrialists.

The power and prestige acquired by labor brings it to the incipient fifth stage of the evolution of its rights in the United States. This is likely to be characterized as the stage of *Social Responsibility*. When labor unions were openly suppressed and had to struggle for their daily existence, it was highly unrealistic to expect unions to assume social responsibility. But the situation has changed radically. Labor is out of its swaddling clothes. It is now in a position seriously and effectively to resist inequities. The millions of members in the ranks of unions constitute a positive power of great economic force and even greater political potential. Labor has matured and is a force to be reckoned with.

But the acquisition of power in a democracy imposes responsibilities. The balancing of power by responsibility is basic to the existence of a democratic system. All actions—"internal" as well as "external"—of any powerful group within a democratic society are properly subject to public accounting. The actions of powerful groups cannot be said to be merely of private concern or of "no concern" to society. This principle applies to all powerful groups. Labor now being among such groups, to what extent will it undertake to share in "social responsibility" to the community?

During this period of the evolution of its rights labor's struggle will revolve around the *degree* of power it is likely to obtain and the degree of social responsibility it is willing to assume. Those groups which traditionally have had social and political power are not likely to part with it willingly. They will gladly saddle labor with greater social responsibility, but they will resist sharing "sovereignty." On the other hand, labor may seek greater power without showing willingness to assume a larger share of responsibility to the community.

But both labor and management must be conscious of the vital interest of the community in the effect of all major industrial disputes. In his book *Trade Unions in the New Society* Professor Harold J. Laski points out that "The smooth running of social life depends upon matters like transport, mining, agriculture, sanitation, the provision of a meat supply. . . . That is why all industry that is directly clothed with a public purpose cannot involve itself in a major dispute without bringing the certainty, at some stage, most usually an early stage, of government intervention." What will be labor's attitude to the government's role in all such disputes?

Sober analysis of social and industrial development must lead to the inescapable conclusion that labor unions are an inextricable outgrowth of our economic system. They are part and parcel of an expanding economy in a democratic society. Big business begot big unions. As a democratic force within a democratic society unions are here to stay within the democratic system. Any attempt by big businessmen to "cut unions down to size" while they retain their own bigness will, viewed historically, prove a failure.

Labor, on the other hand, by virtue of the power it has acquired and which it seeks to expand, must be ready to share social responsibility and must prepare for it. It must have an economic policy based on long-range planning in which industry-mindedness is an integral consideration. A positive program for adjustment of industrial disputes will have to be high on its agenda. "Survival of the fittest" in an industrial dispute benefits neither the contestants nor the spectators, and is hardly a sound public policy today. A method of adjustment of industrial disputes must be suitable to the modern economy and consonant with public interest. A policy of "hands off by the government," to which employers *fully* and unions *partly* subscribe, is a heritage of days long past. To leave the government powerless and helpless in an industrial struggle involving a national emergency or public health and welfare must result in adverse public opinion. And public opinion in a democracy is, in the long run, a basic force without which no dominant group can maintain and retain leadership. Power must bring responsibility, and the degree of responsibility must be commensurate with the degree of power that group enjoys.

No less a liberal and friend of labor than Mrs. Eleanor Roosevelt, on June 16, 1949, at the inauguration of radio station WFDR, owned and controlled by the International Ladies' Garment Workers' Union, expressed the sentiment of the thinking progressive:

Because labor has come to maturity, however, a great responsibility now rests on its shoulders. It is not only the big businessmen in these days who carry political and economic responsibility. With each new acquisition of power, labor acquires greater responsibility.

Labor has come a long way from the *Philadelphia Cordwainers.* The road it traveled is marked by milestones, records of historic cases. These records throw light on the workings of the social forces within our democracy. They may perhaps serve as a guide to an intelligent solution of industrial conflict within our democratic society.

CASES AND AUTHORITIES CITED

Adair v. *United States*
208 U.S. 161
28 Sup. Ct. 277 (1908)
Allen Bradley Co. v. *Local Union No. 3, I.B.E.W.*
145 F (2d) 215 (C.C.A. 2d, 1944)
Allen Bradley Co. v. *Local Union No. 3, I.B.E.W.*
325 U.S. 797 (1945)
American Federation of Labor, et al. v. *American Sash & Door Company, et al.*
69 Sup. Ct. 258 (1949)
67 Ariz. 20
American Steel Foundries v. *Tri-City Central Trades Council*
257 U.S. 184
42 Sup. Ct. 72 (1921)
Apex Hosiery Co. v. *Leader, et al.*
90 Fed. (2d) 155 (C.C.A. 3d, 1939)
Associated Press, The v. *NLRB*
301 U.S. 103
57 Sup. Ct. 650 (1937)
Bedford Cut Stone Co. v. *Journeymen Stone Cutters' Association*
274 U.S. 37 (1927)
Bucks Stove and Range Co. v. *A.F.L., et al.*
219 U.S. 581
Commonwealth v. *Carlisle*
Court of Nisi Prius, Brightley's Rep. 36
(Pa. 1821)
Commonwealth v. *Hunt*
4 Metcalf 111
45 Mass. 111 (1842)
Coronado Coal Co. v. *United Mine Workers of America*
(second *Coronado* case)
268 U.S. 295 (1925)

Danbury Hatters case
(see *Loewe* v. *Lawlor*)
In re Debs
158 U.S. 564
15 Sup. Ct. 900 (1895)
Dueber Watch Case Manufacturing Co. v. *E. Howard Watch and Clock Co., et al.*
55 F 581, 584 (1893)
66 F 637 (C.C.A. 1895)
Duplex Printing Press Co. v. *Deering, et al.*
254 U.S. 443
41 Sup. Ct. 172 (1921)
Fansteel Metallurgical Co. v. *National Labor Relations Board*
98 F (2d) 375 (C.C.A. 7th, 1938)
Friedman-Harry Marks Clothing Co.
1 NLRB 802 (1937)
Gompers v. *Bucks Stove and Range Co.*
221 U.S. 418 (1911)
Hitchman Coal Co. v. *Mitchell*
245 U.S. 229
38 Sup. Ct. 65 (1917)
Jones & Laughlin Steel Corp., et al.
1 NLRB 503 (1936)
Leader v. *Apex Hosiery Co.*
302 U.S. 656
58 Sup. Ct. 589 (1938)
Leader v. *Apex Hosiery Co.*
108 F (2d) 71 (C.C.A. 3d, 1939)
Lincoln Federal Labor Union No. 19129, et al. v. *Northwestern Iron and Metal Co., et al.*
69 Sup. Ct. 251 (1949)
149 Neb. 507
Loewe v. *Lawlor* (*Danbury Hatters* case)
U.S. Cir. Ct. 148 Fed 924 (1906)

Loewe v. *Lawlor*
  208 U.S. 274
  28 Sup. Ct. 301 (1908)
NLRB v. *Fansteel Metallurgical Corp.*
  306 U.S. 270
  59 Sup. Ct. 491 (1939)
NLRB v. *Friedman-Harry Marks Clothing Co. Inc.*
  301 U.S. 58
  57 Sup. Ct. 645 (1937)
NLRB v. *Fruehauf Trailer Co.*
  301 U.S. 49
  57 Sup. Ct. 642 (1937)
NLRB v. *Jones & Laughlin Steel Corp.*
  301 U.S. 1 (1937)
People v. *Fisher*
  14 Wendel 9 (N.Y. 1835)
Philadelphia Cordwainers case
  Commons and Gilmore
  Documentary History of American Industrial Society, Vol. III (1910)
Rex v. *Journeymen Taylors of Cambridge*
  8 Modern 10 (K.B. 1721)
Senn v. *Tile Layers' Protective Union*
  301 U.S. 468 (1937)
Steele v. Louisville & Nashville Railroad
  323 U.S. 192 (1944)
Thornhill v. *Alabama*
  310 U.S. 88 (1940)
Truax v. *Corrigan*
  20 Ariz. 7, 176 Pac. 570 (1918)
  257 U.S. 312, 42 Sup. Ct. 124 (1921)

United Mine Workers of America v. *Coronado Coal Co.*
  (first *Coronado* case)
  259 U.S. 344
  42 Sup. Ct. 570 (1922)
United States v. *American Tobacco Company*
  221 U.S. 106 (1911)
United States v. *Debs*
  64 Fed. 724 (N.D. Ill. 1894)
United States v. *Hutcheson*
  32 F. Supp. 600 (D.C. Mo., 1940)
United States v. *Hutcheson*
  312 U.S. 219 (1941)
United States v. *Standard Oil Company of New Jersey, et al.*
  221 U.S. 1 (1911)
Wallace Corp. v. *National Labor Relations Board*
  323 U.S. 248 (1944)
Whitaker, et al. v. *State of North Carolina*
  69 Sup. Ct. 251 (1949)
  228 N.C. 352
Wolff Packing Co. v. *Court of Industrial Relations*
  262 U.S. 522, 43 Sup. Ct. 630 (1923), and
  267 U.S. 552, 45 Sup. Ct. 441 (1925)
United States v. *United Mine Workers of America and John L. Lewis*
  70 Fed. Sup. 42 (1946)
  330 U.S. 258 (1947)

STATUTES

Clayton Act
  Act of October 15, 1914, 38 Stat. 730, 15 U.S.C. 12 et seq., 28 U.S.C. 381 et seq., 29 U.S.C. 52
Erdman Act
  Act of June 1, 1898, 30 Stat. 424
Labor-Management Relations Act (Taft-Hartley Act)
  Act of June 23, 1947, 61 Stat. 136
National Industrial Recovery Act
  Act of June 16, 1933, 48 Stat. 195

National Labor Relations Act (Wagner Act)
  Act of July 5, 1935, 49 Stat. 449, 29 U.S.C. 151, et seq.
Norris-La Guardia Act
  Act of March 23, 1932, 47 Stat. 70, 29 U.S.C. 101 et seq.
Sherman Antitrust Act
  Act of July 2, 1890, 26 Stat. 209, as amended, 15 U.S.C. 1 et seq.

BIBLIOGRAPHY

The following limited selected list of reading material will greatly aid in securing a broader view of the background of labor rights and of the specific issues in the cases discussed in the book.

FOR GENERAL BACKGROUND:

COMMONS AND ASSOCIATES, *History of Labour in the United States*. New York: The Macmillan Co., 1921.

DANKERT, C. E., *Contemporary Unionism*. New York: Prentice-Hall, Inc., 1948.

DOUGHERTY, C. R., *Labor Problems in American Industry*. Boston: Houghton Mifflin Co., 1941.

DULLES, FOSTER RHEA, *Labor in America*. New York: Thomas Y. Crowell Co., 1949.

GOMPERS, SAMUEL, *Seventy Years of Life and Labor*. New York: E. P. Dutton & Co., 1925.

GREGORY, C. O., *Labor and the Law*. New York: W. W. Norton & Co., 1946.

LANDIS, JAMES M., AND MANOFF, MARCUS. See historical introduction to: *Cases on Labor Law*. Chicago: The Foundation Press, Inc., 1942.

MILLS, C. WRIGHT, *The New Men of Power*. New York: Harcourt, Brace and Co., 1948.

McNAUGHTON, W. L., *The Development of Labor Relations Law*. Washington: American Council on Public Affairs, 1941.

MILLIS, H. A., AND MONTGOMERY, R. E., *Organized Labor*. New York: McGraw-Hill Book Co., Inc., 1945.

PERLMAN, SELIG, *A Theory of the Labor Movement*. New York: Augustus M. Kelley, 1949 (orig. printed 1928).

ROE, WELLINGTON, *Juggernaut*. Philadelphia and New York: J. B. Lippincott Company, 1948.

TAFT, PHILIP, *Economics and Problems of Labor*. Harrisburg: Stackpole and Sons, 1942.

TELLER, LUDWIG, *Labor Disputes and Collective Bargaining*. New York: Baker, Voorhis & Co., Inc., 1940.

TONER, JEROME L., *The Closed Shop*. Washington 1941.

WARE, N. J., *Labor in Modern Industrial Society*. New York: D. C. Heath and Co., 1935.

WITTE, E. E., *The Government in Labor Disputes*. New York: McGraw-Hill Book Co., Inc., 1932.

YELLEN, SAMUEL, *American Labor Struggles*. New York: Harcourt, Brace, 1936.

FOR THE SPECIFIC ISSUES:

In addition to the bibliography on the general background above cited, see also the list of *Cases and Authorities Cited* and the following:

CHAPTER I COMMONS, JOHN R., AND GILMORE, E. A., *Documentary History of American Industrial Society*, Vol. III, *Labor Conspiracy Cases,* Cleveland: Arthur H. Clark Co., 1910.

CHAPTER II The outstanding article on this subject is NELLES, WALTER, "Commonwealth v. Hunt" (1932) 32 *Columbia Law Review* 1128. See also FELLER, A. H., "Lemuel Shaw," *Encyclopedia of Social Science*, Vol. 14, p. 17, and WARE, NORMAN J., *Industrial Worker, 1840-1860.* (Boston, 1935).

CHAPTER III BERMAN, EDWARD, *Labor Disputes and the President of the United States* (New York, 1924) ; BROWNE, WALDO R., *Altgeld of Illinois* (1924); COLEMAN, McALISTER, *Eugene V. Debs* (New York, 1930); FRANKFURTER, FELIX, and GREENE, NATHAN, *Labor Injunction* (New York, 1930); GINGER, RAY, *The Bending Cross*, a biography of Eugene V. Debs. New Brunswick: Rutgers University Press, 1949; LINDSEY, ALMONT, *Pullman Strike* (Chicago, 1943).

ALLEN, CHARLES C., "Injunction and Organized Labor (1894) *American Bar Association Journal* 399; GREGORY, CHARLES O., "Government by Injunction," (1898) 11 *Harvard Law Review* 487; GREGORY, S. S., "The Debs Case," 27 *Chicago Law Notes,* 82.

CHAPTER IV FISHER, C. O., "Use of Federal Power in Settlement of Railway Labor Disputes," *Bureau of Labor Statistics, Bulletin No. 303* (Washington, 1922); O'CONNOR, J. J., *Supreme Court and Labor* (Washington, 1932); WITTE, E. E., *Government in Labor Disputes* (New York, 1932).

DARLING, C. R., "The Adair Case," (1908) 42 *American Law Review* 884.

CHAPTER V BERMAN, EDWARD, *Labor and the Sherman Act* (New York, 1930); BOUDIN, LOUIS B., "The Sherman Act and Labor Disputes, (1939) 39 *Columbia Law Review* 1283; (1940) 40 *Columbia Law Review* 14; GREGORY, CHARLES O., *Labor and the Law*, (New York: W.

W. Norton & Co., 1946); HAMILTON, ALICE, *Exploring the Dangerous Trades* (Boston, 1943) and *Industrial Poisons in the United States* (New York, 1925); MERRITT, WALTER G., *Struggle for Industrial Liberty* (New York, 1922); ROBINSON, DONALD B., *Spotlight on a Union* (New York: Dial Press, 1948); WOLMAN, LEO, *Boycott in American Trade Unions* (Baltimore, 1916).

CHAPTER VI   See titles under Chapter V. See also AMERICAN FEDERATION OF LABOR, *Buck's Stove and Range Company Injunction Suit* (Washington, 1910); GOMPERS, SAMUEL, *Seventy Years of Life and Labor*, 2 vols. (New York, 1925); HARVEY, R. H., *Samuel Gompers* (New York, 1935).

GREGORY, S. S., "The Courts and Free Speech," (1913) 8 *Illinois Law Review* 141.

CHAPTER VII   FRANKFURTER, FELIX, and GREENE, NATHAN, *Labor Injunction*, (New York, 1930); FREY, JOHN P., *Labor Injunction*; GLUCK, ELSIE, *John Mitchell, Miner, Labor's Bargain with the Gilded Age* (New York, 1929); McDONALD, D. J., and LYNCH, E. A., *Coal and Unionism* (Silver Spring, Md., 1939); SEIDMAN, JOEL, "Yellow Dog Contract," *Johns Hopkins University Studies in Historical and Political Science, Series 50* (Baltimore, 1932).

Notes: (1918) 3 *Cornell Law Quarterly* 317 ("Persuading Employees in Non-union Shop to Join Union") ; (1918) 16 *Michigan Law Review* 250 ("Inducing Breach of Agreement by Employees Not to Join a Labor Union, in Order to Compel Unionization of Plaintiff's Business"); (1919) 3 *California Law Review* 78 ("Master and Servant, Note to *Hitchman* v. *Mitchell*").

CHAPTER VIII   GREGORY, C. O., *Labor and the Law* (New York, 1946). See also TELLER, LUDWIG, *Labor Disputes and Collective Bargaining* (New York, 1940); KOVNER, JOSEPH, "Legislative History of Section 6 of the Clayton Act," (1947) 47 *Columbia Law Review*, 749.

CHAPTER IX   SLOSSON, PRESTON, *The Great Crusade and After* (New York, 1930).

CARRINGTON, WALTER, "Injunctions in Labor Controversies" (1922) 8 *Virginia Law Register*, new series 401. Notes: (1922) 70 *University of Pennsylvania Law Review* 101 ("The Effect of the Clayton Act on Picketing"); (1922) 10 *California Law Review* 237 ("Validity of Statute Forbidding Use of Injunction against Picketing"); (1922) 31 *Yale Law Journal* 408 ("The Arizona Labor Decision").

CHAPTER X   FAULKNER, H. U., *Quest for Social Justice* (New York, 1931); PRINGLE, H. F., *Life and Times of William Howard Taft*, 2 vols. (New York, 1939).

Notes: (1922) 22 *Columbia Law Review* 252 ("Limitations on State

Police Power under the 'Due Process' and 'Equal Protection' Clauses");
(1922) 7 *Cornell Law Quarterly* 251 ("Boycott and Picketing").

CHAPTER XI ALLEN, HENRY J., *Party of the Third Part* (New York,
1921); GAGLIARDO, DOMENICO, *Kansas Industrial Court* (Lawrence,
1941); *Kansas Court of Industrial Relations, Second, Third, Fourth,
and Fifth Annual Reports* (Topeka, 1922-1925); NATIONAL ASSOCIATION
OF MANUFACTURERS, *Compulsory Arbitration of Labor Disputes* (New
York, 1938); NATIONAL INDUSTRIAL CONFERENCE BOARD, *Kansas Court
of Industrial Relations* (New York, 1924).

  WHEELER, E. P., "Injunctions in Labor Disputes and Decisions of
Industrial Tribunals," (1922) 8 *American Bar Association Journal* 506;
YOUNG, J. S., "Industrial Courts: With Special Reference to the Kansas
Experiment," (1920) 4 *Minnesota Law Review* 483; (1920) 5 *Minnesota
Law Review* 39.

CHAPTER XII Notes: (1922) 10 *California Law Review* 506 ("Suability of a Labor Union as a Legal Entity"); (1922) 32 *Yale Law
Journal* 59 ("The Coronado Coal Case"). On the second *Coronado*
case, see brief comment in: Notes (1925) 11 *American Bar Association
Journal* 423; (1925) 35 *Yale Law Journal* 111.

CHAPTER XIII Notes: (1927) 4 *Wisconsin Law Review* 250 ("Strike
against Use of Products"). (1927) 26 *Michigan Law Review* 198 ("Secondary Boycott"); (1927) *1 St. John's Law Review* 189 ("Further Development of the Doctrine of *Duplex* v. *Deering*"); and (1927) 14 *Virginia
Law Review 112* ("Enjoining Labor Unions from Refusing to Work
on Non-Union Products").

CHAPTER XIV CLARK, M. R., and SIMON, S. F., *Labor Movement
in America* (New York, 1938); MITCHELL, BROADUS, *Depression Decade:
From New Era to New Deal* (New York, 1947).

  See also comment on the *Senn* case in Notes: (1937) 6 *Fordham Law
Review* 474; (1940) 9 *Fordham Law Review* 95 ("Recent Trends in the
Law of Picketing"); (1938) *Wisconsin Law Review* 170.

CHAPTER XV BOWMAN, D. O., *Public Control of Labor Relations*
(New York, 1942); BROOKS, ROBERT R. R., *As Steel Goes* (New Haven,
1940) and *Unions of their Own Choosing* (New Haven, 1939); EBY,
HERBERT O., *Labor Relations Act in the Courts* (New York, 1943);
LORWIN, L. L., *Labor Relations Boards: the Regulation of Collective
Bargaining Under the National Industrial Recovery Act* (Washington,
1935); NATIONAL LAWYERS' COMMITTEE of the American Liberty
League, *Report on the Constitutionality of the National Labor Rela-
tions Act* (Pittsburgh, Sept. 5, 1935); ROSENFARB, JOSEPH, *The National
Labor Policy and How it Works* (New York, Harper & Brothers, 1940);

TWENTIETH CENTURY FUND, *Labor and the Government*, (New York, 1935).

FUCHS, R. F., and FREEDMAN, W., "The Wagner Act Decisions and Factual Technique in Public Law Cases," (1937) 22 *Washington University Law Quarterly* 510; SAWYER, S. W., "The Commerce Clause of the Constitution: The Old and the New," (1940) 8 *University of Kansas Law Review* 229. Notes: (1938) 11 *Southern California Law Review* 240 ("National Labor Relations [Wagner] Act"); (1937) 17 *Boston University Law Review* 710 ("Wagner Labor Act"); and (1937) 22 *Cornell Law Quarterly* 568 ("National Labor Relations Cases").

CHAPTER XVI HART, H. M. JR., and PRICHARD, E. F. JR., "The Fansteel Case: Employee Misconduct and the Remedial Powers of the National Labor Relations Board," (1939) 52 *Harvard Law Review* 1275; SUGARMAN, N. A., "The Fansteel Decision and the Development of Employees' Rights Under the National Labor Relations Act," (1939) 14 *Ohio Opinions* 202. Notes: (1939) 39 *Columbia Law Review* 1369 ("Employee Misconduct Under the Wagner Act: Developments Since the Fansteel Case"); (1938) 33 *Illinois Law Review* 187 ("The Fansteel Decision: Protection of Striking Workers Under the Wagner Act"); (1939) 1 *Louisiana Law Review* 577 ("From Nose-Thumbing to Sabotage—The Fansteel Sit-Down Decision").

CHAPTER XVII FEINBERG, I. R., "Picketing, Free Speech, and 'Labor Disputes,' " (1940) 17 *New York University Law Quarterly Review* 385; GREGORY, C. O., "Peaceful Picketing and Freedom of Speech," (1940) 26 *American Bar Association Journal* 709; DODD, E. M., "Picketing and Free Speech: A Dissent," (1943) 56 *Harvard Law Review* 513; SHERWOOD, W. K., "The Picketing Cases and How They Grew," (1942) 10 *George Washington Law Review* 763; TELLER, LUDWIG, "Picketing and Free Speech," (1942) 56 *Harvard Law Review* 180.

CHAPTER XVIII KIRSCH, BENJAMIN, *Anti-Trust Laws and Labor* (New York, 1941); HODGES, E. P., *Antitrust Law and the Supreme Court* (St. Paul, Minn., 1941).

BROWN, A. L., "The Apex Case and Its Effect upon Labor Activities and the Anti-Trust Laws," (1941) 21 *Boston University Law Review* 48; COHEN, C. E., "Labor and the Anti-Trust Laws in the Light of the *Apex* Case," (1940) 74 *New York Law Review* 561; GREGORY, C. O., "The Sherman Act *v.* Labor," (1941) 8 *University of Chicago Law Review* 222; McNUTT, E. B., "Labor and the Antitrust Laws—the Apex Decision," (1941) 49 *Journal of Political Economy* 555; SCHULMAN, HARRY, "Labor and the Anti-Trust Laws," (1940) 34 *Illinois Law Review* 769; Notes: (1941) 39 *Michigan Law Review* 462 ("The Apex Decision and Its Effect on the Application of the Sherman Act to Activities of Labor Unions"); Comment, CAVERS, D. F., (1941) 8 *University of Chicago Law Review* 516 (" 'And What of the Apex Case Now?' "); (1940) 49 *Yale Law Journal* 518 ("Labor and the Sherman Act"); (1941) 9 *George Washington Law Review* 948 ("The Apparent Finale of the Application of Anti-Trust Laws to Labor—Need for Remedy").

CHAPTER XIX　ARNOLD, THURMAN W., *Democracy and Free Enterprise* (Norman, Okla., 1942); GREGORY, C. O., *Labor and the Law.*

NATHANSON, N. L., and WIRTZ, W. W., "The Hutcheson Case: Another View," (1941) 36 *Illinois Law Review* 41; LASHLEY, E., "Rights and Obligations of Labor Unions under the Anti-Trust Acts of Congress," (1946) 17 *Oklahoma Bar Association Journal* 803. Notes: (1941) 29 *Georgetown Law Journal* 770 ("Labor Provisions of the Clayton Act Revived"); (1941) 4 *University of Detroit Law Journal* 209 ("Jurisdictional Dispute between Labor Unions in Restraint of Trade"); (1941) 26 *Washington University Law Quarterly* 375 ("The Hutcheson Case").

CHAPTER XX　CAYTON, H. R., and MITCHELL, G. S., *Black Workers and the New Unions* (Chapel Hill, N. C., 1939); EMBREE, E. R., *American Negroes* (New York, 1942); NORTHRUP, H. R., *Organized Labor and the Negro* (New York, 1944); ROSS, MALCOLM, *All Manner of Men* (New York, 1948); SEIDMAN, JOEL, *Union Rights and Union Duties*, (New York, 1943); SPERO, STERLING, and HARRIS, A. H., *Black Worker* (New York, 1931). See also AMERICAN FEDERATION OF LABOR, *Convention Proceedings, 1943*, pp. 140-142, 230-231, 416-425; *1944*, pp. 174, 495-507, 592-593.

Notes: (1945) 23 *Texas Law Review* 287 ("Union Contract Discriminating against Interest of Non-Union Members of Craft"); (1945) 33 *Illinois Bar Journal* 239; (1945) 43 *Michigan Law Review* 982.

CHAPTER XXI　MILLS, C. WRIGHT, *The New Men of Power* (New York, 1948).

Notes: (1945) 58 *Harvard Law Review* 448 ("Discrimination by Labor Unions in the Exercise of Statutory Bargaining Powers"); (1945) 40 *Illinois Law Review* 149 ("Discrimination by Labor Unions"); (1945) 43 *Michigan Law Review* 819; (1945) 3 *National Bar Journal* 148.

CHAPTER XXII　ARNOLD, THURMAN, *Democracy and Free Enterprise* (1942).

Notes: (1944) 58 *Harvard Law Review* 273 ("Restraint of Trade by Combinations of Unions and Employers"); (1945) 45 *Columbia Law Review* 272; (1945) 43 *Michigan Law Review* 818; (1946) 19 *Southern California Law Review* 256.

CHAPTER XXIII CARNES, CECIL, *John L. Lewis, Leader of Labor* (New York, 1936); PERKINS, FRANCES, *The Roosevelt I Knew* (New York, 1946) ; SULZBERGER, C. L., *Sit Down with John L. Lewis* (New York, 1938); WECHSLER, JAMES H., *Labor Baron: A Portrait of John L. Lewis* (New York, 1944). See also WILLIAMS, S. T., and HARRIS, HERBERT, *Trends in Collective Bargaining* (New York, 1945).

WATT, R. F., "The Divine Right of Government by Judiciary," (1947) 14 *University of Chicago Law Review* 409; GREGORY, C. O., "Government by Injunction Again," (1947) 14 *University of Chicago Law Review* 363; Notes: (1947) 60 *Harvard Law Review* 811 ("Jurisdiction to Determine Jurisdiction: *United States* v. *United Mine Workers*"); (1947) 22 *Notre Dame Law Review* 432 ("*United States* v. *United Mine Workers of America*"); (1948) 23 *Indiana Law Journal* 114 ("Criminal vs. Civil Contempt"); (1947) 22 *New York University Law Quarterly Review* 337 ("Power to Punish for Criminal Contempt"); (1947) 42 *Illinois Law Review* 372 ("Substantial Doubt Doctrine of the Lewis Case and the Norris-La Guardia Act").

CHAPTER XXIV DANKERT, CLYDE E., *Contemporary Unionism in the United States* (New York, 1948); METZ, HAROLD W., *Labor Policy of the Federal Government* (Washington, 1945); METZ, H. W., and JACOBSTEIN, MEYER, *National Labor Policy* (Washington, 1947); RESEARCH INSTITUTE OF AMERICA, *Taft-Hartley Labor Law, Its Effect on Labor Relations* (New York, 1947), ROE, WELLINGTON, *Juggernaut: American Labor in Action* (Philadelphia, 1948); WATT, R. F., "The New Deal Court, Organized Labor, and the Taft-Hartley Act," (1947) 7 *Lawyer's Guild Review*, 193; 237-251.

CHAPTER XXV MCNAUGHTON, W. L., *The Development of Labor Relations Law* (Washington, 1941); TONER, JEROME L., *The Closed Shop* (Washington, 1944). AMERICAN FEDERATION OF LABOR, *Convention Proceedings, 1946*, pp. 139, 538; *1947*, 223, 257; KILLINGSWORTH, CHARLES C., *State Labor-Relations Acts* (Chicago, 1948).

ROSS, G., "The Right to Work: It Must be Supreme over Union Security," (1949) 35 *American Bar Association Journal* 10; Notes: (1947) 42 *Illinois Law Review* 505 ("State Regulation of Labor Unions"); (1947) 96 *University of Pennsylvania Law Review* 101 ("Union Security Devices and the Taft-Hartley Act"); (1949) 62 *Harvard Law Review* 886 ("State Laws Prohibiting Union Security Agreements Held Constitutional").

CHAPTER XXVI COMMONS AND ANDREWS, *Principles of Labor Legislation* (New York, 1920); DULLES, FOSTER RHEA, *Labor in America*

(New York, 1949) ; LASKI, HAROLD J., *Trade Union in the New Society* New York, 1949. MILLS, C. WRIGHT, *New Men of Power* (New York, 1948); TELLER, LUDWIG, *Labor Policy for America* (New York, 1945); WITTE, E. E., *The Government in Labor Disputes* (New York, 1932).

Index

Adair, William, 46, 48, 50
Adair v. The United States, 48-52, 54, 254
Adamson Act, 131, 134
Administrative procedure, 198, 212, 214, 268-270
Agent, responsibility of union for, 242, 323
Alabama antipicketing law, 218, 221
Alcorn, George, 8, 9
Allen, Governor Henry J., 127
Allen Bradley Co. v. Local 3, et al., 276-286
Alschuler, Justice Samuel, 109, 166
Altgeld, Governor John P., 33-35, 42
Amalgamated Association of Iron, Steel and Tin Workers, 182-184, 187, 204, 206, 209
Amalgamated Clothing Workers' Union, 227
Amalgamated Meat Cutters (AFL), 129
American Anti-Boycott Association, 58-60, 62, 63, 72, 79, 83
American Civil Liberties Union, 176, 259
American Federation of Hosiery Workers, 226, 227, 230
American Federation of Labor (AFL), 44, 45, 56, 58, 60, 62, 66, 69, 71, 73-75, 83, 94, 164, 182, 184, 201, 218, 220, 221, 226, 243, 253, 263, 272, 288, 309-311, 328, 334, 337
American Federation of Labor, et al. v. American Sash and Door Company, 334-335
American Federationist, 73-75, 77, 139
American Railway Union, 30-32, 36, 38, 39
American Steel Foundries Co. v. Tri-City Central Trades Council, 110-117, 162
Anderson, Judge Albert B., 166
Anheuser-Busch Brewing Co., 243-244, 246, 248, 250
Anselm, A. J., 205-208
Anti-injunction acts, *see* Clayton Act; Norris-La Guardia Act.
Antilabor legislation, 201, 305, 311, 332, 334, 335, 337, 349
  See also Taft-Hartley Act

Antitrust laws, 154, 162, 166, 168, 172, 195, 248, 277, 280
  See also Clayton Act; Sherman Act
Apex Hosiery Co. v. Leader, et al., 229-239, 247, 284
Arbitration, 31, 33, 43, 51, 52, 290, 292
  compulsory, 127, 128, 136, 138-140
  voluntary, 25, 139-140, 244
  See also Trade agreements
Arizona, 118-119
  anti-injunction law, 119, 123-126
  ban on union security, 334
Arnold, Thurman, 244, 246
Assembly, freedom of, 338
Associated Indiana Quarries, 165
Associated Press v. NLRB, 198

Bache, Franklin, 141-146, 153, 154, 156, 157, 160
Bakery and Pastry Drivers' Union v. Wohl, 224
Bargaining, *see* Collective bargaining; Individual bargaining
Bargaining agent, 184, 255-257, 264, 270, 341, 342
  duty to represent entire craft, 259-261, 271
Bargaining power, equality of, 53, 54, 134, 185, 233, 242, 339
Bargaining unit, 207
Barnes, Underl, 6
Bedford, John, 6-9
Bedford Cut Stone Co., et al., v. Journeymen Stone Cutters of North America, et al., 165-171, 241, 251, 347
Berman, Edward, 67-68
Bill of Rights, 223
Black, Justice Hugo L., 213, 268, 283, 297, 299, 338, 340, 342
Blacklisting, 45-46, 54, 73, 280
Blue Eagle, *see* National Industrial Recovery Act (NIRA)
Bootmakers, *see* Cordwainers; shoemakers
Borsari Tank Corporation, 243-244
Boston Journeymen Bootmakers' Society, 17-20, 23
Boudin, Louis B., 68

Boycott, 32, 33, 36, 39, 57, 58, 60, 65-67, 69, 72, 73, 75, 76, 78, 82, 166, 233, 280, 285
  primary, 244
  secondary, 101, 102, 104, 107, 122, 236, 239, 240, 248, 250, 277, 286, 314, 320-322
Boyer, Royal, 189
Brandeis, Justice Louis D., 91, 92, 103, 105, 106, 125, 169, 170, 177, 179, 194, 223, 342
Brandy, Domenic, 189
Bredenbach, Judge Otto H., 175
Brewer, Justice David Josiah, 40, 42, 49
Bucks Stove and Range Co. v. *Gompers, et al.,* 71-77, 204
Business as property right, 103, 104, 124
Butler, Justice Pierce, 178, 198

Caffrey, Judge Francis C., 280, 281
Captive mines, 287, 289
Cardozo, Justice Benjamin F., 194, 346
Carpenters and Joiners Union v. *Ritter's Cafe,* 224
Carter v. *Carter Coal Company,* 195
Checkoff, 206, 315, 323
Christian American Association, 305, 332
CIO (Committee for Industrial Organization; Congress of Industrial Organizations), 201, 226, 253, 263, 288-290, 309-311, 337
Clark, Judge Charles E., 281
Clark, John Kirkland, 278
Clark, Tom, 294
Clarke, Justice John H., 91, 105, 125
Class legislation, 48-49, 102, 122, 123, 176
Class struggle, 83, 169
Clayton Act, 70, 114, 123, 124, 126, 149, 165, 167, 169, 170, 173, 231, 233, 235, 245, 247-249, 281, 284, 302, 314, 322
  ambiguity of, 107
  injunctions under, 98, 101, 106
  labor immunities under, 97, 102-104, 109, 112, 117, 237, 241, 248-251, 285
Cleveland, President Grover, 34, 42, 44
Closed shop, 20, 206, 229, 265-268, 270, 331, 332
  legality of, 25, 269, 313, 323
  right of state to prohibit, 314, 336, 338-342
Coal mines, government operation of, 290-292, 297, 298
Cochran, Justice Andrew M., 47
Codes of Fair Competition, 182, 273, 303
  See also National Industrial Recovery Act
Collective agreement, *see* Trade agreements

Collective bargaining, 1, 182, 185, 186, 192, 194, 198, 206, 216, 233, 238, 239, 242, 273, 288, 313, 315-318
  See also Taft-Hartley Act; Wagner Act
Collison, N. H., 293
Combination, justification of, for labor, 11, 15, 17, 21, 53, 114-115, 242
  lawful, 21-22, 25, 27-28
  unlawful, 11, 13, 15, 16, 19, 20, 23, 91
  See also Conspiracy; Monopoly; Unions
Combination in restraint of trade, 229, 238
Commerce, *see* Interstate commerce
Common law, 247, 344
  binding effect of, 11, 14, 15, 20, 22, 88, 89
Commonwealth (Pa.) v. *Carlisle,* 27
Commonwealth (Pa.) v. *Cordwainers,* 5-14
Commonwealth (Mass.) v. *Hunt,* 24-27, 346
Company towns, 31, 187, 201, 217, 219, 302
Company unions, 94, 166, 167, 183, 184, 187, 189, 209, 210, 215, 216, 256, 263, 264
Competition, 283
  among employers, 99, 304
  among workers, 163, 235, 238, 239, 247
  codes, *see* Codes of Fair Competition
  freedom of, 180, 235
  standards of, 182, 273
Compulsory arbitration, *see* Arbitration
Conspiracy, 87-91, 111, 114, 120, 123, 147, 148, 156, 168, 229, 231, 232, 251, 280
  criminal, 37-41, 102, 244, 245, 345
  doctrine of, 15, 22, 26, 28
Constitution, U.S., 40, 47, 112, 124, 190, 222, 339
Contempt of court, 36, 38-41, 75, 77, 78, 294, 299-301, 311
  civil, 79, 298
  criminal, 76, 80, 81, 297, 298
  defined, 295
Contract, breach of, 90-92
  freedom of, *see* Freedom of contract
Cooling-off period, 307, 314
Coppage, O. B., 46, 48, 50, 53
Cordwainers (Phila.), 1-4, 6-8
Coronado Coal Co. v. *United Mine Workers of America,* 141, 158-161, 237
Cox, Ronald, 189, 190
Coxe, Justice Alfred C., 64
Creel, Judge E. M., 256
Cunningham, Justice D. L., 121, 122

Danbury hatters, 62-66
  See also Loewe v. Lawlor
Darrow, Clarence S., 37, 39
Davenport, Daniel, 58

Davis, Judge Charles B., 245
Davis, Justice J. Warren, 229, 230
Davis, William H., 290
Dayton, Justice Alston G., 87-89, 92, 94
Debs, Eugene V., 29-30, 32, 35, 36, 38, 39, 41
Deering, Emil J., 99, 100
Democratic party, campaigns, *1932*, 303
  1936, 192
  1946, 309
  platforms, *1896*, 42
  1908, 96
Depressions, *1893*, 31
  1929, 182, 254, 272, 303
Discrimination, against union members, 49, 54, 189, 190, 194, 211, 269
  racial, 252-253, 257-258, 261, 262
Dodrill, Harvey, 264
Douglas, Justice William O., 224, 297, 299
Dowd, A. S., 147
Dred Scott v. *Sanford*, 261, 262
Dubinsky, David, 328
Dubois, John, 6
Due process, *see* Fourteenth Amendment
Dueber Watch Case Manufacturing Co. v. *E. Howard Watch and Clock Co., et al.*, 69
Dulles, Foster Rhea, 344
Duplex Printing Press Co. v. *Deering*, 99, 101-106, 114, 126, 169, 171, 241, 244, 251, 347

Economic concentration, 70
Economic conflict, allowable area of, 104-106, 114, 116, 169, 171, 242, 243, 245, 248-250
Economic interest, *see* Unity of interest
Elections, collective bargaining, 184
  majority in bargaining unit, 216, 255, 265, 266
  majority eligible to vote, 319, 320
Electrical Contractors' Association 272, 273
  voluntary code, 274, 275, 279
Electrotype Molders and Finishers Union, No. *17*, 72
Employer-employee relationship, 94, 181, 199
  See also Master and servant relations
Employers' associations, 1, 10, 71, 72, 164, 204, 205
  See also American Anti-Boycott Association; National Association of Manufacturers
Employer, liability of, 51
  natural rights of, 50, 330, 346
Ends and means, doctrine of, 26, 346

Equality, economic, 53
  legal, 50, 52
Equity courts, and labor disputes, 42
  legislative regulation of, 96, 98, 119, 242, 243, 250
  power of, 40-41, 113, 121
Erdman, Constantine Jacob, 44
Erdman Act, 44, 51
Estoppel, 269-270
Evans, Justice Evan A., 109, 110, 116

Fact-finding boards, 291
Factory system, 345
Fair competition, *see* Codes of Fair Competition
Fairchild, Justice Edward T., 175
Fairless, Benjamin, 192, 290
Fansteel Metallurgical Corp. v. *NLRB*, 211-213
Federalist-Jeffersonian conflict, 1, 5, 14, 15
Fifth Amendment, 47-50, 152, 176, 178, 199
Finley, et al., v. *United Mine Workers of America, et al.*, 157-158
First Amendment, 222, 338, 339
Foster, Judge Henry B., 220
Foster, William Z., 182
Fourteenth Amendment, 121-125, 130, 133, 134, 137, 177, 179, 222, 223, 338, 339
Fowler, Justice Chester A., 176
Frankfurter, Justice Felix, 224, 248, 250, 251, 270, 297, 299, 340
Franklin, Walter, 11, 13
Freedom of assembly, 338
Freedom of contract, 47-52, 131, 134, 137, 195, 199, 202
Freedom of press and speech, 74, 80, 112, 121, 123, 136, 178, 187-189, 217, 220-222
Frick, Henry C., 182
Friendly societies, 1
Fuchs, Martin, 57, 60
Fuller, Chief Justice Melville W., 49, 61
Furuseth, Andrew, 44

Gardner, F. W., 79
Gardner, Chief Justice Lucien D., 258
Garland, Judge John E., 147, 148
General Managers' Association, 30, 32, 33, 36, 37
Giebelhouse, Dan, 336
Girdler, Tom, 187
Goldsborough, Judge T. Alan, 294-297, 301, 311
Gompers, Samuel, 30, 36, 37, 44, 70, 71, 75-77, 80-82, 97, 139, 328

Gompers v. *Bucks Stove & Range Co.*, 221
Good will, right to, 91, 122
  See also Boycott
Gould, Justice Ashley M., 73
Government policy toward labor, *see* Injunction; National Labor Relations Act; Pullman strike; Taft-Hartley Act
Green, William, 86, 94, 184
Gregory, Charles O., 106, 346
Gregory, S. S., 39
Grosscup, Judge Peter S., 34, 37
Guilds, 2

Habeas corpus, 39
Hamilton, Alexander, 5
Hand, Judge Augustus N., 281
Hand, Justice Learned, 101, 102
Hanraty, Pete, 155, 157, 159
Harket, John, 6
Harlan, Justice John Marshall, 49, 52-54
Harrison, Job, 6-9
Hartley, Fred E., 310, 312, 315, 323
Harvey, Justice W. W., 136
Hatmaking, hazards of, 56
Hatters, Danbury, 62-66
Henderson, William, 13
Hepburn, John, 6
Hill, Hugh J., 46
Hill, James J., 30
Hire and fire, right to, 48, 197, 320
Hitchman Coal & Coke Co. v. *Mitchell*, 84, 91, 92, 94, 95, 111, 112, 114, 171
Hoffman, Clare E., 310
Holden v. *Hardy*, 53
Holly, Arnold, 174
Holmes, Justice Oliver Wendell, 52, 66, 82, 91, 94, 105, 124, 169
Hopkinson, Joseph, 6, 7, 11
Horne, Jeremiah, 18, 19, 21, 25
Hough, Justice Charles M., 101
Hours of labor, controversies about, 71-73
Howard, George W., 29, 30, 36
Howat, Alexander, 138
Hughes, Chief Justice Charles Evans, 151, 194, 212, 234, 237, 250
Hughes, Thomas, 86
Hughes, William, 96
Human rights, 70
Humphreys, Justice Otto, 109
Hutcheson, Judge Joseph C., 190
Hutcheson, William L., 244, 250

Independent Mine Workers of West Virginia, 85
Individual bargaining, futility of, 212, 242, 330

Industrial espionage, 204-205
Industrial relations, effect on interstate commerce, 196
  federal regulation of, 50, 181, 193
  legislative power to regulate, 52, 124, 340, 342
  patterns of, 1, 139, 140, 182
  state regulation of, 115, 123, 127, 128, 138
Industrial unionism, 263, 388
  See also CIO
Industrial Workers of the World (IWW), 225
Industries affected with public interest, 128, 130, 133, 134
Inflation, 16, 17, 306
Ingersoll, Jared, 11
Injunction, 28, 34, 41, 72-74, 82, 97-103, 108-110, 112, 113, 119, 120, 123, 124, 143, 145, 165, 167, 170, 176-178, 208, 224, 227, 229, 232, 241, 245, 247, 249, 250, 256, 257, 261, 277, 280-282, 293, 294, 296, 297, 299, 300, 314, 321, 322
  abuse of, in labor disputes, 35, 42, 78, 86, 87, 93, 95, 106, 124, 171
  government by, 42
  labor's effort to check, 96-98, 107, 172, 242
  See also Clayton Act; Norris-La Guardia Act
Innskeep, John, 6
International Association of Machinists (I.A.M.), 99, 100, 243
International Brotherhood of Electrical Workers (IBEW), Local *3*, 272, 277-280, 282-284
International Juridical Association, 176
International Ladies' Garment Workers' Union, 227, 351
International Stereotypers and Electrotypers Union, 72, 74
Interstate commerce, 36, 38, 41, 47, 49-54, 60-62, 67, 68, 103, 131, 146, 153, 156, 167, 182, 187, 191, 193, 197, 202, 249, 250, 277, 280
  free flow of, 185, 194, 196, 199, 203, 229, 238
  intent to restrain, 156-161, 166, 168, 228, 231, 237, 244, 246
  See also Antitrust laws; Clayton Act; Sherman Act; Wagner Act
Interstate Commerce Commission, 45
Interunion disputes, effect of, *see* Jurisdictional disputes
Iron and Steel Institute, 183
Iron Molders' International, 71

Jackson, Justice Robert H., 224, 270, 297, 299
Jefferson, Thomas, 4, 5
Johnson, A. R., 209
Johnston, Alfred, 205
Journeymen Stone Cutters' Association, 164-166
Jurisdictional disputes, 243, 246, 249
Jurisdictional strikes, 244, 245, 247, 320

Kansas Court of Industrial Relations, 127-131, 135, 136, 138
Kansas Industrial Relations Act of 1920, 127, 128, 132-138
Keenan, Joseph D., 328
Keimer, George, 6
Keliher, Sylvester, 30, 36
Kenyon, Judge William S., 157
Kirkpatrick, Judge William G., 228
Kondrath, John, 207
Krug, Julius, 292-294
Krug-Lewis Agreement, 292-294, 298, 311

Label, see Union label
Labor, unfair practices, see Unfair labor practices
Labor leaders, psychology of, 348-349
Labor legislation, 107, 174, 185-187, 242, 243, 311-315
Labor-Management Conference of 1945, 307
Labor-Management Relations Act, 1947, see Taft-Hartley Act
Labor movement, failure to achieve unity, 309-311
    judicial attitudes toward, 12-13, 16, 22-23, 25-27, 54, 90, 201, 331, 345, 346
Labor standards, 58, 99, 160, 174, 180, 239, 286
Labor unions see Unions
Labor's League for Political Education (LLPE), 328
Labor's Non-Partisan League, 288
Lacombe, Justice E. Henry, 63
La Follette, Robert M., 46
La Follette Civil Liberties Committee, 205
Lamar, Justice Joseph Rucker, 79, 80
Laski, Harold J., 350
Lawlor v. Loewe, 65-66, 104, 171
Lawson, Thomas S., 221
Leader, William, 227, 230
Legislative power to regulate industrial relations, courts' attitude toward, 52, 124, 340-342
Leibel, Judge Vincent, 277
Lend-Lease bill, 289
Levy, Recorder Moses, 5, 12-14

Lewis, John L., 86, 138, 192, 287-294, 298, 301, 302, 311, 312, 326, 328
Liberty League, 186, 201
Liberty of contract, see Freedom of contract
Lincoln Federal Labor Union No. 19129 v. Northwestern Iron & Metal Co., 336
Lindley, Judge Walter C., 211
Little Steel Formula, 291, 306
Lloyd, Thomas, 14
Lockouts, 142, 165, 218
    See also Strikes
Lockwood, Judge Alfred C., 120
Locomotive Firemen and Hostlers, 254, 258
Locomotive Firemen and Enginemen, Brotherhood of, 29, 30, 253-255, 261
Loeb, William H., 221
Loewe, Dietrich E., 57, 58, 60, 66, 67
Loewe v. Lawlor, 60, 63, 233, 347
Louisville & Nashville Railroad, 46, 53, 254, 256

McAdoo, William G., 253
Mack, Justice Julian W., 109
McKenna, Justice Joseph, 51, 52
McNamara, James K., 155-157
McReynolds, Justice James C., 168, 178, 198, 199, 237
Magna Carta, labor, 97, 106, 165, 241
Maintenance of membership, 332
Majority rule, 183, 197, 255
    See also National Labor Relations Board
Make-work policy, 275, 276, 282
Manton, Justice Martin T., 100, 101
Market, control of, 235, 238, 276, 283, 284, 286
    protection of, 61, 154, 236, 247
    See also Restraint of trade; Sherman Act
Marshall, Justice John, 130-132, 135, 136
Mass production, 1, 226, 262, 263, 288, 302, 330
Master and servant relations, 47, 48, 51, 52, 344, 345
Mayfield, James J., 220, 221
Meany, George, 328
Mediation of disputes, 45
Membership, maintenance of, 332
Merritt, Walter Gordon, 57, 59, 62
Metal Polishers Union, 71
Milk Wagon Drivers Union v. Meadowmoor Dairies, Inc., 224
Mills, C. Wright, 348, 349
Mines, captive, 287, 289
Mitchell, John, 71, 75, 76, 77, 80, 81, 86

Monopoly, 38, 88, 89, 148, 285, 286
See also Sherman Act
Morrison, Frank, 71, 75, 77, 80, 81
Motive and purpose, doctrine of, 26
Moyer, John S., 188
Murphy, Justice Frank, 221, 261, 285, 297, 300, 302, 340, 341
Murray, Philip, 192, 200, 326

National Association for the Advancement of Colored People, 259
National Association of Manufacturers, 72, 83, 186, 201, 305, 331
National Bituminous Coal Wage Agreement of *1945*, 291
National Defense Mediation Board, 290
National Federation of Railroad Workers, 255
National Industrial Recovery Act of *1933* (NIRA), constitutionality of, 173, 184-186, 189, 192, 274
   purpose, 303, 305
   section 7(a), 182, 183, 218, 226, 304
National Labor Relations Act (NLRA), 173, 185, 187, 188, 193, 194, 197, 199, 201, 203, 209, 211-214, 216, 218, 219, 231, 232, 233, 238, 262, 267, 269, 270, 305, 309-313, 320, 321, 323, 332, 347, 348
   attack on constitutionality of, 186, 193
   enactment of, 185, 304
National Labor Relations Board (NLRB), 186-188, 194, 197, 198, 203, 210, 213, 214, 265, 267, 287, 305, 314, 348
   v. *Friedman-Harry Marks Clothing Co., Inc.*, 198
   v. *Freuhauf Trailer Co.*, 198
   v. *Jones & Laughlin Steel Corp.*, 186, 193-200
National Mediation Board, 255, 256, 260
National Metal Trades Association, 204, 205
National Recovery Administration, 226
National War Labor Board, 290, 291, 306, 307, 332
Nebraska Small Businessmen's Association, 335
Negro, discrimination against, by organized labor, 253, 254, 261, 262
   in industry, 257, 258
   political and social, 252
Neider, William, 174
Nelson, Justice George B., 176
Nettles, Judge Zeb B., 337
New Deal, 182, 192, 200, 218, 239, 263, 287, 303, 304, 307, 310

New York City Electrical Contractors' Association, 274, 275, 279
Noble, A. L., 131, 133
Non-Communist affidavits, 314, 317, 324, 326-327
See also Taft-Hartley Act
Norris-La Guardia Act, 245, 248, 249, 250, 277, 280, 282-287, 294, 295, 297, 299-302, 314
   applicability to government, 297-301
   provisions, 242, 243, 247, 322
   purpose of, 173, 241, 250, 251

Office of Price Administration (OPA), 291, 306
Oil Workers International Union, 322
Olney, Richard B., 33, 34, 54
Open shop, 331

Padway, Joseph A., 221
Page, Justice George T., 166
Parker, Alton B., 77
Parker, Justice John J., 267
Parker, Samuel D., 19
People v. *Fisher*, 20, 24, 25
People of the State of Alabama v. *Byron Thornhill*, 219
Perkins, Frances, 288, 289
Persuasion, peaceful, 87, 90, 98, 100, 109, 111, 112
   See also Injunction; Picketing
Phelps, Judge M. T., 335
Philadelphia Cordwainers case, 6-15, 20, 345
Picketing, 128, 132, 175, 176, 218-221, 245, 249, 276
   courts' right to regulate, 109, 115-117
   freedom of speech and, 80, 112, 121, 123, 217, 222
   lawful, 110, 174, 177, 213
   states' right to regulate, 119, 120, 125, 178, 179, 222, 224
   unlawful, 113, 123
Pinchot, Gifford, 187
Pitney, Justice Mahlon, 82, 91, 103, 125
Platt, Judge James P., 59, 60
Police power, 131, 136, 137, 179, 336, 342
Political Action Committee (PAC), 328
Political activity (AFL), 42, 44, 45, 70, 83, 95-97, 108, 328
Pollen, Peter, 6
Pollock, Judge John C., 155, 156
Portal-to-portal pay, 291
Porter, Judge Rufus E., 190
Pound, Roscoe, 55
Prairie Creek riots, 142, 143, 145
   See also Coronado Coal Co. v. *UMWA*

Prejudice, *see* Race discrimination
Primary boycott, *see* Boycott
Pritchard, Justice Jeter C., 89
Production, directly or indirectly affecting interstate commerce, 61, 151, 191, 199, 234
  intrastate, 94, 190
Propaganda, antilabor, 306, 309, 333
Property, broadened definition of, 42, 48
Property rights, 49, 126, 138, 345
  business as, 103, 104, 124
Public opinion, 214, 309, 333, 351
Public relations, *see* Public opinion
Pullis, George, 4, 6
Pullman, George, 30-33, 37
Pullman strike, 31, 32, 36, 54
  committee to investigate causes of, 41, 44
  federal intervention in, 33-35
  injunction, 34-37, 41-43
Purchasing power, as factor in economy, 182, 273
  as economic weapon, 59, 67, 82

Race discrimination, and labor, 252, 253, 257, 258, 261
Railroad brotherhoods, 30, 44-46, 54
Railroad Labor Board, 45
Railroad Trainman, 54
Railroads, industrial relations in, 29-30, 33, 44-46, 53, 54, 253, 254
Railway Labor Act, 255-260
Railway Conductors, Order of, 30
Rantoul, Robert, Jr., 20-25
Rare Metal Workers' Union, Local 1, Inc., 210, 211, 213
Recall of judges, 118, 119
Reed, Justice Stanley, 213
Representative bargaining, *see* Collective bargaining
Restraint of trade, *see* Interstate commerce; Sherman Act; Unreasonable restraint of trade
Rex v. *Journeymen Taylors of Cambridge*, 20, 25
Rice, Judge James, 220
Richwood Clothespin and Dishworkers' Union, 264-270
Right to do business, 42, 178
Right to organize, 25-28, 185, 186, 195, 201, 202, 233, 330, 348
Right to work, 176, 333, 334
Robb, Justice Charles H., 74
Roberts, Justice Owen D., 194, 237, 250, 270, 284, 285
Robinson, Donald B., 67
Rodney, Caesar A., 11

Roosevelt, Eleanor, 351
Roosevelt, President Franklin Delano, 173, 182-184, 191, 273, 288-291, 303, 304, 307, 309, 348
Roosevelt, President Theodore, 46
Rule of reason, *see* Sherman Act; Unreasonable restraint of trade
Rutledge, Justice Wiley B., 297, 300, 340, 341

Sanford, Justice Edward T., 169
Scab, 7, 8
Schechter Poultry Corporation v. *United States*, 184-186, 195
Scott, J. M., 46
Secondary boycott, *see* Boycott
Seniority rights, 254-259
Senn, Paul, 174-178
Senn v. *Tile Layers' Protective Union*, 175-179, 223, 342
Shaw, Chief Justice Lemuel, 24-27, 346
Shepard, Chief Justice Seth, 78, 81
Sherman, John, 68
Sherman Antitrust Act, 60, 66, 103, 145, 146, 149, 151, 160, 161, 163, 167, 169-171, 201, 228, 229, 230, 237-239, 244, 245, 249, 250, 251, 282, 284, 302, 346
  application to labor, 38-40, 61-64, 67, 68, 86, 89, 90, 94, 102, 147, 148, 230, 232-237, 240, 241, 286
  labor's campaign to amend, 70, 95, 238, 241
  original purpose of, 42, 69, 235, 239, 283
Shoemaker employers, 2-3, 8, 10
Shoemakers, journeymen, Boston, 17-20
  Philadelphia, 3-4, 6-10
Sibley, Judge Samuel H., 190
Sit-down strike, 207-209, 211-216, 227, 228, 230
Slankart, James, 143
Smith-Connally Act, 291, 292, 297-299, 307
Snyder, George, 6
Social welfare, 349-350
Societies, friendly, 1
Society of Master Cordwainers, 10
Sparks, Judge William M., 211
Speech, freedom of, *see* Freedom of speech
States' rights, 48, 125, 193, 199, 202, 342
Statute of limitations, 81, 82
Steel industry, labor relations in, 182-184, 187, 189, 190, 192
Steel Workers' Organizing Committee (SWOC), 192, 200, 219, 227
Steele, Bester William, 257-260
Steele v. *Louisville & Nashville Railroad*, 259-261
Steelman, John R., 290

Stone, Chief Justice Harlan Fiske, 169, 194, 213, 234, 238, 239, 249, 259, 270
Stonecutting, hazards of, 164
Stove Founders' Defense Association, 71
Strike, right to, 91, 92, 103, 139, 199, 233, 248
Strikes, cooling-off period before legality of, 44-45, 307, 313
  injunction and, 35, 41, 100, 162, 163
  post-World War I, 127
  post-World War II, 291, 308, 333
  sympathetic, 32, 35, 104, 244, 207
  Taft-Hartley Act and, 325
  use of federal troops in, 34-35, 145
Supreme Court, 60, 117, 132, 141, 181, 182, 215, 217
  labor resentment of decisions by, 54, 55, 126
  policy toward legislative experiment, 52, 124, 125, 340-342
Sutherland, Justice George, 168, 178, 198
Swan, Judge Thomas W., 282, 283
Sylvin, Ted, 209

Taft, Robert A., 310
Taft, Chief Justice William Howard, 112, 116, 118, 123, 124, 134, 151, 158-163, 168
Taft-Hartley Act, 302, 311, 312, 349
  aims, 315, 321-323, 329
  analysis of, 313-315
  background, 308-312
  evaluation, 316-320
  political expediency and, 323, 324
  significance of, 327-329
Taylor, Myron C., 192
Tennessee Coal & Iron Co., 218, 219
Textile Workers' Organizing Committee (TWOC), 227
Tharel, Buck, 156, 157
Thatcher, Judge Peter Oxenbridge, 19-22
Thompson, B. E., 264, 267
Thompson group, see Richwood Clothespin & Dishworkers' Union
Thornhill, Byron, 217, 219, 220, 222, 223
Thornhill v. Alabama, 221-224
Trade agreements, 57, 71, 88, 89, 141, 142, 175, 266, 267, 272, 273
Trade Unions, see Unions
Transportation, see Adair case; Debs case; Interstate commerce; railroads, industrial relations
Treanor, Justice Walter C., 212
Tri-City Central Trades Council, 108, 109, 111, 112
Truax, William, 119, 120-122
Truax v. Corrigan, 119, 122-126, 179, 342

Truman, President Harry S., 291, 292, 307, 308, 309, 311, 318, 322
Trumbull, Lyman, 39
Trusts, see Sherman Antitrust Act

Udall, Judge Levi S., 335
Unfair labor practices, 186, 188, 189, 201, 210, 212, 264, 267, 268, 270, 313
  See also National Labor Relations Board; Taft-Hartley Act
Unionization, obstacles and encouragement to, 59, 61-62, 67, 82, 84, 106, 201, 203, 348
  See also Blacklisting; Discrimination; Yellow-dog contract
Unions, aims of, 161
  attacks on, 12-14, 20, 21, 58, 59, 72, 88, 306, 309, 333
  attitude to judiciary, 26, 55, 83, 95, 126, 202
  attitude to society, 344, 349-351
  company, see Company unions
  craft, 29
  duty to represent entire craft, 259-261, 271
  individual members' responsibility for acts of, 58, 59, 63-66
  industrial, 36
  judicial attitudes toward, 12-13, 16, 22-23, 25-27, 54, 90, 201, 331, 345, 346
  judicial power to restrain activities of, 26-28, 95
  label, 57, 65, 275, 276
  leaders, 310, 311, 348
  legality of, 25-28, 51, 65, 88, 114, 115
  liability to damages, 149, 150, 153, 154, 159, 314
  open-union policy, 271
  political activity, 42, 44, 45, 70, 83, 95-97, 108, 314, 328, 348
  public relations, 214, 273, 302, 320, 321, 348, 349
  recognition of, 196, 348
  regulation of, 203, 313-315, 332-338
  security, 318, 319, 332-338, 342, 343
  social attitude toward, 344, 345, 348, 349
  social responsibility, 349-351
  suability, 73, 147, 148, 151-153
  union shop, 331, 332
United Brotherhood of Carpenters and Joiners, 243, 334
United Construction Workers Organizing Committee, Local 129 (UCWOC), 263-266
United Hatters of North America, 56, 58, 60-62, 64

United Mine Workers of America (UM-WA), 76, 78, 85, 86, 89, 92, 114, 141, 145, 146, 149, 151-154, 158, 218, 287, 288, 296, 301, 307
District No. *21*, 146, 151, 154-156, 158-160
United Mine Workers of America, et al., v. Coronado Coal Co., et al., 150-155
United States Chamber of Commerce, 201, 305
United States Shoe Manufacturing Company, 170
United States Steel Corporation, 170, 192, 219
United States Strike Commission, 41, 43, 44
United States v. Adair, 46
United States v. American Tobacco Company, 69
United States v. Hutcheson, 244-251, 282, 286
United States v. Lewis, et al., 296-301
United States v. Standard Oil Co. of New Jersey, et al., 69
United Textile Workers of America, 225, 226
Unity of interest, 116
See also Economic conflict
Unreasonable restraint of trade, 68, 170, 171, 237, 247

Van Arsdale, Harry, Jr., 273, 279
Van Cleave, J. W., 71-73, 79
Van Devanter, Justice Willis, 82, 137, 178, 198
Van Orsdel, Justice Josiah, 75, 77, 81
Vinson, Chief Justice Fred M., 297, 301
Volpe, Angelo, 189
Voluntarism, *see* Gompers, Samuel
Voluntary arbitration, *see* Arbitration

Wages, 13, 17, 58, 85, 99, 108, 119, 129, 132, 135, 293, 336
as source of industrial unrest, 131
Wagner, Robert F., 185
Wagner Act, *see* National Labor Relations Act
Waite, Isaac, 18, 25
Walker, Edwin, 34, 37
Wallace, Henry A., 289
Wallace Corp. v. NLRB, 267-271
War Labor Board, *see* National War Labor Board
War Powers Act, 306
Washington, Va. & Md. Coach Co. v. NLRB, 198
Watkins, A. R., 86
Webster, Daniel, 21
Welfare funds, 292, 323
Whigs, 19
Whitaker, et al., v. State of North Carolina, 337
White, Chief Justice Edward D., 49, 82
White, John P., 156, 158
White, William Allen, 135
Willkie, Wendell, 289
Wilson, Clarence R., 80
Wilson, President Woodrow, 97
Wisconsin Employment Peace Act, 305
Wisconsin Labor Code, 174, 176-178
Wolff Meat Packing Co. v. Kansas, 133-138
Woods, Judge William A., 38
World War I, 127, 253
World War II, 289-291, 305-307
Wright, Carroll D., 45
Wright, Justice Daniel Theu, 71, 76, 80

Yellow-dog contract, 45, 84, 87, 91, 94, 95, 287, 335, 340
Youmans, Judge Frank A., 147

Zalenka, John, 86